Göttsch
Business Strategy in the Online Industry

I0014125

GABLER EDITION WISSENSCHAFT

Internationalisierung und Management

Herausgegeben von Professor Dr. Hans A. Wüthrich

Die Schriftenreihe präsentiert Ergebnisse der betriebswirtschaftlichen Forschung zu den Themengebieten Internationalisierung und Management. Im verbindenden Diskurs zwischen Theorie und Praxis verfolgt die Reihe das Ziel, Organisationen praxisnahe Lösungsansätze zu aktuellen Managementherausforderungen bereitzustellen und gleichzeitig einen Beitrag zur theoretischen Fundierung von Fragestellungen der Führungspraxis, nicht zuletzt im internationalen Kontext, zu leisten.

Christian Göttsch

Business Strategy in the Online Industry

Market and Network Strategy in Multi-Layered Industries

With a foreword
by Prof. Dr. Hans A. Wüthrich

Deutscher Universitäts-Verlag

Die Deutsche Bibliothek - CIP-Einheitsaufnahme

Göttsch, Christian:
Business strategy in the online industry : market and network strategy in multi-layered industries
/ Christian Göttsch. With a foreword by Hans A. Wüthrich. - 1. Aufl..
- Wiesbaden : Dt. Univ.-Verl. ; Wiesbaden : Gabler, 2000
   (Gabler Edition Wissenschaft : Internationalisierung und Management)
   Zugl.: München, Univ. d. Bundeswehr, Diss., 2000

1. Auflage Dezember 2000

Alle Rechte vorbehalten
© Betriebswirtschaftlicher Verlag Dr. Th. Gabler GmbH, Wiesbaden, und
   Deutscher Universitäts-Verlag GmbH, Wiesbaden, 2000

Lektorat: Brigitte Siegel / Stefanie Brich

Der Gabler Verlag und der Deutsche Universitäts-Verlag sind Unternehmen der
Fachverlagsgruppe BertelsmannSpringer.

www.gabler.de
www.duv.de

Höchste inhaltliche und technische Qualität unserer Produkte ist unser Ziel. Bei der Produktion und Verbreitung unserer Werke wollen wir die Umwelt schonen. Dieses Buch ist deshalb auf säurefreiem und chlorfrei gebleichtem Papier gedruckt. Die Einschweißfolie besteht aus Polyäthylen und damit aus organischen Grundstoffen, die weder bei der Herstellung noch bei der Verbrennung Schadstoffe freisetzen.

Die Wiedergabe von Gebrauchsnamen, Handelsnamen, Warenbezeichnungen usw. in diesem Werk berechtigt auch ohne besondere Kennzeichnung nicht zu der Annahme, dass solche Namen im Sinne der Warenzeichen- und Markenschutz-Gesetzgebung als frei zu betrachten wären und daher von jedermann benutzt werden dürften.

ISBN-13: 978-3-8244-7318-2   e-ISBN-13: 978-3-322-85209-0
DOI: 10.1007/978-3-322-85209-0

to my parents

Foreword

„The Internet is like a 20-foot tidal wave
coming thousands of miles across the Pacific
and we are in kayaks. "

Andi Grove

In the course of the commercial distribution of Internet technology since the year 1995 new business models emerged and ultimately established the on-line industry as a distinct economic environment. The author defines this new marketspace as „.....a multi-layered industry consisting of five main layers: network, hosting, software, content and devices. Each layer consists of sub-layers. Players from the converging industries telecommunications, computer hardware/software, media and consumer electronics conduct on-line business units offering a set of on-line services." (S. 17). Significance and growth of the on-line industry are enormous.

The market for multimedia products and services represents approximately 10% of the US GDP already today. The industry volume is expected to double every 12 to 18 months. The increasing relevance of the on-line industry is driving the interest of academia in a theoretical foundation of the observed economic phenomena. The term **network economics** establishes a new scientific area. Due to the specific structure and logic of the industry traditional business concepts and strategy approaches can be translated only in a limited way. At this point the work of Christian Göttsch comes in play, which – by utilizing the theoretical concepts of network economics and game theory – models the structure of the on-line industry and delivers a methodic set of instruments to develop marketing strategies. These conceptual components together with a host of case studies delivers deep insight for executives and professionals being involved in the New Economy.

Prof. Dr. Hans A. Wüthrich

Preface

Coming up with the plan to approach such a rapidly moving and changing space as the Internet with a rather slowly developing medium as a dissertation seemed to be a very challenging decision. Hence I decided to stay away from hype and hectic of the day to day business in the Internet time and tried to find the general patterns and mechanisms in this space. This preface is written for the publication of the book one year after the actual dissertation was finalized and some statements and advice can already go through a reality check.

The surprising fact in an environment where windows of opportunities to create new businesses seem to close so rapidly, is that many things do not change all that fast and enduring principles can be perceived. All of us still have to cope with an unsatisfying user experience, for example when we do not find what we want, sites deliver poor service quality, net software turns out to be unstable or too complex, and purchases in the virtual space are neither faster nor cheaper than in the real life store next door. The lesson here is that speed is not everything and that there is still way space for improvement. Opportunities are still out there, if creativity and quality comes in play. For new businesses as well as the established players the enduring economic principles of the **networked economy** and a **co-opetitive conduct**, as it is laid out in this book, will provide guidance in navigating through this space. This becomes even more true as large "info economy giants" representing the current paradigm, such as AOL and Time Warner or Microsoft's ".net strategy", as well as a host of "start up davids", representing the potential future paradigm (page 259), obviously follow these rules. In this sense the increasing prominence of the **notion of network effects** underpins the emphasis of this book.

This book was written during my professional involvement with CompuServe Europe and as a visiting scholar at the Berkeley Round Table on the International Economy (BRIE) at UC Berkeley. I want to thank my mentor Professor Hans A. Wüthrich for the freedom and advice he gave me during the whole research project. Thank you also to Professor Arnold Hermanns for being the co-corrector of the dissertation. At CompuServe and AOL Europe I would like to thank specifically Dr. Konrad Hilbers and Dr. Klaus Hommels for supporting the research with the resource and goodwill, which was required to make it happen. At Gruner + Jahr thank you to Martin Stahel for carrying over the provision of this support. For all the joint research I would like to express my special appreciation to the research fellows at BRIE and the mcm institute in St. Gallen, Switzerland. At BRIE I would like to thank the co-directors for having me there and particularly Professor John Zysman for continuously challenging my thoughts. To initially kick-start this academic project and continuously reminding me to deliver results thank you to Dr. Christian Horn. For the never-ending editing efforts I would like to thank Brigette Buchet at mcm and my girlfriend Maria.

Ultimately I want to thank my parents for always being there and supporting all my academic efforts over the years. This book is dedicated to you.

Christian Göttsch

Table of Contents

List of Figures

List of Case Studies

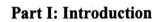

Part I: Introduction

Introduction

Up until the middle of the 1990ies the on-line service industry was a fairly unknown business operating in a relatively small and protected niche, which ensured its high profitability. The market was stable and clearly defined with only a few experts involved in this – very predictable – business. However, a sudden change occurred, enabled by innovations in the information communication technology framework and the presence of open Internet standards. This created enormous possibilities with high expectations from various perspectives. An overwhelming dynamic developed in a short period of time with 'multimedia', 'Internet', 'e-commerce', and 'on-line' becoming ubiquitous buzz words all describing related phenomena. A trend began with companies, policy institutions and the public in general developing their particular interest with the Internet. The new technology creates a groundswell of change and results in opportunities and threats for vast areas of the economic as well as social life. From an economic standpoint, it is expected that new business and jobs will be created in a large scale. On the other hand, one can assume that existing businesses, processes and structures are threatened by the new technologies. Over time social life will face fundamental changes.[1]

It is significant that economic theory is about to start reacting to these adjustments, while it is apparent that the aggregate economic contribution of this sector will be enormous in the long run. Firms are facing new challenges, which the theory of business administration has not had to consider previously. Moreover, it is as yet unclear to which extent the empirical challenges will lead to adjustments in the theoretical frameworks. Neither business theory nor practice have yet developed a common framework of instruments to deal with these problems.

This work addresses these issues from a strategic management standpoint and presents a business strategy framework for the on-line industry in the Internet paradigm. This research is necessary as the scientific community has so far widely overlooked this growth area. In this sense, the author analyzes the recently converging area from the standpoint of the on-line industry and not only from the perspective of the converging industries, as the majority of the research which oversees crucial factors does. The author also employs experiences from past proprietary on-line service and considers the technological parameters of the field.

The author develops conceptual instruments for analytical and applied purposes. Based on empirical findings and the theory of network economics, a multi-layered model of the industrial structure is designed. Mainstream business strategy and most recent theories developed in the context of the Internet will be applied to develop the strategic framework of a tool set used to derive business strategies. In order to develop such strategies, this work first lays out a set of tools, which influence industrial structure with respect to the chosen strategy. In this sense, the structural and strategic instruments dynamically work together.

---

[1]   OECD (1998a) assumes $1.000 Million in total revenues by 2003 – 2005. See Margherio et. al (1997) A1 24-43 for a detailed quantitative macro economic analysis. The market for multimedia products and services is characterized through the convergence of formerly distinct areas, increasingly globally operating industries and firms. It represents 10% of the US GDP and will generate revenues of $1.47 Billion in the US by the year 2005 (see Tapscott 1996, p. 9). Current assumptions for 1998 presume over 1. Mio. open positions (Margherio et. al. 1998, OECD 1998a). E. g. new Internet based procurement and distribution changes classical ways of handling these processes and the related jobs significantly (OECD 1998a, Andersen 1998).

Due to the infancy of the industrial environment, this work frequently applies fundamental theories and focuses on the significant aspects of the field from a high level perspective, ignoring the detailed views of rapidly changing functional areas. Microeconomic foundations, such as those found in Industrial Economics and Network Economics dominate large parts of the discussion where they are enhanced by resource-based aspects and game theoretic implications. The positioning of this thesis, with its applied aspects, includes technological implications. For empirical and illustrative purposes, the thesis will introduce various business cases and examples, with the goal of enhancing the general analysis. This defines the direction taken in this thesis. Ultimately, an alternative view to what is generally considered on-line, Internet or multimedia business in the current scientific and practical discussion emerges. This picture will open a wider and more comprehensive perspective of the business environment by explaining the industrial framework for business, which is conducted on-line in the Internet.[2] This new paradigm of on-line business will ultimately describe the platform upon which e-commerce and the new digital e-conomy will be built.

This first part of the thesis develops a preliminary understanding of the field, explains the research and its design and locates this thesis on the academic map. The second part is an empirical and theoretical analysis of the industrial structure and models the industry in a multi-layered constellation. The third part presents the implications for business strategy and provides perspective with the structural model. Part four summarizes the findings and gives an overview for further research.

1. Particular Approach, Research Focus and Methodology

In the course of the first chapter, the authors develops a fundamental approach and explains the basic understanding of the object under analysis. This will show a clear distinction between the current mainstream view towards the on-line environment, which regards it as a rather new phenomenon since it considers only the short commercial history of the Internet. (1.1). With this particular definition of the research object and the respective approach the underlying problem of this thesis will be worked out in 1.2. Scientific positioning, research design as well as the applied theory of the thesis will be presented in 1.3. The structure of the thesis will be outlined at the end of this first introductory chapter (1.4).

1.1. This Particular Approach

As the on-line business environment is a relatively new, highly complex and rapidly changing field, these first definitions are crucial to present a clear picture and generate a preliminary understanding. While this object can be perceived from numerous relevant perspectives the

---

[2] The particular aspects regarding issues of intranets or extranets will not be focused upon. These areas of research focus either on how companies organize their business to business (B2B) processes (Extranets) or how companies organize their internal business processes (intranet), both based on Internet technology. This discussion would lead into an analysis of the virtualization and disintermediation of business in general. This thesis will refer to the existing complementary analysis in this field. Although this does not mean that this thesis has a focus solely on end customer business. Particular business-to-business aspects, which are part of the value system for on-line services, e. g. dial-up network wholesale, server software, client software etc., and their strategic aspects will be analyzed.

4

final picture will vary enormously depending on object definition and particular standpoint.[3] The definition of these two factors will significantly influence the clarity and the added-value of the results. Therefore, the following will analyze this aspect. Stemming from the early stage of research into the on-line industry in the context of strategic management, object definition as well as agreed upon standpoints have not been clearly worked out yet. It is a prerequisite to develop a set of definitions for this thesis. This will avoid ambiguity and will finally lead to a precise set of answers for the chosen problem. For these reasons a clear and unambiguous set of definitions is a fundamental element of this thesis.[4]

While the current discussion is characterized by the frequent application of "buzz words" 1.1.1 will clarify their meaning and relation. Using this first definition of a **terminological context** 1.1.2 will work out a particular view as **perspective definition**, which will be called the "genuine perspective". Complementary to this perspective definition the **object definition** is representing an understanding which is partly different to the current perception of the on-line industry. It will not be regarded as an entirely new phenomenon and it will be suggested to utilize significant experience curve effects of proprietary on-line services of the past. While the on-line business will be considered as a business with existing traditions the reasons and results of the technological convergence will eventually be regarded as **the truly new phenomenon** (1.1.3).[5]

1.1.1. The Context of "Buzz Words"

The Internet has created enormous expectations regarding the possibilities and impact of the digital future. Emphatic statements often characterized the early stages of academic debates as well as the general public understanding.

> "Today we are witnessing the early, turbulent days of a revolution as significant as any other in human history. A new medium of human communications is emerging, one that may prove to surpass all previous revolutions - the printing press, the telephone, the television - in its impact on our economy and social life. (...) Interactive multimedia and the so-called information highway, and its exemplar the Internet, are enabling a new economy based on the networking of the human intelligence. In this digital economy, individuals and enterprises create wealth by applying knowledge, networked human intelligence, and effort to manufacturing, agriculture, and services." (Tapscott 1996:xiii)

Not only hopes but also a deep skepticism is associated with the rise of this "brave new world", for example drastically displayed in the debate regarding privacy. The overwhelming

---

[3] Winter (1998) outlines this cohesion of standpoint and object definition, the shape, from a organizational and management perspective in a very differentiated way.

[4] It is a fundamental aspect that the underlying context and the particular hypothesizes of a standpoint are crucial to determining perception. Dependent on existing information and accepted hypothesizes, the perception of an object will be adjusted accordingly. See Graumann (1956) for the cognitive aspects of individual perception and the shaping influence of the underlying hypotheses.

[5] This framework of definitions is a fundamental source of differentiation of this thesis from the existing scientific work. This is a vital aspect as the number of research projects in the on-line and multimedia area are growing steadily.

interest has created a large number of buzz words, all describing phenomena in the context of the Internet. Observers of this growing business, which is emerging in the framework of the Internet are confronted with verbal clutter. One can summarize that:

> "Multimedia and the Information Superhighway are terms used so broadly that they have come to mean absolutely everything and, as a result, are beginning to mean virtually nothing." (Hagel / Eisenmann 1994:39)

The following will put the most frequent terms into perspective in order to distinguish this approach from other academic work, which also analyzes aspects in terms of on-line[6], Internet[7], multimedia[8]; e-commerce[9]; e-business or e-conomy.

The digital economy, recently "**e-conomy™**",[10] is taking place in the global virtual space created by the Internet. This defines the main boundaries of this economy. It is embedded in the global economy and therein responsible for a small, but growing, contribution.[11] Aside from the economic and business issues this digital e-conomy, demands issues from social science as well as natural science perspectives are on the research agenda. The economic and business aspects can be structured from a standpoint of the value chain.[12] Figure 1-1 distinguishes two main areas in the e-conomy which are relevant from a business standpoint.

The first area considers the **virtualization of the value chain** using the infrastructure of the Internet. This debate is encompassing an entirely new dimension with the presence of ubiquitous Internet standards and a growing adoption of this technology throughout the economy.

---

[6] The terminology around the term "on-line" will be elaborated in 2.3 - 2.5.

[7] See 2.1.2 for a deeper explanation of this term.

[8] Multimedia combines static and dynamic media and enables interactive applications whereas interactivity and cross media integration are the distinct particularities. See Booz Allen Hamilton (1995), pp. 24-25.

[9] In general "Electronic commerce is the ability to perform transaction involving goods or services between two or more parties using electronic tools and techniques." (Schutzer 1997:521).

[10] The term "e-conomy" was introduced by the University of California at Berkeley which is running a comprehensive interdisciplinary research project (http://e-conomy.berkeley.edu) covering this new economic and social environment. The author took part in the kick-off team for this project as a visiting scholar contributing to the aspects of business strategy and comparative issues of the US - European business practice to the research agenda.

[11] OECD (1998a) predictions assume approximately 1% of the global economy is being generated in the digital e-conomy. This number appears relatively low but distinguishes between real data and hyperbole. Nevertheless, one should take into account that this sector is highly innovative and fuels a multiplier into other future sectors of the economies.

[12] This refers to Porter's (1985) model of the value chain. This concept assumes that each company has internal activities which add value to the product or service. Porter structures them in a chain of primary activities like production or R & D and secondary overhead activities which support the primary activities. At the boundaries of the **firm's value chain** it connects with the **supply chain** and the **distribution chain**, which establishes a **value chain system**. The vertical dimension of this value chain system describes the sequential steps of the value adding process. The horizontal dimension describes activities at the same level of value adding activities. The configuration of this value chain is a source to generate competitive advantage. Porter's framework will be further introduced and discussed in 2.2.2 and 3.2.1 as a fundamental analytical component.

It is being embraced by players ranging from large corporations to small firms and the end customer.[13]

> We are in the midst of a fundamental shift in the economics of information - a shift that will precipitate changes in the structure of entire industries and in the ways companies compete. This shift is made possible by the widespread adoption of Internet technologies, but it is less about technology than about the fact that a new behavior is reaching critical mass. Millions of people are communicating at home and at work in an explosion of connectivity that threatens to undermine the established value chains for businesses in many sectors of the economy. (Evans / Wurster 1997:70)

Related research closely aligns these phenomena to the emergence of information and communication technology (ICT). Traditional research has analyzed the aspects of decreasing transaction costs enabled by this technology, which allows firms to redefine their boundaries and value creation processes.[14] In the context of this thesis this approach is termed the "lateral perspective" (see 1.1.2 below). The term **e-business**[15] is even more related to Internet terms as it was invented to describe electronically conducted business, based on Internet technology. This area describes traditional business processes of any kind when they are conducted in a virtual way. From the standpoint of a firm, the value chain can be divided into three areas: inbound supply chain, internal firm value chain and outbound distribution chain. On the supply side, value creation is researched under the headline of **electronic procurement**.[16] The firm value chain is analyzed in terms of a **virtualized e-enterprise** and the term **e-commerce**[17] describing the on-line based distribution chain activities.[18]

---

[13] See Evans / Wurster (1997), Rayport / Sviokla (1996), Rayport / Sviokla (1997), Zerdick (1999, eds.) for a new trend in the traditional discussion about the virtualization of firms (see footnote 26) by focusing the Internet as a ubiquitous and shared platform for transactions.

[14] See Williamson (1975, 1986, 1999, eds.) for the underlying economic models, Coase (1937) as the theoretical foundation and Picot / Reichwald / Wigand (1996) for an management application with strong IT references.

[15] The term "e-business" was coined as an overall umbrella label for IBM's new strategy to supply a complete suite of products to support business processes with products and services based on Internet technology. Due to IBM's massive marketing effort, this term experienced very rapid diffusion. It can be used to refer to business processes in the digital economy according to interview with Stuart Feldman, Director of the IBM Advanced Research Lab, 4th of March 1999, Berkeley.

[16] See Selz / Klein (1997).

[17] In the presence of an exploding amount of literature discussing the issues on e-commerce, the author recommends a host of publications, which appear fundamental rather than hyperbolic and which were in part responsible for spawing a widespread theoretical discussion such as Hagel / Armstrong (1995, 1996, 1997a, 1997b), Hagel / Bergsma / Dheer (1996), Hagel / Rayport (1997a, 1997b), Hagel / Sacconaghi (1996), Hagel / Singer (1999), Sacconaghi / Abela 1997), Harrington / Reed (1996), Harrington et. al. (1998). In general, the author would commend the activities of the following major players who are claim to be the "pioneers" of ecommerce with a positioning as a gateway (e.g. AOL, @Home), a web portal (e.g. Yahoo!, Excite), an etailer (e.g. Amazon, etoys), an auctioneer (e.g. eBay, Onsale), a buying network (e.g. Priceline, Mercata) or a direct to customer business (e.g. Dell.com). Goldman Sachs (1999a) provides an excellent overview and structural analysis of these different approaches. Each of these categories differ significantly in their positioning and it yet remains to be proven which position will be the best over the long run. The theoretical discussion in this footnote provides some indications.

[18] See Kalakota / Winston (1996), pp. 219-222 for a distinction of three types of electronic businesses and references to the Internet, Extranet and Intranet as the according on-line platforms.

The second research area shown in Figure 1-1 describes the **on-line environment,**[19] where virtual value creation activities take place. Thus, both areas have to be seen in a complementary manner. Due to divergent market constellations and different technological designs, it is powerful to distinguish the following three environments: **Extranets**[20] running between companies and connecting supply-side activities with an **Intranet**[21] based firm value chain. The created products and services then flow into the **Internet**[22] based virtual distribution chain.

The on-line industry is shaping the open Internet where individual users gather information, communicate and purchase goods and services. Therefore, on-line services are a natural complement of the distribution chain of the e-commerce activities of an e-business. An analogy might help to illustrate this relationship: just as streets, traffic lights, signs, cars, bikes and so forth serve people as a network, which provides mobility, the Internet serves as a network, which provides companies with the possibility for virtual value creation and the conduct of e-business. Among all players, the on-line industry has the closest relationship to a large numbers of end customers.

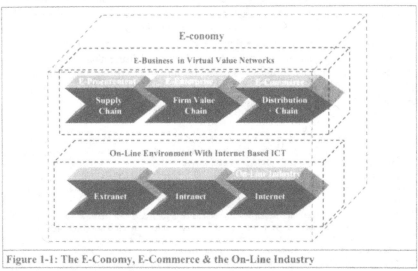

Figure 1-1: The E-Conomy, E-Commerce & the On-Line Industry

The main distinction between the e-business area and the on-line area is, that players in the former regard the Internet as yet another way of organizing the value creation of their tradi-

---

[19] This on-line environment can be seen as an evolutionary progress from proprietary EDI systems, which were related to general research on the virtualization of value chains. Schutzer (1997, pp. 521-523) points out that EDI technology is gradually being replaced by the shift towards Internet technology. In the context of the Internet, new, open standard technology is incrementally superceding these EDI systems with the accompanying technological life cycles and related research is focusing on Internet technology. This logic underlies the research activities of the UC Berkeley e-conomy project and the research of the Stanford Computer Industry Project at Stanford University.

[20] The adoption rate of this technology in the large industrial sectors in 1998 shows an expected growth from 35% to 70% by the year 2000, which underpins the importance of this environment (see Deloitte 1998, p. 5).

[21] The adoption rate of 20% in 1998 is expected to grow to 42% in 2000 (see ibid., p.5).

[22] The adoption rate of 15% in 1998 is expected to grow to 70% in 2000 (see ibid., p. 4).

tional businesses. **Players of the on-line industry consider the Internet based ICT environment as their core business** (see 1.1.3) and can be seen as **the builders of the Internet** and New Information Infrastructure (NII)[23]. This thesis discusses business strategy issues regarding the on-line industry on the e-conomy research agenda. It will analyze this part of the e-conomy which can be described as a virtualized system, which establishes the Internet as huge on-line service, based on a network of complementary components with an open standard technology platform. This view will transfer experience curve effects from past on-line services and will explain how convergence created a new on-line service paradigm, namely the Internet. Thus, this thesis will provide understanding on the research on the "virtualization of the value chain" which creates virtual "marketspaces"[24] where "new infomediaries" (Hagel / Rayport 1997b) connect the virtual world to the global economy of the real world. In this context, the on-line industry creates an environment where information and communication products and services as well as e-commerce opportunities are on offer to end users. While the process aspect of the industry is not in the focus of this work, the network aspect of players adding value in a complementary structure will be analyzed. The particular perspective on the on-line industry will is outlined in 1.1.2.

1.1.2. Research Perspective and Object Definition

Many businesses from different industries are looking into this environment all of a sudden. However, their underlying motivations fundamentally vary. Different buzz words label their rationale behind these adjustments of business strategies. Depending on firms' positioning, these changes result in different opportunities and risks and lead to action items according to the external changes. A clear and distinctive standpoint towards the research object and a context of different views is required to clarify the research perspective of this dissertation. Depending on the perspective taken in an analysis of the on-line business, different perceptions and findings will result. Therefore, it is important to lay out how this thesis distinguishes itself from other research and to define its positioning in the spectrum of perspectives towards the on-line business. For this purpose, the **value chain**[25] is applied as a **reference system,** in order to derive a generic perspective towards the on-line business.

According to the structure of the value chain system, changes in the ICT area can be perceived as a new technology, which provides companies with the possibility of reinventing its value creating structures as shown in Figure 1-1. Possibilities to virtualize part of the business arise, fostering higher degrees of market mechanisms within value creation.[26] Value webs[27] or

---

[23] See e.g. Bar / Borrus / Steinberg (1995) and Donahue (1997).

[24] Rayport / Sviokla (1994) created this term of "marketspace" which describes the new form of virtual marketplaces, which are located in the cyberspace of the Internet. Section 2.3 will show that past on-line services were the predecessor of these new Internet-based marketspaces and suggests deriving experience curve effects from that proprietary online service tradition. The use of the term marketspaces is in its plural, as these past services were isolated, closed systems without significant capabilities to interconnect the users of each platform.

[25] Porter (1985).

[26] This discussion was become more and more popular since the new institutional economics were developed, based on Coase's (1937) ideas, and expounded by Oliver Williamson (1990, eds.) and others. Since the Internet is becoming such an overwhelming economic phenomenon, this research was recently revitalized and enhanced with an increasing analysis of new Internet-related forms of value creation in the virtual marketspace.

value networks with the blurring of boundaries increasingly shape the value creating structures. It is significant for this standpoint that neither on-line services nor information and communication technology are the core business. Both are only seen as **enablers** to change the way business is conducted with a higher degree of virtualization leading to increased efficiency and flexibility.[28] Value creation becomes increasingly desegregated while physical and informational flows of goods become more and more disintermediated. This results in the possibility – if not the necessity – of the "deconstruction of the value chain" (Evans / Wurster 1997:76).

> "In any business where the physical value chain has been compromised for the sake of delivering information, there will be an opportunity to create a separate information business and a need to streamline the physical one. Executives must mentally deconstruct their businesses to see the real value of what they have. If they don't (...), someone else will. (Evans / Wurster 1997:70)

The package delivery players are a prominent example. Industry leaders like FedEx enter:

> "(...) the online retail bazaar. (...) become full service logistics providers that specialize in orchestrating the flow of goods *and* information between customers, retailers, and suppliers. (...) [FedEx, C. G.] is a company rooted in the world of information technology and distributed networks. (...) FedEx [has a, C. G.] physical network of jets and vans, and it's information network of computer, databases, and operations management tools. (...) FedEx is a network" (Lappin 1996:241).

> "It's a core tenet of FedEx gospel that the data about each shipment is just as valuable as the shipment itself." (Lappin 1996:284)

But this deconstruction of value systems does not mean destruction as Evans / Wurster note referring, when they refer the example of on-line retail banking[29]:

> "The integrated value chain of retail banking will have been deconstructed. Deconstructed but not destroyed. All the old functions will still be performed, as well as some new ones. Banks will not become obsolete, but their current business definition will -- specifically, the concept that a bank is an integrated business where multiple products are originated, packaged, sold, and cross-sold through proprietary distribution channels." (Evans / Wurster 1997:76)

This kind of research generates insight for the improvement of structural and procedural aspects of existing business. From that perspective, the actual implementation of the value chain may lead to more virtualized patterns, although their fundamental definition as an outcome of the business concept is not necessarily affected. The Internet and on-line services itself appear

---

This new research on the virtualization of enterprises is becoming extremely **web centric**. See Evans / Wurster (1997), Rayport / Sviokla (1996) and Hagel / Rayport (1997b).

[27] See Selz / Klein (1997/1998) and Selz (2000).

[28] See Picot / Reichwald (1994) regarding the virtualization of the firms boundaries due to ICT, Picot / Reichwald / Wigand (1996) for a general organizational approach with extensive notions of the technology aspects.

[29] See furthermore on on-line banking Johnson et. al. (1995), Hagel / Hewlin / Hutchings (1997).

as enablers in a **lateral perspective.** Currently, there is extensive ongoing research in this area that is especially **relevant for information intense businesses.** Thus, this is a complementary general view which may be applied to better understand the value creation issues in a highly information based environment such as the on-line industry.

A second view of the on-line industry can be described as the **horizontal perspective.**[30] This standpoint mainly **represents companies from the converging industries:** media, telecommunications, computer hardware, software and consumer electronics (see Figure 1-4). These companies perceive that their respective industries are converging and that the corresponding implications of the product market portfolio[31] is to potentially expand into on-line businesses. Although the core business is not conducted in the on-line area, the value chain is affected at its horizontal boundaries, which drives the necessity for adjustments. From this standpoint the on-line area appears as a means to offer new products or services derived from the traditional business. This new business is considered an expansion of the existing product market range. The emerging value chain structures are identical or similar to the known industry, with the on-line business perceived as a horizontal enhancement. The fundamental design of the value chain is not affected by these new businesses.[32] The most prominent example in this context is the definition of a "multimedia value chain", assuming that telecommunications services and media value chains merge.[33] First, this perspective is dominated by the existing traditions of large industries, which do not consider the genuine uniqueness and alternative factors of on-line services. Second, completely overlooked is the influence of software, and computer and consumer electronics players. And third, by so doing, they do not grasp the crucial strategic interdependencies of a multi-layered industry and hence will deliver irrelevant output.

Contrary to this approach, it is possible to regard the on-line business from a fundamentally different standpoint, which believes that the on-line industry has a significant history with traditions stretching back more than 25 years as described below. This view will consequently be called the **genuine perspective** as it **acknowledges a business mission targeted to conduct business in the on-line industry.** From this standpoint, the issues reach far beyond singular improvements of the value creating structures, like the lateral perspective focuses on above. It also goes beyond the view of regarding on-line based business as solely a product market expansion. From this position, the vital core of the business is designed around on-line based business. Mission critical aspects of business strategy are based in the structure of the on-line industry. The fundamental business context and the general mind set behind the logic

---

[30] The majority of the current research projects are approaching the on-line industry from this horizontal perspective where existing and established industries, especially from the media or telecommunications sector view the on-line industry. Usually they research the new aspects for the existing business from a known and familiar position, which is gaining in relevancy through on-line and multimedia development. From this standpoint, the on-line business is typically considered a new phenomenon in the environment of existing businesses. Traditional knowledge, like market structure, market mechanisms, and value adding structures are applied and singular enhancements are made from a particular industrial view.

[31] See Ansoff (1965).

[32] This statement refers to the underlying logic of the value chain and not to the potential virtualization of its structure. The later aspect is related to the lateral perspective and is of course also valid for the converging industries, which may increase the degree of virtual value creation within their business system.

[33] See for example Squire, Sanders & Dempsey (1998a), pp. 84-93, Squire, Sanders & Dempsey (1998b), p. 210-227, KPMG (1996a), pp. 83-141and European Commission (1997a), pp. 1-2.

of the business value system are solely orchestrated to compete successfully in the on-line industry. The particular logic and mechanisms of the on-line industry define the rules for the players. From this standpoint, the on-line business is perceived in an authentic and holistic manner, which understands the environment with its particular constellation. The structure of the value chain is designed in a way that meets the demands of the on-line business. This view is relevant for every company, which wants to execute business in the on-line field and considers this to be the prime activity of the company. So far very limited research has occurred utilizing this point-of-view. As a consequence descriptive and prescriptive scientific work lags behind business practice. This thesis will, therefore, present an extensive analysis of the on-line business from this perspective.

Figure 1-2 summarizes the key factors of each perspective. It shows the shift of the viewpoint results in an increasing interest in the product market area and the core business for the Internet and on-line industry. Furthermore, it becomes obvious that a decreasing number of industries is relevant for the analysis of this thesis. The two right columns indicate the logic of the value chain definition and the related research areas as outlined above.

Generic Perspectives	Resulting Relevancy For			Primary Affected Industries	Logic of Value Chain Definition	Research Area
	Value Chain	Product Market Strategy	Mission & Core Business			
Lateral				• Any industry • Appropriate industries for organizational virtualization • Especially information intense industries	Typical structure of a value chain of the specific industry. Increasingly value webs	• e-conomy (Figure 1-1)
Horizontal				• Convergence industries (telecommunications, computer, media, consumer electronics)	Convergence value chain Multimedia value chain	• Convergence • Multimedia
Genuine				• On-line Industry	Layered value networks. Differentiated value chains, compliant with the on-line industry framework.	Strategic management in the on-line industry. Not analyzed yet.

Figure 1-2: Generic Perspectives Towards the On-line Business and the ICT Area

This thesis is aimed at developing an alternative view that will be called the genuine perspective. While the lateral and the genuine perspective are complementary, the horizontal and the genuine view are in a competitive relation.

After outlining this research perspective the second preliminary step is to deliver a **definition of the particular research object**. It is a fundamental difference if one approaches the problem from a perspective of established industries and considers the Internet as a new meta-phenomenon, which overlaps several industries (lateral / horizontal view) or if one considers on-line based business as an established and independent business, which experienced explosive growth since 1995 (genuine view). The latter approach draws conclusions from a broad basis of experience of on-line service as a business environment. It considers a significant on-line business experience of more than 25 years. From that standpoint an on-line service consists of a bundle of components such as information, communication, community services, usage software, network access, and all the necessary structures at the back-end, which supports the visible elements of such an offering. The following **definition of the term on-line service** (see 2.3.2) is used in the context of this thesis:

> A complete on-line service is a **bundling** which offers **interactive content** in applications serving **information, communication and community needs** over a **data network** infrastructure in **digital technology** with a **computerized usage device**. Singular content applications as components of a complete bundling can be referred to as on-line service.

The term on-line services describes a product, which serves customer needs and which is the outcome of a business concept and the base for an on-line business. For the term **on-line business** the following **definition** (see 2.3.3) will be applied:

> An on-line business is the underlying business model and the execution of an on-line service. This business offers singular on-line services either as stand-alone or in a bundle with other on-line service components.

This thesis includes an analysis of past consumer oriented on-line services and derives corresponding conclusions. The following table gives an overview of the commercial on-line service past by showing the most significant examples with their general market definition, time of existence, and the development of their customer base. It is significant that all of these players reacted to convergence by incrementally integrating web technology into their system around 1995, at a time when the Internet, as a "non-proprietary on-line service alternative", was serving just 2-3 million subscribers.[34]

One can distinguish two categories of fully integrated service bundles. On the one hand, there were end-consumer oriented services with distinct positioning, such as AOL as the "easy to use and entertaining service", or CompuServe as the "professional service for those serious about on-line". They targeted customers for private or semi-professional purposes. On the other hand, there were business-to-business services, which targeted vertical markets such as Bloomberg or Reuters for the financial markets and the news sector.

---

[34] See ibid.

SEGMENT	EXAMPLE	MARKET	EXISTING SINCE	WEB TEC SINCE	USER BASE 1990	USER BASE 1995
Consumer On-Line Services	CompuServe[35]	Global	1969	1995	2.7 M	4.8 M
	AOL	USA	1985	1995	0.3 M	1.1 M
	Prodigy	USA	1984	1995	-	1.3 M
	Minitel	France	1981	1988/1999[36]	10 M	16 M
	T-Online	Germany	1984	1996	0.7 M	0.8 M
Business On-Line Services	Bloomberg, Reuters Knight Ridder	Vertical	-	1995	2.1 M	3.1 M

Figure 1-3: Overview of Classical On-line Services[37]

This clear distinction between business and consumer on-line services was incrementally blurred during the course of convergence (see 1.1.3 and 2.4) as both types of services were moving to the Internet. Furthermore, it is a strong trend in the Internet to become a market-space for a growing number of services designed for vertical markets.[38] Ultimately the table proves that virtual marketspaces developed for a long period, before the Internet transformed from a non-profit to a commercial network. This industry developed incrementally in a relatively **stable institutional and technological framework** (see 2.1). Specific know-how, proprietary technology and high initial investments built up **high entrance barriers**. A very limited number of players developed the market with **high** – but compared to the later Internet development not as explosive – **growth rates** of around 30% per year. Within these 'market-spaces,' business online services generated $13 billion with 3.1 million subscribers and consumer on-line services generated $0.9 billion with 5.6 million subscribers in the United States in the year 1994.[39] Within this comfortable business environment, **stable laws of the market-place** evolved with a comprehensive portfolio of **solid business models**. In order to establish a solid environment, **stable business processes** were developed around these business models. The companies operated these business processes in a **value chain** with a **high degree of vertical integration**. Part II will use comprehensive empirical data to describe the details of this environment and will frequently use examples for illustration, often employing the example of the CompuServe on-line service.

This thesis will utilize existing experience curve effects from that era of on-line services (see 2.3) and will "look into the past to see the future" (Zerdick (1998:36) [translation C. G.] pat-

---

[35] Including Japanese licensee NiftyServe, which is based on CompuServe technology.

[36] Minitel has one difference to the other services as the service bundling includes the access device as well. Minitel offered its application via Internet technology since 1988 whereas this usage did not really grow until 1990 (see OECD 1998, pp. 26-27). Minitel plans to introduce a service based on Internet technology with IBM as network supplier and Alcatel as the device supplier in 1999 (see Andrews 1998 and interview with Benoit Raimbault, Marketing Manager Alcatel Screenphone, 24th of July 1999, Paris).

[37] Sources: OECD 1998, BCG (1995b) and internal company data.

[38] This is a plausible development, since in the past business on-line services were able to generate revenues per subscriber 15 times as high as consumer online services (see BCG 1995b).

[39] See BCG 1995b. In 1996, US on-line services alone still outnumbered the 10 million Internet users with its combined user base of 12 million subscribers according to Morgan Stanley (1995).

terns of the digital economy. It will analyze the well-defined institutional framework of the past business that was the appropriate environment to establish stable laws of the market place and a clear structure of the industry. This environment had a customer base of appproximately 25 million users in the year 1995, just prior to the Internet gaining commercial relevancy. This stable framework led to high returns on investment and to solid and enduring business models. Furthermore, it will be shown that the organization of value creation in a highly vertically integrated value chain worked for a long time.

But as fundamental parameters in the framework of the on-line industry have changed in the course of convergence, a large part of the analysis needs to examine these changes as well. This will explain the new constellation, which created the Internet as a quickly growing environment for a huge variety of on-line services and will show how this marketspace hosts e-commerce and the new e-conomy. These aspects will be briefly introduced as a preliminary base in the next point while 2.4 presents an in depth analysis.

1.1.3. The Internet and the Emergence of a New Constellation in the Process of Convergence

The year 1995 was mentioned above several times.[40] This date refers to the transition of the Internet from a non-profit network into a commercial on-line service platform and the drive towards the "information superhighway".[41] Analytically there are two drivers which have to be distinguished for this process.

Convergence is the first driver. Dowling / Lechner / Thielmann state:

> "Convergence is an often used but rarely defined concept. Ideas such as the creation of synergies, disappearance of industrial boundaries, integration, or overlapping of markets, are all used to describe this phenomenon." (Dowling / Lechner / Thielmann 1998b:31)

The following definition of the term convergence serves in the course of this thesis:

> "Convergence is an on-going process whereby the scarcity of the distribution of information, communication and entertainment services diminishes over time.
> This process entails the coming together of:
> - the 'logical' convergence of physical information distribution infrastructures (such as broadcast television and telecommunications) to carry similar sorts of information at increasingly lower costs;
> - the interactive information storage and processing capabilities of the computer world;
> - the ubiquity and ease of use of consumer electronics; and content from the audiovisual and publishing worlds." (KPMG 1996a:87)

---

[40] It seems plausible to set this date, as by this time all on-line service providers started to offer Internet access and the adoption rates of internet service providers started to grow dramatically, while the Internet was just privatized. See also BCG (1995b).

[41] See MacKie-Mason (1995) and Varian / Shapiro (1998) p. 13.

Four main sources in the industrial environment are responsible for these changes: (1) technological environment, (2) public policy, (3) industrial and economic environment and (4) the social context.[42] These factors will be analyzed in 2.1. They are driving forces in the processes, which result in the increasing overlap of telecommunications, media, computer, software and consumer electronic industries.[43] From a computer industry perspective Applegate states in this context that:

> "Computers now can process all types of information (...) This has enabled digital transmission of information that was formerly the domain of the television, telephone and entertainment industry." (Applegate 1997)

With interactive services expanding into alternative usage devices such as Personal Data Assistants (PDA's) and set top boxes (see 2.1.2) consumer electronics become part of this industry as well. These large industries develop by increasingly merging information and communication technology (ICT[44]), which is where new on-line based business is initiated in a large scale. Figure 1-4 shows this convergence phenomenon, shaping the ICT sector.

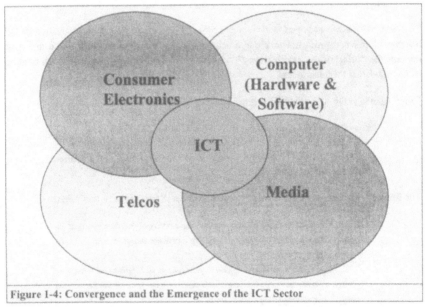

Figure 1-4: Convergence and the Emergence of the ICT Sector

Since approximately 1995, an increasing part of this business has developed in **open standard Internet technology**, which has to be identified as the second driver. This growth was

---

[42] Ibid. p. 89.

[43] See also Messerschmitt (1996) for a computing and telecommunications perspective and Dowling / Lechner Thielmann (1998a) for a media perspective. Dowling / Lechner / Thielmann additionally differentiate the technological dimension, the needs dimension, the industrial dimension, and the firm dimension of convergence (ibid., pp. 3-4).

[44] The term multimedia has a large overlap with the term ICT, although multimedia rather the describes the convergence of telecommunication and audiovisual applications.

kick-started by the enhancement of the Internet with the **world wide web**. This graphical user interface, based on the html language, dramatically improved usability and functionality of the Internet as an information and communication platform. It introduced an easy way to navigate through interactive content via hyperlinks. This made the Internet suitable for mass market adoption. The visual and navigational improvements quickly reached a stage where old style on-line services appeared old fashioned and unappealing. Moreover, the usage costs were significantly lower as charges for content did not apply. Open standard technology provided new players with low entrance barriers to the system. This demand and supply side enhancements were an effective enabler for the adoption of Internet based on-line usage.

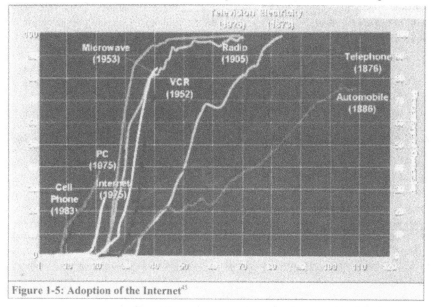

Figure 1-5: Adoption of the Internet[45]

Figure 1-5 shows in an effective way how the Internet started to enter a rapid adoption period when the world wide web was introduced and when the converging industries started to fuel this growth. This take-off point was in the year 1995, which misleadingly supports the common perception of the Internet as a suddenly emerging phenomenon, but in fact:

> "The internet (...) which has far reaching and profound social potential, is (...) based on technology that took time – some 35 years, in fact – to achieve broad market fitness" (Zimmerman 1998:5).[46]

Hence, as a result of convergence, the adoption rate of the Internet suddenly exploded after a period of two decades of stagnation on a low level. Figure 1-5 puts this speed of adoption into perspective with other new technologies, in order to emphasize this particularity.

---

[45] Microsoft (1998). See Rogers (1995) for the underlying aspect of diffusion of innovations in a social system.

[46] See also Figure 1-5 which shows that the adoption rates stagnated over 20 years but have rapidly increased since 1995.

17

Clearly both factors have resulted in an enormous boom for the on-line business, since the middle of the 1990s and have initiated the overwhelming growth of Internet based activities. For example, AOL has built a global customer base of subscribers for its on-line service of over 20 million before the year 2000. Ultimately, both factors were redefining the rules of the traditional on-line business and finally **reshaped the economic logic of the entire industrial framework** and caused the **transition to the Internet paradigm**.

Within this new framework, which connects a host of players like customers, businesses and communities, a new digital e-conomy is emerging. The term e-commerce currently drives the analysis of these phenomena. The on-line industry itself is developing the commercial platform for these new economic activities. To assure a common understanding of the term **on-line industry** the analysis in chapter 2 will present a model, which follows the **definition**:

The on-line industry is a **multi-layered industry** consisting of **five main layers**: network, hosting, software, content and devices. Each layer consists of sub-layers. Players from the converging industries telecommunications, computer hardware / software, media and consumer electronics conduct **on-line business** units offering a set of **on-line services**.

Together with the other definitions presented above, the preliminary **object definition** is completed at this point. The corresponding analysis is conducted in the course of chapter 2. This work with definitions assures the reader that one can refer to it on several levels. The definition of the term "on-line service" can be utilized on a **product level** where customer needs and product components of an on-line service bundle can be discussed. This will bridge the **business level** where internal aspects, market needs and relationships to other market players will be condensed into a business strategy, which includes a business model and value creation aspects. This level has to be seen in context with the **industry level,** which frames the business environment.

1.2. Research Problem: Structure of and Strategy in the On-line Industry

Ketelhöhn's notion on the appropriateness of the systemic view of an industry, or in other words the way one models an industry and derives a business strategy, reflects the underlying motivation of this thesis. Driven by the insufficiency of existing industrial models and strategy tools with respect to the highly complex on-line industry, this thesis presents a novel view of these matters. It derives a conceptual model of the industry and tools for business strategy to develop a strategy with this model. The following will define the research problem in a structural manner and starts with a short example of an actual business constellation in Case Study 1-1, which illustrates the problem:

The consumer electronic unit of Alcatel is planning to offer an "Internet Screen Phone" as a combined telephone, answering machine and Internet device. The product will be positioned as a consumer offering and as such priced below $500, which is significantly lower than competing products (e. g. the competing Siemens Online Terminal at $800). Utilizing the price sensitivity of the consumer segment and some strategic distribution partnerships, Alcatel plans to sell approximately 2 million. units (Siemens: approximately 40.000 units) during the product life cycle. Scale effects for lowered production costs are considered. Alcatel faces two main problems. First, the economics behind the product are negative as with given projected prices, there will be a negative delta to overall costs of the product of around 25%. Second, its competencies are based on experiences with other telephony consumer products and are not sufficient for the target market. Content, network access, subscriber management, value added applications, online technology and the laws of the marketplace are unknown areas for the company. The competitor Siemens faces the same problem. The companies need to partner with other players in the online area in order to subsidize the business model and to gain the required competencies and market access to succeed.

In order to solve its problem, Alcatel is developing value network partnerships. For the French market the following constellation is set up: the proprietary online service Minitel (the online service of France Telecom) serves as the access provider of choice and expects to sell approximately 2 million units as an upgrade to older Minitel terminals in the existing customer base. This will increase the retention rates of the Minitel service. New customers acquired with the Screen Phone will be rewarded with a payment to Alcatel. Sun Microsystems is selected to supply a Java based operating system and browser for the device. This is considered a significant step to claim market share to the detriment of Microsoft products for non-personal computer (PC) Internet devices. The French Media company Havas supplies major parts of local French content for the desktop of the device. Yahoo! supplies a localized Internet catalogue and sells advertising on the desktop through its successful sales department. La Redoute is the e-commerce partner of choice on the desktop and offers distribution of the device in exchange. Barclays Bank offers online banking as a killer application on the desktop and pays fees (so called "bounties") for new customers. Each of the partners offers market access to its existing customer base. Meanwhile, Siemens develops a similar constellation with the competitors of the partners of Alcatel.

The overall constellation is a win win situation for all partners. Depending on the role of the partners, they exchange market access, retention factors, financial contributions, specific competencies and they all gain competitive advantages. The business model connects all partners on several layers (R & D costs, production costs, marketing expenses, outsourced customer service, ongoing revenues). The units of the participating companies are run as profit centers. Together they bundle a complete on-line service offering in a virtual value network.[47] The constellation seems to be optimal. The strategic problem is that each of the partners has a different perspective towards the business. Each player applies the value chain from its specific traditions: a traditional media company (Havas), a consumer electronic manufacturer (Alcatel), a telecom (FT), a proprietary online service (Minitel), a software company (Sun), a bank (Barclays), an Internet online service (Yahoo!) and a retailer (La Redoute). The underlying business assumptions of each business differ significantly and the business will be perceived in different ways. Therefore, the business direction and the value chain for this virtual system are not consistent. Although each of the partners considers a different value chain, the customer perceives the product bundle as a product that is produced in a system of a virtually closed value chain. Consequently, the virtual value network suffers from inconsistent business models and insufficient business processes. As a result, by the year 1999 there is no offering as described available on the market. A consistent view towards the business system has to be developed.

Case Study 1-1: Integrated On-line Services in a Multi Firm Value Net

---

[47] This example describes the overall business system behind Alcatel's Internet Screen Phone, which was awarded "Product of the Year" at CeBIT 1997. The background is based on interviews with Benoit Raimbault, Marketing Manager Alcatel Screenphone, 24th of July 1997, Paris and Rony Vogel, Marketing Manager Siemens Online Terminal, 27th of July 1997, Munich. The strategic partner of Siemens for telecommunication was CompuServe. Additional background information can be found at Andersen (1998d).

This example shows a bundled on-line service offering, which integrates several complementary partners. Together they produce an on-line product and service offering in a virtual network constellation. This scenario reveals the complexity of the on-line business and the need to define a clear structure of the business environment. It shows how each of the contributing partners considers its contribution as part of the on-line focused product-market – strategy and differences in the related business focus become apparent. Furthermore, it illustrates how players in the ICT area need to share competencies and have to build up value network relationships, in order to participate in on-line service offerings in the Internet. The synergy of the overall network constellation adds additional value to each singular contributor. Finally, it reveals the problem of miscellaneous standpoints with different underlying traditions towards the on-line business, which leads to inconsistent perceptions of the actual business. Therefore, a view relying on the genuine perspective as described above should be developed in order to provide a consistent view towards the business environment. This perspective does not yet exist and consequently there is no clear understanding of strategic management in the online business within the scientific community. This thesis analyzes these aspects and focuses on the strategic management of the product-market area and the value creating structures, summarized as follows:

> Model the structure of the on-line industry and work out a set of tools to derive and conduct a product-market – strategy and networking strategy!

This problem implies a path forward in several steps. The first step is to take an **aggregate industry perspective** and to derive a framework, which structures the entire business environment in a way that reveals the product-market and value creating relationship. The second step of this general framework is to utilize a **specific company perspective**, in order to explain the corporate positioning, the product-market strategy and the related value creation strategy of a company and its business system. For this purpose a set of tools has to be developed, which takes external market factors into account as well as internal resources. As a consistent and verified view of the on-line business does not exist yet, the problem ultimately requires a solution that approaches the online business in a holistic way, explaining issues from an aggregate industry standpoint as well as a specific company standpoint. This view has to consider especially the dramatic speed of change, the highly virtualized value creating structures as well as the vast technological and regulatory implications. Figure 1-6 illustrates the cohesion of the problem:

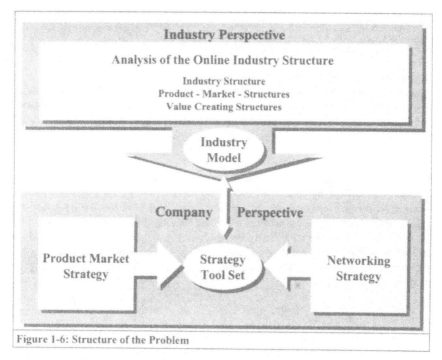

Industry Perspective

Analysis of the Online Industry Structure

Industry Structure
Product - Market - Structures
Value Creating Structures

Industry
Model

Company | **Perspective**

Product Market
Strategy

Strategy
Tool Set

Networking
Strategy

Figure 1-6: Structure of the Problem

Thus the formulation of the problem is focused on the business practice rather than the business theory. This is appropriate for two main reasons. On the one hand, the on-line area is an economic sector which is highly relevant for the future and so far the scientific community has not devoted comprehensive analytical efforts to this area. The theory of strategic management as an applied theory still needs to deliver conceptual input with strategic models and strategy tools to the business practice. On the other hand, the actual practice of the on-line business has a high degree of innovation and creativity, which needs to be examined as there might be implications, which lead to adjustments of basic premises of business and economic theory. Answers to these problems may be found with a strong focus on the practice of the business rather than by primarily utilizing existing theoretical concepts.

The solution of the problem will lead to an overall model of the on-line business and a set of tools, which can be applied for the strategic management of a company and which can be used to derive the competitive strategic potential for an individual company. It will also further deliver input to the current scientific discussions with implications for economic and business theory. The following will outline the theoretical context, position this thesis in the scientific community, and lay out the research design of the underlying research project.

1.3. Applied Theory, Scientific Positioning & Research Design

1.3.1. Applied Theory & Scientific Positioning

Which theories and methodology are appropriate? Which theories can be applied and how do they relate to each other? Although the definition of the research problem focuses on rather practical issues, it, in fact, implicitly raises theoretical problems as well. Does the industry indeed require a new set of theories as some publications suggest (Kelley 1998) or do old economic principles still guide the directions (Varian / Shapiro 1998a) of this infant industry?

Examining the problem one finds two main clusters. The first cluster seeks to understand the industry and to develop a model. In this sense, a neutral concept which helps to grasp the **general scope and mechanisms of the industry** is required. The second cluster seeks to understand the incorporated issues, which need to be solved, in order to derive strategy for individual firms. In this respect, one needs to be able to comprehend the strategic challenges from the **individual view of firms**. For these purposes a set of tools for the product market strategy and the network strategy needs to be developed. Ultimately, chosen theories need to be compatible, in order to develop a model of the industry combined with a set of tools for a firm to make strategy in a consistent way.

It remains a question as to whether the problem should be analyzed from a microeconomic market-based view, which looks at the industrial economics of the business environment. Or is it more a question of business strategy of individual companies conducting business in a highly complex world, which is exhibiting evolutionary patterns of a complex autopoetic system? This indicates quite different choices of theoretical paths on offer for the solution of the problem.

As the central conceptual framework, this work chooses to apply the **most recent theoretical framework of network economics** (Katz / Shapiro 1985, Economides 1996, Varian / Shapiro 1998a), which **are an "updated version" translating traditional industrial economics and the accompanying market-based view of business strategies into the new information economy**. Therefore, microeconomic concepts dominate this dissertation.

In the context of modeling the industry in part II, the theory is extended with further components of industrial economics, mainly the five forces framework (Porter 1980) and an adapted version for converging competitions (Dowling / Lechner / Thielmann 1998a). Aside from this theoretical background, extensive areas of part II are of a descriptive nature, which document the empirical findings.

In the context of part III the particular challenges rooted in the on-line industry are solved from an individual firm perspective. Highlighted are appropriate components of the **market-based view** and the **resource-based view**, with the aim of showing to which extent business strategy can be based on these mainstream approaches of business strategy. Namely, the insights of the market-based view are discussed and translated into insights from microeconomic theory for the specifics of the industry. Initially, the traditional concept of the neoclassical theory of markets and the Structure - Conduct - Performance (SCP) - Paradigm (Bain 1956, Sutton 1991) tells a great deal with regards to the strategic implications of the industry structures and exogenous parameters found in the field. In order to consider the market dynamics, the ideas of Hayek (1937, 1945) will be put into perspective with the industrial facts. Given this the central role of friction on firms' profits and Hayek's notion of the distribution and use of knowledge with respect to market dynamics will be the conceptual bridge from the outside-in to the inside-out approach of the resource-based view (Penrose 1959, Prahalad / Hamel 1990). This emphasizes the knowledge aspect for an industry, which is driven by intangible assets, such as know-how, human resources, and capital. The idea of a competence configuration (Krogh / Roos 1992), which dynamically compares internal resources and the required tasks in the field builds a bridge to the empirical findings of the field. These insights from mainstream business strategy theories will be combined into a tool set designed to work on the industry model. **The surprising finding is that these – in some cases very old – mainstream theories can explain the majority of the strategic issues.**

Nevertheless some of questions remain unanswered and therefore the analysis extend these insights with **the most recent work which has a very (Inter)net-centric focus.** This work discusses the technological implications of the innovative Internet area. Moreover, the **particular economics of information and communication technologies** lead to specific implications. Namely, the work on **business strategy in the context of network economics** (Varian / Shapiro 1998a, Economides 1996) and the concept of **co-opetition** (Brandenburger / Nalebuff 1997) are applied. Both concepts highlight the **salient role of complementors**, where the former approaches the issues form a microeconomic standpoint and the later from a **game theory** driven perspective.

Although vast areas of this thesis utilize microeconomic theories, which are usually based on analytical models, **the findings are translated into a conceptual model.** Different from the ceteris-paribus, duopoly models of microeconomists, the work of Brandenburger / Nalebuff lays out a conceptual framework, which considers all factors dynamically. Therefore, this is an excellent extension of the conceptual approach utilized by this work and ultimately is well suited for the empirical patterns of the on-line industry.

In order to put these theoretical components into perspective, Figure 1-7 presents a structure of four layers, which explain the **cohesion of economic practice and theory in complex environments.**[48] The layers move downwards from a very abstract and general view to a more concrete and specific view. It shows how **knowledge is transferred between theory and practice** through cases, which connect academia with the practical sphere. The multiple arrows show the **evolving character of the system,** which is embedded in the economy, continuously adjusting and co-evolving with the environment. The figure illustrates the underlying understanding of the relationship between theory and practice. The research design (1.3.2) of the underlying research project was set-up accordingly.

---

[48] This figure is an applied version of the evolutionary relation of business practice and theory in complex environments (Kirsch 1992). It is presented at this point of the thesis to illustrate how the applied scientific program of the research project has utilized synergies between the practical and theoretical spheres in this complex environment.

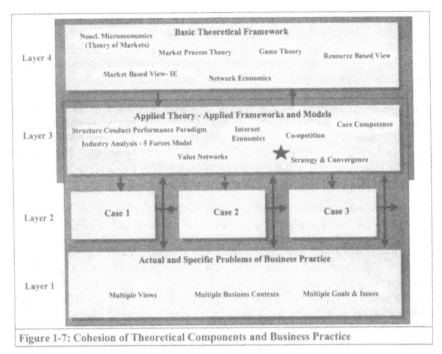

Figure 1-7: Cohesion of Theoretical Components and Business Practice

As was stated above under many aspects the on-line business practice is more creative and more advanced than are the discussions within the scientific community so far. While practice continues to drive this development the scientific community has to catch up with this process. Because of this reason, a **major part of the scientific work is descriptive** at this point in time.[49] The scientific community is challenged to describe the business practice in a general way, to **discover significant trends and** to **increase the level of abstraction, while modeling the real world.** On this more abstract layer, existing economic and business models can be utilized in order to enhance and adapt them for the on-line environment. **Nevertheless the author also presents prescriptive insights** which are based on the conclusions the author has derived from the empirical and theoretical findings.

Only limited research from a strategic management standpoint has occurred so far.[50] For this reason, the formulated problem focuses the on-line environment in a holistic way and puts an

---

[49] This also reflects the approach of the scientists who were part of the cooperative research network during the course of the underlying research project. The research area is considered to have a high degree of novelty and current research tries to approach the business practice in a descriptive way in order to develop models with higher levels of abstraction.

[50] At this point in time, the majority of research concentrates on the third layer. The reason is that the scientific community has adopted the topic only recently, with a much stronger emphasis in the United States. So far, primarily the consulting companies and investment banks are generating abstract knowledge about the on-line business in a significant way. The particular approach of consultants especially on value chains, technology life cycles, adoption rates, various matrixes and so forth have focused on layers two and three. The projects are usually run under the headline of multimedia or e-commerce. Opposed to this, investment banks have developed a more convincing understanding of the fundamentals of this industry and usually combine these

emphasis on business practice. This thesis is a contribution to the **applied theory of strategic management** and will present a **conceptual framework** and **application tools** for business strategy in the on-line industry. Referring to Figure 1-7, it is positioned in layer 3 where it connects business practice and the scientific community and gains insights from both perspectives. The star symbol represents this and shows a close positioning to concepts like Internet economics, complementary networks in co-opetitive constellations and research on convergence.

Moreover, **a host of cases and business situations** (layer 2) are introduced. They will be analyzed, in order to derive general patterns that can be transferred into the theoretical framework and frequently illustrate theoretical conclusions. This bottom up process will ensure that the creative potential of the actual on-line business will be utilized and the derived models are robust and able to represent problems occurring in actual practice (layer 1). In a top down direction, the models and frameworks will incorporate insights, which will be broken down from frameworks of higher abstraction (layer 4). This will be formulated with practical terms which will match the needs of the on-line business environment.

Finally this thesis serves as an interface between the rapidly changing business environment and the scientific community. Utilizing theoretical methods and frameworks, abstract models and tools on how to conduct business on-line will be developed for actual practice. The scientific community will gain a structured picture of strategic management in the on-line business, which makes it possible to derive further insights for economic and business theory in this new environment. According to this academic goal, the research design has been set up which is outlined below.

1.3.2. Research Design

The research was designed in such a way as to take into account the rapid speed of **change of the field, international dimension** of the industry, insights from **industrial practice** as well as **academia** via **field and desk research**.

The novelty and complexity is a challenge for the design of the underlying research project. The international dimension required observations in Europe and the United States. In addition, conducting applied research in an infant industry required intense exchange with industrial practitioners and academia with a wide scope rather than a narrow focus. Furthermore,

---

insights with powerful value driven considerations. Most of the European research and consulting projects funded by companies in the converging industries: telecommunication, media, computer and consumer electronic or by political institutions (e. g. the US Department of Commerce, the European Commission DG III, DG XIII, DG XV, BMWi, UK ministry for trade and industry). Due to the particular background of these industries, the perceptions are heavily influenced by the convergence industries. This thesis will prove that the on-line business needs to be analyzed in an authentic way and the horizontal views of the converging industries systematically reduces this perspective. This is the main reason why consulting projects overlooked some major aspects so far. The majority of the US consulting projects approach the on-line business form a lateral perspective such as banking or automotive. They usually analyze this environment with regards to e-commerce or virtual value creation aspects. Considering these sources, extensive internal documentation from different companies was used as background information for this thesis.

the reliability and validity of the available quantitative data exhibited extremely poor quality, therefore it was insufficient to develop quantitative conclusions.[51]

In order to manage this scientific challenges the following research design was set-up, where four sources representing the spectrum between theory and practice were integrated into a cooperative situation in order to exchange information and add value from several perspectives. The following groups were selected within this spectrum in order to utilize knowledge from different levels of abstraction and complementary expertise:

Scientific community
Analysts
Consultants
Business practitioners

The research problem (1.2) was analyzed and approached in knowledge exchange with these groups aimed to work out the significance of the research object as illustrated in Figure 1-8:

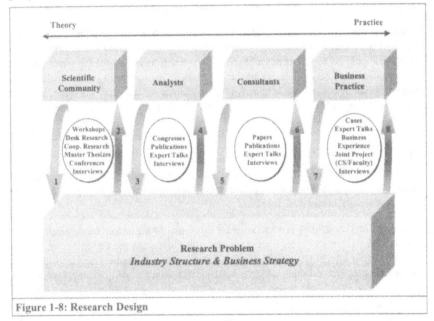

Figure 1-8: Research Design

Within this constellation various activities to utilize insights from all knowledge sources as outlined below were undertaken:

---

[51] This refers not only to the available value of topical data but even more to the quality of forecasts covering future developments. Most of the quantitative statements of market researchers, analysts and consultants usually have the quality of roughly plausible assumptions based on scenario techniques. It is especially insufficient that the quantitative data about mission critical and strategically crucial factors (see 3.1.4) is unreliable. It is still a common phenomenon that one is exposed to almost a "menu of choices" of a singular business planning factor. It is obvious that the on-line business, although being based on data processing, cannot be analyzed and managed as is a mature business environment. As a consequence, quantitative data was applied in singular aspects but not in the fundamental part of this thesis.

▪ To generate insights with the **scientific community** (arrows 1 & 2), comprehensive desk research was undertaken and a cooperative research network[52] was established, which connected scientists with similar research interests in the United States and Europe. This network was used for ongoing exchange and discussion, with several workshops and conferences being organized around it.[53] Particular aspects were further analyzed in a joint research project between graduate students and CompuServe, plus several master theses, which emerged.[54] Finally, a host of interviews with academic scholars in the United States and Europe (see appendix) were conducted.

▪ The exchange with **analysts** (arrows 3 & 4) was conducted at congresses, round table discussions, interviews, and an ongoing review of their publications.[55]

▪ **Consultants** are a typical interface between academia and industrial practice (arrows 5 & 6), which holds particularly true in a growth industry.[56] This work integrates a large number of their publications, analyzed extensive documentation from company internal projects[57] and conducted several interviews.

▪ Finally, an intense exchange with the **business practice** (arrows 7 & 8) via expert talks and interviews (see appendix) is maintained. Furthermore, a simultaneous professional involvement with the CompuServe on-line service – the sponsor of this research project – developed a profound understanding of the business fundamentals. Relevant practical responsibilities and research interests established enormous synergies in this relationship. Expertise from strategic business planning, business operations and detailed insight into actual business situations contributed a great deal. These insights are integrated in an implicit as well as explicit manner, which provides the empirical foundation of this thesis. Conceptual discussion with experts exposed the premises, assumptions, and conclusions of this thesis to a constant process of criticism, which helped to keep the conceptual framework of this dissertation robust and relevant.

---

[52] The author took part in the research team of the University of California "e-conomy" project as a visiting scholar of the Berkeley Round Table on the International Economy (BRIE) at UC Berkeley from February 1999 through May 1999. Furthermore ongoing joint research efforts were undertaken with the Media and Communications Management Institute (MCM), University of St. Gallen from August 1998 through September 1999, and the University of Regensburg from March 1998 through September 1999. Furthermore the author worked together with researchers from the London School of Economics, Stanford University and the University of Piacenza.

[53] 6th / 7th of July 1998, 11th / 12th of February 1999 and 26th / 27th August 1999 in St. Gallen, 4th / 5th of November 1998 in Munich, 4th / 5th of May 1999 Los Angeles.

[54] Graduate students of the Institute of International Management of the University of the German Armed Forces and CompuServe – the sponsor of this project – conducted a research program analyzing product and pricing issues of a content based on-line service offering.

[55] See Communic (1997a, 1997b), BCLT (1999), Baack / Eberspächer (1999, eds.), Cioffi / Berg (1999), and a host of publications from financial analysts.

[56] As the consulting companies expect that the entire Internet framework will be a huge source of future consulting projects they are starting to analyze the field and publish the findings to convince future customers of the necessity to react and to prove their expertise.

[57] Comprehensive information and documentation of consulting projects in the multimedia and telecommunications sector from the following consulting companies was accessible: McKinsey, AT Kearney, KPMG, Booz Allen & Hamilton, Deloitte Consulting, Coopers & Lybrand, Squire Sanders & Dempsey, and Andersen Consulting.

Applying this methodology, comprehensive empirical information and integration of scholarly insight from practical as well as academic perspectives in Europe and the United States were combined. Ultimately, this dissertation is developed by exposing a conceptual model, framework and tools based on a solid foundation of qualitative and quantitative data to a wider audience. This work declines to develop quantitative models as the available data (see above) does not yet support such a modeling. Therefore, it uses quantitative data rather for illustrative purposes within the text.

For easier comprehension and illustrative purposes, large parts of the analysis and discussion are enhanced with short cases. These **cases serve as illustrative examples** and not as comprehensive case studies, although the analysis of past proprietary on-line services (2.3, 2.4) is comprehensively built on the case of CompuServe.[58]

Based on this underlying research agenda the author develops the structure in 1.4.

1.4. Structure of the Thesis

The structure of the thesis mirrors the structure of the problem defined above.

Part I covers the introductory chapter of this dissertation. It presents a set of preliminary considerations describing the particular approach (1.1) of this thesis. Section 1.2 illustrates the research problem of the corresponding industry structure and strategy in the on-line industry with a short case study and structures the problem. Section 1.3 places this dissertation into perspective with other research and economic and business theories and outlines the methodology of the underlying research project.

Part II holds forth on the general perspective and analyzes the industrial framework of the on-line business, working out a conceptual model. It is of purely descriptive nature and contains comprehensive empirical components. Section 2.1 presents a snapshot of the overall situation of the field in the late 1990s and explains how external factors policy, technology, society, and economy interplay with the on-line industry. Based on these findings, Section 2.2 introduces the concept of network economics, extends this with the idea of market forces in converging industries, and ultimately lays out a conceptual model for multi-layered industries. In Section 2.3 it argues that proprietary on-line services tell a great deal about on-line business in general and analyzes past technologies, drivers of business models and the underlying vertically integrated business system. Section 2.4 extends this, by focusing on the adjustment processes affecting the industry in the mid-1990s, as they occur in the course of convergence of the ICT area and rapid adoption of Internet standard technology, which changed the industrial economics and industrial structures in an unbundling process. Ultimately, Section 2.5 lays out the structure of the new Internet paradigm of on-line services, as it exhibits networked openness, change, and growth and finally presents an applied model representing the structure and mechanisms of the on-line industry.

---

[58] As Eisenhardt (1989, pp. 538-539) points out, data collection and processing are not discrete and sequential tasks in the course of case studies. They occur ongoing during the process of research. This describes the character and proceeding of the underlying research activities of this thesis as continuous access to data of the field which was used for the practical examples and cases was provided.

Part III switches to the perspective of an individual firm and prepares a set of tools for business strategy in the on-line industry, enabling firms to navigate in this competitive arena. Section 3.1 catches up the empirical and conceptual findings of the industry structure and outlines the resulting challenges for business strategy. Section 3.2 discusses the relevant parts of the market-based view and the resource-based view, finally deriving a high-level strategy tool set from these mainstream business strategy theories. Section 3.3 switches to a level of finer granularity and introduces several net-centric strategy concepts, discussing firm conduct with respect to product, networking, pricing, adoption, and complementary strategies with each resulting in a strategy tool. Ultimately, the instruments worked out in the course of this dissertation pulling together the industry model, tool set and tools and enhancing them with an extensive case study, are summarized in Section 3.4.

Part IV summarizes the findings in Section 4.1 while Section 4.2 points out the issues, which remain unsolved and require further research.

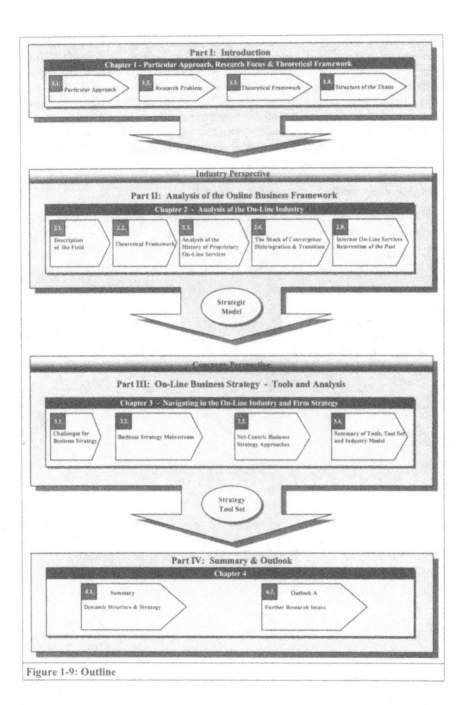

Figure 1-9: Outline

Part II: On-line Industry Structure - Analysis & Model

2. Analysis of the On-line Industry

The second chapter will develop a **comprehensive picture of the on-line business as a multi-layered industry, which is virtually constituted out of five vertically related layers.** In addition, it will show how each of these layers contains several sub-layers. This chapter is a **descriptive view of the on-line business industry,** which generates data on the field and discloses the underlying structures. The ultimate aim, however, is **to construct a model of the industry.** In the process of so doing, insights of the most recent practice of the wider field as well additional insights from proprietary online services will be presented, as these tell a great deal about conducting on-line based business.

Section 2.1 approaches the on-line industry as a black-box and presents an analysis of the **exogenous parameters,** which shape the development path of the on-line industry with respect to the impact of size as well as structure of the markets.

Section 2.2 lays out the **theoretical framework** for the descriptive part and the main methodological foundation by introducing the theory of network economics. This framework will be extended with a novel concept to analyze competitive forces in converging industries. On these grounds, a **conceptual model** for multi-layered industries will be worked out.

Section 2.3 analyzes the **history of proprietary on-line services** to present a picture of past commercial traditions, which may lead the direction in the further commercial development of on-line services in the Internet framework.

Section 2.4 focuses on the processes which impacted the on-line industry in the middle of the 1990s when the forces of technological **convergence and the advent of the Internet** created a fundamental discontinuity in the evolution of interactive media and on-line services.[1]

Section 2.5 presents the structure of the **on-line industry in the Internet framework** and combines the empirical and theoretical findings of part two in an **applied model.** This model generates a clear picture of the industry and can be applied to analyze industrial constellations. However, this model must be viewed with the strategy tools presented and worked out in part III.

2.1. Description of the Field

The function of the following aspects within this thesis is to point out the vital **exogenous parameters** of the overall environment, which will influence the endogenous variables of the industry system.[2] The first issue is to identify the respective parameters and to **disclose their relevancy for strategic management purposes.** The second issue is to analyze the **current state** of their development path. A third issue is to discuss how adjustments of these exogenous parameters may have an **impact on the outcome of the endogenous variables** of the

---

[1] See Bar / Borrus (1997), Bar / Cohen / Cowhey / DeLong / Kleeman / Zysman (1999).

[2] Regarding a wider research agenda, these exogenous parameters can be central for other research activities in the context of the e-conomy (Figure 1-1). The analysis below shows that most of these factors are uncertain or at least not finally analyzed in the late 1990s. This indicates that further research is needed in these areas.

focal system "on-line industry". As the Internet is a new, rapidly changing and highly complex system, most of the parameters are only at the early stage of discussions. Most of the factors of the system are still far from being stabile enough to provide certainty in the conduct business. Figure 2-1 shows the **on-line industry as a black box,** which is embedded into an environment consisting of the political and institutional framework (2.1.1), the technological environment (2.1.2), the industrial framework (2.1.1), the technological environment (2.1.2), the industrial framework (2.1.3) and the overall socio-economic environment (2.1.4) impact this black box.[3]

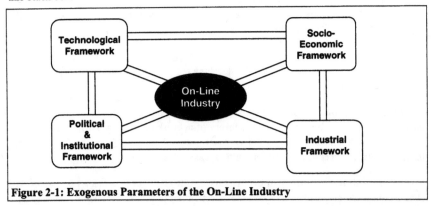

Figure 2-1: Exogenous Parameters of the On-Line Industry

The following analysis empirically approaches and discuss these exogenous parameters and summarizes conclusions for the development path of the on-line industry. In the consecutive course of the thesis this black box will go through an analysis, which will enlighten this area.

2.1.1. Political & Institutional Framework

Crucial external parameters, which are mainly a concern of public policy,[4] will affect the industry. Their current state will be introduced in the following and a brief discussion will provide the relevant conclusions for the purposes of this thesis. Although the majority of the companies will not play an active role in the development of these parameters most of their business models will be directly or indirectly affected by them. Companies, familiar with the

---

[3] It is reasonable to select these four factors, which represent the major sources of influence to the industry. In addition to their impact on the on-line industry, they furthermore correlate with each other, which creates a very complex cause and effect setting. The same factors were identified by the government sector in the United States (Margherio et. al 1997 and USA 1998), and in Europe (KPMG 1996a, European Commission 1997a, Squire, Sanders, Dempsey 1998a, 1998b and 1998c, BMWi 1996b and 1996c, UK Department of Trade and Industry 1996, 1997, 1998) as well as supranational organizations (OECD 1998a). Academia is also analyzing these external parameters in Europe (see Zerdick 1997, eds.) as well as in the United States (see BCLT 1999).

[4] Numerous sessions rounds at the Berkeley Round Table on the International Economy (BRIE) substantially contributed to these institutional and public policy aspects. Furthermore, the panels and discussions during the congress on the legal and public policy framework on e-commerce at UC Berkeley, March 5th - 6th 1999 provided a comprehensive overview. For a conference summary see Cioffi (1999a). The sources outlined in footnote 3 include a complete in depth discussion of all factors.

rules of the political sector, are equipped with the resources to play an active role and need to understand the crucial parameters for their business.[5]

The positive result of the analysis of the **status quo** is that the **main issues are identified**.[6] International governments, academia as well as global industrial players agree on the issues, which need to be solved. A negative finding has been that the process to a solution is in a **very premature stage**. The matters are characterized by **conflicting interest** and **divergent prioritization** from political, legal and industrial positions with different national interests. Furthermore, there is as yet no organization[7] or institution in existence, which could handle a political problem solving process, which considers social, legal, economic and technological in such a supranational scope. Enormous complexity and uncertainty exist. Therefore, the main contribution in this thesis is to outline the factors and show their implications:

- **Security:**[8]
- **Tariffs & Taxation**[9]
- **Privacy**[10]

---

[5] See BMWi (1998) for the positions of companies to the European Greenbook (European Commission 1997a). Furthermore, see (USA 1998) for postings of industry positions towards the US government. See Section 3.2.2 for the resource-based implications for business strategy.

[6] Concurring factors were outlined by the sources mentioned in footnote 3.

[7] Just to name a few relevant – but yet insufficient – institutions: OECD, IEC, ISO, ITU, WTO, WIPO, European Commission, US Government agencies. An interesting model is the very efficient work of the supranational and independent IETF (Internet Engineering Task Force) or W3C (WWW Consortium), which oversee the global http protocol, the html and many more standardization processes, which is recognized by all commercial players.

[8] The technology of the Internet (2.1.2) was initially not designed for commercial purposes and hence is lacking secure standards (see Perrine 1997). This is necessary to provide a solid environment for further commercialization of on-line services and the growth of e-commerce. (a) Secure authentication is needed to identify partners in exchange relations. (b) In order to support confidentiality and to protect privacy (see below) encryption enhancements are necessary. (c) For clear digital signatures a common and secure design for contracting is needed. To provide these secure and authenticated transactions, the process needs to be based on confidentially, authentication, integrity, a time stamp and non-repudiation (see Baker 1999 and Merrill 1999). For a further insights see Margherio et. al (1997), p. 39, USA (1997), pp. 14-15, KPMG (1996a) pp. 57, 225.

[9] The main issues with tariffs and taxation are: (a) some areas are not appropriate for increased taxation or tariffs, in order not to crowd out the future growth potential, while other areas seem to appear as normal business which should be taxed traditionally. (b) If a party plans to introduces taxes the relevant location is unclear in many respects. It is possible to use the legal seat of a company, the location of the server, or the location of the end user of a transaction. The plausibility of which factor seems to be the most appropriate varies enormously depending on the specific taxation issue. (c) Due to the nature of the web as a distributed system, these factors are usually desegregated and international as well as trade issues become relevant. For further detail see USA (1997), pp. 4-5, Squire, Sanders, Dempsey (1998a) pp. 23-27, OECD (1998a), pp. 13-14. Finally, the current state of tariffs as well as taxes can be described as exploratory phase and as a reaction to the new environment (see Frost 1999).

[10] Privacy is a vital parameter. „Many current business trends (and consulting buzz-phrases) reinforce this notion: Customer intimacy, intranets, extranets, multi-firm value nets, knowledge management and on-line community all depend on trusted relationships, mutual disclosure, identity management and other thorny issues that remain unsolved in cyberspace." (Dyson 1999). Three main roadblocks can be identified. (a) First there are many different standpoints regarding this issue, which are culturally bound or simply vary enormously upon individual preferences. Currently, the industry and policy sectors are mutually working to solve these issues. (b) Second there is a trade off between increased privacy protection rules and the possibilities to personalize products, which is increasingly the individual value added of products. (c) Third there is a conflicting trade off between increasing privacy and business model adoption. For further reading see Margherio et al. (1997) pp. 39-40, USA (1997), pp. 12-13, Lessig (1998a), Dyson (1997, 1998) and Dyson et. al.

- **Jurisdiction & Code**[11]
- **Intellectual Property Rights**[12]
- **Governance of Antitrust and Deregulation**[13]

(1998). For the European perspective see Squire, Sanders, Dempsey (1998b), pp. 17-18, 204-205 and KPMG (1996a), pp. 220-225. For an excellent and detailed empirical analysis on privacy protection within on-line services see Gauthronet / Nathan (1998). For a European comparative analysis see Reidenberg / Schwartz (1998). It is ultimately worth noting, that a total annual turnover of $1.5 billion (see Reidenberg 1999) is generated with the sales of personal information in the US alone.

[11] There is an ongoing debate addressing whether there is a need for a new code regarding cyberspace or not. Squire, Sanders, Dempsey (1998b), p. 229 support the position that "(...) there is little need for new laws or regulations to be adopted with respect to the Internet. What is required, however, is that the existing body of laws and regulations throughout the multimedia spectrum be adapted so as to reflect common principles across all sectors." Although in addition they propose to adjust the definitions underlying the existing code as "Existing regulatory definitions are fundamentally ill-suited to deal with the phenomenon of convergence." (ibid.:238). Contrasting to this standpoint Lessig (1995, 1997b, 1998b and 1999) elaborates on a new code defining the cyberlaw. But taking a pure business standpoint, it has to be stated that it is an issue that existing cases provide precedence for future business, while they are working around a formal legislation process. This reasoning from case to case is rather common for the US but other countries e.g. Germany have major methodical problems with these aspects. As a result, Germany issued a federal code (see IUKDG 1997). The impact on the industry is far felt, because the judiciary is sending strong signals to commercial players, who adjust their behavior accordingly. The most prominent example so far was the conviction of the German CompuServe Country Manager for the support of child pornography and illegal nazi propaganda. An enormous uproar resounded throughout the entire global Internet community. As a result, the German market lost significant attraction to commercial players. Furthermore, as a result of IUKDG, a large majority of German ISP's are operating their hosting business outside the country. Finally, legal uncertainty (Burkert 1994) is a large issue for economic development.

[12] The issue of intellectual property rights includes primarily the aspects of (a) copyrights, (b), trademarks and domain names and (c) patents (see USA 1997, pp. 8-11). Companies from different areas, such as Hollywood's entertainment industries, hardware companies, software developers (e.g. the Linux open source movement vs. Microsoft's proprietary approach), telecommunications carriers up to the individual content creator have indeed conflicting interests. Depending on the final solution, different type of players will either be better or worse off. Samuelson (1999:16) comes to the conclusion: "We are currently witnessing the emergence of new forms of commerce in information and new means by which to distribute it. As a consequence, new rules governing commerce in information are inevitable. (...) Intellectual property law and policy will (...) be an integral part (...) if the information economy is to achieve its full potential." For further discussion see Dyson (1994), Dyson (1996), Dyson (1997), Lessig (1995), Lessig (1997a) and Merges et. al. (1997). Squire, Sanders, Dempsey (1998b), pp. 203-204 present the European perspective. For recommendations in the strategic application of copyrights and patents in the ICT area see Hayes (1999). For deeper reflection and an alternative view on intellectual property rights see Barlow (1994).

[13] Subsection 2.2.1 will explain how the particular economics of networks carries strong tendencies of horizontal and vertical concentration along the value chain. This leads to anti trust issues. But while regulation should support consumer choice and economic efficiency, the logic of network economics leads to a concentration of markets which can have beneficial aspects for all players. The theory of network economics will highlight the highly valuable interconnections and bottlenecks as the central variable for these issues. As a conclusion "The future regulatory framework should address the risks of market failure and/or the creation of bottlenecks. To this end, targeted regulation should focus on high value activities in the multimedia value chain." (Squire, Sanders, Dempsey 1998b:230) Furthermore, "The existing static model of 'vertical' regulation of the respective telecommunications, broadcasting and publishing sectors requires re-evaluation. A new "horizontal" regulatory model is needed that reflects the commercial and technological realities of multimedia and addresses the new industry configurations which are emerging in the marketplace." (ibid.:261) The same position is supported by KMPG (1996a), pp. 110, 146-147 and 149-150. In addition to the current research, this thesis will deliver a model of the industry, which makes it capable of comprehending these horizontal and vertical aspects of the value layers (Figure 2-38). It also has to be stated that "The widely held view that the Internet is "unregulated" is incorrect. Although the current system of Internet governance is relatively anarchic, it is wrong to assume that the Internet is not subject to any regulation." (Squire, Sanders, Dempsey 1998b:238) For further reading see Lessig (1997b) or for the European perspective Squire, Sanders,

The order of these factors does not imply any prioritization as this is finally a matter of a given standpoint. As it was stated above, there is a wide spectrum of organizations and institutions that are playing a role in their development process. Currently there, is a **problem of how these factors should be developed**. Obviously, there is no controlling overseer in existence, who is able to handle the complexity of the Internet. An ideal path would be the design of an *a priori* framework in a social and public policy process and a subsequent development of the industry. Obviously this is impossible while the on-line industry and related business is developing simultaneously with the exogenous variables. Answers will be found in the spectrum between complete political governance and complete self-regulation within the industry. Political governance could easily crowd out the growth potential and strong self-regulation carries a threat of a resulting market failure, which could lead to economic inefficiency or social discrepancies.[14] The United States government has defined five **policy principles** in this context:[15]

- The private sector should lead
- Governments should avoid undue restrictions
- Where governmental involvement is needed, its aim should be to support and enforce a predictable, minimalist, consistent and simple legal environment
- Governments should recognize the unique qualities of the Internet
- Electronic Commerce over the Internet should be facilitated on a global basis

Overall this seems to be a wise general guideline to ensure a development path of an infant industry. It is significant that European positions are concurrent in many aspects although the European governmental sector seems to reflect more on social and political implications of the Internet. This is due to greater experience with regulating the media industry and controlling the content in public TV networks, where, for example, issues of plurality of opinions, general access to information, or prosecution of particular content are traditionally controlled aspects. Furthermore, stronger traditions in customer protection are already leading to a more restrictive management of the growing privacy issues in Europe and growing problems in the United States.[16] On the other hand the United States has more comprehensive experience in the governance of telecommunications, hardware, and software industry. Facing the overall

---

Dempsey (1998b), pp. 143-158. For an economic analysis see Economides (1995a) and Economides / White (1994).

[14] See KPMG (1996a), p. 159. The term efficiency refers to the concept of economic (Pareto) efficiency, which is a situation where is no way to make one consumer better off without making some other consumer worse off. For many cases of interest, Pareto efficient outcomes can be thought of as those that maximize the sum of economic benefits minus costs (see Varian 1992, pp. 222-223).

[15] USA (1997) p. 2-3 and Margherio et. al (1997), pp. 50-51.

[16] For an overview see Europe (1997), European Commission (1997), KPMG 1996a, Squires, Sanders, Dempsey 1998c and Raab et. al. (1998) for an international comparison which was conducted for the European Commission. The following quotation shows strong evidence for future Internet related privacy problems in the USA: "Complete fair information practice protections including enforcement for consumers who are the subject of marketing data in the United States are rare. This conclusion is the same for online and off-line activities. Marketing is, for the most part, an unregulated activity so no external fair information practice requirements exist." (ibid.:164).

complex challenge, it seems appropriate for all responsible players to take a humble position and consider the long term effects of their current conduct.[17]

Nevertheless, this area is a complex matter, which is constantly changing. No factor is stabilized and many parties have different views and expectations. Furthermore, the factors are correlated in multiple ways. The procedure and the right kind of organization to manage these issues is still a large problem. It has to be summarized that the **development of the political and institutional framework** of the on-line industry is a highly political process and **will take many years** while the **industry will double its volume every 12 to 18 months.**[18] **A cooperative approach** between governments, industry, social groups and nations promises the best outcome possible.[19] However the crucial result for businesses is that the **political sector cannot provide certainty for a significant time,** regarding the six factors, which are discussed above. Individual players from the industries neither know their preferences nor see the opportunities. Consequently, entrepreneurs will develop a business in an environment with few rules. Without the existence of exogenous parameters, companies establish their own rules and try to keep these stabilized. This is currently a significant empirical aspect of the industry: Companies make their own rules for their business as only few rules have been established to this point. Even the existing rules are often adjustable. Some companies also have the know-how and resources to participate in the political process and influence the exogenous variables from within the industry.[20] As long as the political environment is not stabilized **competitive strategy** has to **consider the impact of these exogenous variables to generate competitive advantage from these external factors in a reactive and proactive way** (see also 3.2.1). The following illustration shows, how an "exogenous" factor influences the firms business models, by using the example of the regulation of interconnection fees:

> The WTO telecommunications negotiations ended successfully in 1997. All countries agreed to privatize the telecommunications monopolies and open their markets under terms of equal treatment and most favorable nations to foreign firms. The countries of the European Community specified that new entrants will be allowed to use the incumbent's network at reasonable cost. In order to regulated that constellation each country installed local regulators – comparable to the Federal Communications Commission (FCC) in the United States – to decide what that cost might be.[21] The difficulty is to set up interconnection rates

---

[17] The statement of humbleness is taken from the interview with Eliot Maxwell, Special advisor to the United States administration on the digital economy, 4th of March 1999, Berkeley. It seems to be the wisest guideline for the conduct in policy issues for all players in this complex challenge.

[18] See Feldman (1999) with additional contribution from the interview with Elliot Maxwell, special advisor to the United States federal administration, 4th of March 1999, Berkeley. Data about growth rates is provided by the commercial analysts and organizations like the OECD. They concur regarding growth rates but they differ regarding the projected total numbers.

[19] See KMPG (1996), Andersen (1998). An additional contribution to this aspect was the interview with Peter Harter, Global Public Policy Counsel of Netscape Corp., 5th of March 1999, Berkeley.

[20] See e.g. BMWi (1998) for a comprehensive overview of the positions of the industry regarding the EC Greenbook. Although companies will support their particular positions, contributions from companies have to be well analyzed. It should be taken into account that the industrial sector has the largest experience with the Internet, gained in everyday business situations.

[21] Additional background by interview with Peter Cowhey of UC San Diego, former advisor to the FCC WTO negotiations, 20th of April 1999, Berkeley. For an overview of the strategic landscape of entering telecom players in the German market shortly before deregulation (see Communic 1997a).

and conditions, which allow for fair competition and do not artificially distort the performance of the firms. However, it is highly problematic to generate these terms to regulate competition. Even if costs are calculated by similar methods, the results may differ widely, depending on the assumptions made regarding cost of capital or the funding of access deficits, which result from unprofitable local line rentals.[22]

"A comparison of local interconnection rates carried out by the European Union in 1997 showed that BT's interconnection fee was 0.52 pence per minute, for example, while NYNEX in Massachusetts charged 2.26 pence. Yet both companies used more or less the same methodology. The fee set is crucial, as differences as small as a tenth of a cent per end (of a phone line) per minute can translate into hundreds of millions of dollars of value lost or won. Not surprisingly, disputes abound. Deutsche Telekom, for example, is opposing its regulator's decision to halve its proposed local interconnection fee. Further arguments are inevitable as costs and traffic volumes change and the focus shifts to negotiating the fee for connecting [data networks, C. G.]. These fees are at present relatively high." (Beardsley 1998:34).

Shortly after Beardsley's observations, the result of the WTO telecom deregulation agreements immensely affected the European on-line markets, because on-line services were allowed to run their data access networks under a telecom license and thus were able to claim interconnection revenues. These revenues are created by the margin between interconnection rate for the local loop a telecom player has to pay to the incumbent and the end user rate, which is captured by the telecom player. The regulation of these interconnection fees results in arbitrage possibilities for the involved players. Of importance in this case is that the on-line services are traditionally operating the telephone numbers, which generate the highest usage hours. Owning a telecom license places them in the position to play in the telecom arena and to capture part of the interconnection arbitrage.

Some volume numbers for the German market in early 1999 are: 0.5 million usage hours for a Free ISP (germany.net), 1 million usage hours for an on-line service (CompuServe) and 2 million (Mobilcom) and 1 million (Arcor) for "call-by-call" offers of telecom providers (internal data). If one considers a subscription of 2 million users for a combined AOL / CompuServe service in Europe, which exhibits an average usage per month of approximately 6 hours, then one receives a call volume of 12 million hours per month.[23]

These volumes put into the perspective of end customer and interconnection prices show how small adjustments in the interconnection regulation directly influence the business model of the on-line access business. Depending on the end customer and interconnection rates, the larger Internet access providers are placed in the position where they can generate huge interconnection revenues.

For example for July 1999, the German Telecom regulator defined the following parameters: Deutsche Telekom charges 2.6 Pfennig per minute for the telephone local loop, while the end user price is set at 9 Pfennig. In addition Deutsche Telekom offers a wholesale ISP network at 2.6 Pfennig per minute, which leaves a margin for the end user service provision for ISP resellers of 3.8 Pfennig. Service providers with larger volumes can negotiate for better rates depending on their bargaining position. At given fixed cost the regulation directly determines the breakeven to profitability for this type of business.

The position of "owning" the largest aggregation of calls in a country is hence a very attractive, but also risky position, which was drastically shown in the UK market in 1998/1999. The UK telecom regulation (OFTEL) was setting interconnection prices in a way that first the large existing on-line services and

---

[22] The deficits in some local regions usually results from the "universal service" requirement, which obliges the incumbent telecom to provide service to every household. For example, the economics of an urban financial area widely differ from the economics of a widespread rural mountain area.

[23] According to interview with Konrad Hilbers, CEO CompuServe Europe and COO AOL Europe, 9th of February 1999, Munich. Data does not show exact, but realistic data due to nondisclosure agreements.

ISP's (AOL, CompuServe, Demon) could suddenly capture an interconnection margin, which subsidized their Internet access business. This affected existing business models of on-line services and traditional ISP's in an extremely positive manner. As an example, the interconnection revenue generated by the access business fueled the business of AOL UK, then the largest access provider in the UK, in a way that it could capture approximately 25% profit per revenue in 1998.[24] As this expert knowledge regarding a lucrative opportunity spread over the time, other players saw possibilities for an ISP start-up and created a market for "FREE ISP's," which attracted a large number of entrants. The presence of open Internet standards and a growing demand in the public enabled these new players to enter competition.

The end user was charged only the local call – thus called "free" – and the ISP captured the margin of the interconnection fee – thus not really "free". The most prominent example was an offspring of the consumer electronics retailer "Dixons", branded "Freesurf". Freesurf could leverage Dixon's retail channel and the aggressive pricing, which resulted in 1 million subscribers in the first year. CompuServe and AOL combined needed 6 years to reach that level. Ultimately, within one year this regulation policy boosted the UK market volume for Internet access by 2 million users in addition to the already projected growth. As a result, AOL UK has a host of new competitors, significantly lost market share and the profits are eroding.[25]

Case Study 2-1: Regulation of Interconnection Rates Shaping Market Size & Structure

This example shows a substantial discontinuity in the market development created by public policy. It shows how public policy – in this case the regulation of telecom interconnection rates – created a new market for "Free ISP's". It is questionable, if this outcome was originally intended by policy but regardless, it changed the competitiveness, the market volumes, the usage levels, and the mind set of the consumers in a positive way. Other public policy issues have comparable impacts on firms' business models and market efficiency.

As all the exogenous variables discussed above are highly correlated with technological, industrial and social aspects, a summary of their impacts on the on-line industry will be presented at the end of Section 2.1. Nevertheless, many aspects are fundamentally dependent on technological standards and how the products are technically designed. These technical parameters often set the framework for what is possible and what may be desirable but unrealistic. Especially the aspect of **interoperability**[26] of networks – a central public policy issue – will substantially be determined by technological design. This will be discussed in subsection 2.1.2, which analyzes the technological framework.

---

[24] According to interview with Klaus Hommels, Assistant Managing Director of AOL Germany, 19th of September 1997, Hamburg. Due to non-disclosure purposes the figure is not exact but provides a reasonable understanding of the profitability.

[25] According to interview with Chris Hill, Executive Vice President Corporate Development AOL Europe, 23rd of June 1999, London.

[26] Interoperability is the ability of two or more given systems (including devices, databases, networks or technologies) to act in concert with one another in accordance with a prescribed method in order to achieve a predictable result. Interoperability allows diverse systems made by different vendors to communicate with each other so users do not have to account for differences in products or services. Interoperability does not lead to the lock-in effect (see 2.2.1) since purchasing components from one system does not preclude communication with components from a different system.

2.1.2. Technological Framework

The technological framework of on-line services and the Internet is a complex issue. In order to keep the following discourse on a reasonable level, only the most essential points, which are salient to the purposes of business strategy will be introduced. After a short introduction of the historical background of the Internet, the technological structure will be outlined. Three major technological issues will be highlighted, which have a heavy impact on future business strategy: First is the issue of availability of bandwidth, second it is the question of the future access network structure, and third is the question of the evolution of standards.

The **history of the Internet** has a non-profit past which leads back to the early 1960s.[27] It is a world-wide **distributed network** of computer networks which use a common communication protocol, **TCP/IP**. TCP/IP provides a common language for interoperation between networks that use a variety of local protocols. The initial idea of a decentralized data network that connects computers, which led to the development of the Internet of today, was driven by the US defense department and later further developed by United States universities. The concept of **data packet-switching** (1962) was enhanced with the application of **hypertext** (1968). The ARPANET[28] (1969) was the predecessor of the Internet which linked together universities and high-tech defense contractors. In the following years the scientific part, NSFNET[29], evolved until the National Science Foundation funding ceased and **the network was privatized on April 30, 1995**. Applications like telnet (1972), ftp (1976), Usenet/newsgroups (1979) were followed by the **http-protocol** and the **World Wide Web**[30] using the hypertext language **html** (1992 presented by CERN scientists) and Mosaic (1993) as the first web browser (ibid.). Due to the standards highlighted above the Internet achieves a high degree of **interoperability between the components of partial systems.** Internet applications gained commercial relevancy since 1995 as all major consumer online services (see Figure 1-3) and Internet service providers (ISP's) introduced Internet applications to a wider audience.

The following will explain the **technological infrastructure** of the Internet and the further necessary **components to provide on-line services.** The technological infrastructure can be divided into three aspects[31]:

> **Data communication aspects of the network:** This describes the sole **network structure of the Internet,** which supports the flow of digital data in telecommunications net-

---

[27] This part covers the history of the Internet although traditional on-line services were not at all equal with the Internet of the past. Section 2.3 will provide an analysis of the traditional proprietary online services and Subsection 1.1.2 gave a brief overview of their business past. Section 2.5 will show how on-line services are experiencing a reincarnation within the framework of the Internet. Therefore an overview of the Internet is sufficient. See Zakon (1999) and Abbate (1994) for a comprehensive overview of the history of the Internet.

[28] Advanced Research Projects Administration (ARPA), a division of the U.S. Defense Department. See Abbate (1994) for a in depth analysis of the development from the ARPANET to the Internet.

[29] Similar developments to the NSFNET scientific networks occurred throughout the international research area, e. g. the German DFN.

[30] Note: Although the WWW is just a graphical user interface to the Internet it is to that which most people refer when considering "The Internet".

[31] As the data is rapidly changing 2.1.2 does not include quantitative data and refers to references. Spectrum (1998) provides a comprehensive overview of topical data on the different technological components.

works. The networks carry bits and bytes and depending on the application type this data can be generated by a phone call, or via a file attachment, or so forth. Within this structure, enormous **backbone networks** transport the aggregated data traffic over long distances. **Routers** organize the flow of data packets and ensure that information is transported in singular data packets, which are then reconfigured into the original information. Telecommunication carriers[32], such as MCI Worldcom or Sprint, usually provide these services based on technology, provided by companies such as Cisco, Lucent, or Siemens[33]. This traffic is aggregated either in **local networks** (e.g. LAN's or local telephone networks) or **dial up networks** of Internet or on-line service providers.[34] This digital telecommunications infrastructure is designed to transport data in a manner, where data has to be allocated in order to utilize backbone capacities and router processing power to the highest level of efficiency.

▨ **Informational and data management aspect of the network:** The network structure described above connects computers and/or computerized digital devices and enables the exchange of information between them. The information in the Internet is contained in computers.[35] They are solely set up to manage large data amounts of content (databases, websites, email boxes, video clips and so forth) to deliver content to a wide audience. These **host computers**[36] are running different types of **operating systems** and **server software**[37] for the on-line service applications (further analyzed in Section 2.3. They are designed to manage large amount of requests and users at a high level of efficiency.[38] Whereas the network structure laid out above can be compared with a network of streets, which transports cars and so forth, the hosts can be compared with a library, which is organized in shelves and the catalog system represents the servers in this analogy.

▨ **The usage aspect of the network:** The usage aspect analyzes the final end user perspective of the on-line service network infrastructure. First, there are the **hardware** components: Usually it is a **usage device** (e. g. computers, PDAs, cellular phones, "webyfied" telephone terminals and many future multimedia devices), which the user can apply to operate services like reading / sending email, chatting with friends, browsing a web site, listening to a sound clip or watching a news clip. These components work together with an **access device** (e. g. a modem or a LAN card). Both devices are usually combined, whereas this would be assembled by one manufacturer or the user itself is assembling open standard components. To operate these services accompanying **client software** needs to be installed on the device. These software pieces are based on Internet technol-

---

[32] See OECD (1998b), pp. 18-24, 34-35 for an overview about the carrier market.

[33] See Eugster et. al (1998) for a current overview of the Telecom equipment market.

[34] See MacKie-Mason (1997) and Burg (1998).

[35] Basically each computer once connected to the Internet is an added resource of information, although most of the computers are not mainly intended for an information provision to the network of other computers. e. g. most of the end users connecting to the Internet either retrieve information (e.g. a stock quote) or use the network for communication purposes (e.g. email). These computers are discussed below as usage devices.

[36] For topical data on the hosting market see Network Wizards (1999).

[37] For topical data on the server market see Netcraft (1999). For the strategic implications of the operating system and server market in conjunction with client operating systems and application software see SPA (1999).

[38] See Spectrum (1998), pp. 81-82.

ogy and work together with the usage device, the network infrastructure and the hosting facilities. The main client software categories are applications for access (e.g. the Windows DUN dialer), content (a.k.a. browser), email, chat and multimedia (players for audio/video streams). These components can be assembled (e.g. AOL, MS Internet Explorer Suite) or the user can assemble them in a tailored way (e.g. DUN, Netscape Navigator, AOL Instant Messenger, Eudora Mail). The software connects the hardware device over the network infrastructure with the servers on the data hosts.

It is crucial that all of these components are computerized, digital components, which work with technology mainly based on Internet standards. As a result, information and communication technology converges. This has widespread implications for the industries under consideration as will be discussed in Subsection 2.1.3. As the entire area is currently in a period of rapid change **the only constant factor is the aspect of change**. Therefore, for the purpose of this thesis it is crucial to consistently structure the technology field as presented above. This identifies the main areas of change and outlines a constant framework for this purpose. Figure 2-2 illustrates this technological framework:

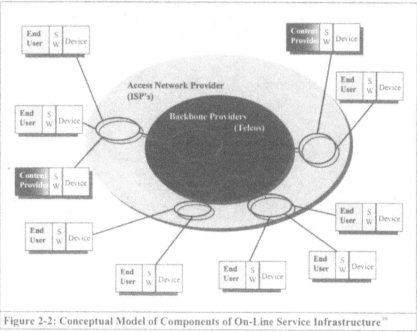

Figure 2-2: Conceptual Model of Components of On-Line Service Infrastructure[19]

Whereas this framework structures the areas into categories where the development will occur the following will **predict general trends** of this change which characterize the **velocity** of the development path.[40]

---

[39] Adapted from Werbach (1997), p. 11.

[40] See also Werbach (1997), pp. 4-7.

1. Data and information management

Computer processing power determines the speed of data processing, which affects all areas of the technological infrastructure: Routers send the data packets faster and more efficiently. Servers handle information requests faster and in a larger variety, while devices offer more information faster and in a more complex way. Gordon Moore, the co-founder of Intel, defined **Moore's Law**. He predicted, in 1964, that the density of transistors on a silicon chip would **double every 18 months to 2 years**. This has held true since.

2. Data transport

The available **bandwidth** determines how long it takes to transport information to the user. Limitations in bandwidth constrain how rich and complex multimedia features of on-line services can be, in order to ensure a satisfying user experience. John Metcalf, the inventor of the Ethernet and founder of 3Com, defined **Metcalf's Law** (Metcalf 1993). He predicted that the **network power is the square of the computing power**. UUNet and its mother company MCI Worldcom, as the leading ISP and data carrier probably with the closest practical insight, are planing their infrastructure according to a doubled of data traffic every 100 days.[41]

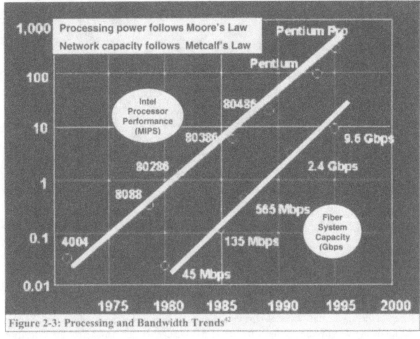

Figure 2-3: Processing and Bandwidth Trends[42]

The two rules as shown in Figure 2-3 give a good general idea regarding the velocity of the development of the Internet. Both can be further analyzed, but for the purposes of this thesis,

---

[41] See Inktomi (1997).

[42] See (Microsoft 1998).

the basic understanding of both laws is sufficient. In addition, to these drivers of velocity, one can identify three major areas of technological evolution, which influence the **direction of the development path** of the on-line industry:

1. Standardization

Standardization is a complex and central issue. It can be perceived that the most significant technological factor, aside the continued growth in computer performance, is the trend towards **open standards,** based on Internet technology. This lowers the entrance barriers of new players significantly. Moreover, the evolution of these standards has widespread **effects on the interoperability**[43] between networks and according services. Currently, the basic standards of the Internet, such as TCP/IP, http, or html, increase the standardization and diversity of products tremendously. Although it has to be stated that in particular areas,[44] the outcome of the technology standardization process is unclear.[45] This aspect is highly interdependent with the three other exogenous variables of the on-line industry as well as with the industry itself.[46] Ultimately, the design regarding the underlying technology – especially the fundamental decision to apply closed proprietary technology or open technology – has **widespread implications and potential for industrial structure and business strategy** as it will be discussed in Chapter 3. In general it has to be summarized that currently the evolution of standards is still in a very high uncertainty stage.

2. Networking technology

The traditional network technology for on-line services provides connectivity in a low bandwidth technology environment, employing dial-up networks over copper telephone lines. In the past, high bandwidth access was provided only via leased lines. In addition to these fixed

---

[43] Discussions on interoperability reflect standards and their overall fit with attractive economics of technology, policy regulations (see above), and social desirability (see below). The overall economic added value of the system is an aggregate measure. Anti-trust issues are closely related with issues of interoperability and the interconnection of networks. Policy issues, as described above, have to be considered, while technological design itself defines a large portion of what can be realized and what cannot. Furthermore, the embedded bottlenecks have to be identified. This, on the one hand, appears as business opportunities for the owners of the bottlenecks, who can charge gate keeper fees. However, on the other hand, it appears as a policy issue where interconnection regulations have to be defined.

[44] Particularly crucial commercial technologies such as billing and open standard MIS / collection system interfaces, security and authentication were not available in standard formats by the close of 1999.

[45] See Squire, Sanders, Dempsey (1998b), p. 126.

[46] "Standardisation in the multimedia sector is driven not simply by the electronic interoperability requirement, but also by the need to satisfy the conditions for open markets in products and services for the ultimate benefit of users. The full realisation of the economic potential of the multimedia market will depend both on technical interoperability and on product diversity. These goals can best be achieved in a competitive market in which users and operators are aware of, and demand access to, standards-conforming products." (Squire / Sanders / Dempsey 1998b:225-226). They (ibid.) conclude that standardization in the multimedia environment needs to support (a) the interoperability of products in distinct markets to avoid confusion in the delivery of multimedia services, (b) the interchangeability of multiple products for the same applications, in order to promote price competition, (c) the interoperability within national environments between different networks comprising multimedia platforms, and (d) the interoperability between national networks to maintain openness of multimedia services regardless of national boundaries with fully interchangeable products in seamless end-to-end services provided nationally and internationally, on multiple network platforms.

access methods, wireless technology is responsible for a small portion of the usage.[47] Metcalf's Law gives a clear prediction regarding bandwidth development. Thus one can assume that "bandwidth will be there". It is a predictable trend – the backbone infrastructure of the transport networks will be converted into Internet technology.[48] Application of enhanced compression technology and packet switching technology will lead to an **increase of bandwidth on the backbone side.**[49] The major issue is the **uncertainty relating to the** market development of different possible **access network technologies.** The development of the alternative platforms for the provision of connectivity remains wide open. Dempsey et. al. (1998) point out that **bandwidth will move to the broadband world,** which:

> "(...) represents a **major discontinuity in the Internet** access (, software, and content, C. G.) business." (Dempsey et. al. 1998:10) [emphasis added]

However it is impossible at this point in time to give a solid prediction regarding the market share of different broadband access network technologies for the future. Therefore, the following outlines potential **options for increasing the bandwidth of the local loop,** which will remove the bottleneck problem found in the common low bandwidth, fixed access via the telephone copper wires:[50]

- **Fixed access:** There are two main options to increase bandwidth: either by enhancing the telephone copper lines with DSL technology or by enabling the existing TV cable networks for telephony and Internet services. A third option is to utilize the electricity networks.[51]

- **Wireless access:** Current wireless technology (e.g. GSM or CDMA) will be replaced by new technology with significantly enhanced bandwidth (e.g. W-CDMA, UMTS)[52]

---

[47] See Spectrum (1998), pp. 45-51.

[48] The telecommunications infrastructure is currently moving away from old ways of networking to Internet technologies. Old data protocols are being replaced by IP protocols and packet switching is replacing circuit switching, which is in fact converging content and communication on a common infrastructure. The voice traffic is digitized and transported in data packets just as regular data (see Eugster et. al. 1998, p. 95).

[49] Current and predicted distribution for backbone traffic between voice, data and Internet in the US in 1998 is 100 GB for data as well as voice traffic and 14 GB for Internet traffic. In 2008 voice traffic is expected to be 200 GB, data traffic over 10 TB and Internet traffic over 100 TB. Or in other words the annual growth rates for voice are 5%, for data 30% and 100% for the Internet. See Baack (1999), p. 9. See also Nortel (1998).

[50] See Werbach (1997), pp. 68-75 and Squire / Sanders / Dempsey (1998a), pp. 45-52 for an overview. See Dempsey et. al (1998) who discuss strategic scenarios. See European Commission (1998b) for a comprehensive international comparative analysis regarding broadband platform scenarios in the European countries, the United States, Australia and Japan.

[51] To better understand the genesis of these platforms the following data provides an impression of the current adoption rates: Household cable penetration is (USA:70%, Germany 50%, France 12%, United Kingdom 10%, Japan 8%) significantly lower than the nearly fully adopted copper telephone technology. Electricity networks are only tested in small range field trials so far (see Spectrum 1998, p. 46). Ultimately 99.3% of the local loop for Internet access in the OECD countries is provided over incumbent copper lines (ibid. p. 48). Wireless technology is still extremely insignificant (see footnote 52). This current constellation, combined with the current access device technology of computers and modems, indicates significant advantages for new technologies that fit into this constellation, such as DSL technology. This path dependency of technological developments will be further introduced in the context of the theory of network economics.

[52] Nevertheless the current wireless access technology is still not significant. According to internal data, less than 0.05% of the on-line connections to the German CompuServe network in Spring 1999 used wireless GSM technology when compared to analog modem or ISDN technology.

Satellite access: Currently, satellite is only rolled out on a very small scale (e.g. Iridium). In most industrialized countries the economics of satellite technology will also be inferior in the future. Satellites will be primarily used in locations with poor infrastructure and low population densities.[53]

Figure 2-4 gives an overview of the development path of access technologies. These technologies will upgrade from the current narrowband technology, which is described above:

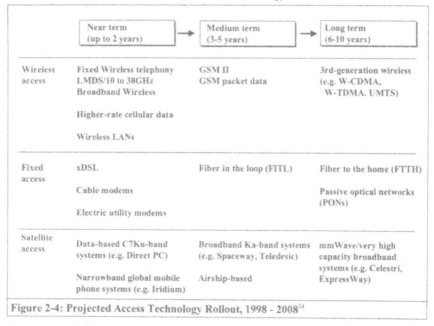

	Near term (up to 2 years)	Medium term (3-5 years)	Long term (6-10 years)
Wireless access	Fixed Wireless telephony LMDS/10 to 38GHz Broadband Wireless Higher-rate cellular data Wireless LANs	GSM II GSM packet data	3rd-generation wireless (e.g. W-CDMA, W-TDMA. UMTS)
Fixed access	xDSL Cable modems Electric utility modems	Fiber in the loop (FITL)	Fiber to the home (FTTH) Passive optical networks (PONs)
Satellite access	Data-based C7Ku-band systems (e.g. Direct PC) Narrowband global mobile phone systems (e.g. Iridium)	Broadband Ka-band systems (e.g. Spaceway, Teledesic) Airship-based	mmWave/very high capacity broadband systems (e.g. Celestri, ExpressWay)

Figure 2-4: Projected Access Technology Rollout, 1998 - 2008[54]

Considering this, an enormous increase in telecommunications access technologies can be expected in the next years. This has to be understood as one of the underlying trends of the on-line industry.

> "Twenty years ago, telephone services relied on one access technology: twisted copper wire. Today, there are many technologies, and all will coexist at the global level. At the local level, however, it is clear that different markets will have different mixes of technologies, and in any given segment, only a limited number will be able to compete successfully." (Beardsley / Evans 1998:30)[55]

Figure 2-5 shows, different access technologies providing bandwidth differentiated depending on the market and product definition of the services.

---

[53] See Evans et. al (1998), Spectrum (1998), pp. 57-58 and Eberspächer (1999), pp. 210-211.

[54] Taken from Beardsley / Evans (1998), p. 21, see furthermore Margherio et. al. (1997), p. A2 – 14.

[55] Peter Cowhey stated (in the interview) that the number of three competing alternative network technologies, regardless of fixed, wireless or satellite, would be a good "wide oligopoly" in this respect.

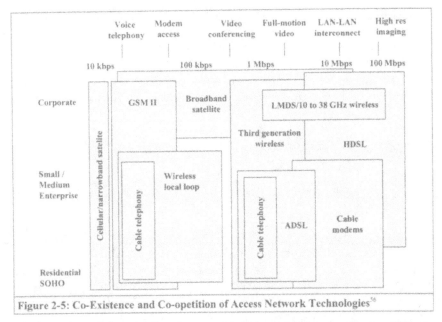

Figure 2-5: Co-Existence and Co-opetition of Access Network Technologies[56]

This figure shows the coexistence of many technologies and their competition on different customer segments. The strategic position of these technologies and their complementary and/or competitive relationship depends on the specific market particularities.

3. Usage Devices

The third big issue in the technology environment of the on-line industry is the development of usage devices. While computers with modems are the main usage devices at this point, a variety of alternative devices will emerge in the future. At the end of the 1990s the first "we-byfied" cellular phones, smart phones, personal digital assistants (PDA) and TV set top boxes entered the market. Due to the economics of complex needs and products, it is very unlikely that one "super-device" will penetrate the market.[57] Rather, it is likely that a variety of devices will emerge in the future, which will integrate a smaller or larger portfolio of Internet applications.[58] Seven main categories for future devices can be identified:

Computers
Cellular phones
Telephone consoles (see also Case Study 1-1)
TV Set Top Boxes
PDA's
Game consoles
Hybrids / Combinations

---

[56] See Beardsley / Evans (1998), p. 23.

[57] See Forrester (1997a).

[58] See Forrester (1997b).

Due to its computing power, the computer is the device with the richest portfolio of Internet applications among them. The others emphasize certain killer applications specializing in the devices' nature, such as email and directory services for telephone consoles or TV listing and weather reports for TV set top boxes. This basically depends on the main need, which the producer is aiming to fill, and the technological capabilities of the device.[59] It is still uncertain in the late 1990s, which device will eventually be the most successful killer applications in any specific product type.[60] However, it is certain that the future will bring a variety of devices, which will support the use of Internet based on-line services.

Policy, industry and society have an impact on these factors and depending on the constellation of specific markets different effects will result.[61] Summarizing the technological framework it has to be concluded that the on-line industry will face an **increase in bandwidth, a growing number of access devices, and better access network technologies**. Furthermore, an **increase in products and services will occur**, including the **converging telecom and**

---

[59] See Margherio et. al (1997), pp. A2 – 15-16. The computer is still the predominant access device, which accounts for almost 100% of the Internet usage in 1999. Therefore, the adoption rates of Internet usage are still constrained by the adoption rates of computers with access devices (see the following data for comparison of household penetration rates in 1996/1997: USA: 19% (PC) / 26% (therein PC with Modem), Japan: 15% / 10%, UK: 15% / 10%, Germany: 11% / 12%, France 11%/ 6%, see Spectrum 1998, pp. 42-43). The potential is the multiplication of both factors as they are both conditio *sine qua non*. This illustrates the interdependence of the development path of the usage device technology and the Internet as a market. As soon as other devices significantly start to enter the market, overall market size will grow accordingly. This will automatically have a positive effect on the other technology components. This is one of many network effects, which results in positive feedback within the industry system, as Subsection 2.2.1 will further analyze. Innovations in the cellular phone area market have been providing the integrated Internet applications since 1998, however significant usage is did not occur until 1999. Case Study 1-1 provided an overview regarding telephone access device scenario. By 1999, no major player had introduced a product in large scale, although this appears to be just a question of short time. TV set-top boxes still have not entered the mass market significantly. But as soon as prices, content formats, and access technologies are more suitable for mass markets, the predictions range for about 35% of the device market share (according to interviews with Patrick Bonaire, Business Development Manager WebTV, 5th of April 1997, Palo Alto, Matthias Herfet, Project Manager Grundig TV Set Top Box, 19th of August 1997, Munich and Wolfgang Schneider, Business Development Manager Microsoft, 16th of June 1998, Munich. See Donahue (1997) and Ecker / Mobley (1997) for a roll out scenario for TV-based devices. Digital TV set top boxes are still encountering extensive hardware limitations regarding disk space and software upgrade potential as well as encryption problems (according to interview with Dr. Jan Traenkner, Managing Director Pro7 Digital, 9th of March 1997, Munich). In general it can be summarized that the introduction of non-PC devices will reduce the complexity of Internet applications, which will open additional growth potentials into new customer segments (see Wössner 1999a). See Donahue (1997) for a projected roll out plan for TV based devices.

[60] The following examples illustrate the uncertainty in this area. e. g. it is that the WebTV set top boxes were designed to integrate interactive Internet content into traditional TV sets. Although 43% of the service usage is email, content appears not to be the killer application (according to interview with Wolfgang Schneider, Business Development Manager Microsoft, 16th of June 1998, Munich). Current state of the art PDA's support email usage. The majority of the users do not use this feature. It is unclear if customers perceive future cellular phones/PDA's as a telephone at first or rather as an "webyfied" information and organization device with mobile phone capability. Currently, there is neither conjoint analyses available, which analyze these issues, nor is there sufficient market experience.

[61] The development of transport networks, access networks and devices as enabling technology areas will heavily impact the development path of the on-line industry. Furthermore, depending on the regulatory environment, industrial environment and social environment, which are obviously divergent in different countries, according technologies will experience greater adoption rates. Of course, the underlying economics of technologies still plays a strong role in general when it comes to determining a potentially successful technology, but obviously not the only one.

audiovisual sectors. The area exhibits **high uncertainty regarding** the development path of **standardization** and the resulting level of **interoperability** between the different platforms.

2.1.3. Industrial Framework

To understand the larger industrial context, the following discusses the exogenous industrial variables and their impact on the on-line industry system. The industry framework has obviously shifted dramatically. Global usage of on-line services in the Internet is experiencing a dramatic increase on both the demand and supply sides. Thus, the market faces explosive growth. Considering the past proprietary on-line service traditions, the world has changed dramatically. Figure 1-4 shows the convergence of telecommunications, media, computer and consumer electronic, which developed into the information and communication technology sector (ICT). This technological **convergence** dramatically affects the on-line industry.[62] Basically the computer hardware and software, media, telecommunications and consumer electronic industries represent underlying industrial forces. They are converging towards the ICT sector, where they are establishing a new economic environment. Subsection 2.1.2 analyzed the technological innovation, which results in three basic **tenants of** the economic setting:[63] Growing (1) **connectivity** and (2) **digitalization** are shaping the ICT sector as new economic environment. Furthermore, the emergence of open (3) **Internet standards** (see Subsection 2.1.2) substituted for the proprietary on-line technology, which created the Internet as the new platform for on-line business. **This technological innovation opened up the on-line industry space for additional players. The rapid growth of this alternative on-line business environment consequently pulled the relatively small on-line industry into the center of the giant ICT constellation as a new competitive arena.** Hence, it is plausible to conclude that many of the on-line industries' **exogenous variables are now internalized** and the on-line industry is part of the ICT area. This has resulted in a rapid and fundamental change for the traditional industry framework and created a very disorderly environment, which is presented in Figure 2-6:

---

[62] See McKnight / Bailey (1995).

[63] See also Werbach (1997), p. 5, KPMG (1996a), p. 101.

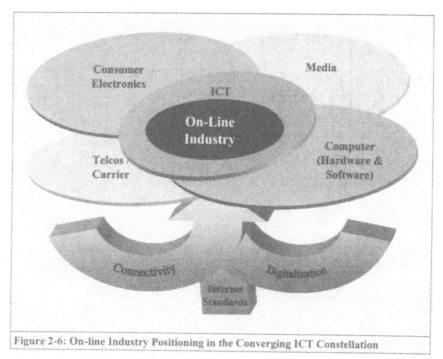

Figure 2-6: On-line Industry Positioning in the Converging ICT Constellation

Figure 2-6 illustrates the main origins of new players entering the on-line business competition in the second half of the 1990s. The **enormous forces** brought to bear by these players work on the industrial framework and affect the entire setting. In order to give a quantitative impression, Figure 2-7 shows the total annual turnover of 812 billion ECU in the European Community alone. This impressively illustrates the power and origin of the market forces behind this converging environment. It, further, shows the particular areas where this revenue is traditionally generated. The figure allocates the categories according to their product or service character and their content or infrastructure character. These numbers, when compared with $ 0.9 billion in revenues of consumer on-line services generated in the US in the year 1994 (see 1.1.2) show the ratio of forces and evidently the declining power of the original on-line industry within the emerging ICT constellation.

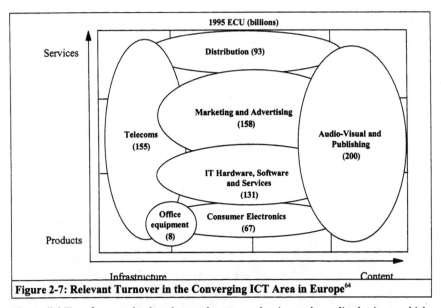

Figure 2-7: Relevant Turnover in the Converging ICT Area in Europe[64]

The availability of open technology lowers the entrance barriers to the on-line business, which formerly relied exclusive on proprietary on-line platforms. The players behind the turnover summarized in Figure 2-7 are shifting part of their business to the emerging Internet platform. This increasingly develops towards a new virtual marketspace with new players. Consequently, the on-line industry is more and more shaped by the converging industries into a quasi-virtual industry. Furthermore, the **economic logic** within the different layers of the industries is increasingly **influenced by the underlying economic laws of the converging industries.** These new entrants are experiencing the changed economics, which essentially affects the business models of the on-line industry. This has caused a fundamental shift of the laws of the marketplace. An analysis of this constellation reveals three **general effects** of the causes described above:

1. The on-line industry is a multi-layered environment

> "The Internet is a virtual network (...) More generally, the layered structure (...) leads to a recursive relationship in which the cost structure of services provided in any layer is determined by prices charged by providers one layer below." (Gong / Srinagesh 1995)

Gong / Srinagesh highlight the virtual structure and multi-layered of the underlying industries of the Internet.[65] Consequently, their economics as well as their distinct competitive skills are vertically related and interconnected. As described above, the technological innovation

---

[64] See EITO (1995).

[65] See also Richardson (1999), who emphasizes the vertical and horizontal aspects of the multi-layered Internet environment; furthermore Bane / Bradley / Collins (1996) who use and extend the example of Yoffie's model of the ICT area.

changed the industrial constellation and pulled the converging industries towards one another. Hence Gong / Srinagesh observe that:

> "Technological advances are rapidly blurring traditional industry boundaries and ena-
> bling competition between firms that did not previously compete with one another."
> (ibid.) [66]

Within this overlapping area with **blurring boundaries,** the intersections are constantly changing. Players from formerly distinct industries contribute complementary as well as competitive business activities to the Internet on several layers of the industry.[67] Due to an increase in number and type of players, the **complexity has increased** enormously. Within this area, open standard Internet technology enabled the production of on-line services on the Internet platform. The overwhelming interest in the Internet positioned these new on-line based businesses right in the center of the ICT area. Consequently, the on-line industry was heavily pulled into this area and was fundamentally adjusted according to the different layers of this constellation.

2. Enormous growth

As a part of this heavily growing economic sector, the on-line industry participates in this growth. Hence:

> "(...) the most confident predication that can be made about the Internet is that it will
> continue to grow." (Werbach 1997:21).[68]

But according to the new constellation this growing pie of the on-line industry is also sliced into more layers and segments which are divided between a growing number of players.

3. Rapid change

All of these layers belong to industries with different industrial traditions. All of them are currently experiencing a high degree of change. Hence, the on-line industry, as a combined and multiply interconnected system of these changing industries, experiences rapid processes of changes in an additive if not even multiplied way. Furthermore, Figure 2-6 shows a certain dynamic within this constellation, which indicates that the entire industrial cohesion is also in constant motion around the axis'.[69]

---

[66] See furthermore Werbach (1997) p. 5 and Wössner (1999a).

[67] Ibid.

[68] The continuous growth of computers connected to the Internet (average host growth rates 1993 - 1999: 31.1 % every six months, see Network Wizards 1999) and "landmarks" at the world wide web (average domain name growth rates 1993 - 1999: 29.6 % every six months, ibid.) quantifies this growth very evidently and precisely. For a comprehensive overview and an international comparative analysis see OECD (1998b).

[69] This refers to the aspect of the ongoing shift of the entire converging industries as it is visible with media companies adjusting there mission to become telecommunications companies as well (see e.g. Middelhoff 1998) or telecom carriers entering the media industry (e.g. AT & T acquiring the cable company TCI which acquired the cable on-line service @Home which acquired the Excite portal site) and so forth.

In addition to these general characteristics, **four specific economic effects** affect the on-line industry now. In the past, these effects could be described as external parameters determined by the converging industries, which heavily translated these economics from the external industrial framework into their internal structures:

- **Virtualization of the value chain**
- **Economies of scale**[70]
- **Economies of scope**[71]
- **Competency based competition**

On-line services were yet another distribution channel for the respective firms of the converging industries and their value chain was the transmission mechanism (see 2.3.4). In the course of convergence, the laws of the marketplace of these industries were internalized into the on-line industry system (see above). Moreover, this process translated the particular economics into the on-line environment. Hence, these industries now have to be considered as part of the black box shown in Figure 2-1. Therefore Section 2.4 will present a deeper analysis, which examines the inside of the black box to discover internal mechanisms, which characterize the industry.

Summarizing the economic environment it has to be stated that the resulting growth potentials of the on-line industry make it **an attractive industry**. The **multi-layered constitution** results in various **network effects**[72] between the different layers. **Complex laws of the marketplace** are determined by the converging industries. Highly problematic is that the rapid speed of change and the overall complexity determine that the industry will be a difficult environment in which to conduct business. In order to complete the exogenous variables of the industry system, Subsection 2.1.4 will outline the parameters determined within the social framework.

2.1.4. Socio-Economic Framework

Referring to the socio-economic framework within this context means looking into the specifics of the industry, which are determined by people as individuals or as collective. This widespread area implies issues from a wide field of scientific aspects such as the social sciences or the behavioral sciences. At this point in time, the implications are on the verge of

---

[70] A system exhibits economies of scale, if a proportional increase in the inputs increases the output amount by more than the same proportion. Typically they are assumed as supply side economies of scale of the production function. Subsection 2.2.1 will introduce the additional concept of "demand side economies of scale" which are particular for network markets. Both are associated with increasing returns to scale as an economic particularity of networks.

[71] A system exhibits economies of scope if an increase in the inputs increases the output scope by more than the same proportion. In other words, to increase the output scope of the product, the amount of effort (input) required is only a fraction of what it would take to develop the product from scratch, without the leverage provided by the existing product. For example, consider the Microsoft's Windows operating systems, including Windows for desktop, laptop, and notebook computers, Windows NT for servers, and Windows CE for palmtops and handheld devices, or Deutsche Telekom's ability to bundle ISDN, the T-Online on-line service, voice long distance, wireless and devices under the same brand using the same telecommunications network.

[72] See 2.2.1 for the discussion of network effects in the theoretical context of network economics.

being analyzed from a scientific standpoint.[73] Yet, as this will have fundamental effects on the development of the on-line industry, the following outlines the most critical factors for the economy and for companies conducting business therein. Obviously, the reaction of individuals and entire societies to a new technology has widespread implications.[74] In order to focus on the intersections between the economic framework and implications for individual firms, the following will analyze the two critical microeconomic factors: the production function and the consumption function. The corresponding implications for firms, which arise out of the social framework will be broken down into major issues[75]:

1. Effects on the production function

a) **Labor**: Depending on the availability of workers who are (aa) willing to work under certain condition (wages, flexibility and so forth) and (bb) appropriately skilled according to the requirements of the on-line industry, individual firms are able to utilize this resource to produce a certain output in a given market.[76] Although this is a basic insight from classical microeconomic theory, it needs to be mentioned here. The reason is that the availability of skilled workers or the lack thereof is a **major limiting factor** in the current development of the industry. The availability of an appropriate work force is basically rooted in the social framework; or to transfer this into business terms: 'location matters'.[77] Stemming from social aspects such as education and the unemployment rate, industries are able to produce. The Silicon Valley, for example, offers a large number of appropriately skilled workers for the on-line industry. However, the large number of players demanding labor in this area is rapidly driving up labor costs. Other areas, such as Germany, still suffer from the low availability of specifically qualified workers.[78] In both cases, labor is a limiting factor, which determines the growth of the on-line industry. This factor is

---

[73] See NRC (1997), for a research agenda on social impacts of the Internet, a catalogue of indicators (ibid., pp. 20-63, 74-79), and a first comparative analysis of differences between the United States and Africa. NRC (1998b) mainly illustrates "unanswered questions", (ibid.) pp. 21-77, provides some data (ibid.), pp. 78-100 and refers to the lack of comprehensive analysis (ibid. p. 2). This suggests the premature stage of this area of research. See also Gräf (1997).

[74] NRC (1998a), pp. 21-22 also suggests focusing the analysis on the economic and market drivers rather than on the social sectors as education, governance, etc. at this point in time. There are especially strong intersections with the political area (see ibid.). Issues such as availability and access to information, plurality and democratic principles are also highly political issues which are fundamentally affecting the social framework. This thesis does not discuss these points. For further reading, see European Commission (1997a), USA (1997), pp. 10-18, Spectrum (1996), OECD (1998a), and NRC (1998b).

[75] Just as the development of the Internet as an economic space is dependent on this external factor, the Internet will also have profound effects on social norms and culture in exchange. See Dery (1996), Slouka (1995) and Turkle (1997).

[76] See Varian (1992).

[77] See Margherio et. al (1997), pp. 46-45 and A1 9-16 for a detailed comparative analysis of skills, wages, growth etc. This aspect is a vivid example for the globalization and internationalization of business.

[78] See Cohen / Fields (1998) and Cohen / Fields (1999) for the effects of labor and skill sets fueling growth in the Silicon Valley. See Wäsche (1999), pp. 4-5 for a comparative analysis of the labor situation in the United States and German multimedia environment, particularly for a start-up perspective. Furthermore, see Egan (1996) for the "Seattle Perspective". See Castells / Aoyama (1993) on a comparative analysis of trajectories of employment structure in the G7 countries based on technology from 1920-2005.

interdependent with the political and industrial parameters as described above. Ultimately social structures are the underlying forces driving these processes.

b) **Technology**: Available technology **shifts the production function**.[79] This is especially true for business conducted in the ICT area. Overall, availability of technology in a social framework enables firms to operate on a higher level of productivity. The diffusion of this technology is extremely dependent on the social framework, which provides for a certain technological environment.[80] Obviously, this aspect is very interdependent with the long term settings of political and technological parameters in a society. Therefore, the potential for firms to operate their business is very dependent on this underlying structure.

c) **Funding & Start-Up Potential**: In this early stage of the industrial development, the funding of new businesses and the overall start-up potential is a **crucial driver**. The start-up business is dependent on (aa) the availability of financial resources, (bb) the presence of entrepreneurs willing to capture "windows of opportunities", and (cc) the social reward for entrepreneurial conduct and the absence of social remedies for failure. Currently, the two predominant ways of acquiring start-up funding are: (aaa) investments from large corporations in the context of their portfolio management, or (bbb) the venture capital method. In a second stage, after the first start up period, growing businesses require larger capital amounts where either (ccc) large corporation have to invests in the growth of business units, (ddd) or units need to go public to get access to large amounts of capital.[81] The presence of these factors in a socio-economic framework determines both the potential and direction of the economic development. If one compares both the United States and European economic development, both regions exhibit different patterns. The first wave of the European Internet business in the mid 1990s was driven by investments from large corporations (e.g. Europe Online, AOL/Bertelsmann, British Telecom, Deutsche Telekom, Microsoft, CompuServe, Cegetel) in the absence of venture capital and a stock market accessible to smaller firms. Opposed to this, the market in the United States was proactively shaped by small venture capital funded companies, which later went public, at the NASDAQ (e.g. Netscape, Yahoo!, Lycos, eBay, Doubleclick). In most cases, large corporations were followers in this market (e.g. AT&T, Microsoft, Disney) with a few exceptions such as Cisco or Worldcom.[82] With the advent of ubiquitous venture capital in the European markets and instruments, such as the German "Neuer Markt" stock exchange, innovation is increasingly driven by small start-ups.[83]

---

[79] See Varian (1992).

[80] See Deloitte 1998, pp. 40-57 for an international comparative analysis of the relevant technologies and usage patterns. These comparative aspects are crucial for regional market strategies in international businesses with diverging markets.

[81] See Wäsche (1999), Cohen / Fields (1999).

[82] "America Online and other Internet service providers, not the Regional Bell Operating Companies, popularized mass subscriptions to the Internet. Personal computers, the Netscape browser and Cisco, not AT&T, drove the architecture of data networking and the Web." (Bar / Cohen / Cowhey / DeLong / Kleeman / Zysman 1999:1). Nevertheless, now in the second wave of the Internet on the verge of broadband exactly these large corporations are developing momentum to capture their position in the future Internet economy.

[83] According to an interview with Klaus Hommels, Investment Manager Internet Ventures, Apax, 19th of August 1999, Munich.

2. Effects on the demand function

a) **Overall adoption rates** of relevant technologies such as on-line services or complementary platform technologies (e. g. penetration of telephones and PCs with Modem), determine the current market volumes and the future **market potential**. An analysis of the adoption of products in detail indicates which product categories have chances to develop into a mass market product, and which will emerge to fill specialized niches. Ultimately, the suitability of the technology to people's needs determines the market potentials.

b) **The social framework** is the sophisticated underlying structure, which determines the evolution of a market.[84] It is the area where "soft facts" develop their subtle power in their translation into the market constellations. The consumption of goods and services is dependent on needs, particular buying and usage patterns (on-line or off-line), demand for choices, convenience, style of communities and so forth. If accepted by the people any particular technology of the on-line services allows for personalization and mass customization, which enables firms to address needs in a more sophisticated manner. Hagel / Armstrong (1996) describe how the rules of certain communities can enable firms to expand "markets in online communities". This determines the "net gain" (Hagel / Armstrong 1997) in the "virtual marketspace" (Rayport / Sviokla 1994) of a society. Microsoft created the term **"Web Lifestyle,"**[85] which describes the adoption of the Internet, and in particular, the general **mind set** rooted in a social framework. It serves as a very illustrative term in this context. Ultimately, the demand side of the social framework is represented by particular adoption rates, which exhibit economic potential.[86]

These two factors in combination outlined above will support a market equilibrium, based on certain price and volume levels. This determines the aggregate welfare from an economic standpoint and the overall market volume from a firm's standpoint, based on the socio-economic framework.

Due to its subtle nature, which is deeply routed in the social structures, **the adjustment processes of new technologies will take decades rather than years** as Bill Gates points out:[87]

---

[84] See Margherio et. al (1997), pp. 41-45 for a comprehensive discussion.

[85] See Koll (1999) and Higgins (1998).

[86] For illustrative purposes the example Yahoo!. Its United States's Yahoo! site creates approximately 200 times the amount of page views to customers compared to the German site (according to interview with Karsten Weide, former Senior Producer Yahoo! Germany, 23rd of June, 1999, San Francisco). This cannot solely be explained with a lower adoption rate of access (app. 6 times higher in the US). A more complex setting of drivers has to be taken into account. Significantly higher access costs (ca. $4 per usage hour in Germany compared to $45 flat rate (($20 for Internet access)) including all local phone calls, see Werbach 1997, pp. 48-49) support this bias. As a result average monthly online usage e. g. within AOL in the US is more than 6 times higher compared to Germany (AOL internal data). Also worthy of consideration is German users viewing the US site (according to internal data ca. 3%) cannot fully explain the disparity. Obviously a Web Lifestyle, when the Internet becomes an integral part of daily life, has already become a reality in the USA compared to other countries e.g. in Europe.

[87] See also Feldman (1999).

"Technological advances alone aren't enough to drive social change. At least some people have to embrace change or it won't happen. Two tendencies cause new products to be adopted over prolonged periods rather than immediately. Products evolve slowly to meet the needs of the market, and the market adapts slowly to new opportunities. People only slowly adapt their patterns, mindsets, skills and expectations to match the opportunities afforded by a new product. It takes years for people to hear about a product, try it, get used to it, rely on it." (cited from Zenith 1999)

The following will summarize the analysis of the structural framework and will condense the main findings that effect the on-line industry system.

2.1.5. Conclusion from the Industry Environment

The analysis of the exogenous variables reveals the character of the overall environment of the on-line industry. It shows that this area is experiencing extreme growth. Due to the strong attraction in this area a growing number of players – from small start-up companies to large corporations – are entering the arena. This results in an increasing differentiation of the area. Furthermore, due to an overall incomplete definition and stabilization of the exogenous parameters, the industry has to deal with a high level of uncertainty and a rapid rate of change. While most of the exogenous parameters are interdependent the motion in the overall cohesion accumulates in its complexity and change. Thus, the industry has to deal with a changing set of exogenous variables, which will constantly affect the endogenous variables. Overall the industry is far away from having approached an equilibrium.[88] Looking into the projected timeframe, it will be years and/or decades until the major parameters reach a higher level of stability. Therefore, it appears reasonable to define the four **general characteristics of the environment** of the industry as the focal system:

- **Growth**
- **Change**
- **Complexity**
- **Uncertainty**

These general characteristics are valid for all of the four areas of exogenous parameters. A closer analysis of the four particular areas of the external environment highlights a **host of specific factors**. Primary among them is **interdependence**. They can be complementary to each other, as in an increase in the availability of skilled labor, which supports an accelerated development of technologies, markets and competencies. On the other hand, they can also result in a negative trade-off as, for example, when privacy regulations constrain the development of advanced personalization technologies and vice versa. Few of them have a neutral relationship.

Overall the environment is a complex and fluid setting, which will evolve and stabilize over time. **In the process of transfer to the on-line industry, adjustments of these exogenous factors have a strong influence on firms. Depending on the underlying business model, adjustments will cause fundamentally different results for individual firms.** In this context, Booz Allen Hamilton highlights the exogenous parameters:

---

[88] See Economides / Himmelberg (1994) p. 11.

"(...) technological transformation, deregulation and increasing competition, increasing customer demands, and globalization (...). Changes in these key drivers will likewise determine future market developments." Booz Allen Hamilton (1998a)

Hence it is crucial for players within the industry to understand that these factors exist in the external environment and how adjustments of these exogenous parameters will specifically affect their business. Figure 2-8 gives a general impression regarding the impact of the discussed exogenous factors on firms operating in the on-line industry:

EXOGENOUS DRIVERS	FACTOR	GENERAL COMPANY IMPACT ON	DESCRIPTION EXAMPLE
Political Framework	▪ Security	Demand Costs	Increased trust in e-commerce Costs for secure technology
	▪ Tariffs	Costs	Internationalization
	▪ Taxation	Costs	Growth
	▪ Privacy	Demand Product Features	Trust in services Personalized services
	▪ Jurisdiction & Code	Clarity Potentially wrong signals	End of wild west mentality, Irritating business development
	▪ Intellectual Property Rights	+ Large player, Creators – New style publishers	Hollywood, Prince, MP3.com
	▪ Governance & Anti Trust	Costs Demand, Market Size Market Structures	Controlled Growth vs. Planning Failure (Freesurf, @Home European Digital TV)
Industrial Framework	**mainly internalized through convergence (see 2.4)**		
Technological Framework	▪ Converging Infrastructure	Costs Product / Services	Email via Cellular phone, Video-conference via automobile PC
	▪ Backbone Capacity	Costs	Price for Videoconference
	▪ Access network Capacity	Costs Products / Services	Multimedia Development (Internetradio, Internet VOD)
	▪ Network technology platform	Costs Products / Services	Differentiated product and prices / conditions bundles
	▪ Host & server capacity	Costs Products / Services	Multimedia Development Mass Customization
	▪ Usage devices	Products / Services	Service types: Handy email, stock quotes, PC videoconference
	▪ Standards development & Interoperability	"Make or Buy or Partner"	Wireless Access Protocol (WAP)
Socio-Economic Framework	▪ Labor supply	Speed / Type of Growth	Recruiting and retention issues
	▪ Capital supply & start-up potential	Market structure Speed / Type of Growth	Start-Up climate Silicon Valley vs. Central Europe in 1999
	▪ Overall technology deployment	Market size Costs	Installed base of PC, cable TV , modem households
	▪ Adoption rates	Market size Investment intensity	Adoption of Internet access
	▪ Web lifestyle ("Internet mindset")	Market size Investments intensity	Usage intensity of news, weather, mail via web (and not via TV, paper, snail mail)

Figure 2-8: "Exogenous" Variables and Impact on the Firms Business Models

Adjustments in these factors result in adjustments in products and services, cost structures, market volumes, market structures. These are crucial aspects for the industrial development as summarized in the following thesis:

The political, technological, industrial and social environment will set exogenous parameters, which shape the size and structure of the future on-line industry.

The on-line industry is far from maturity. The evolution of industrial, political, socio-economic and technological environment – the exogenous parameters – will heavily influence the development of the respective endogenous parameters of the on-line industry. Aggregated forces will shift the overall setting in such a way as to determine the size as well as the internal structure of the on-line industry. This indicates the influence of policy on the future business generated within this area.[89] This process opens **windows of opportunities** in the online market space.

This is ultimately the pie for which the players in the industry are competing and that which this thesis discusses from a business strategy standpoint. Figure 2-9 displays the four areas in the shape of triangles which shift in a horizontal manner as indicated by the horizontal arrows. The triangles overlap to represent their interdependence. Motion of one area will cause motion in another area. At any given point, the cohesion will reach a temporary equilibrium, which will determine the size of the central black box – the focal system of this thesis. The size represents the current volume of the industry or to place it in an economist's terms, it represents the contribution of the industry to the overall economy, which equals the size of the central square area.[90]

---

[89] Additional information taken from the interview with John Zysman, Co-Director of BRIE, 27th of April 1999, Berkeley. See also Case Study 2-1.

[90] Most of the research on the framework of the multimedia and on-line industry ends at this point of the analysis. The general recommendation is usually to target the **highest level of interoperability**. This will maximize the overall economic value added and support systemic efficiency. This thesis outlines the critical parameters, which work as influential exogenous variables to the endogenous variables of the industry system. To model the interdependence would be rather an issue of political economy, which is not central for this thesis. For a comprehensive discussion see e. g. KMPG (1996a), pp. 159-241. In general, it is an agreed position that the most fruitful approach to orchestrate the external industry setting involves a mutually cooperative approach of all participating players (see e. g. ibid., Wössner (1999c), KMPG (1996), Andersen (1998).

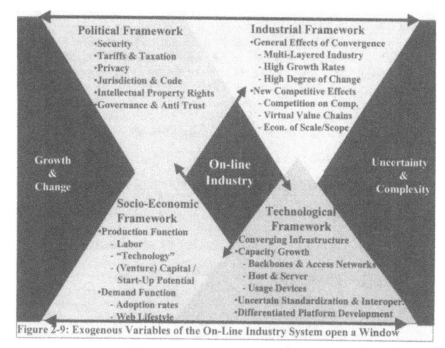

Figure 2-9: Exogenous Variables of the On-Line Industry System open a Window

As the entire setting is in constant motion on all axis', the diagonal arrows around the industrial black box represent these complex friction. They do not only change the size of the industry but also its internal structure. These general and specific trends in the industrial environment create a complex structural framework which results in **enormous challenges for business strategy** (Subsection 3.1.1). A main conclusion for firms is the insight about the unreliability of the exogenous variables, which imply a host of conclusions. Hence, firms have to deal with a high degree of uncertainty. They should be aware of the impact of the exogenous parameters on their business models. There are two approaches to handle this: adaptive, or in a proactive way. Proactive handling is the case of firms with capabilities to influence the exogenous parameters, like when the media firm Bertelsmann, negotiates with the political sector or Microsoft controls the developments of standardization due to market power. But this will be further analyzed during the discussion of the strategic conduct of firms in chapter 3. Many business models have yet to be invented and rules often do not exist. Thus **players often have to define their own rules** and need to try to leverage off the uncertainty and immaturity of the environment.[91]

After this analysis of the logic and mechanisms given by the external environment of the online industry **the following analysis looks into the black box** in order to analyze the laws of

---

[91] This finally means that in some cases the endogenous variables will shape the exogenous variables. Or in other words: The exogenous overlayer will be shaped from within the system that it plans to shape. This is due to the premature stage of the industrial environment, but appears mainly as a concern of public policy. "Policy-makers must address this issue quickly because the competitive development (...) is so rapid that decisions made now will profoundly shape the future trajectory of its development." (Bar / Cohen / Cowhey / DeLong / Kleeman / Zysman 1999:5).

the marketplace dominating the internal system environment. The view on the external environment indicated that the industrial framework has shifted. Different economics, the ICT driven trend of value chain virtualization, competency based competition and many interdependencies, or in other words – network effects, now dictate the economic and strategic laws of the market. The technological framework enables and drives a large part of this cohesion. These components will be analyzed in the consecutive course of chapter 2. Initially Section 2.2 will introduce the theoretical components to work out the conceptual model able to deal with these complex analytical challenges of the structural framework in the on-line industry.

2.2. Theoretical Framework for an Industry Model

This section lays out the theoretical framework. The central point is the introduction of the theory of network economics which is an excellent framework to conceptualize the economic mechanisms of the multi-layered - networked -.on-line industry. In combination with a novel approach of industrial analysis of the market forces in converging industries the author will present a conceptual model for multi-layered industries at the end of this section.

The analysis in Section 2.1 revealed that convergence internalized crucial factors of the convergence industries and established a multi-layered environment where several layers are vertically connected. In addition to these vertical network structures the horizontal layers of the business exhibit network aspects as well which is caused by the particular network technology. For example telecommunications networks are vertically connected with the community networks of Internet media companies. From a value chain point of view their connection establishes a vertical network structure. Each layer alone follows the logic of a horizontal network. In order to conceptualize such a structure in an economic way the theory of **network economics** will be introduced in Subsection 2.2.1. This theory can explain the economic logic – such as network externalities – within horizontal and vertical networks. It can build a logical bridge from the laws given by the exogenous parameters discussed above, to technological and traditional business strategy aspects, as they will be introduced in the consecutive course of this thesis. In order to enhance this with the appropriate tools to analyze the economic and strategic logic of the industrial competition Porter's (1980) five forces framework will be introduced and adapted as a conceptual framework for an **industry analysis** in Subsection 2.2.2. These two components will be combined to a **conceptual model** for the analysis of the industry in Subsection 2.2.3. Both components will serve as an analytical framework for an abstract model of the industry which is compatible with the according web-centric and market-based business strategy components introduced in part III.

2.2.1. On Network Economics

Over the past hundred years successful players in the industrial economy have been driven mainly by economies of scale while market structures were mostly characterized by more or less wider oligopolies. Market shares in mature settings adjusted only gradually. In contrast in the new information economy temporary monopolies dominate market structures.[92] An attractive position is captured by one initial player, who breaks through with a **level of critical mass** and gains a **dominant position**. This in return attracts other players who try to adjust

---

[92] See Varian / Shapiro (1998), p. 173.

market definitions and market shares. But in network markets players who are able to lever-age the network economics the best, have the opportunity to maintain the dominant position. However due to (network) economics these temporary adjustments can result in transitions into new dominant network structures.[93] According to the particular economics of the network and the strategic conduct of the players, constellations evolve in different patterns than in non-network markets.[94]

> "What has changed? There is one central difference between old and new economics: the old industrial economy was driven by *economies of scale*; the new information economy is driven by *economics of networks*." (Varian / Shapiro 1998:173)

But does this imply that we need new economics to understand this new economic space? Varian / Shapiro, and the majority of microeconomic community does not think so.

> "We think that many of the most important effects in the Information Economy have been present in the Industrial Economy. But there is a difference. Effects which are relatively uncommon in the Industrial Economy - like increasing returns to scale and network externalities - are the norm in the Information Economy." (Varian 1999b:25)

Varian points to the **increasing returns to scale** and **network externalities** as the particu-larities, which dominate the economics of the Internet. Whereas the relevancy of returns to scale will be formulated in terms of traditional Industrial Economics in the course of this the-sis, network externalities have to be identified as the truly new aspect in network economics. This new economic principle generates **network effects**, which are dominating the laws of the marketplace, market dynamics and competitive strategy in the network economy.

The underlying traditions of network economics are purely of microeconomic nature. A majority of the work is predominantly analytical and extends traditional microeconomic is-sues such as welfare analysis, market regulation, or game theoretic strategies into the particu-lar economic and technological situation of network markets. After the formulation of the network effects and its consequences on competition, network adoption and its concomitant technological compatibility, subsequent research analyzes a host of issues in the context of

---

[93] So far the theory has not delivered a model which explains a stable equilibrium (Economides 1996, p. 30). The empiric discontinuities (ibid.), which solve monopolies can be described in terms of monopolistic com-petition (see Economides / Wildman 1995 who particularly describe the pricing patterns during the entry of new players). Although particular network effects support the emergence of new monopolies on different network structures. This leads to another concentrated market situation based on a new network.

[94] See Katz / Shapiro (1985), Economides (1994, 1996), Economides / White (1994b), Economides / Flyer (1997). The two most common analytical approaches to market structures look either into monopoly struc-tures from a anti trust perspective or into duopolies in order to analyze the strategic conduct of players in this environment. Game theory is usually applied to analyze the strategic conduct of the players (see chapter 3). The performance, which arises from this conduct in different market structures tends to have different results in the presence of network externalities. An increase of market share and a higher degree of horizontal and vertical integration often results in a higher aggregate welfare, which distinguishes these markets from non-network markets (see Economides 1996). Positive feedback (see below) tends to support monopolies or stra-tegic coalitions and at the same time results in higher welfare: "We also find that the presence of network externalities dramatically affects conventional welfare analysis, as total surplus in markets where these exter-nalities are strong is highest under monopoly and declines with entry of traditional firms." (Economides / Flyer 1997:1). For a particular analysis of vertical integration see Economides (1994, 1998).

network economics and the accompanying business strategy. Figure 2-10 gives an overview of the main authors and their research focus.

AUTHOR	FOCUSED ISSUES
Arthur	• Path dependence • Increasing returns, positive feedback
Bakos / Brynjolfsson	• Bundling & demand-side economies of scope, pricing information goods
Borrus / Bar	• Value chain, international production networks, NII
Church / Gandal	• Complementarity, standards, adoption, entry
David	• Path dependence and standards
Economides	• Further research on the nature of network externalities • Industry structure, compatibility, anti trust • Extension into the field of value chains • Discussion of vertical and horizontal network dimensions • Elaboration on complementarity and its causal roles for externalities
Farrell / Saloner	• Standards, compatibility, competition and industry structure, IPR, adapters, adoption
Katz / Shapiro	• Initial definition of network externalities • Focus on adoption, technology, standards, compatibility, and anti trust
Varian	• Internet focus: IPR, economics of information goods (content, software) • Focus on product, pricing and adoption strategy (versioning, signaling) • Conceptualized "positive feedback" for business strategy • Comprehensive conceptual work in addition to analytical modeling
MacKie-Mason / Varian	• Technology structure, pricing

Figure 2-10: Authors in the Context of Network Economics[95]

The following section will introduce the concept of network economics and will put it into a perspective with the on-line industry. This forthcoming analysis will lay out the fundamental economic mechanisms in the industry and will be applied to model the industry in a structural way. The particular implications for the strategic conduct of firms will be further analyzed in part III during the course of the development of the business strategy tool set which will be designed to work with the industry model.

The first attempt to analyze and conceptualize the particular effects of networks, which also coined the term "network externalities", came from Katz / Shapiro (1985, 1986a,b). Both authors are microeconomists with practical expertise in telecommunications policy, which reveals the empirical background. Their research has disclosed the particular nature of economics of networks in general and for telecommunications in particular. Further observations focused on other network industries such as transportation, information, financial and railroads.[96] Understanding the dimension of these industries Katz / Shapiro conclude that for the theory of economics of networks, the role of network externalities is central:

---

[95] Arthur (1989, 1990, 1994, 1996), Bar / Borrus (1995), Bakos / Brynjolfsson (1996, 1997), Bar / Borrus / Steinberg (1995), Borrus / Zysman (1997), Church / Gandal (1992a, 1992b, 1993, 1996), David (1985, 1986, 1989), Economides (1989, 1991, 1992, 1993, 1994, 1995a,b, 1996, 1997, 1998a, 1998b, 1998d, 1998e), Economides / Flyer (1997), Economides / Himmelberg, (1995a, 1995b), Economides / Lehr (1994), Economides / Salop (1992), Economides / White (1994a, 1994b), Economides / Woroch (1992), Farrell / Saloner (1985, 1986, 1992), Farrell / Shapiro (1988, 1989), Katz / Shapiro (1985, 1986a, 1986b, 1992, 1994), Varian / Shapiro (1998a, 1998b), Varian (1978, 1993, 1995, 1996, 1997, 1998a, 1998b, 1998c, 1999), Varian / MacKie-Mason (1994a, 1994b, 1994c),

[96] See Economides (1996), pp. 675. With respect to network industries an important factor is that their development is often interdependent. Michael Janes, VP of electronic commerce for Federal Express states this in

"We have developed a simple model to capture what we believe is a very significant element of competition in several important markets." (Katz / Shapiro 1985:439)

Since then the theory has seen further development. **Most recently, the majority of the research focuses on phenomena in respect to the Internet, which intensively exhibits the network patterns described in network economics.**[97] The economic relevance and growth of the Internet has resulted in an enormous academic interest in the theory. Since the publication "Information Rules" (Varian / Shapiro 1998), the theory has also garnered serious attention from a wider audience.

The main effect in networks is that the value of the network to a customer increases with the number of users on it. These networks can be real such as communication or transportation networks or virtual as the network of users on the AOL buddy list. Or described generally, networks are composed of complementary nodes and links. The crucial defining feature of networks is the complementarity between the various nodes and links. A service delivered over a network requires the use of two or more network components. The goods and services, which can be described as networks, generate greater value with being used by an increasing number of users.[98] In general the term externality describes a situation where the conduct of one player affects the utility function of another player without a compensation being paid. This term is usually used to describe negative external effects of – to use the classic example – environmental pollution by a firm. In the case of network economics the externalities are positive.[99] A higher number of people using email will positively affect each user. Each additional user is not paid for their value added to the network, although each user benefits from this added value. Metcalf's Law (see 2.1.2) can be interpreted as follows: The value of a network goes up as the square of the number of users on it.[100] In fact

---

the following manner: "When the telegraph came along there was a corresponding development of the rail system. The telegraph created the connections and the railroad allowed fulfillment. Well, today the Internet creates connections, and we [FedEx, C. G.] provide the fulfillment." (Lappin 1996:286) In this sense FedEx proclaims "FedEx is a network" (ibid.).

[97] See Economides (1996:2).

[98] See Katz / Shapiro (1985), p. 424 and Economides (1996), p. 682.

[99] See Varian / Shapiro (1998), p. 183.

[100] See ibid., p. 184. This refers to the economics of a two-way network. The formulas cited below also describe a two-way network as for example the network of email users. n users determine the potential goods and hence the value of this network. The first user can not send email to no one. Two users can send and receive email between user one and user two. Hence the potential goods are 2 (2-1) = 2. Three users can send up to 6 (3 (3-1)=6)potential goods. The super-linear progression becomes evident. But this describes the **potential** goods, because when high numbers of users are acquired, the majority of the potential combinations / goods stays unused. Therefore the formulation states the potential value of a network is proportional to n x (n-1) = n^2 –n. The externality created by the (n+1) additional user is 2n in a two-way network. User n+1 can send email to n existing users and vice versa, which results in 2n potential added goods. Neither new user nor existing users on the network are compensated for this additional value created by joining the network - hence its externality.

"If there are n people in a network, and the value of the network to each of them is proportional to the number of *other* users, then the total value of the network (to all users) is proportional to n x (n-1) = n^2 - n" (Varian / Shapiro 1998:184)[101]

"In this component network, there are n (n-1) potential goods. An additional (n+1st) customer provides direct externalities to all customers in the network by adding 2n potential new goods through provision of a complementary link (...) to the existing links." (Economides 1996:675-676).

This last quotation refers to direct externalities which go back to different types of networks. Katz / Shapiro (1985) and Economides (1996) classify **two types of networks**, which generate different network effects. One is **two-way networks** where the exchange flows in both directions. There, users are not only receiving content, but they are also contributing content. This contribution can be a file upload, a chat, participation in a message thread or other activities (see also Case Study 2-2). With an increasing number of network components (such as community members or email users, see footnote 100) the network effect described above is the outcome. This type is called the **direct network effect**. On the other hand, different economic effects can be perceived in **one-way networks**. A one way network, such as the CNN News Site, which broadcasts information will not directly generate greater value if more user use the network. The indirect effect in this example is caused by the greater number of viewers, which in return establishes a larger market with a higher revenue potential. Thus a supplier of a one-way network can spend more money on the supply side and therefore is able to deliver higher value, e.g. better TV. This effect in return adds value to the customer in an indirect way caused by an increased number of users. This is referred to as the **indirect network effect**. [102]

Varian / Shapiro (1998:173) point out that network externalities result in **positive feedback**, which rewards players who utilize network externalities. The first telephone in the world had very little value to its users as there was no one else to call. With a growing number of telephones the telephone network was increasingly commoditized and each additional user could derive a higher utility.[103] This effect can be called **demand side economies of scale**. [104] Hence users can realize scale economics in networks with **growing adoption rates**. Another term used for this phenomenon is "positive consumption"[105]. The growing adoption increases the utility of the network and ignites a growth trend. A crucial factor is that a certain **critical**

---

[101] See also Economides (1996), p. 675 who derives the same equation. This definition can be used to derive the overall value of a network. To describe the individual utility from a user's point more precisely. Economides (1996, p. 681) notes that the exact interpretation of network externalities in fact would not exhibit a downward sloping demand curve. He shifts the definition to a higher level of precision, by stating that to the individual customer, the value of a unit sold increases with the *expected* number of units sold. This results in a demand function which slopes downwards but shifts upwards with an increased expectation of the number of sold units. For example, as PC users expect others also to use Microsoft's Windows as a dominant operating system, then the perceived future value of Windows (and all its compatible software products) is perceived as superior to others, such as a Linux operating system.

[102] See Economides (1996), pp. 6-7.

[103] See Katz / Shapiro (1985).

[104] See Varian / Shapiro (1998), pp. 175-190.

[105] See Economides (1996), p. 682.

mass must be reached in order to fuel the supply side economies of scale, demand side economies of scale and enjoy the positive feedback. Once this critical mass is reached the positive self-reinforcing dynamic of network externalities kicks in.[106] Varian / Shapiro illustrate the break even of the critical mass and the initiation of positive feedback with the feedback of a signal of a microphone, which passes through the amplifier and returns to the microphone. Once a critical factor is reached this feedback process fuels itself until the maximum amplification. Or to translate this into market terms:

> "(...) positive feedback in the marketplace leads to extremes: **dominance of the market** by a single firm or technology." (Varian / Shapiro 1998:176) [emphasis added].[107]

On the other hand if this critical mass is not reached a network will not realize sustainable economics. This can be due to weak marketing efforts in the absence of competition if a player fails to push the network components to the break even point. It can also be due to a competitor with better competitive position in the network constellation, who receives stronger positive feedback (see Figure 2-12). This illustrates, on the one hand, that the value of the system is increasing when there is a growth trend and as positive feedback begins. On the other hand it shows that, if a network does not to reach a certain level, the potential to survive will be diminished. Booz Allen Hamilton analyzed the facsimile market with regards to this and state that the take-off occurred at an adoption rate of approximately 30%.[108]

In the on-line industry positive feedback is supported not only by demand side economies of scale (positive consumption) but also by classical supply side economies of scale (production externalities). Telecommunications networks, software production, content creation are all products, which exhibit high initial fixed costs and very low variable costs for each additional incremental unit. This results in strong economies of scale on the supply side.[109] **Demand and supply side scale effects combined result not only positive feedback from the market side but also from the economics of the business** (production externalities). Hence,

> "Supply-side and demand-side economies of scale combine to make positive feedback in the network economy especially strong." (Varian / Shapiro 1998:182)

---

[106] See Varian / Shapiro (1998), pp. 175-179. The term critical mass has been developed in studies of the communications market (Rohlfs 1974, Oren / Smith 1981). See Economides / Himmelberg (1994) who discus the influence of number of players, standards and level of variable costs as alternating variables which influence critical the mass of network size. They explain the phenomenon of critical mass with the "chicken and egg" paradox from their observations that the expected network size is too small to induce consumers into the network. In turn, because no consumers are willing to join the network, network providers are not willing to invest into a network. Thus a solid marketplace cannot be established. For exactly these reasons the largest trial project on cable broadband infrastructure by Vebacom in Germany in 1996-1998 did not succeed. The projected network size was 10.000 users which was too small to motivate content providers to generate high bandwidth content. Due to a lack of attractive content, which could differentiate the network from the low bandwidth Internet, potential users were not interested to join the network. Obviously the critical mass was over 10.000 users (according to CompuServe internal data).

[107] See also Economides / Flyer (1997) who discuss the effects of compatibility on market dominance.

[108] Booz Allen Hamilton (1995), p. 47.

[109] See 2.1.3, Varian / Shapiro (1998), pp. 1-19 and Varian (1995).

These particular economics will result in **increasing returns** (Arthur 1990, 1996), which fuel a self-reinforcing growth trend once a player reaches the level of critical mass.[110]

Market dominance is the likely outcome. Consider AOL: the more people subscribe to the system, the increased the probability that friends or colleagues can share the interactive proprietary features, such as chat, multimedia email, and buddy lists, of the system, all of which make a subscription more attractive. Thus, a large number of users increase the demand-side value of the network. This results in a market-side positive feedback. The growing number of users generates an increasing amount of traffic on the telecommunications network, which supports positive feedback on the supply side as AOL benefits from lower costs for network traffic, which follows strong economies of scale.[111] The same effect appears in costs for content: The larger the traffic through AOL's Internet gateway the better the position to negotiate favorable content deals and capitalize advertising opportunities. Figure 2-11 shows how this positive feedback results in AOL assuming a dominant leader position against competing, narrow bandwidth providers in the United States, who trail by a wide margin.

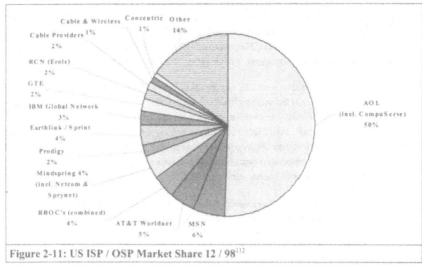

Figure 2-11: US ISP / OSP Market Share 12 / 98[112]

---

[110] Different from the traditional definitions in Industrial Economics, which focuses on production-side scale driven increasing returns (the cost per unit decreases as more units of the good are produced), in the context of network economics the term is used to describe more generally a situation where the net value of the last produced unit [= (dollar amount consumers are willing to pay for the last unit) - (average per unit cost of production)] increases with the number of units produced.

[111] As stated above, the business model for Internet traffic is based on extremely high initial costs for the network owner who establishes it. The variable costs are comparatively low. Hence an increasing amount of traffic generates increasing returns per unit as the fixed cost allocated per variable unit decrease drastically. As the high initial fixed costs are sunk costs, the provider of the network will try to capitalize the investment as much as possible. This position provides an on-line service, which may be viewed as a giant traffic aggregator, with a strong bargaining position from which it may drive down prices for traffic. See Case Study 2-1 for bargaining in an interconnection situation in a deregulated market and footnote 235 for the volume based costs digression in data network rentals.

[112] Goldman Sachs (1999c), p. 9 showing data of IDC.

The critical issue in this constellation is the difficulty of reaching the level of critical mass. If there is a market, where a player has already reached critical mass and receives positive feedback its growth gets fueled by a dynamic process. This typically **does not support a market constellation with a large number of players**. Market share determines the level of positive feedback, which results in a constellation where **the strong get stronger and the weak get weaker** as Figure 2-12 shows:

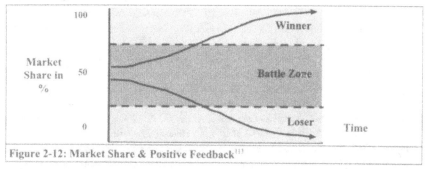

Figure 2-12: Market Share & Positive Feedback[113]

In the case of the on-line industry Booz Allen & Hamilton (1998b) was predicting a tough "survival" or "shake out" perspective for regional and national players due to "unfavorable economics" (ibid.). Moreover Figure 2-11 already includes the takeovers of Sprynet and Netcom by Mindspring and of CompuServe by AOL. Furthermore IBM Net was sold to AT&T while analysts expect further transactions and consolidation in this field.

The following case study illustrates a typical two-way network situation of an on-line service community, which exhibits the particular economics of the Internet:

"Communities" seemed to be the buzz word in the Internet and on-line service industry in 1996. But different from many other trends in this area, which are subject to hyperbole, the notion of communities as success factor is still around five years later - and for good reasons. Aside from a service provider, a web site, or since interactive e-commerce, any normal firm needs to build a relationship to their community. The prediction stemmed from the emergence of "virtual marketspaces" (Rayport / Sviokla 1994) where "new infomediaries" (Hagel / Rayport 1997), who are the "commercializers" of a community, capture the "net gain" and the "real profits from virtual communities" (Hagel / Armstrong 1995, 1996, 1997a, 1997b). This was the salient insight. Much has been written about it since it became popular, but the mentioned references comprehensively captured the novel insights at an early stage. The related highlights, such as user generated content, virtual networks, positive feedback and increasing returns indicate that the power behind communities is fueled by network effects. The case study outlines the stages of the commercial evolution of on-line communities and finally highlights an on-line trading community: the on-line auction site of eBay.

In fact, on-line communities are the perfect example for a two-way network system with strong increasing returns to scale on the supply-side and the demand-side, which exhibits critical mass issues and results in dominance of a market or market segment. Hence, network externalities are the driving force in the economics and commercial success of a community.

---

[113] See Varian / Shapiro (1998), p. 177.

A community is basically a group of people, who share a common interest, either via exchanging information or communicating in relations with like-minded persons.[114] Initially virtual communities were driven by personal interest groups, usually without commercial motivations. The Usenet newsgroups are the most prominent examples.[115] The first example for commercial on-line communities emerged within the CompuServe on-line service during the late 1970ies. CompuServe developed an integrated proprietary forum technology supporting chat, message threading, file sections, and search tools. "Community managers" could set up their forum to build their **community in a CompuServe Forum**. They were compensated with a pay-out of 10% of the connect-time revenues, which their community members generated on the CompuServe network while accessing the communities of their interest. Communities could use the content provided by their members in the file sections and message boards while community managers just needed to organize on-line events and control the quality of the posted content. The common term for this phenomenon is user generated content. This effect of user generated content increases with the number of users. Over time there is more content and more people to meet, which makes more people join. In return the manager of such a community gets content for free and the variable costs for delivering this content are zero. With an increasing number of users on a community platform, the attraction of joining this community increases. The community member acquisition is frequently conducted by existing community members, which are inviting new members in the specific community of interest. This shows how the traditionally high costs for the creation of content are shifting towards zero in some areas in the on-line framework. The community membership by and large gets increased by its own usersbase, which invite new users Furthermore the incremental costs for the distribution of this content are almost zero. There are fixed costs for the production of the content which are generated by providing a technical environment to support these community functions. Once people join a community and provide content via their actions, these actions create a cycle attracting additional users, which will generate additional content, which attracts additional users and so on. The incremental costs for these actions are almost zero once a technical production platform for a community is set up.

Over time the community members are generating their content on a specific technology / production platform, and develop their network of personal relationships. Both aspects combined makes users unlikely to change the platform as their switching costs are increasing. This lock-in effect makes a community a business opportunity with not only low customer acquisition costs, low maintenance costs, low investments, but also a very strong retention.

Hence such communities exhibit demand side and supply side economies of scale and are an ideal example for a virtuous cycle as described by Varian / Shapiro (1998), p. 180. This self-reinforcing dynamic characterizes the network economics of interactive on-line services. Popular CompuServe communities with 10-20.000 users, such as regional chat and socializing forums, generated 50.000 usage hours per month resulting in more than $15.000 per month for the community manager.[116] But ultimately these two early community types lost relative importance in the late 1990s due to the rise of the world wide web. Stronger commercial communities took over their role. The reason is that these new community types

---

[114] See Figure 2-23 for the fundamental needs of on-line services which are completely covered in on-line communities, such as a forum.

[115] See Dyson (1997) for a comprehensive description of the nature of these not-for-profit communities.

[116] CompuServe internal data. Sample calculation: 50.000 usage hours based on a rate of $2.95 per hour adds up to $147.500 for the on-line service generated over the network access. A ten percent revenue share for the content and service community manager is $14.750. Based on 10.000 users, this assumes a monthly presence of 5 hours per user (see also Figure 2-22).

were built on different business models, utilized the coverage of the Internet and the more appealing graphical interface of the world wide web. Therefore they carry stronger commercial incentives for the community managers as well as better distribution and visual creatives for the user

The first web **communities, such as Geocities or Tripod**, were set up as free services connecting people under one "umbrella". Users are setting up free homepages, which generate content at almost zero costs. The community managers organize these websites in an editorial way and add events, topical news, and search functions. An increasing number of members using these communities add content and potential personal relations, which increase the attraction of joining the community - a typical demand-side scale effect. If one defines the network as the community of users, then according to the theoretical discussion above, the network value increases proportional to $n2-n$ to the number of users. Additional users were not rewarded for joining, which makes this scale effect an externality captured by the community manager. Fixed costs were generated by the initial system set-up and are increasing linearly– but are relatively negligible – variable costs are generated by the hosting space and editorial activities. As these communities run on advertising-based models they need to scale-up to be profitable. More users joining boost the revenues at a stronger rate than the costs. Hence communities like Geocities also enjoy supply side economies of scale. This creates increasing returns. In addition the growing number of users, combined with salient word-of-mouth marketing effects of the in the web[117], the network effects also fuel their marketing functions, which overall results in positive feedback corresponding to the growing number of users.

Considering the potential purchasing power of the community on a site, the sole advertising business model promises only comparatively limited commercial prospects. Considering potential revenue streams **trading communities** meeting on **auction sites** provide opportunities for better business models in the late 1990ies. The most prominent one is the eBay trading community which is based on a consumer-to-consumer e-commerce business model[118] A site like eBay is based on very generic back-end technology, which is available as an Internet technology off-the shelf software component.[119] Furthermore, the costs for editing a host of auction categories and technically maintaining the site is relatively small and rather fixed. Variable costs for additional auctions do not apply, because the costs accrue to the seller and buyer of an auctioned good. This reveals that an auction site has one-time set up costs and fixed costs for ongoing maintenance. These costs are sunk costs. Each additional unit - in this case a transaction - generates revenue with no concomitant costs. The results is predictable: increasing returns after break even is reached, caused by supply side scale effects. This is a crucial strength of the business model of auctions: It is only the virtual part of transaction which generates no incremental costs. It excludes the real actions of the transaction which do generate incremental costs.[120] This determines the success factors in the eco-

---

[117] Interview with Karsten Weide, former Senior Producer of Yahoo! Germany, 5th of March 1999, San Francisco.

[118] See Goldman Sachs (1999a), pp. 20-28 for a categorization of e-commerce business models.

[119] Off course in terms of scale like the eBay site, tailored components apply, but in general the software is available for anyone at low cost.

[120] Additional benefits are aggregation of purchasing power: A large auctioneer generates enormous demand in certain product categories, demand for shipping, demand for escrow, demand for insurance and so forth. These positions can be used as a strong bargaining position against suppliers to generate additional revenue streams. If one considers for example that eBay handles more than 1.5 million auctions per day it evidently owns market access to an enormous demand for shipping and handling. To be the preferred provider of these services for eBay is a very attractive position which can be sold by the auction company. These are indirect network effects which can be utilized as well, but corresponding details are left out in this case study in order

nomics of the production function. The crucial point lies with the demand-side externality of auction sites: The more people offering something in a trading community, then the more sellers will join this community and vice versa. Users of this platform will start spreading the word, depending on how well such a platform performs for buyers and sellers, which in return is a "self-reinforcing" mechanism (Arthur 1988) in the marketing of such a site. The obvious essence of these trading communities for all participants is: 'the bigger the better.' - better for the seller, better for the buyer and better for the community provider. Size provides the positive feedback, which is typical for network markets. Early movers have the advantage to shape the business model, the laws of the market place and will ultimately break through to critical mass first. Meg Whitman, CEO of eBay, points out: "[But] we created this market and we know it really well. We have a bit of a "network effects" business here: The more buyers you have, the more sellers you have, [and] in turn, [that] attracts more buyers." (Whitman 1999:3). The community members are the salient success factor for this kind of on-line business: "EBay is more about building a community than about e-commerce per se" (ibid.:2), which is highly recognized by eBay. Its software, web site and services can all be imitated - but an active community of several million traders cannot be easily generated. Hence eBay's crucial asset is its lively, interactive, and virtual network of community members. [121]

In general one can conclude for communities, that once the growth has reached critical mass and has begun to generate positive feedback, a provider can gain a dominant position. But as the subsequent discussion of network economics will show: these dominant structures exhibit no stable equilibrium and hence can disappear as fast as they emerged. These networks are "tippy" (Benson / Farrell 1994) and can shift to new dominant network structures. In the three analyzed cases of on-line communities, CompuServe forums, Geocities homepages, and eBay auctions, which dominated the community model at different development stages of the on-line market, fundamental changes in technology, products and business model made previously attractive combinations look less attractive relative to the new combinations. CompuServe offered proprietary technology, which provided the most comprehensive information, communication, and relationship-fostering product in forums generated from a time-based business model. Geocities provided an open standard Internet technology product offering content, homepages, email and search functions based on an free / advertising business model. EBay offers open standard technology auctions sites where people can meet and trade collectibles, based on low (almost no) costs running a transaction share business model.

From a commercial standpoint the crucial question is the design of the business model as most communities are free of charge. This implies the necessity of locating alternative revenue streams, which are not based on content subscriptions or similar approaches. Advertising is so far the most common business model, in the case of web communities. New infomediaries who are the agents initiating and participating in transactions in the e-commerce scenarios, are probably the most promising ones (Hagel / Rayport 1997). The consumer-to-consumer approach of eBay is obviously a strong example for this model.

To provide a taste how these community models are valued in the late 1990s, it is worthwhile pointing out that CompuServe (including network, approximately 2000 communities, approximately 1000 additional content sites, technology, ISP unit) was sold for $1.2 billion in early 1998 (see Case Study 2-5),

---

to focus the pure web-based parts of the business model. In fact eBay's competitors, such as OnSale, focus on this kind of foregoing.

[121] Background information for this case study from interviews with eBay executives Brian Sweete (Executive Vice President Marketing), Scott Barnum (Vice President International) and Reed Maltzman (Director Strategic Planning), 12th of May 1999, San Jose.

while in March 1999 Geocities – one of the Internet's early high-profile companies - has a market capitalization of $ 3.462 billion while eBay is valued at $20.625 billion.[122]

Case Study 2-2: Positive Feedback in Two-Way Networks: The Case of On-Line Communities

The fundamental aspect of networks is the complementarity of network components:

> "A good, or a network component, is more valuable when more complementary components are available." (Economides 1998a:2).

In networks, goods and services must be used in conjunction with other products at the same time. Their independent value in isolation of this network is little or none. Thus the singular components of the network exhibit a complementary relation. Hence,

> "The key reason for the appearance of network externalities is the complementarity between the components of a network." (Economides 1996:6)

The consumers using these products constitute the network in which the utility derived from consumption of the goods and services increases with additional users of complementary components. In this context the influence of **technical standards** (see 2.1.2) and their critical relation to network economics becomes evident. Standards create compatibility of components.[123] If these components exhibit a complementary relation they can be connected to a larger network extending the network effects. In this respect

> "(...) compatibility (...) can be understood through the lens of complementarity (...)." (Economides / White 1994b:22).

Due to network externalities the definition of standards and the possibility to **interconnect networks** affects the fundamental economics of markets. Within this issue network economics exhibit the same outcome as described above: larger networks generate higher value. Consequently increased compatibility will interconnect networks to form still larger networks, which will, in general, increase the value of the network. Economides (1998) translated this into terms of competitive strategy and points out that vertical complementarity of components equals **economies of scope.**

Networks have this strong tendency to generate economies of scale. Consequently the ability to enlarge the scale of the network, which expands the network externalities, is a very valuable potential. Hence **the position as a bottleneck** which is created at the interconnection points of networks **are extremely valuable.** A bottleneck can be defined as a part of the network for which there is no available substitute in the market, hence there is no way around.

---

[122] See Goldman Sachs (1999a), using data of March 19, 1999. It is significant that eBay's stock was valued at $159,75 on that day while it peaked at $234.00 on May 23, 1999 and dropped to $98.00 until August 15, 1999, which shows not only volatility but also the overall value of that player.

[123] Definitions of compatibility vary in the literature covering network economics (e.g. Economides (1989, 1996a and Bailey et. al. 1995). It is commonly said that two products are compatible when the cost of combining them to generate services is free. This implies gradual steps of compatibility depending on the costs to achieve the full level of compatibility at no costs. Adapters (see below) are a typical example which generate costs to accomplish compatibility.

Players who play the function of a gate keeper to other networks can capitalize on this position. This can either happen by charging **interconnection** fees to connect compatible networks or by building a business around an **adapter**, which is able to connect formerly incompatible networks.[124] The **control over standards** can enable players to design the bottlenecks in their favor. This puts them in the position to capitalize on their gate keeper position by charging other players to interconnect.[125] One example is the computer desktop, an extremely valuable bottleneck, which is owned by the operating system vendor. In the case of Windows, Microsoft can use this bottleneck to negotiate favorable terms with Internet services by giving access to this desktop, e. g. by bundling a logo or even pushing content as in the case of the active desktop channels of Microsoft's IE 4 generation. In this case Microsoft was not charging money but bartering presence and visibility on the desktop against co-marketing efforts and technology adoption.[126]

How are networks structured? Economides states that networks can be seen as systems (composite goods) consisting of components (elementary goods):

> "Many complex goods are composed of simpler *elementary goods*, which in many
> cases are sold separately." (Economides 1991:2)

For example, the good "email sent from X to Y" requires the use of an email appliances consisting of hardware and software at X and at Y as well as the use of a network that allows the transmission of data from X to Y. This network usually includes the local access networks of locations X and Y plus a backbone network. **Each of these elementary goods is complementary with the others,**

> "(...) since their combination allows the consumer to purchase the *composite
> good*"(ibid.)

or in other words, the "bundled good" in order to send and receive email from X to Y.

> **The elementary goods can be thought of as** *components* **and the composite goods**
> **as** *systems*." (Economides 1991:3, emphasis, C. G.)

In the on-line industry many bundlings appear as a system or a composite good. Email was given as one example. Another one is the commercial infrastructure consisting of the components access network, backbone network, client software technology and user management system, which can be seen as a composite good consisting of complementary system components. On-line services and ISP's are packaging these complementary bundles. **In this context the influence of technical standards and their influence on compatibility becomes evident:**

> The ability of all elementary goods (or components) to be combined costlessly with
> all elementary goods of a different type to produce functioning composite goods (or

---

[124] See Economides / Woroch (1992), Economides / Lehr (1994). For further analysis on the bottleneck function of standards see Katz / Shapiro (1985), pp. 436-437 and Economides (1996), p. 29 who analyze the strategic influence of adapters to realize compatibility in non-standard networks.

[125] See Varian / Shapiro (1998), pp. 228-236.

[126] Based on CompuServe internal data.

systems) is defined as *full compatibility*. Compatible elementary goods can be thought
of as constituting a *network*." (Economides 1991:3)

Consider, for example, the composite good "email sent via website", such as
www.hotmail.com. This action is composed of at least four elementary goods that are complementary with each other - the use of a mailbox, the use of a website, the use of a browser,
and the use of a device. Full compatibility of all elementary goods means that any mailbox
can be used from any website, with every browser with any access device.[127]

Given such a structure of compatible components which can be connected to a system in
complementary ways one can distinguish a **horizontal dimension** and a **vertical dimension**.
Under full compatibility there is an on-line service network vertically connecting backbones,
access networks, contents, hosts, corresponding server and client technology. Each horizontal
layer is connecting complementary and compatible components with complementary and
compatible components of other vertical layers.

" Thus, the existence of a (vertical) network is contingent upon compatibility between
complementary elementary goods." (Economides 1991:3-4)

In the case of the on-line industry the network of complementary components with a horizontal dimension could be the number of users using email or a buddy list. But one can also
distinguish a network in a vertical dimension such as the network of modem users and the
network of PC users that vertically establishes a network, which can be connected to the
Internet access networks. Complementarity between components in the horizontal and vertical
dimension is crucial in the on-line industry as the technological framework (2.1.2) revealed.
User need devices to connect via networks to retrieve or exchange information. The networks
need traffic, devices need networks and value-added applications such as email and websites.
If all these components are based on compatible standards, then their complementary relationship will initiate positive feedback based on network externalities.[128] The Internet delivered
such standards, which caused the fundamental adjustments of the entire industrial setting (see
2.1.3). This indicates that complementarity in networks and network structures themselves
have a horizontal and a vertical dimension. Consequently the network constitution of the
Internet with the horizontal and vertical dimension make the theory of network economics
extremely suitable for the multi-layered on-line industry in the Internet framework.

In this context, Economides (1996) and Economides / White (1994b) argue that **vertically
related industries** can also be regarded as a network:

---

[127] Note in this context the "AOL anywhere" strategy or the recent Microsoft strategy "Information on your
fingertips anytime, anywhere, from any device".

[128] Another – very prominent example – is the bundling of the Microsoft Internet Explorer browser with the
Windows operating system. Competitors of the browser market, like Netscape cannot benefit from the resulting vertical network effects and thus suffer from a lack of a positive vertical externality compared to the
competing Microsoft product. This example shows how vertical markets affect each other. For an in depth
discussion of the technical, legal and economic aspects of this particular case see Bork (1999), SPA (1999)
and Economides (1998a) and Case Study 2-6.

"Most industries involve vertically related components and thus are conceptually similar to one-way networks." (Economides / White 994b:Abstract)

This expands the theory of network economics to non-network industries by simply defining the virtual network caused by the complementarity of vertically related layers. This is a crucial aspect for the industry structure in the virtually constructed on-line industry in the Internet (see Figure 2-38).

In this sense the strength of the network relationship between vertically related industries is dependent on type and degree of their complementarity. Economides points out that two-way complementarity result in direct, and thus stronger externalities, and one-way complementarity in indirect, and thus weaker, network externalities.[129] Accordingly, it is possible to regard a typical supply chain as a one-way network. Opposite to this a complex virtual value "web" structure which bundles a product with two-way complementary components can be understood as a two-way network.[130] **Economides (1998a) argues that the bilateral complementarity of components in the multi-layered computer industry can be understood as a two-way network, which exhibits the resultant strong positive feedback. The same applies for the multi-layered on-line industry as all layers exhibit two-way complementarity.**[131]

The question of the cause of bilateral complementarity with respect to demand-side economies of scale and scope is worth looking into more precisely, because it is a source for the strong network externalities in vertically related industries. It is argued that complementarity results when the final product is a bundled – or in Economides' diction: composite – product. This assumes that product bundlings assemble a product of components, which have a complementary relation, often across firms' boundaries.[132] For example, customers who by modems are happy to find free trials of on-line service providers, Internet software for content and email and so forth bundled with the modem. The modem purchaser gains added–value, as does the software producer, as does the access provider. Together they bundle a package across firms, which delivers a valuable product for a customer who wants to go on-line. This describes two-way complementarity between each component in a nutshell. But what constitutes the two-way complementarity, which results in strong direct network effects? It is the complementary relationship of product value with regards to the same customer. It has to be understood that the product components add value to a set of needs, which are meeting a bundle of related needs of the customer. Each singular **component** serves one **need's dimension** and the **bundling** serves the complex of correlated needs. This is an extremely novel finding, which was so far been widely overlooked in the discussion on the network economy. The first authors to discover this aspect were Bakos / Brynjolfsson:

---

[129] Economides (1996), p. 6.

[130] See Economides (1996) and Economides / Salop (1992) who analyze the microstructure of complementary products between firms explain the aspects of integration and competition between the firms.

[131] Richardson (1999) and also the interview with John Richardson, Director of International Computer Services Research, Stanford Computer Industry Project, 6th of May 199, Los Angeles, supported the thesis that the according conclusions can be translated to the on-line industry in the Internet framework.

[132] See Economides (1993) who analyzes the positive economic effects of product bundling. Compatibility and technical standards are an enabler for these effects (see Economides / White 1994b).

> " (...), bundling of information goods can substantially increase profits even when the valuations of individual goods are highly correlated, but not to the same underlying variables" (Bakos / Brynjolfsson 1996)

Or in other words, there is no complementarity if "My Yahoo!" offers another location's weather information to the variable "need for weather information", but there is high complementarity when "My Yahoo!" offers local news to the respective area of the user, including weather, which serves the highly correlated variable "need for further information on the specific area". In addition to this rather horizontally located need, one can expand this to a vertical needs dimension of on-line services where the product bundling consists of a device, access provision, interactive services and the according usage software. It can be argued that the **targeting of the same customer segment is the crucial aspect in bundling / networking**. If players who have a complementary position bundle their products and services together, they will enjoy a two-way complementary relationship, which establishes a direct network effect on the demand side. The corresponding network externality fuels everyone's businesses. Consequently, if the degree of complementarity is asymmetrical the network effect is asymmetrical.[133] For example, the bundling of an on-line service provider is only slightly complementary to a PC, but extremely complementary for the on-line service provider who is constrained by the PC as an exclusive access device. This explains the strong interest of AOL to be bundled with each windows operating system which is bundled with (almost) each PC. In this case the PC is the limiting factor, the bottleneck to the AOL market. PC manufacturers can leverage this position. In the case of the PC, the manufacturer lost control of this integral link in the value web, which is now controlled by the monopoly position of Windows. For these reasons, AOL continues to integrate the Microsoft Internet Explorer browser into its software package, although it owns Netscape, which is the competitor of Microsoft. The position on the PC desktop is more valuable for the AOL on-line service offering, than is the market share of the Netscape Navigator browser (which is also an AOL product line).

Horizontal and vertical network effects are extremely significant for the on-line industry. For example, the adoption of email is supported by horizontal network effects. The more people using email, then the higher the resulting aggregate network value is, as well as the particular value for each individual email user. In addition, the value of the email network is influenced by complementary components, which are positioned in a vertical position. For example the growing adoption rate of devices, which bundle email functionality – today mainly PC's, but in the future a growing number of non-PC devices (see 2.1.2) – will increase the penetration of email. This externality from a vertical layer will positively affect the email network. Due to its bilateral complementary nature, the existence of a largely accepted email network adds value to the email components of the device network. This exhibits multiple two-way network relations and therefore creates strong positive feedback. In case of a one-way complementarity, for example, the above mentioned classical one-way supplier relationship, the externality will be indirect and hence will provide weaker positive feedback. Complete on-line service consists of a bundle of on-line services, which complement each other

---

[133] See Economides (1991) and Bakos / Brynjolfsson (1996) who analyze asymmetrical demand and asymmetrical value in respect to composite, bundled goods.

(see Figure 2-25). It is further argued within this thesis that **the vertically differentiated layers in the on-line industry exhibit mostly two-way complementarity-ness, which increases the strong network externalities already existing in the horizontal layers of the industry and vice versa.**

Figure 2-13 gives an overview of the different findings with respect to one-way and two-way networks. It highlights the fact that one-way networks usually have one (or few) senders and many receivers. This can be understood by the broadcasting example of television or a news site, which has no interactive components. Furthermore, a classical supply chain can be seen in this manner. One company manufactures goods for a host of customers. Due to its interactive nature two-way networks enable each receiver automatically to be a sender as well. If the same news site has interactive components, like boards to "post your opinion here!" or "join the discussion", it invites a receiver to contribute content and changes the media logic to a multicast manner. This community aspect of user generated content, as described in Case Study 2-2, changes the economics of the site on the supply side as well as the demand side.[134] The effects of the particular arithmetic which result in strong positive feedback and increasing returns is also shown in Figure 2-13 which summarizes the particular network economics analyzed above.

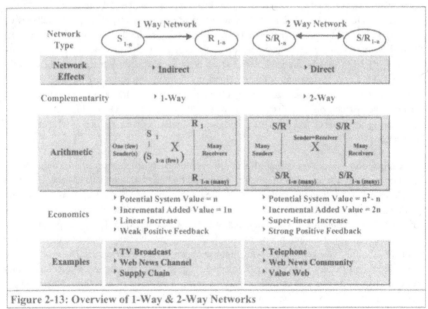

Figure 2-13: Overview of 1-Way & 2-Way Networks

In addition to these general mechanisms

> "In network markets, and more generally in markets with network externalities, when firms and consumers interact in more than a period, [because, C. G.] **history matters.**" (Economides 1996:26) [emphasis added]

---

[134] See Hagel / Armstrong (1995, 1996) for an in-depth analysis of the particular economics of communities.

This factor has a particular influence on the adoption and retention of networks and their underlying technologies. The analysis above discussed the influence of network externalities in respect to adoption rates. It highlighted the break even to critical mass as a crucial factor. The following discussion introduces demand side and supply side aspects which influence the adoption rates of networks.

On the demand side it is crucial that the demand for a network good is a function of price and the expected size of the network or its complementary networks.[135] In general one assumes demand sloping downwards regarding the prices. As Economides[136] states, expectations do not adjust the slope of the demand curve but increased expectations for future network adoption shift the demand curve upwards in a "bandwagon effect" (Leibenstein 1950). For example the massive signaling of Deutsche Telecom regarding their determination to expand their proprietary ISDN technology convinced users that a large number of other ISDN users would come into existence in the German market. This large number of compatible components added value to the enhanced, features of the technology. These expectations did not exist in markets outside of Germany. Therefore, the international adoption rates of ISDN technology are much lower. This phenomenon shows that **initial adoption requires customers expectations** to be positive about the overall adoption of a network technology. For example, if customers believe that a new technology will be the de facto standard, like an upgrade from Microsoft Office 95 to Office 97, they will have less resistance towards investing in the new technology. However, on the other hand, if the users expect that not many others will buy the technology, the adoption of this new network experiences a massive start-up problem. This problem is intensified as the network good has little value in isolation. Therefore bundling (see above) is an important factor to introduce network goods to the market. Successful examples of bundling can be seen via Microsoft's Internet Explorer browser with the Windows operating system or through the bundling of the Instant Messenger software with the Netscape Communicator browser and later the AOL software package.[137]

On the supply side

> "The pattern of adoption depends on whether technologies are sponsored. A **sponsor** is an entity that has property rights to the technology and hence is willing to make investments to promote it." (Katz / Shapiro 1986a:822) [emphasis, C. G.]

---

[135] See Katz / Shapiro (1985, 1994), Bensen / Farrell (1994), Economides (1996).

[136] Economides (1996), p. 6, see also footnote 101.

[137] This successful bundling combined with compelling value of the Instant Messenger buddy list helped to create a network of over 30 million users and later justified an acquisition through AOL for $420 million in 1997. This example shows that the value of a network is driven by the number of compatible components. In the case of the buddy list / Instant Messenger the components are the millions of subscribed users and the installed software base. Neither the technology itself nor the hardware infrastructure nor the human resources alone could have justified such a capitalization. This case was all about network size and the super-linear economics of Internet communities (see Case Study 2-2). Mirabilis' ICQ system was based on a similar concept of higher sophistication and could accomplish similar subscriber rates. It was also acquired by AOL in 1998. Competing services like Yahoo! ("Yahoo Pager", 1998) or MSN ("Microsoft Instant Messenger", 1999) introduced similar services. The economics of all these examples are mainly driven by network scale. The Instant Messenger example shows dramatically how bundling of complementary components – like a browser and a chat / community tool – can create a network value in a short time.

In the case of ISDN, Deutsche Telecom was the owner of the technology and sponsored this technology by massive marketing investments. Depending on the constellation, early market entry, fast adoption fueled by a sponsor, and the relevant network externalities often result in a **winner with inferior technology** as an outcome in the market.[138] Consequently **time to market** as well as **speed of adoption** are critical in network markets, while expectations of the market players and the sponsorship of new networks are the central variable controlling this process.

A crucial effect of networks and their underlying technologies is that users typically experience lock-in effects into a certain network once they have decided to use it.[139] This stems from the fact that adoption and usage of technology creates costs. These costs are mostly irreversible – in other words they are **sunk costs**.[140] Once customers use the technology, they begin to invest resources into the network. This investment can be in form of time, such as becoming accustomed to a certain email software or the user interface of an on-line service. Furthermore, these can also be hard costs, such as investments in a new analog modem to use AOL via copper access, which does not work with the cable network of @Home. Usually the decision to invest into a certain technology creates additional investments in complementary goods based on compatible technology. For example, a Macintosh user buys software for Macintosh. These secondary investments into compatible network components increase the costs of switching to another network technology. Time as well as the money spent are costs, which are sunk and irreversible. These costs determine the particular **switching costs**[141] for the user. Switching costs can include costs of physical replacements (changes in equipment, etc) as well as costs incurred in the transition (learning/training, loss in productivity, etc.) An example is the marketing costs to sign-up a member from Prodigy to AOL. The user has to install new software, rebuild all the email contacts, bookmarks, and has to get used to the new user interface. AOL has to spend marketing resources to convince the user to switch. These costs sometimes can exceed $200 per member depending on the marketing channel. Typical sign-up costs per member vary between $20 and $100.[142] Varian / Shapiro define the total switching costs as the costs incurred by the user and the new network supplier, which in turn

---

[138] See Katz / Shapiro (1986). As network externalities support one dominant network (see Figure 2-11) this leaves basically just two main options: The equilibrium is reached at the start if the network reaches the level critical mass or a change occurs at a later point in time of the network development (see Economides / Himmelberg 1995). In the case of two competing network technologies (one established inferior and one new superior technology) the development is dependent on the conduct of the players (in the case of a duopoly). Both players can support the old and inferior technology which is called excess inertia. If both are supporting the new technology the situation is called excess momentum. If both players support competing technologies, old technology can benefit from network externalities induced by the installed base while the new technology can utilize superior quality (see Economides 1996, pp. 27-29 and Farrell / Saloner 1985).

[139] See Varian / Shapiro (1998), pp. 103-134.

[140] Referring to Sutton's (1991) analysis on the effects of sunk costs on market structures and the corresponding implications for conduct and performance Schmalensee notes that "(...) Sunk Costs (...) (have, C. G.) robust implications for game-theory models of free-entry equilibrium for the dependence of minimum viable levels of seller concentration on market size, set-up costs, and other factors." (Schmalensee 1991:125). The discussion of network economists in this context on market structure in network markets and the role of sunk costs can be seen in the same line of these traditions from Industrial Economics.

[141] See Varian / Shapiro (1998). Switching costs are the costs that a player of an alternative network technology has to spend to make a user switch.

[142] According to AOL internal data.

determine the rent the original supplier can capture.[143] Switching costs will occur in case of a change to a new network. If the added-value of the alternative network is lower than these switching costs, the user will remain with the old network. Users experience **lock-in** once the initial choice has been made.[144] This in return creates additional positive feedback for a growing network and makes the position of a follower particularly hard.

These mechanisms have strong effects on the development path of networks for the following reasons:

> "Both consumers and firms make production and consumption decisions based on sizes of installed base and on expectations of its increase over time. The same underlying technology and consumers preferences and distribution can lead to different industrial structures depending on the way things start. Thus, strategic advantages, such as first mover advantages, can have long run effects." (Economides 1996:27)

This shows that the development of network markets follows a phenomenon which Arthur (1989) coined **path dependency**, which refers to the dependence of a system or network on past decisions of producers and consumers. Path dependence leads to irreversible or difficult to reverse paths, which are sensitive to initial conditions.[145] For example, the more people use on-line services via their PC and (today's narrow bandwidth) telephone copper lines, the more the users become accustomed to it, the more devices will be offered for this type of usage, the more customers will be locked-in by their service providers and the more content will be programmed for this constellation. This path dependency will potentially support a 'PC based AOL on-line service via RBOC DSL high bandwidth modem' path development. On the other hand, this path will make the introduction of an offering such as "Web TV via high-bandwidth cable network @Home" much tougher.

The increasing returns of markets based on strong positive feedback – as in the on-line industry – make this trend particularly strong.[146] Consequently, historical events have a crucial influence on the development of network markets. In any case, path dependence defines another crucial mechanism in the on-line service industry, which is illustrated by the following case study:

> This is a fictitious case which tries to anticipate patterns of path dependence which will influence the battle between copper and cable as the local loop technology in the path dependent transition from low bandwidth Internet into the broadband world (see 2.1.2). After the first noncommercial phase of the Inter-

---

[143] Varian / Shapiro (1998), pp. 111-115.

[144] See ibid.

[145] See Arthur (1989, 1994, 1996) and Liebowitz / Margolis (1995). One can distinguish three degrees of path dependence: (a) First-degree path dependence: Instances in which sensitivity to starting points exists, but with no implied inefficiency. (b) Second-degree path dependence: Sensitive dependence on initial conditions leads to outcomes that are regrettable and costly to change. They are not, however, inefficient in any meaningful sense, given the assumed limitations on prior knowledge. (c) Third-degree path dependence: Sensitive dependence on initial conditions leads to an outcome which is inefficient – but in this case the outcome is also "remediable." That is, there exists or existed some feasible arrangement for recognizing and achieving a preferred outcome, but that outcome is not obtained (see ibid.).

[146] See Arthur (1994), Varian / Shapiro (1998).

net and the second phase of the commercial world wide web in a low bandwidth world the Internet will enter the next phase. "The third phase of the Internet's evolution will see the mass diffusion and adoption of broadband technologies (...) when a critical mass of users are about to experience 'always-on' high speed Internet access from their home." (Bar / Cchen / Cowhey / DeLong / Kleeman / Zysman 1999:6).

In a broadband world the "PC via telephone dial-up over a narrow-band access network" constellation will change. Multiple devices, no longer limited to the PC, will have broadband access via fixed and wireless telephone networks while the cable network will provide multiple access network infrastructure combinations.

The big question with respect to networks is which of the competing technologies will be the predominant network. While 2.1.2 provided an outlook regarding the technological developments in the upcoming years, the reality is that there will be competition between two broadband technologies, copper vs. cable, which will occur in the context of the old narrowband paradigm.

Nevertheless, it is a fact that as of 1999 a low-bandwidth copper network is still the predominant access technology for the local loop. If the notion on installed base is correct, the narrow-band Internet will have effects on the diffusion of broad-band technologies in general, and will affect each one differently. E. g. in markets with high PC and modem penetration, DSL technology can play the role of the logical successor as an access technology. It uses the same socket in the wall of the room where the existing usage device is placed and hence inherits competitive advantages from the past low bandwidth constellation of competition e.g. a cable – set top box – TV – constellation. The US local telephone service providers (RBOC's) for example build their strategy on this effect and team up with narrow-band ISP's to use them as marketing partners and to share their service provision expertise. On the opposite side, in markets with low PC penetration but high cable TV adoption, a scenario with TV set top boxes and cable modems seems to be more likely. E.g. ATT with its @Home franchise or Time Warner with its Road Runner franchise drive down this path. Hence, a TV audience is used by the cable provider, as these people may not own a PC but are interested in interactive services - for the first time a good market segment for such cable providers. Switching costs will be low and the position to the customers is close, due to past business relations. In markets with low penetration of fixed copper or cable technology wireless solutions might have better chances to succeed. One can, for example, think of many African or Asian markets. In this sense wireless broadband technologies will hit the market later but will be easier to role out. In cases of very low population density satellite has its advantages.

The standard constellation of the networked components has two ends, which will determine the trajectory of future development paths. On the first end is the user, who applies a PC and analogue modem dialing into a copper telephone connection. On the other end is the ISP, who operates a dial-in POP's with modems of the same dial-in technology. This system design determines potential switching costs to alternative technological constellations.

First the installed base on the user end determines the current potential were new access technologies meet existing usage devices. If, for example, a market is dominated by PC usage devices which connect via dial-up modems the machines are using a telephone socket. Changing to DSL technology would not change the socket and could use the PC at the same position in a house. Usually the cable network sockets are fewer and not in the same room. In other words users switching to copper will frequently be forced to extend their cables, move their device or buy a device like a TV Cable Set Top Box, which will be used more as a TV supplement. The installed base of PC's with modems in the room with the telephone socket, which is the most common constellation of narrowband Internet in the home, is a great advantage for

DSL. Finally the users are used to the "PC-Modem-Telephone Socket" setting which would cause a marketing challenge to communicate the added value of alternative scenarios such as broadband via Set Top Boxes. The switching costs on the user end are the lowest in a transition to DSL technology. Providers of competitive network technology need to work out incentives (e.g. a free cable modem and a free TV Set Top Box) to convince users to switch.

On the side of the service provider the notion on installed base is easier to measure as compared to the end user. A service provider has an installed base of narrowband modems in the access network infrastructure. In a broadband constellation this infrastructure needs to be replaced. Bar / Cohen / Cowhey / DeLong / Kleeman / Zysman (1999:17) provide an overview of the technology which needs to be replaced and the corresponding installation costs in the case of DSL and cable technology. DSL has a better position in this respect. It needs to be said that the US market has the highest global penetration of cable households (over 70% compared to 50% in Germany, which is the European market with the highest cable penetration see Morgan Stanley 1999). Moreover the majority of the European networks needs to be upgraded with a back-channel to provide interactive services, which creates additional investments.

One can conclude that in a comparison cable versus DSL, the provider of cable technology needs to have deeper pockets as a the switching costs from the current narrowband world to DSL is cheaper and the development path hence runs in this direction. To change this direction requires large expenditures into investments for the technological infrastructure and the end user marketing.

In addition to this notion on switching costs the time lag which will be created by infrastructure upgrades on networks infrastructure will be another crucial factor in resect to path dependence. Considering that the path will be directed into the broadband direction the technology, which will redirect this development at first will leverage path dependence for its technology.

Furthermore it can be assumed that the three factors (1) society, (2) industry and (3) policy heavily determine the adoption of technology in markets: (a) Customers are used to the application of certain technologies and hence prefer certain technologies because of usage habits (see the path dependence illustration above). (b) The market position of players behind different technologies (e. g. cable provider versus local loop of telecom providers versus wireless telephone provider) will have an effect on success of technologies and (c) the policy environment will determine parameters (e .g. local loop interconnection regulations, privacy regulation and so forth) which favor certain technologies (e. g. cable vs. telephone lines vs. wireless[147]).

Overall each market has its own situation which is in this respect more "compatible" to the different broadband network technologies. In this sense the battle to be the winner in the broadband world is heavily influenced by the effects of path dependency.

Case Study 2-3: Path Dependency & the Battle "Copper vs. Cable Broadband Networks"

Switching costs on the customer side as well as on the side of the providers of a technology support the retention of the old technology, which is called "excess inertia".[148] However, as it

---

[147] For example, the constraints of stronger privacy regulations in Europe have lead to a limited development of certain markets like personalized services. Other examples are the FCC regulation in the early 1990s which led to lower low bandwidth charges in the US compared to Europe, or Deutsche Telecom's state monopoly, which supported a stronger cable roll out. Furthermore, the European Commission's anti trust regulations slowed down digital pay TV and constrained business models for cable technology and so forth.

[148] See Farrell / Saloner (1985).

was stated above (see footnote 93) the economics of **networks do not exhibit one single stable equilibrium.**[149] Benson / Farrell (1994) describe these discontinuities in networks as "tippy", to emphasize that dominance of a technology today does not guarantee continued success forever due to system instability. For example, the overwhelming dominance of **AOL**, who's growth is **fueled by positive feedback, will not automatically remain constant.** It is a known fact that AOL's technology is inferior, but its dominance overcomes this weakness. However, over time comparable alternative networks, like @Home, with **broadband** via cable infrastructure, might be both technologically superior and also powerful **enough to break up AOL's dominance.** The market would "tip" over into a new equilibrium – with @Home as the new dominant player. The structural change created by the presence of broadband network technology and the sponsorship of it by a powerful player like AT&T could push this market to "tip" over. Hence **AOL needs access to broadband networks, technology, and content** to deliver an online service package, which is competitive in the next decade.

The overall insights on the theory of network economics can be outlined under a structure - conduct – performance pattern[150] as shown in Figure 2-14. The figure summarizes the general findings of the analysis of network economics and their implications for general mechanisms and, according to the laws of the marketplace in industries, which exhibit network externalities. First, there are neutral **structural factors** occurring in network markets, which determine the performance of a market according to the conduct of the players. The dominating factor here is network externalities. They occur in horizontal and vertical network structures, which are based upon compatibility of components. Depending on the network type (one-way or two-way) they result in weak or strong network effects. This network constellation determines strong economies of scale and scope, whereas demand-side economies of scale is a phenomenon particular to network industries, such as the on-line industry. As it also experiences strong supply-side economies of scale, the resulting network effects are extremely strong. Due to imperfect information, players coordinate their conduct on expectations regarding the future and fail to coordinate in a fully efficient way. Upon this given industry structure, players can influence the following core parameters with their **conduct.** Compatibility can be controlled via standards or the design of adapters. Adoption rates are dependent on time to market, where first mover advantages have a strong impact on the speed of adoption. Positive expectations support the adoptions rates, while in many cases a sponsor of a new network needs to drive the adoption process. The creation of switching costs causes the lock-in of users to certain networks. Players can capitalize on the control of bottlenecks in network constellations with interconnection charges or utilize this asset for a stronger bargaining position. The crucial parameter, which is dependent on the orchestration of the other

---

[149] Different from non-network markets, network markets exhibit several equilibria at the same time (see Economides 1996, p. 27).

[150] The structure conduct performance (SCP) paradigm was developed by Bain (1956). It is part of the school of Industrial Economics. It is employed at this point of this discourse, because it shows that the conceptual structure of network economics follows traditional microeconomic strategy traditions. Its fit with the SCP pattern underpins this finding. Moreover 2.2.2 will introduce the Five Forces Framework (Porter 1980) as analytical framework for the analysis of the competitive structures of the industry. Both are fundamental contributions to business strategy from a microeconomic standpoint. This anticipates the introduction of the market-based view of strategy making in 3.2.1, which in turn is a fully compatible component to the conceptual model worked out in the course of part II.

parameters, is critical mass. Once critical mass is achieved in a network market, **performance** is fueled by the underlying network externalities and players enjoy positive feedback and increasing returns, which in turn leads to a dominant market position. They can then leverage path dependence of technology adoption and use this to protect their market. But as other market equilibria exist, the constellation is not a natural monopoly. The system can tip over into another constellation, which favors another dominant player. All factors are correlated over feedback loops.

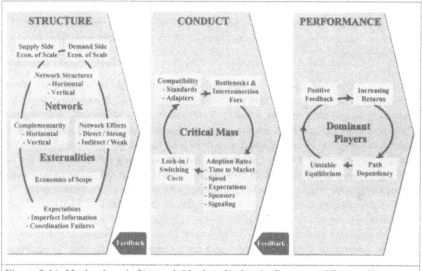

Figure 2-14: Mechanisms in Network Markets Under the Presence of Externalities

Overall the theory of networks can provide strong indications on the particular **economic logic** and **general dominating laws of the marketplace in network industries** such as the on-line industry. Although the theory flows from microeconomics, it displays a strong difference from the conventional neo-classical view, which avoids increasing returns and path dependence and tends to model decreasing returns in competitive market structures. Diametrically different, network economics embraces a dominant player, who enjoys increasing returns and positive feedback.

A closer look reveals that many of the **arguments follow the argumentation of Industrial Economics** (see 3.2.1). First, the notion on the role of customer lock-in through switching costs is basically identical to the classical mobility and entrance barrier, as it is discussed in Industrial Economics (Porter 1980, 1986). Second, real network markets usually exhibit dominating scale effects, due to high sunk costs and low incremental costs. The discussion on the role of sunk costs, resulting in returns to scale, creating concentrated industry structures, and was discussed exactly along these lines in Industrial Economics (Sutton 1991). Third, Economides correctly points out, **network effects cause a bundling of vertically and horizontally related components, which is virtually equivalent to scope effects**, which is another key concept of Industrial Economics.

It has to be noted that traditional microeconomic strategy tells one a great deal about the theory of the firm and how the production function can be used to derive economies of scale and scope. Traditionally, the theory translates this into the market constellations, from which a strategy can be derived.

Traditional Industrial Economics looks into the economics of the microeconomic hemispheres "firm" and "market" and so far has widely overlooked the economics of the household. In markets, which exhibit network externalities, this is a crucial gap. Network economics fills this gap. The real novel aspect is the formulation of demand-side scale and scope effects, which are a crucial parameter with respect to network goods.

Hence the truly novel aspect is the formulation of demand side scale and scope effects with respect to network goods. These externalities are a new aspect in economics, which is a dominating factor in the network economy. Furthermore a host of research, analyzing particular aspects along these lines, are relevant for the Internet framework: the **role of the path dependent adoption of technological standards and their impact on complementarity and industry structure delivers tremendous insights regarding the mechanisms for the growing business in the Internet.** In particular the work of Varian and Varian / Shapiro adds **salient insights on product and pricing strategies with respect to information goods.** The work of Economides contributes enormous insights on **horizontal and vertical industry structures** with regards to complementary goods in compatible multi-layered network structures. Although the theory provides a lot of insight it has so far by-and-large overlooked or neglected research on the demand-side source for demand-side externalities. Modeling the household side of microeconomics simply seems not to appear on the radar screens of the respective authors and scholars. **The theory only describes demand-side economies of scale. Demand side economies of scope and complementarity of bundled needs at its root, has been widely overlooked so far.** The complementarity of needs was identified as the crucial source for scope-effects network externalities and the work of Bakos / Brynjolfsson pointed towards the right direction. **With respect to a multi-layered industry, these scope effects will play a crucial role** as these reflections on business strategy reveal. Overall business strategy can utilize these insights in order to better understand network markets and in order to derive competitive advantages, which will be addressed in part III.

Understanding the academic background of the authors it becomes self-evident that large portions of network economics are nothing more than an off-spring of microeconomic theory, in particular of Industrial Economics with extensions with respect to the demand side economies of scale and scope as well as technological and product / market particularities.[151] Therefore **the general focus of the theory is the particular aspects of a market logic and market mechanisms, mostly from an efficiency and not business strategy standpoint.** Although

---

[151] The underlying mindset and methodology of authors in network economics is traditional microeconomic business strategy. This can be explained by the academic background of the authors which are all microeconomists, often with assignments in business schools teaching business strategy. They frequently hold a practical background in telecommunications policy and anti trust gained at governmental agencies like FCC or FTC.

terminology partly differs, many of the strategic implications are, due to its theoretical back-ground, identical with the market-based view of business strategy (see 3.2.1). Nevertheless the theory provides particular implications for business strategy, which focus the product, market, and pricing aspects of network goods, which will be further applied in 3.3.

Furthermore, the theory does not provide sufficient explanation of long term market devel-opments and maturity processes, which lead to a market equilibrium with higher degrees of consolidation, stabilized distribution of market share and somewhat stable and profitable business models. Economides concludes in this context:

> "One of the most important issues that remains largely unresolved is the joint deter-mination of an equilibrium market structure (including the degree of vertical integra-tion) together with the degree of compatibility across firms." (Economides 1996:30)

The theory of network economics discusses and formulates the power of vertical and hori-zontal bundling of compatible components and the resulting scale and scope effects for these units. But the question of firm size and industrial structure is left open. The general implica-tion is the following: bundling to achieve horizontal and vertical scale is good. But **how flexi-ble and in which manner shall these multi-layered network structures shall be bundled in a rapidly changing environment, ultimately remains an unsolved issue.**

Moreover, because of its microeconomic nature, the theory does not analyze internal aspects of the firm, as they are ultimately condensed in the production function of a firm and how it configures its input factors and underlying production technology. Along these lines **re-source-based aspects of business strategy are entirely neglected**, which seems as a salient shortcoming for the development of a successful business strategy, based solely on network economics. Enhancements are required and will be worked out in 3.2.2.

In order to proceed with the modeling of the industry, **Figure 2-15 presents a model A of a multi-layered network structure.** It highlights the horizontal and vertical dimensions of a multi-layered cohesion of singular components in a network structure as it is exhibited in the on-line industry (see 2.1). Applying the terminology suggested by Economides (1991) it can be described as a **two-dimensional network** consisting of many **components** (elementary goods) which are combined to a **system** (composite good). The system is exhibiting network externalities in horizontal and vertical dimension, within which their multiple connections determine their strong interdependence. **Analytically each horizontal layer can be seen as an isolated market. The vertical dimension connects the horizontal layers.** Each dimen-sion has a spectrum from 1 to n. In this conception, **n determines the complexity as well as the potential network externalities.**

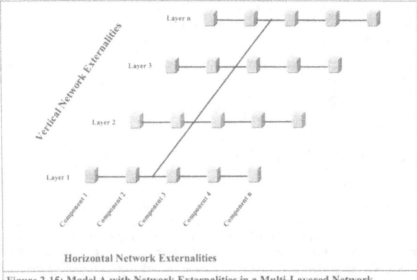

Figure 2-15: Model A with Network Externalities in a Multi-Layered Network

While 2.2.1 outlined the general economic mechanisms and laws of the marketplace in such a network constellation. 2.2.2 will enhance this model with a conceptual framework for the analysis of the competitive situation of an industrial constellation which exhibits a multi-layered constitution. For these purposes some components of Porter's (1980, 1985) framework will be enhanced with respect to industries with blurring boundaries and overlapping areas as it is exhibited in the ICT / convergence area.

2.2.2. Competitive Industry Analysis in Overlapping Industries

Although the on-line industry is a networked industry, its structural mechanisms with respect to business strategy are not completely described by the rules network economics. Network externalities, the race for critical mass, and the resulting dominant players supported by path dependency would be a fairly poor framework to derive a comprehensive set of tools for business strategy. **The theory of network economics is capable of explaining economics and effects within a network constellation, but it does not focus on how this translates into competitive strategy. While the structure of the on-line industry also follows traditional competitive patterns of industries,** it seems wise to enhance the framework with common methods for the analysis of industries. For this purpose, Porter (1980) developed his famous model of the Five Forces. It is a tool used to analyze an industry in a way, which delivers strategic implications for individual firms.[152] However, one must keep in mind that **the**

---

[152] Part II of this thesis focuses on the structural aspects of the industry rather than the strategic implications which are discussed in part III. Hence the following draws an analytical distinction between Porter's component for the analysis of industries – the Five Forces – and the according components, including the generation of generic strategies as well as the concept of the value chain as a tool to derive competitive advantages (Porter 1985) according to the generic strategies. They will be further discussed in part III which analyzes the strategic implications from an individual firms perspective.

multi-layered construction with horizontal and vertical network effects requires some adjustments of the common tools. Both theoretical components combined will deliver a framework, which is capable of explaining the underlying structure and laws of the on-line industry from an overall industry perspective.

Figure 2-15 incorporates model A, which includes horizontal networks with n components vertically connected over n layers. This stage of the model is able to explain the network effects in a multi-layered industry. But,

> "[...] little analysis has been done on competition in a multi-layered structure of vertically related components. Nevertheless, it is exactly this kind of modeling that is needed for an analysis and evaluation of potential structures of the "information superhighway"." (Economides 1996:39)

To include the aspects of competition in this construct, several enhancements need to be made. In order to incrementally work out a framework, the following will first discuss the aspect of a competitive market situation within an industry and then turn its attention to the aspect of the vertical interconnection in these singular markets.

1. Analysis of competitive market constellations in horizontal layers

It can be argued that within a multi-layered industry, **each particular layer can be understood as a distinct competition,** which can be analyzed with Porter's framework. This is an issue of the definition of the object "industry". This thesis coins the single horizontal layers as "markets" or "competitions" and the overall vertically integrated cohesion an "industry". Pümpin argues that the term industry characterizes the supply side of a competition.[153] In this context an industry would establish an exchange with the demand side of a certain marketplace. The aspect a marketplace where demand and supply meet results in an equilibrium of volumes and prices and is the central factor. Referring to model A each of the horizontal layers can be perceived as a analytically distinct network market. The model includes only the number of components within these layers but does not express the demand and supply side in a competitive constellation.

While Pümpin focuses on the firms of the supply side, Porter (1980) formulated a constellation of the **Five Forces,** which determine the competitive structure of an industry. The five factors are: the bargaining power of suppliers, the bargaining power of the demand side, the threat of substitutes and entrants as well as the rivalry within the existing competitors. While this thesis defines the overall cohesion as an "industry" and the embedded layers as "markets", each layer can be understood as a distinct, but interdependent, competitive arena. Therefore, by defining distinct competitions, Porter's framework is applicable, when it can be analyzed according to his framework. The reason being that it is basically a question of terminology and definition of a model. Furthermore, it is crucial to define the boarder of an industry to apply Porter's framework. This is equally the case for the horizontal market layers. They need to be defined in a way that facilitates interpretation and analysis under the framework of the Five Forces. While a clear definition needs to be assumed at this point as model A

---

[153] See Pümpin (1992), p. 104.

only models n layers in a general way, it must be realized in the empirically driven application of the industry model (see Section 2.5) that only concrete layers based on factors of the specific field will be defined. Thus a concrete definition in the sense of Porter's industry term will be given in order to be able to apply his framework.

The underlying idea of the Five Forces is built on the microeconomic theory of markets.[154] However, it differs from the neoclassical position of the adaptive behavior of players, which assumes a friction free market with perfect competition and perfect information, where demand and supply meet at an equilibrium price. Porter's model points out Five Factors, which can be used to **derive strategic implications for a proactive behavior of a firm to influence a firm's position and the underlying market structure.** Depending on certain conduct a performance of the firm will result. This allows one to **translate the underlying industrial structure of this marketplace into a firm's profit equation** as each of the Five Factors has an impact on costs, intensity of investments, prices and finally the units sold.[155] At any given point in time, an industry experiences the Five Forces in a particular way. This determines the attractiveness of an industry to a firm.

While Porter analyzes the internal factors of an industry Kirsch (1988) **enhanced** this **by adding exogenous parameters,** which influence the endogenous industry structure.[156] He added factors from the "socio-economic field" (ibid.:224) [translation C. G.] as external parameters influencing the industry structure: socio-demographic, economic, political, and technological factors of the field. This intends the same enhancements undertaken in Section 2.1 of this thesis where technological, industrial, socio-economic, and political factors of the field were discussed with respect to their influence on the overall size and structure of the on-line industry. As these factors obviously impact the endogenous parameters of the industry, the application of Porter's analytical framework is enhanced by this exogenous parameters as suggested by Kirsch. An empirical analysis these factors was conducted in Section 2.1, in order to generate a preliminary understanding of the overall environment.

Finally this analytical concept is a widely shared theory in the scientific community of strategic management and has proven to be a powerful tool. Considering the fundamental influence of the exogenous parameters in the infant stage of the on-line industry as described above, it is important to integrate this influence. Figure 2-16 conceptually summarizes this cohesion according to Porter including exogenous parameters given in the external environment which are influencing the endogenous parameters.

---

[154] See Varian (1992).

[155] The bargaining power of suppliers to a company influences the resulting sourcing costs. The bargaining power of the demand side is aligned to the prices which can be charged in a market. The competition among existing firms playing in the same industry influences speed of innovation and the accompanying investments, and the bargaining conduct towards the customers affects prices and finally the aggregate experience curve affects the cost structures. The entrance barriers determine how protected the current competition within this industry is while high investments and specific know-how typically increase entrance barriers. If they are low, market position is less sustainable and threatened by potential new entrants. The threat of substitutes endangers future units sold and hence the sustainability of current profits by alternative products or services.

[156] See also Porter (1990), p 127 who increased the emphasis on the environmental factors compared to his former work.

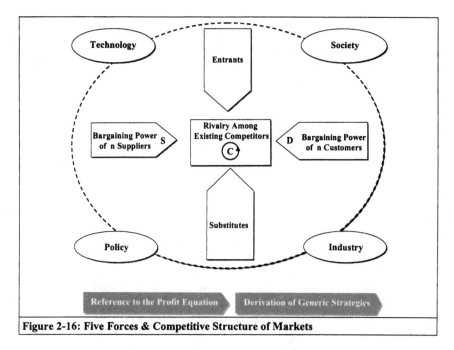

Figure 2-16: Five Forces & Competitive Structure of Markets

In this context, this text argues that the implications of the Five Forces can be transferred into the constellations of horizontal market layers of network industries, which exhibit characteristics as represented in model A (see Figure 2-15). This will be conducted in Subsection 2.2.3, which will **bridge Porter's framework to an enhanced version of network markets**. Yet, as the industry operates in a multi-layered environment, with interdependencies of the vertically interconnected horizontal layers, Porter's framework requires adjustments considering the multi-layered constitution.

2. Vertical interconnection of singular horizontal market layers

With respect to the multi-layered constitution of the on-line industry, the following will derive an applied version of Porter's Five Forces for the converging industries – those with significant overlap, a blurring of boundaries, and strong interdependencies of several layers. Referring to the Five Forces, the following factors need to be analyzed, in order to be able to translate Porter's framework into a multi-layered network industry (2.2.3) such as the on-line industry:

- Definition of boundaries of an industry
- Demand side
- Supply side
- Role of entrants
- Role of substitutes

and referring to network economics the aspect of interconnection of market layers considers

- Interdependence of vertically related competitions with analytically distinct boundaries.

In order to provide differentiated terminology it is suggested above to apply the term "market" or "competitions" for the horizontal layers and to use the term "industry" for the competition in the overall structure. As a first step, this enables the application of the Five Forces within each layer and in as second step it enables the analysis of the influence among the interconnected layers on each of the Five Forces. Through this addition, the accompanying vertical network effects can be integrated within a model of the industry.

The analysis of the field (2.1) revealed that convergence (see Figure 2-6)[157] was the main driver for the establishment of the multi-layered ICT area, which determines the rules for on-line services in the presence of ubiquitous standards. In the context of the structural analysis of industries Dowling / Lechner / Thielmann (1998b:31) ask:

> "Where is convergence occurring and what effects has this phenomenon for the industries involved?" (Dowling / Lechner / Thielmann 1998b:31)

They (ibid.) analyze this issue in an applied way for the converging on-line and television industries and discuss adjustments to Porter's Five Forces in this context.

> "The Porter "The Five Forces Model" (Porter 1980) is an often cited and used analytical framework, however that model assumes that industry boundaries are relatively clearly defined. Dealing with converging industries, where the industry boundaries are changing, the framework has to be reevaluated in order to be modified or extended." (Dowling / Lechner / Thielmann 1998a:5-6)

Hence, they analyze the ICT area and use the Five Forces framework as an analytical tool. Referring to the complexity of the ICT area as it was discussed in 2.1, they raise the question:

> "Can Porter's model be applied to converging markets (as in this case)? Does this even help to structure more clearly the high complexity? (...) Porter's model shows some limitations for the purposes of analyzing convergence because of the high complexity involved. The five forces do not reproduce adequately the complex and interlocking relationships inherent in converging markets. The interactions (...) are also not considered. Instead, the focus of the analysis is the rivalry between existing competitors within an industry with relatively clear boundaries. Porter discusses the difficulty of defining the boundaries of an industry and suggests the method of functional definition of the boundaries. He does however not deal explicitly with the definition of an industry relevant for the formulation of strategies." (Dowling / Lechner / Thielmann 1998a:16) [emphasis in the original]

Furthermore they argue that **in the case of converging industries the model must be modified with respect to industry boundaries, threat of substitutes and market entry** in order to identify and differentiate these factors more specifically.

---

[157] See also Messerschmitt (1996) for the ICT and particular computing perspective and a discussion of the layered constellation in a vertical and horizontal dimension of the converging industrial sector, where he is particularly refers to the OSI model.

> "As a consequence Porter's abstract model has to be modified and expanded in order
> to analyze these influences" (Dowling / Lechner / Thielmann 1998a:17)

The following will present the approach of Dowling / Lechner / Thielmann, will discuss its appropriateness, and will add aspects, which are overlooked within the suggested model. They analyze the problem of converging industries – their example being the converging industries of digital TV and on-line services – in order to derive a modified version of the Five Forces framework. The initial point is the decision to focus on the customer and the underlying needs, hence to prioritize the **demand side**.

> "The customer as focus point for an industry analysis must be analyzed in terms of
> his/her current and/or potential needs. Competitive advantage can then be achieved by
> meeting these needs in new ways through innovation." (ibid.:17)

This seems to be a wise decision as the other parameters are underlying a continuous, often rapid change and the demand side appears as rather predictable as well as the most fundamental force in the whole scenario.

Their main statement regarding the **supply side** is unfortunately rather indifferent. They highlight their assessment of the shifted bargaining power of suppliers in the TV and on-line industry, which, in fact, proves just the opposite given the current competition as prices for content production are constantly declining.[158] Furthermore, although they mention the attempt of large media players to achieve high levels of vertical integration[159] within the value chain system in this context and although they comprehensively discuss the aspect of complementary-ness, they fail to discuss network effects of complementary components within networked value chains as discussed in Subsection 2.2.1. This is an obvious oversight in this approach as these influences heavily impact the on-line and digital TV industries. Therefore, the subsequent discussion needs to enhance these aspects of complementary components and their role in a Five Forces framework.

Regarding the components **threat of entrants**, **threat of substitutes** and **rivalry within the competition** they are redefining Porter's framework with consideration of the influence of complementary and substitution effects between converging – or in other words networked - components. Referring to Greenstein / Khanna (1997), two basic forms of convergence can be distinguished:[160]

- **Convergence through complements**
- **Convergence through substitutes**

---

[158] According to interviews with Jan Traenkner, Managing Director Pro7 digital, 9th of March 1997, Munich, Christoph Mohn, CEO Lycos Europe, 21st of November 1997, Munich, Klaus Hommels, Assistant Managing Director AOL Germany,19th of September 1997, Hamburg, Karsten Weide, Senior Producer Yahoo! Germany, 23rd of June 1997, Munich, and Matt Rightmire, Director Strategic Planning Yahoo!, 28th of April 1999, Santa Clara and Varian / Shapiro (1998) for an analytical explanation.

[159] See e.g. Middelhoff (1998) who outlines the Bertelsmann strategy of vertical integration.

[160] See Dowling / Lechner / Thielmann (1998a), p. 4.

They relate the complementary constellation to cooperative scenarios of players and the substitution constellation to competitive scenarios. In the case of the substitution / competitive paradigm they talk about a 1+1=1 situation. They state that:

> "from two separate industries a new single industry emerges (1+1=1) – often referred to as "the blurring of industries boundaries" or "industry collision". Such convergence is often followed by mergers or acquisitions of firms from the two formerly separately industries." (Dowling / Lechner / Thielmann 1998b:4-5)

The example of the telecom giant, AT&T, which attempts a highly vertical integration by taking over the cable company TCI, the cable on-line service @Home, and the Web Portal Excite, is an example where boundaries of several industries are blurring. However, it can be debated if this convergence of formerly distinct businesses is a substitution process or rather the attempt of a large player for vertical integration with the aim of internalizing potential network externalities. In any respect, it is a strong point to distinguish the type of relationships in which distinct but interdependent or convergent markets are exhibited. In this context, Dowling / Lechner / Thielmann describe the complementary paradigm as:

> "The Cooperative Paradigm or Complementary Convergence (1+1=3). Complementary convergence occurs when two products or services from different industries are merged to meet a larger set or new set of consumer needs simultaneously. In this sense, a new market emerges (1+1=3) that requires the combination of resources and competencies from previously separate industries. In such cases, strategic alliances are often the mechanism for firm in different industries to merge such resources." (Dowling / Lechner / Thielmann 1998a:5) [emphasis in the original]

Given the two basic relations – complementary or substitution – the aspects of separate competitions, threat of market entry and substitutes between distinct industries is dependant on the relationship of the entities involved. In the case of multi-layered industries, the distinct horizontal markets exhibit the same constellation of blurring boundaries and converging characteristics. This aspect can obviously be illustrated by the fact that a telecommunications player like AT&T, a software player like Microsoft, a media player like Bertelsmann and a hardware player like Compaq all run their own on-line business or Internet business units.[161] The difficulty is to model these added complexities into the Five Forces framework.

As mentioned above Dowling / Lechner / Thielmann (1998a:17) suggest to "focus on the customer" and model an example with two industries, or to apply the suggested terminology for this thesis, they model a case with two market layers. Figure 2-17 highlights this focus as the other forces are based on the customers and their underlying needs. Two separate industries have their suppliers but the influence of **convergence results in a constellation of potential bilateral market entry**. Depending on the relationship of the industries – and of course their respective players – convergence results in either a competitive or cooperative market entry, or to use Porter's terminology: given the standpoint of one industry, players from the other industry are perceived as new players entering the competition. Although their

---

[161] Dowling / Lechner / Thielmann (1998a) distinguish technology, needs, firm and industrial dimensions of convergence, which underpin these examples.

nature can be **complementary,** which will result in a positive perception, for example, the opportunity of new partners with whom cooperate. Hence, **different to the traditional Five Forces framework, entrants are not threats per se. In case of substitutes the perception remains threatening.** In other words, converging industries lead to interconnected markets, with blurring boundaries with the level of complementary-ness as a fundamental factor, which determines if the market entry is "hostile" or "friendly",** as visualized in Figure 2-17:

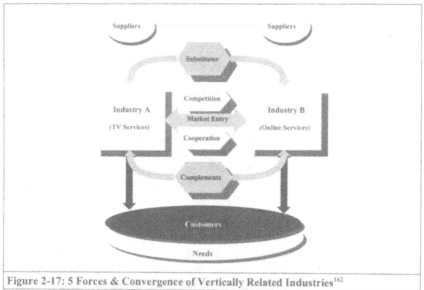

Figure 2-17: 5 Forces & Convergence of Vertically Related Industries[162]

It has to be stated that the approach of Dowling / Lechner / Thielmann discusses the issue of limitations for the definition of a industry's boundaries in Porter's framework, which is particularly relevant in converging environments such as the ICT area. They provide enhancements to the Five Forces framework and discuss the aspect of complements and substitutes in competition with converging constellations. These **extensions** point to fundamental issues of the field, **which were not sufficiently discussed in the traditional Five Forces framework.** They are obviously **highly relevant for** the ICT area, as well as respective industries such as **the on-line industry.**

Unfortunately **the authors do not discuss the aspect of complementary-ness and the respective implications** further than that. While this work argues that their **substitution scenario is ultimately identical** with the threat of substitutes in the traditional Porter framework, their **complementary scenario lacks a complete discussion** of the effects on the overall constellation. As a consequence, **they overlook the depth of the crucial network effects, which are created by complementary relationships.** Although they discuss technological convergence[163] they **fail to mention technological compatibility** and the accompanying network

---

[162] See Dowling / Lechner / Thielmann (1998a:17).

[163] Dowling / Lechner / Thielmann (1998a), p. 3.

interoperability **as enabler and source for complementarity** in a sufficient manner. Furthermore, **they do not generalize** their findings into a scenario of more than two converging areas. There are more than two industries in the discussed on-line industry and TV industry. Microsoft, in addition to competing in the software industry, has a stake in AT&T, Qualcomm and NBC (MSNBC), operates an on-line service (MSN) and several interactive media entities (MSN.com and vertical services such as Car Point or Expedia). Moreover, AT&T is integrating into cable TV (TCI, Media One), on-line services (@Home) and Web portals (Excite); and AOL is buying Netscape, ICQ, Instant Messenger and planning AOL TV. These obvious examples indicate that **there are more than two industries / layers, which need to be modeled** in a Five Forces framework, in order to serve as an analytical tool for the multi-layered Internet environment. Thus, the following will present a general, multi-layered model of the Five Forces framework, enhancing the approach of Dowling et. al.

Instead of focusing on the operational problem with a clear definition of the boundaries of a competition – especially in the presence of blurring boundaries in the convergence area – it can be stated that this problem is not new at all with respect to the application of the Porterian framework. The convergence area just exhibits the problem to a strong degree. It seems plausible to understand the Five Forces framework as a highly consistent analytical tool, which is applicable as soon as boundaries to the object "industry" can be defined. Consequently, it is suggested that one apply the framework of Porter, but to be aware of the difficulties in the process of implementing it.

Nevertheless, the **interdependence of one industry to another vertically-related industry needs to be integrated** in order to be able **to discuss network effects within this framework**. If this is possible, a multi-layered network industry can be analyzed regarding the network effects **in both horizontal and vertical dimensions,** as well as regarding the five market forces in the distinct markets. In order to implement this, the findings of Dowling et. al. regarding the influences of complements need to be integrated and enhanced. As stated above the effects of substitution in the process of convergence seem to be identical to Porter's interpretation. Hence, they do not need to undergo a redefinition.

The following suggests to define a multi-layered set of n times Five Forces. Each layer consists of the five forces. The forces of convergence create multiple connections between these layers. Dowling et. al. emphasis that the needs dimension and the accompanying **convergence of needs** must be considered as the most influential factor and conditio sine qua non.

> "The complexity of the structure and dynamics of influencing variables in converging markets makes the problem of identifying relevant competitive forces and their relationships very difficult. However the analysis above suggest that for converging markets the starting point for industry analysis should be the customer and his/her needs (...). From this customer focus perspective it then become possible to analyze the structure of the industry and the relationships implied depending on whether competitive or complementary convergence is occurring." Dowling / Lechner / Thielmann (1998a:17)

With respect to the market definition, this work concurs with Dowling et. al. Regarding the imperative to focus the needs dimension. This seems to be a well-set priority as the customers' needs are the fundamental source for a business. This holds ever more true in the presence of such rapid speed of change and complexity as exhibited in the ICT area. Hence, **needs seems to be a relatively stable and strong factor to start a structural analysis**. The customer needs seem to be causal and consistent over time. **Therefore, a bundle of convergent needs should be identified as the starting point for an analysis of a multi-layered** industry with distinct and vertically related markets, whereas each of them can be analyzed under the Five Forces. In the case of the on-line industry, a bundled service offering typically attempts to meet a corresponding needs bundle such as the need to use email as it converges with the need to have an access provider and client software. This example was the foundation for the free email service, Juno, which is solely offering a free bundle consisting of email boxes with corresponding access network and client software.

Furthermore, the analytical procedure of identifying converging needs leads to an overall structure of components, which serve a positively correlated bundle of singular needs. This establishes the cohesion of complementary needs and complementary components. Consequently, an analysis results in a multi-layered industry structure with complementary layers. In return, the resulting definitions of competition define markets in a way, which reveals existing network externalities.

The discussion covering network economics (2.2.1) revealed the strong role of complementarity and its as a source for network externalities. This shows the strategic relevance of this in network industries. If an analysis would not consider these effects, a crucial component of the underlying industry structure would not be modeled.

Although Dowling et. al. Discuss the aspect of market entry in this context they fail to point out that the **technological compatibility of components enables market entry** and is contingent as Economides points out in a network terminology:

> "The ability of all elementary goods (or components) to be combined costlessly with all elementary goods of a different type to produce functioning composite goods (or systems) is defined as *full compatibility*. Compatible elementary goods can be thought of as constituting a *network*" (Economides 1991:3)

In the case of Dowling et. al., Internet standards enable next generation TV set-top boxes to show web sites on TV screens and digital TV programming enables broadcast over streaming media Internet technology. This compatible technology can enable players either

(a) to **enter a competition**, e.g. MSNBC to broadcast their TV shows on a web site with their streaming media technology[164] or

---

[164] According to interviews with Wolfgang Schneider, Business Development Manager Microsoft Germany, 16th of June 1999, Munich and Jan Tränckner, Managing Director Pro7 Digital Business TV, 9th of March 1997, Munich.

(b) to **substitute components of another competition** such as the time sensitive delivery of stock quotes or context sensitive classifieds, which will incrementally disappear from print media and will be substituted by the real time, context providing, full searchable on-line medium.[165]

To describe this cohesion in a more general way, one can analyze the singular components regarding their relationship. Components – or in another terminology: players / products from another competition – can be substitutes if they are "of the same type" (Economides 1991:3), such as the information "stock quote". But the components – products / players – can also be complementary if for example the second component is seen as the channel for the information. An additional channel with different characteristics, e.g. for music, has a complementary relationship. Considering this: one can listen to the San Francisco radio station KKSF in Europe over the Internet, which constitutes the Internet as a complementary component to the terrestrial broadcast network in San Francisco. From the standpoint of the European radio competition, this is seen as a market entry, but from the standpoint of KKSF, the Internet is seen as a complementary component compatible to their one-way network. Therefore **a multi-layered model of the Five Forces needs to interconnect the forces "threat of entry" and "threat of substitutes" and relate them to the contingent factor compatibility of components.**[166]

Different from Dowling et. Al, this work integrates the aspect of complementarity in a different way. Singular industries, or in the terminology suggested in this thesis, components of singular competitions or markets can have a complementary relationship regarding their product and market definition. As discussed above the **bundling of convergent needs is a source to create and leverage complementarity. As a result needs can be used to derive the complementarity and the corresponding network effects** as discussed in Subsection 2.2.1. Obviously the needs dimension: "I want to get on-line and get this email stuff – now! – and easily!"[167] enables a vertically related system of the complementary components, including access, content, email software with the required service provision. In reality, this example results in a bundle of complementary components of Microsoft, AOL, MCI Worldcom, a host of content providers and the largest on-line community of the world. Evidently the complementarity provides synergies that result in a "1+1=3" scenario as coined by Dowling et. al.

The **complementary components** from one competition can support components of another vertically related competition. This can occur in two basic ways, depending on the standpoint:

On the demand side of one layer. In this case, one component of a vertically related layer is a vehicle on the distribution side. It increases demand through additional channels.

---

[165] According to interviews with Martin Stahel, Gruner + Jahr Chief Strategy Officer, 10th of June 199, Hamburg and Tom Tischler, Gruner + Jahr Corporate Development Manager, 17th of March 1999, San Francisco.

[166] A consecutive analysis can then disclose how and for who this convergence changes the competition. This can be perceived as entry, substitution though functionally equivalent goods, or as complements through vertically related components.

[167] Which is the most fundamental need and marketing rationale addressed by AOL according to interview with Klaus Hommels, Ass. Managing Director, AOL Germany, 19th of September 1997, Hamburg.

For example, the bundling with Windows is a superb distribution channel for the AOL software.[168]

- **On the supply side of one layer.** In this case one component bundled from another layer is added in such a way as to appear rather as a supply component. For example, the perception of the AOL software from the standpoint of Windows is as an added component, which adds value to the features which need either Internet access or content. Microsoft does not need to develop the components on its own as AOL supplies this functionality.

Both cases taken together describe a situation equal to the idea of systems (or composite products) as they consist of complementary components as described in Subsection 2.2.1. **The argument upon which this thesis elaborates is the influence of complementary needs bundles. They lead to multi-component structures that create virtually connected competitions following economics with network externalities.** The discussion covering business strategy in part III will further discuss the strategic implications from a product-market and a value net standpoint. In this context, a deeper analysis of complementarity potential conduct of players further reveal strategic insights. The example used here describes a case of reciprocal complementarity. Other constellations and the relevant factors will be discussed in part III. Figure 2-18 illustrates this insight and highlights the underlying and determinant role of a set of convergent needs.

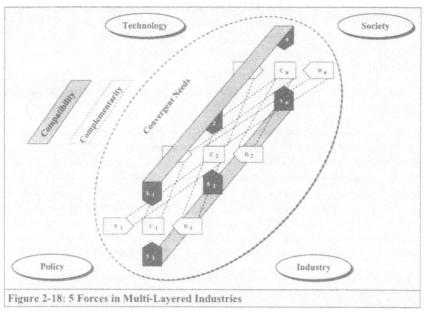

Figure 2-18: 5 Forces in Multi-Layered Industries

On the critical side, it needs to be mentioned that this approach ultimately suffers from the same weakness as Porter's framework. It is difficult and complex work defining concrete boundaries in the application to a specific case. How many layers apply? Where are the

---

[168] See Bakos / Brynjolfsson (1996).

boundaries? These are the critical questions in applied cases. While this thesis is applied research, this theoretical framework will be applied to the on-line industry, which will be conducted in Section 2.5.

The conceptual focus of this thesis is the analysis of the structure and the mechanisms of the on-line industry. Subsection 2.2.1 discusses the economics of networks and reveals the patterns of the Internet and on-line service framework as an ideal example. In order to be able to model these network effects in a way which also considers the related competitive forces, model A (see Figure 2-20) needs to be enhanced by the findings discussed in this subsection 2.2.2. Hence, **this Five Forces framework with several vertically related layers, which are interconnected as either substitutes or complements, needs to be translated and synchronized with the framework of network economics presented in model A.**

2.2.3. Conceptual Model of Multi Layered Industries

Given a multi-layered constitution, Porter's framework of Five Forces will be applied to support the model of the on-line industry with the information and granularity for the competition-based aspects of business strategy. However, as the discussion about network economics revealed the dominant mechanisms and laws of networked markets, this work suggests to integrate the Porterian framework into a network oriented model. Hence, the networking approach will be the dominant paradigm. Consequently, the insights from the enhanced, multi-layered Five Forces model need to be translated into the horizontal layers of model A. In order to conduct this in an incremental way, the following will first integrate the Five Forces framework into horizontal layers of a network model and then will add the aspects of a multi-layered cohesion.

1. **Integration of demand and supply side aspects of competitions in horizontal network markets**

According to model A, n components can be used to define the size of a network market. In two-way networks the potential value of the network growth with 2 x n. Economides (1996) points out the value of a network with this equation. While the network economists only analyze the overall economics of a network from a systems perspective and inflexibly model a monopoly, duopoly, and perfect competition scenarios, a strategic management approach requires a more **flexible modeling of the competitive situation of demand and supply in a market.** Hence, it is necessary to integrate the demand and supply side of horizontal network layers into the model. The analysis above proved that Porter's approach can be enhanced to account for a multi-layered constellation and is able to provide insight on each singular layer.

Network economics teaches that the larger the number of components, then the larger the market. Hence, from the standpoint of the companies constituting this network, it is possible to interpret the number of n components as the demand-side volume of a market. Model A highlights a cube based on the network line for each component. In network markets the component number is usually large. Hence, it is not possible to visualize this number in an applied case. The large number flattens out the number of cubes, which incrementally can then be represented by the size of the accompanying line. Hence, it seems plausible to **visualize** this **large number on the demand side** of n components **by the thickness of the horizontal line** as outlined in Figure 2-19. In a multi-layered cohesion a comparison of the size of the respective horizontal lines is able to represent the market potential on several interconnected vertically positioned market layers.

It could be argued that two-way networks exhibit the particularity that each component can be a sender and receiver at the same time. This could be interpreted that each of the receivers is on the demand side and each of the senders on the supply side. Consequently, the number of players on the demand side would equal the number on the supply side in two-way networks. But as the majority of senders is usually non-commercial and not paid to contribute to the network, they do not represent the supply side from an industrial perspective. Furthermore, this phenomenon represents precisely the positive externality, which is exhibited in network markets. The theory of network economics analyzes either competing networks without interoperability, such as incompatible proprietary on-line services or it discusses interoperable networks competing with the same network technology such as Internet service providers. In the context of a horizontal network market, the field as well as the theory of network economics highlights a **typically very low number of suppliers** (see 2.2.1) whereas a supplier has to be understood as a commercial player, who captures and controls a large portion of this particular network market. [169] Representing the business practice as Ann Winblad in formulating it with respect to Internet investments, writes:

> "If we consider a new venture in the Internet we say: The number one in a market is super hot. The number two is still very cool. The number three is quite nice. The number four is [she yawned]. The number five does not exist!"[170]

In reality, this can be a supplier of a dominant buddy list technology and the accordingly large member data base (e.g. AOL Instant Messenger, AOL's ICQ, Yahoo! Pager and MS Instant Messenger as competing networks on the same horizontal layer) or a supplier of an access network (e. g. a fixed narrowband network such as AOL/Worldcom Versus a fixed broadband such as @Home/AT&T versus a potential wireless broadband network). Hence, the position that each user, who is not only a receiver but also a potential sender needs to be represented on the supply side of a model as well results in a large number on the supply side, but it can be decreased. **Therefore, it can be concluded that a model of a network market needs to represent large number on the demand side and a low number on the supply side. In order to visualize the supply side, small cubes representing the competing players can be used.** The size of the players can be illustrated with the size of the cubes as displayed in Figure 2-19:

---

[169] See Economides / Woroch (1992), Economides / White (1994b) and Economides / Flyer (1997). Economides (1992, 1995a) also discusses the rationale of inviting additional competitors to expand the market volume and to increase the network effects. He points out that in some cases the network effect through increased network size is stronger than the weaker strategic position by increased rivalry within the competition through new entrants (e. g. competition driven price reductions). Obviously, pure industrial economics and pure network economics come to diverging conclusions in this point. As network economics discusses the trade-off between the negative competitive effect and the positive network effect, it integrates both perspectives.

[170] Ann Winblad, partner of Hummer Winblad Ventures, in her lunch speech at the conference on The Legal and Policy Framework for Global Electronic Commerce, International House UC Berkeley, 5th of March 1999. Ann Winblad is a partner at Hummer Winblad Ventures, a leading Silicon Valley venture capital firm.

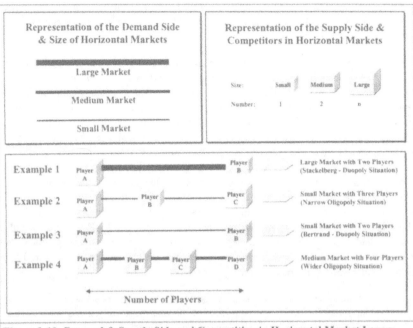

Figure 2-19: Demand & Supply Side and Competition in Horizontal Market Layers

This visualization quickly represents demand side and supply side of a market. The figure shows some examples representing different market volumes and supply situations, which result in different market constellations. This way of modeling visually shows the number and size of competing players, as well as the volume of the market. Furthermore, the ratio of market size (represented by the thickness of the line) and number of players is able to represent the intensity of competition in relative terms to the size of the market. Given a structure of several horizontal network markets, which are vertically interconnected, the attraction of the respective markets will be visible by looking at size of the line and number / size of the cubes. As network markets tend to evolve as narrow on the supply side, the figure shows two duopoly situations: one with relatively equal players and one with a larger leader and a smaller follower (Bertrand vs. Stackelberg).

Consequently Porter's supply side and demand side forces as well as rivalry can be integrated in a network model in a way, which is also able to represent horizontal network effects. In addition, the interdependence of these singular horizontal competitions needs to be added, as well as the Five Forces threats of substitutes and entrants.

2. Integration of interdependence of vertically related competitions

In order to complete the translation of a competitive analysis into multi-layered industries, the Porterian aspect of substitutes and entrants and the interdependence of vertically related competitions needs to be integrated into a multi-layered network framework. In extension of Dowling et. al., a multi-layered Five Forces framework is interconnected with the factors

complementarity and **compatibility**. This results in the network approach and the extended Five Forces framework as being conceptually compatible. **Network effects between vertically interconnected horizontal layers depend on the complementarity and interoperability / compatibility of networks** (see 2.2.1). **Substitution and entry aspects of vertically related competitions which result in their interdependence are similarly dependent.** Therefore, the following develops and integrates the findings of both approaches into a multi-layered network industry model based on the aspects of complementarity.

The cohesion of the Five Forces in several vertically related layers is interconnected as either substitutes or complements. Network economics discusses the causal influence of the complementary relationship of distinct "components" for the creation of externalities. The terminology of a framework of different competitions which discusses respective **"players" and "products" can be understood as "components" that exhibit a relationship within the spectrum of complementarity and substitution. This assumes that layers overall exhibit a certain level of complementarity and are network compatible.** Respective players positioned in these layers can leverage this complementarity to bundle their businesses. Or to refer to a product-market level: to bundle their components to a composite product, which serves to answer a set of related needs.

According to the multi-layered Five Forces framework, network layers can exhibit a relationship **substitution** as described in Porter's framework. For example, do email boxes with a web site interface such as Hotmail or "Yahoo! mail," which are accessible via browser substitute services with email software for downloadable email like AOL email. Reactions such as the production of access to mailboxes via AOL webmail shows a way to react to this threat of substitution. Another example is the threat of substitution for narrowband ISP's, which is created by broadband networks via DSL or cable technology. Using the terminology of network economics, these forces for substitution are equal to the **unstable equilibrium** of dominant networks, when dominant networks suddenly disappear, because they are **"tippy"** as coined by Benson and Farrell (1994).[171] As a result, complete layers disappear as they are substituted by functionally equivalent networks. The strength of lock-in effects, which are determined by switching costs, determine if networks tip and are substituted by other networks or if they remain in place.

In the case of a **complementary relationships of entrants**, which opens up **possibilities of cooperation** as described by Dowling et. al (1998a), it has to be distinguished, of which nature the compatibility of the relationship is. Depending on the type and structural logic of the complementarity in the relation, the cooperation generates vertical network effects for the networked players according to the underlying complementarity. Unfortunately, there is as yet no explicit discussion in the literature on network markets so far, which elaborates on different types of complementarity. Usually the discussion focuses on the compatibility aspect, which has to be seen as a second step enabling network effects. Enhancing the short discourse on complementarity in the context on network economics[172] one can conclude the following types of it:

---

[171] See Noam (1992), for an applied discussion on the instability of dominant telecommunications networks.

[172] Church / Gandal (1992b), pp. 657 and (1993), pp. 242-245 and Economides (1996), pp. 681-683.

■ **One-way complementarity,** defines a relationship when it is only perceived from one end. For example, the growing adoption rates of the Internet result in a higher demand for technical customer support, which is usually outsourced. Therefore, the diffusion of Internet access creates direct network externalities for call centers. On the other hand, the growth in the number of call centers would not be perceived as directly complementary to Internet access business.[173]

■ **Two-way complementarity** is when the interconnection fuels the economics of both players with strong direct network effects. For example, a composite product of the dial-up network of MCI Worldcom and the AOL community uses the AOL client software to connect to the AOL service exhibits a highly reciprocal complementarity. According to Figure 2-18 AOL plays the role of a reseller the dial-up network of MCI Worldcom and is a distribution channel for the network. Furthermore the AOL service adds value by providing content and customer service. Hence AOL is a distribution channel creating demand for the network but also a "complementor" (Brandenburger / Nalebuff 1997), which adds value to the telecommunications network as a vertically related market layer: Compelling services provided by AOL will drive network usage rates, which are generated by the subscribers. The growth and quality of AOL will fuel the growth of MCI Worldcom and vice versa as the growth and quality of MCI Worldcom enables AOL to provide a better network at lower costs.

■ In addition, one can perceive a third type of complementarity which should be called **asymmetrical complementarity.** In this case the complementarity of the relation is received by both layers although the impact is uneven. For example, the bundling of Windows with every Compaq computer is highly complementary – in this case almost vital - to both players. But as both players also integrate Compaq's search engine Alta Vista, MSN.com, and MS Internet Explorer into their network, the complementarities between the search engine, web Portal and web browser layers exhibit asymmetrical complementarities which results in asymmetrical network effects. Or in other words, where Windows has a strong interest to be installed on each Compaq PC and vice versa, the complementary added value of Alta Vista compared to Windows or the complementary added value of Internet Explorer to a Compaq PC is asymmetrical. In addition, both players seem unclear regarding about the positioning of the portal layer MSN.com, which exhibits an obvious substitution effect with Alta Vista.[174]

Ultimately **the level of complementarity of the layers provides players with the possibility of capturing vertical network effects.** Part III will look closer into the competitive scenarios of several players competing on each layer, which creates strategic possibilities for vertical value webs of complementary players from each layer. In order to be able to discuss the complementarities as source for vertical network effects between horizontal layers, one can inter-

---

[173] One may see an indirect network effect through better supply of call centers at lower costs for Internet access firms, if the market for call centers grows, but it does not directly complement the Internet access business, as the functions can also be provided internally.

[174] According to interviews with Andrew Wyatt, Director Electronic Commerce Compaq Europe, 21st of June 1999, Munich, and Klaus Mantel, Business Development Manager Microsoft Germany, 15th of June 1999, Munich.

pret one-way complementarity with a simple arrow, two-way complementarity with a two-way arrow, and asymmetrical complementarity with a connecting line, which becomes slimmer on the less effected side as it is visualized in Figure 2-20. This network cohesion implies compatibility of all included components as it would otherwise not be a (vertical) network. Substitution effects are shown with dotted arrows, with the direction indicating which layer could substitute for which layer.[175] For example, the substitution of narrowband by a broadband local loop results in challenges for AOL and @Home, which are players on the respective horizontal networks. Or to give another example described by Zaret / Meeks (1999): the approach of AOL, Sun and Netscape to embrace through the Internet in a new customer, device, client, network, server, e-commerce technology scenario result in a structure, which aims to substitute Windows.

The above analysis (2.1, 2.2.2) discusses the influence of the exogenous parameters, which determine the size and also the structure of the industry. This is illustrated by the bubbles surrounding the industry cohesion in Figure 2-20:

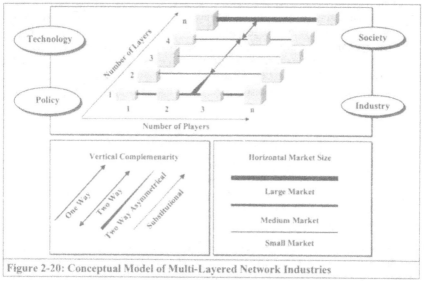

Figure 2-20: Conceptual Model of Multi-Layered Network Industries

Figure 2-20 models a multi-layered network industry, which consists of network markets on each horizontal layer. The vertical interconnections based on inter-layer compatibility and complementarity result in additional network effects. In an intra-layer view as well as in an inter-layer view, the forces of demand, supply, rivalry of competitors, entrants and substitutes determine the attractiveness of distinct competitions. Due

---

[175] This scenario discusses only direct and indirect network effects generated in the primary business activities. According to Economides (1996) secondary overhead activities can exhibit weak indirect network effects. This can describe for example a shared accounting and human resources unit as mutual overhead by several business units. This is the case with AOL, CompuServe, BOL, Lycos and other Bertelsmann multimedia units, which can enjoy a larger and more specialized overhead at lower internal prices. Although these advantages are generated by traditional optimization of value chain processes and are not created by the market structures of the direct business operations. Therefore, they are left out in order to reduce complexity.

to the particularities of the layered network industry, the Five Forces framework, including the enhancements discussed above, is implicitly integrated in Figure 2-20.

While Section 2.1 looked into the exogenous variables of a model for the industry and 2.2 analyzed the general economics exhibited in a network industry the following analysis will take a micro-perspective and will analyze the endogenous factors of the industry. The application of the conceptual model needs to determine which layers can be distinguished in a concrete multi-layered market and how many components each of the layers has. This distinction needs to be derived from the fundamentals of a specific industry. As this thesis is a contribution to applied theory, this next step will incrementally be conducted in the course of the analysis of the fundamental market data of the past and current on-line industry (2.3-2.5).

2.3. Analysis of the History of Proprietary On-Line Services

Rayport / Sviokla (1994) coined the term "marketspace", which describes the new form of virtual marketplaces, commonly understood to be located in the "cyberspace" of the Internet. At the time their article was written, the Internet was, in fact, not a commercial space. The main platform creating virtual marketspaces available to large customer groups, and hence **established significant markets**, were the proprietary on-line services. Subsection 1.1.2 shows clear evidence of these commercial traditions. Prior discussions (1.1.3, 2.1.3) show that convergence indeed shifted the industry in a fundamental way. The outcome is the Internet framework of on-line service business. Players in this field face high uncertainty armed with little experience:

> "The product concepts in these new fields may well consist of combinations of existing technologies, (...) customer needs will have to be defined, identified, or even developed from the scratch before the fruits of technological convergence can be enjoyed. Not only do we not know precisely who the customers are for the newly conceiving products; we also do not know what they are willing to pay, what features they value the most, and how they are best reached." Gomes – Casseres / Leonard – Barton (1996:362)

As most of the current analysis focuses on only the short history of the Internet, this thesis utilizes experience curve effects from the closely related industrial history. While the industry is experiencing outrageous growth rates on the one hand, it has, on the other, lost the stability of business models and value creating structures. Hence, there is still a lack of experience on how to run a stable and profitable business on-line. Nevertheless, this is one of the main concerns of analysts who criticize the "net stock mania" where companies such as Amazon or Yahoo! outnumber the market capitalization of traditional businesses like Barnes & Noble or CBS.[176] Critical here is that the fundamental financial data in many cases shows **growth fueled by the stock market rather than by realistic stable business models, which provide solid revenues from the actual operational business. This all returns to the fundamental immaturity problem of the Internet framework**: a lack of stable business mod-

---

[176] Although some of the options evaluated in Internet stocks might prove to be correct in the long run, the irrationality in this context is significant. See for example Fost (1999:B4) describing the case of ZDNet.

els, as well as a solid structure of the business value system, stabilized behavior of market participants, and the availability of commercial technology.[177]

Thus Subsection 2.3.2 will analyze how the **past on-line business** provided products and services in an on-line environment, which **created a portfolio of business models resulting in a profitable business.** Therefore, the analysis reveals crucial **technological and business insights from the past** (2.3.3). Furthermore, Subsection 2.3.4 rounds off this perspective with an analysis of **vertically integrated value creating structures** from the past. It is crucial to understand that the constellation described below outlines a profitable on-line business, which **indicates potential business patterns emerging in the future development of the Internet framework.** Section 2.4 will show how this business was unbundled and desegregated, while 2.5 the next section shows how the Internet paradigm, in some respects, is merely a reinvention of the past. Those who understand this will be better equipped to understand future models providing profitable business operations conducted in the on-line industry. In order to rediscover the learning curve from proprietary online service traditions, this following analytical part will:

"look into the past to see the future" (Zerdick 1998, eds.:36) [translation C. G.]

2.3.1. Utilization of Experience Curve Effects

Past on-line services had a very **high degree of vertical integration of the value chain.** Consequently, their **broad competence portfolio** as well as their operations included activities in the area of telecommunications players, software companies, media companies and computer hardware manufacturers. On the one hand, their **steadily growing market was extremely protected due to their powerful proprietary technology,** the lack of open standard technology and their particular **experience curves.** Yet, on the other hand, they were forced create a large portion of the value creation within their own structures as it will be outlined in below in Subsection 2.3.4. The Internet as a new and open standard platform for on-line services exhibits the extreme growth patterns described above. Due to an unstable and premature structural framework (see Section 2.1) it does not provide an environment where a portfolio of viable and stable business models has yet evolved. Aside from a small number of players, the vast majority offers services for free and tries instead to sell advertising, cross-sells services, or features e-commerce partners to be successful. Usually the primary goal is to gain market share and to capture future market positions, which has compelling arguments with respect to the lessons told by network economics (see Subsection 2.2.1). But **the Internet framework does not deliver significant experience curve effects with solid business models.** Nor does it provide sustainable revenue streams at this point. Several reasons can be identified for this:

The insufficiency of the available commercial technologies, particularly the technologies for billing & collection, security and authentication, simply do not allow for the most desirable business models. As opposed to the **closed proprietary environment,** which **had feasible technical solutions,** the available open standard technology does not provide such solutions

---

[177] Messerschmitt (1996), p. 34, points out the missing system infrastructure: coherence of the open Internet architecture. Widespread application of a host of business models would require interoperable commercial technologies which does not yet exist(ibid.). See also Hagel / Bergsma / Dheer (1996), p. 64.

as of the late 1990s. Very limited standardization[178] and compatibility of the available technology only raises the uncertainty outlined in Subsection 2.1.2. The superior performance of a network market (see 2.2.1), therefore, cannot be fully captured due to this premature stage of the technology. However, considering the velocity and the corporate drivers behind these technological development processes it is to be expected that a secure framework similar to proprietary on-line services will be available in the near future.[179] Furthermore, the competitive and dynamic market framework produces a rapid speed of change so it does not provide an environment where stabilized expectations relating to the behavior of the market players can evolve. This results in a lack of coordination in the conduct of the players. Patterns of **coalitions** and **competition** are as yet, unclear. Furthermore, the value adding processes are heavily based on constantly adjusting **virtual value creation structures**. The degree of **horizontal** and **vertical integration** is also unclear at this point. Moreover, the distribution of the added value between the players within this structure is undefined. Therefore, the overall business framework of the on-line industry is highly problematic for developing a business strategy, as it is obvious, that significant growth will continue in this sector within the foreseeable future. Unfortunately, the majority of **current industry research** perceives the on-line business solely within the Internet paradigm, coupled with the **reduced perspectives** described in Subsection 1.1.2. Consequently, they perceive an economic environment with an unstable institutional framework and still undefined business models and value chain definitions incorporating an **experience curve of approximately 4 years**.

In contrast, the analysis below will show that many patterns in the new Internet paradigm are identical to many of past on-line business patterns. If one analyzes the on-line business from this perspective, acknowledging that there is a comprehensive business history, it is possible to utilize valuable experience curve potentials. This can help one to understand patterns of current and future developments better, albeit despite the fact that the institutional framework of the future on-line business will indeed dramatically differ from the past, given the influence of the entire convergence.[180] Thus, a contrary standpoint, which considers the on-line business as equivalent with the short commercial history of the Internet and only regards this as a new phenomenon runs into an **experience gap of about 20 years** considering the specific requirements for the "on-line perspective" as described in Subsection 1.1.2. This thesis closes this experience gap, while utilizing experience curve effects from the proprietary on-line past and will transfer on-line business into the new "Internet paradigm". The following figure illustrates the intention described above:

---

[178] See 2.1.1. Weather national institutions like the US IEEE or German DIN nor the industry itself have been able to solve standardization issue yet. So far the most efficient party driving the standardization process is the supranational WWW Consortium (W^3C) based in the south of France, which is mainly supported by industry (according to interview with Josef Dietel, Senior Consultant W3C, March 17th 1998, Hanover.

[179] See also AT Kearney (1998a), p. 2

[180] See also Arthur Andersen (1998a), pp. 28-29.

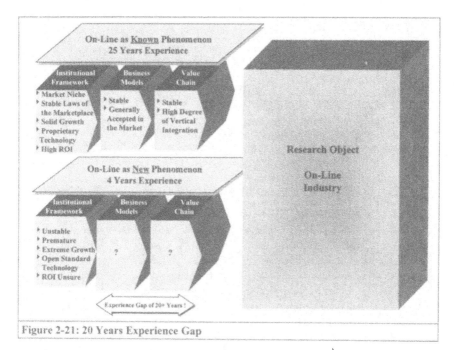

Figure 2-21: 20 Years Experience Gap

On the grounds of these statements one can derive the following thesis:

On-line business is not a new phenomenon. The on-line business is an established business with comprehensive experience curve effects including business models and value creating structures. These experiences can be transferred into the Internet paradigm to avoid the threat of running into an experience gap of 20 years.

Along these lines KPMG sets the on-line business into a context regarding the current convergence processes in the Information Communication Technology (ICT) area and suggests to

„(...) look at parallels between on-line and Internet services and convergence. The on-line industry is considered by many to be an actualisation of the superhighway. (...) The conclusion to be drawn, however, is that on-line businesses show how successful services of this type can be and illustrates how competitive service provision models may work." (KPMG 1996a:103)

Given that one analyzes the on-line business from a perspective which acknowledges a comprehensive business history, it is possible to utilize these valuable experience curve potentials. Therefore, Subsection 2.3.2 provides an overview of a complete portfolio of business models from past on-line services. The subsequent analysis shows the underlying needs structure for this business and leads to the structural model of an on-line service, outlining technological components as well as the role of business partners (2.3.3). Subsection 2.3.4 conducts a closer analysis of the underlying value creating structures.

2.3.2. The Proprietary Online Service Business Model

The following analyzes on which grounds past on-line services conducted their business.[181] Subsection 1.1.2 has already outlined that **past on-line services existed in a small market niche, which exhibited solid growth and returns for more than 25 years.** Yet, during this time on-line services existed as fairly isolated platforms with **limited interoperability,**[182] different market definitions and portfolios of business models, which were attractive for business partners and for users. A crucial commercial difference to the immature Internet environment is that **the past exhibited stable and profitable business models.**[183] The further part of the analysis will look closer into the underlying customer needs structure, which enabled these business models and attracted the vendors.

The following is an empirical overview, structuring the business models, which were implemented by on-line services in the past. It highlights the models of CompuServe, which offered the most comprehensive portfolio of **business models, and which evolved over many years.** It represents models, which in fact created **stable market platforms of significant volume** and were populated by a host of commercial players and millions of customers. Figure 2-22 outlines the set of different models. The left column outlines **business models** in a general way **with respect to media, commerce, service, telecommunication, technology** and **combination**-driven models. This fosters the understanding of future business models in the **convergence** area rather appropriately than does an approach dominated by the isolated perspectives from the convergence industries.[184] The center column presents the applied business models. The surprising fact is that within proprietary on-line services, this variety of models was already applied to specific business relationships with significant volumes, which is illustrated with prominent examples for on-line based business upon the various models in the right column. The related revenue data is taken from the German regional market of the CompuServe on-line service. The data is for April 1995, when the world wide web had still limited commercial significance. In fact, a single application like chat accounted for twice as many usage hours as Internet connections at this time. Thus, this old data should exhibit almost no distortion of the emerging Internet influence. Representing a **comprehensive closed**

---

[181] The author served in several positions in strategic planning and business development for CompuServe. Subsection 2.3.2 will use data from this professional involvement. Thus the analysis of the past will extensively emphasis the CompuServe on-line service. It is an example of on-line services representing the virtual marketspaces of the past, where the past is defined until app. 1995, due to the emergence of convergence and the WWW as discussed in Subsection 1.1.3. This process changed the entire business framework in a way as it is outlined in 2.4. CompuServe's main difference to other on-line services was that it was the only real global on-line service at this time and that it had a much more comprehensive portfolio of business models (see Figure 2-22). In 1995 the combined user base of all services was approximately 25 Million (see Figure 1-3) which demonstrates the commercial significance of on-line business before the World Wide Web evolved so rapidly.

[182] The content of the services was not interoperable due to closed standards. With email the obvious killer application, the services designed gateways between the email hubs of other large email providers. CompuServe also shared some international network agreements with third party networks in order to extend the global coverage of dial-in POP's. For the usage of these third party networks for dial-in purposes, users were charged so called "network surcharges," which functions as a roaming fee to other networks.

[183] See Murphy (1996), pp. 4-6.

[184] See for example Zerdick (1998, eds.), pp. 24-28 who outlines models according to media, telecommunications and the IT sector, which do not apply in the Internet framework.

on-line environment it can serve as a highly coherent sample for a field experiment under real life conditions. The user base at this time was 190,000 users, which represents the market size of the underlying sample. The volumes for different market segments in the right column give an impression of the relative size of different on-line based businesses. Overall business model 14 highlights 3.5 million dollars as monthly revenue. This gives a good general understanding of a revenue stream which could be generated with a complex set of business models in a market with a volume of 190.000 participants.[185] The key message here is that the study of past experience can indeed generate insight about business models and pricing schemes (see the high revenue stream for transaction-based models and look at the type of information) as well as the power of certain applications (see the high usage of email and chat!), or the potential for personalized information (see business model 2) or the user affinity to certain content (see the computing-driven revenues by Ziff and Microsoft or the business database revenues in a technology and business oriented community like CompuServe). This thesis does not intend to fully analyze the particularities of business models, but the data shown below gives clear evidence that past on-line business can provide extensive experience regarding potential future market trends. The conclusion is that **a decade prior the increasing commercialization of the Internet, all on-line service business models emerging in the course of the Internet already existed.** Crucial is that, unlike the premature Internet framework, **on-line services provided a commercial technology platform** (see 2.3.3), which was able to deliver interactive services, mostly provided by third party vendors to fulfill customer needs (see Figure 2-23) on-line. This setting emerged to the virtuous portfolio of business models outlined in Figure 2-22.

Communities (model 1) with its particular economic logic[186] provided a platform in which developed business were fueled by heavy network effects. The early successful players in this arena learned how to manage in that marketspace. They represent the early cases of successful interactive media and demonstrated that first movers could develop core competence for this competition. Most of them leveraged this competence to manage virtual communities later in the Internet space. For example, E-Drive (see business model 1), the largest independent entertainment community on the Internet started within CompuServe. Ziff Davis, as an IT publishing group, used CompuServe as a platform with high user affinity for more than a decade and generated additional profits via on-line subscriptions (see business model 3). All these players were traveling up the learning curve and then transferred to the Internet as a larger platform for interactive media. Because of the existing community in proprietary services, they were able refer their user base to their web presence via web links and the CompuServe Internet gateway provided the transport there. Hence, they started in the Internet with a level of critical mass and a significant learning curve from day one of operations. Hence, these players had the know-how and existing customer base to compete against new entrants.

---

[185] Note that this number excludes advertising (model 10) and most ecommerce revenues (model 7) which can multiply that number depending on the development of these business models within a virtual market platform.

[186] See Hagel / Armstrong (1995, 1996, 1997) and Case Study 2-2.

GENERAL BUSINESS MODEL	APPLIED BUSINESS MODEL	EXAMPLE	REVENUE IN APRIL 95
Content Time Based	1. Community management (low or no rates / minute)	Microsoft Forums[188] Chat Rooms E-Drive	$ 224,792 $ 125,876 $ 37,469
	2. Premium services (high rates / minute)	Executive News Service (news clipping service)	$ 25,000
Flat Rates	3. Content subscription	ZIFF-Net (Computing subscription)	$ 57,000
Transaction Based	4. Pay per view (pure information goods)	IQuest database reselling (incl. e.g. Dun & Bradstreet) Business database plus (incl. e.g. Hoover)	$ 92,000 $ 14,000
Commerce[189]	5. E-Commerce Intangible goods & services	Automotive e.g. Auto by Tel Travel e.g. SABRE, Travelshopper Software e.g. Shareware Reg. Area short messages & paging	N/A N/A N/A $ 4,388
	6. E-Commerce Tangible goods	Flowers e.g. FTD Flowers	N/A
Free Services	7. On-line customer services	Software upgrade[190] Software distribution CompuServe Customer Support (free)	($ 66,000) ($ 40,000) ($ 9,429)
	8. On-line services	On-line banking	N/A
	9. Promotion & advertising	Banners, anchor tenants, Sponsors	N/A
Telecommunication Volume Based	10. Pay per Mbit (typical ISP model)	based on up/download volumes	N/A
Bottleneck Based	11. Congestion Fee	Evening prime time	N/A
Time Based	12. Consumer data transport	Email File transport	$ 444,865 $ 65,000
Technology	13. Local loop based	Modem baud rate	N/A
Combinations of all	14. On-line service bundling	CompuServe	$ 3,500,000

Figure 2-22: Empirical Overview: Evolved and Stable Business Models

An analysis of the different revenue streams of traditional on-line services reveals another significant number: subscriptions were by far the most significant revenue stream. In 1996, CompuServe received 74% of its revenue via subscriptions. Within the Internet framework, subscriptions are still on a mostly free basis, which deprives businesses from an important revenue stream. However, due to the necessity to work around this weakness, the indirect revenue streams of e-commerce and advertising increase drastically. For example AOL – the most significant player who still receives subscription revenue – reported for its third quarter of fiscal year 1998/1999 advertising and commerce revenues of almost one third of the sub-

---

[187] Some items do not show quantitative data, as it was not available anymore for this time period. Nevertheless these business models (5, 6, 8, 9, 10, 11, 13) existed and experience was generated.

[188] This example prominently shows how a software company could tie in customers to the product via an on-line community service function. This increased retention and in this particular case even revenues. Hence, the story tells that a typical cost driver as customer service can be turned into a value driver if conducted well. Rayport / Sviokla (1996) and Hagel / Armstrong (1995, 1996, 1997) provide a good general understanding how this virtual value chain can be managed in virtual communities.

[189] All these examples, with brands well renown in the Internet, used CompuServe as commercial platform for many years before they moved their business to the web.

[190] These three items where not billed but the number showed the actual costs for the delivery of these services. It tells a great deal about how certain services can be shifted to an on-line site at certain costs. In any case the costs of on-line distribution in this particular case were much lower than by physical distribution vial mail.

scription revenues. This shows the shift in business models from direct revenue streams based on communication and information to indirect revenue streams.

As yet it is **not possible to analyze these comprehensive experiences from the Internet framework,** because advertising and recently increasing e-commerce are the only models being implemented on a large scale. As mentioned above, the main reasons are a **lack of commercial technology**[191] and the **overheated and not yet consolidated competitive behavior.** Its nature as an extremely distributed system implies that comprehensive comparative analytical approaches are almost impossible for the Internet. The only exceptions to this are potentially the advertising and e-commerce driven business models. In the case of advertising, leading players like Yahoo! or AOL's AOL.com derive their main revenue stream from a significant volume from this source for the last 5 years. The accumulated experience of these models is certainly significant. In some cases of e-commerce, past experience seems to be transferred directly by the players itself, the successful cases of SABRE or AutobyTel prove. This, in return, supports the hypothesis that utilizing past experiences results in competitive advantage. Other Internet e-commerce examples of new players like Amazon – with a substantial brick and mortar part of its value chain – or auction sites like eBay - with an entirely virtual value chain – are the new models emerging in the Internet framework. In many cases, sustainability has yet to be proven.[192]

When most of the players behind the businesses outlined above moved their business to the web environment in the middle of the 90s, they decided to exchange stable business with constrained market volumes for activities without underlying business models in an environment with enormous growth rates.[193] The network effects of the larger installed base in the Internet obviously worked towards this decision. On the other hand, it is not rocket science to predict that this unstable market will experience the emergence of sustainable business models and a consolidation with fewer players in more market layers in the long run. Depending on the particular positioning of an Internet based on-line business it seems valuable to analyze the logic of past business models. There are good reasons for doing so. Many **business models that are projected for the future** and do not exist in the Internet yet, **were obviously already conducted in past on-line services** in a significant scale. If a firm plans to enhance the business model based on additional revenue streams, a case-to-case analysis of past examples seems highly valuable.

In order to better understand the basic forces, which drove past models, the **underlying structure of needs** has to be analyzed. The following statement of AOL's President Jack Davies clearly points out that on-line services are about much more than just content:

> "The reality with America Online is more than 50 per cent of our usage has nothing to do with content. It is about chat, it is about e-mail, it's about posting messages on message boards. It's people communicating with other people. So anytime you hear somebody say content is king .... that is we believe a substantial myth and that the de-

---

[191] See Varian (1996).

[192] See BCG (1998) for an overview about developments in retail e-commerce with an analysis of a larger number of consumer on-line stores. See Goldman Sachs (1999c) for a corresponding strategic analysis.

[193] Market definition, user interface and back end technologies were adjusted to a web framework. During that process on-line service suppliers became competitors in their specific product area. See 2.4.

velopment of this medium is very much about community. It is about bringing content and community together in an interesting fashion and making it interactive and participatory rather than one way." (OECD 1996:31)

This clearly points out that usage reflects usage patterns far beyond just informational content services, highlighting the **two-way network** aspect. Hence, a definition of content has to be broadened to include **interactive services**. On-line services offered an integrated bundle of components for a bundle of needs.

A closer look reveals that on-line services shows that it basically served four **fundamental needs: information, communication** and **community**. Offerings for electronic **commerce** were served as well. But at the old days, this was still seen rather as an additional service than a fundamental component. **These needs demand the visible components** of an on-line service offering. People want to gather information, talk to people and get–to-know people and are happy to buy something cheaper and quicker. For these purposes on-line services provided a **portfolio of content applications**, which served customer needs such as email, file transfer, gateways to other services (e. g. CompuServe gateway to IBM X-400 network or email to fax, or AOL mail to CompuServe mail), databases (all major scientific databases, Dun & Bradstreet, Hoover etc.), individual and group chat applications, commercial applications (purchasing flowers, flight tickets, cars etc.), forums (integrated community platforms with message sections, chat, email and independent member databases run by independent community managers), editorial content channels (e. g. news, weather, sport) and information agents (e. g. the personalized news clipping agent "Executive News Service," which scanned the main global agency news tickers based on personalized parameters). Airline tickets, flowers, and cars could be purchased in commercial sections. In total for the example of CompuServe, the huge variety of services accumulated to a number of approaching 3.000.

But in addition to the demand for the fundamental needs, there was an implicit demand for – in the best case – an invisible technological platform, to the content applications. Along these lines one can understand the key benefit delivered by AOL as expressed by its COO and president Bob Pittman:[194] **"Convenience is king."** (Zenith 1999)

An on-line service like AOL provides a **comprehensive technology platform**, which combines a highly complex technological system architecture serving **two implicit needs: convenience** and **connectivity**. Business partners and users needed to utilize a network of technology components. Especially in the consumer environment, people do not want to bother. This is a fundamental need and firms need to provide connectivity to the services in the most convenient way. The end user demands a software package (consisting of a dialer and clients for mail, content and chat), to use the content applications, and he expects a network (consisting of dial-up POP's, a transport network and the data processing hosts) to be there in order to connect him. Ultimately all the particular components can be derived from these six general needs cluster as shown in Figure 2-23:[195]

---

[194] See also Case (1998).

[195] Goldman Sachs (1999b), p. 9 developed a similar model to assess Internet businesses which they call the seven C model, whereas they refer to content, community, communication, connectivity, communications, commerce, context.

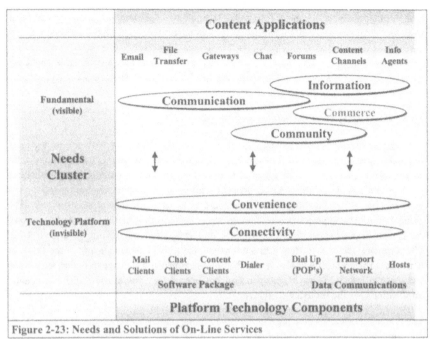

Figure 2-23: Needs and Solutions of On-Line Services

On these grounds, the following thesis is formulated:

Communication, information, community and commerce are the fundamental needs driving on-line services in the Internet paradigm. Invisible technology must provide connectivity for it in a convenient way.

Other needs driving the development of Internet based, on-line services are subsets of these needs such as the need for a browser, the need for access software.

In this context, **the term "content" needs to be defined more broadly** to include interactive applications for communication, community and commerce. In order to consider the presence of network externalities, the term needs to encompass the interactive, two-way aspect of on-line services.

The term content in the context of the Internet describes a variety of **products and services,** which organize a flow of **information** between **complementary components** – or more generally spoken between a **compatible sender and receiver** –in a digital network in a **uni-directional or bi-directional way.**[196] Usually the flow includes a strong **interactive component.**[197]

---

[196] See 2.2.1 and in particular Figure 2-13 for the fundamental shift in the underlying economics.

[197] Varian / Shapiro make a similar decision to broaden the term information which complements the definition of the term content within this context: „We use the term information very broadly. Essentially, anything that can be digitized -- encoded as a stream of bits -- is information. For our purposes, baseball scores, books,

If one further analyzes this needs – content – technology – cohesion, it becomes obvious that although customers were only interested in content applications, a complex technological infrastructure was needed to provide an on-line service. Therefore, Subsection 2.3.3 will analyze this technological infrastructure, which can then be used to derive insights about the entire structure of the industry. Furthermore it can be used to understand many strategically relevant factors in order to generate competitive advantages.

2.3.3. Proprietary On-Line Service Architectures

It is the **technological infrastructure**, which ultimately **enables a network of business partners to conduct their business on-line**. A deeper analysis reveals the enormous complexity of this area and leads to **a host of implications for industry structure and business strategy**. Proprietary on-line services owned extensive infrastructure which provided a complete on-line service bundling. Thus, they could serve as a comprehensive show case. The particular underlying proprietary technology structures will be described in order to enhance the general technological descriptions of the on-line industry outlined in Subsection 2.1.2. The surprising fact is that, from a structural view, the technological structure of the **Internet is not that different**. It will also reveal that the fundamental difference has to be seen in the fact that the Internet is **based on open and not proprietary standards**, which has **crucial implications for the industry structure**.

The following describes how the CompuServe on-line service was configured its technological components to deliver on-line services to subscribers.[198] CompuServe used to coin this structure the "precious gem", which explains the diamond shape shown in Figure 2-24. It shows that the customer was purchasing a highly integrated on-line service bundling[199] based on a complex but mainly invisible technology. The figure gives some specific examples of infrastructure components and reveals that a **complex technological environment** was needed on order to serve the information, communication and community needs as shown in Figure 2-23. It highlights the user as on top of an almost completely **integrated and closed structure**. Aside from the usage and access device the entire structure was closed, proprietary and owned by the on-line service provider which is indicated by the thick line. The actual user was basically only interested in the huge variety of content applications, such as email, news services, airline bookings or participation in a community of interest. These services are indicated by the gray arrows. In order to deliver this content a host of compatible components needed to be assembled in a structure as illustrated in Figure 2-24. **This structure enabled external business partners of the on-line service provider to deliver inputs based on the proprietary standards in order to establish business relations with the on-line service**

---

databases, magazines, movies, music, stock quotes, and Web pages are all information goods. We focus on the value of information to different consumers. Some information has entertainment value, and some has business value, but regardless of the particular source of value, people are willing to pay for information." (Varian / Shapiro 1998:3)

[198] The main sources for Subsection 2.3.3 are several interviews with Dave Bezair (CompuServe, Director Product Management) and Bob Horton (CompuServe, Vice President Technology) and the authors experience from the professional involvement with CompuServe.

[199] Section 2.5 will show how influences of convergence fostered a desegregation of the various bundled components, which are now offered by many players in many different ways but still under similar basic principles.

customers. The on-line service provider owned the technology, as well as the customer, and hence could leverage this position to capitalize on this channel / bottleneck between business partners and subscribers Therefore, this structure was coined the "precious gem". The main industries participating in this structure were the media, telecommunications, computer hardware and software companies or in other words: those very industries, which are now converging as described in Subsection 1.1.3. Commercial partners like airline ticketing and flowers as mentioned above provided their offerings on-line. These players perceived on-line services as additional market channels and, therefore, accepted the proprietary technology of the on-line service providers just as the subscribers who had no alternative choices.

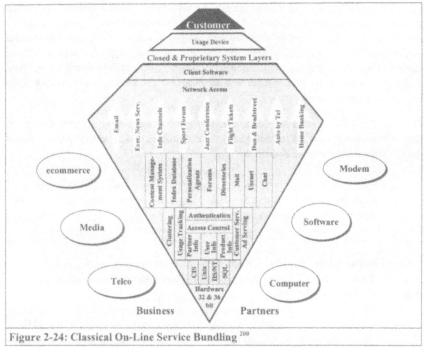

Figure 2-24: Classical On-Line Service Bundling [200]

The figure shows several technological layers with a large number of components. The following will first describe in which way the different layers worked together. Figure 2-25 will then outline the singular components in a more structured way. First the customers needed a **usage device,** which in the past was solely computers. This computer needed to be equipped with a modem or an Ethernet card in case of a LAN connection. This device needed an installed **client software** package to use the service. This client software consisted of a dial-up mechanism that built a connection via a modem / LAN to the **network infrastructure** and was able to authenticate the user at the user database of the subscriber management systems

---

[200] Figure according to material provided in the interview with Dave Bezair, Director Product Management CompuServe, March 26th 1997, Columbus, including minor adjustments by the author. It outlines the view of the system architecture of the CompuServe on-line service. It is derived from the view of the product management group, which was the strategic interface between the business management and the technology and development organizations.

of the service. Next to the dial-up and authentication component, the software had an email client, a chat client, and a content client (=browser), components for the actual information, communication, community, and commerce **applications**. The network infrastructure consisted of a dial-up network with thousands of network nodes, which connected the user to the hosting facilities via the backbone network. These **hosting facilities** consisted of hardware, the host computers, which ran servers on proprietary and standard operating systems. This hosting infrastructure supported several components of **strategic commercial technologies**. In this area, with management information systems (MIS) and customer management infrastructure as the main components, information about the user (e.g. name, address, billing and pricing information), usage (e.g. usage times and transactions), business partner (e.g. content provider, marketing partner), service and products (e.g. addresses, prices) were managed. The next layer was the layer of the **value added technologies,** which was the technical production infrastructure for the information, communication and community applications (e. g. forums, content management systems, personalization databases, index databases, mailboxes, chat). Every component of this infrastructure was computerized and took part in organizing information in a digital environment.

Given the defined understanding of content and information, the underlying needs structure as well as the description of the technological nature of bundled on-line service, one can derive the following **on-line service definition**.

A complete on-line service is a **bundle** which offers **content** in applications for **information, communication and community** needs over a **data network** infrastructure in **digital technology** with a **computerized usage device**. Singular content applications as components of a complete bundling can be referred to as on-line service (singular).

The term **on-line service** describes a product, which serves customer needs and which is the result of a business concept and the base for building an **on-line business,** which can be defined with the following definition:

An on-line business is the underlying business model and the operation of an on-line service. This business offers singular on-line services either standalone or in a bundle with other on-line service components.

Figure 2-25 shows the cohesion of this complex proprietary system infrastructure of past on-line services in a more structured and general way. It shows how the actual **content applications**, which serve the on-line needs (see Figure 2-23), are surrounded by technology as if it were the meat in a sandwich. This is highlighted in the dark gray box in Figure 2-25. This defines the **virtual space,** which is established by the exchange of information goods as defined above. The light gray boxes describe the main areas of system components. Each of them includes a number of subcomponents. Each component is designed as a **compatible technology** in order to interact with rest of the components. Therefore, **each component has a complementary relationship to the other components**. These complementarities are exhibited on a horizontal layer as well a on the vertical layer. For example, sports communities benefit from email communication and sport information in sport channels. Whereas in a vertical relationship the number of email clients benefited from the number of email boxes, which in turn benefits from the number of communities and vice versa. These examples illustrate the complex network dynamic of singular complementary components. In the same manner, the main areas, as represented by the main boxes, benefited, as they also exhibit strong complementarities, as each of them was a *conditio sine qua non* for the others. The **usage software bundling** needed the **telecommunications network infrastructure** in order to use the content, which was produced with according **value added production technology**, so called middleware, which was running upon the hosting infrastructure. The **hosting layer** managed all the data exchanged within this system. The crucial layer, which made this entire cohesion a commercial play, was the **strategic commercial infrastructure** for pricing, tracking, billing, security, authentication and marketing of the on-line services running on top of this infrastructure.

The later analysis of the technological infrastructure of on-line services in the Internet will show that the design of the Internet as initially a non commercial network neglected the development of corresponding layer for a long time and, hence, exhibits technological immaturity for commercial purposes.

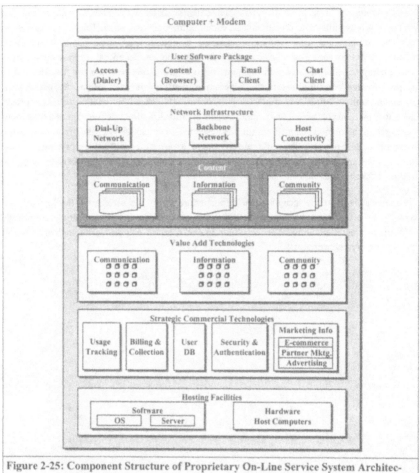

Figure 2-25: Component Structure of Proprietary On-Line Service System Architecture

As traditional on-line services were programmed with their own **proprietary technology,** these environments were **closed network structures** with limited interfaces to other networks. This means that customers, as well as business partners, could only utilize the benefits from a singular service bundle and not all bundles. Hence, on-line business platforms like CompuServe, AOL or Prodigy (see Figure 1-3) were not able to utilize network effects by combining their customer and business partner base to reach larger scale. Section 2.5 shows that this was a major difference and a major disadvantage, when compared to the on-line business environment in the Internet paradigm. However, this foreshadows aspects of the underlying business system, which will be discussed in Subsection 2.3.4.

2.3.4. Structure of a Vertically Integrated Business System

The following analysis of proprietary services looks deeper into the value creating structures, which were build upon the proprietary technology platform. In order to develop a feeling for the commercial volume of such past systems, one can consider the case of CompuServe, where the on-line service served approximately five million customers, maintained more than 3000 business partner relationships and generated revenues of more than $600 million, which resulted in a profit of $140 million in the year 1995.[201]

A closer look into the structure of the value creation of on-line services, such as AOL or CompuServe, reveals that their value chain had a **high degree of vertical integration**. Due to the proprietary nature of their technology, on-line services had either the option to develop and maintain all parts of the business itself as other parties had no access to the technology or to license the technology to third parties (see Case Study 3-3). **Make or buy decision were mostly irrelevant** due to almost no existence of compatible standard technology.[202] The decision for proprietary technology obliges a firm to create solely all according pieces of the value chain. This was dictated by the technological design. Hence, on-line services had no other choice than to do almost everything within internal structures. This in return created high entrance barriers, during the absence of comparable open standard technology.

On-line services designed their technology according to the needs structure of customers and business partners and established themselves as channel in between. In return, the design of the technological infrastructure and **its proprietary nature had a dual influence on the structure of the value creation** within this system. As it was stated above, the proprietary nature led to a high vertical integration, which **defined the outside boundaries** of the on-line service firm value chain to the supply chain and the distribution chain.[203] Service components, which were not available on standard technology, automatically led to internal value creation. An analysis of the firms inside shows crucial effects of the technology setting as well. The different technological layers led to a **differentiation of internal functional clusters** that were determined by the characteristics of the particular technological layer. Hence, the business itself had a multi-layered character and was heavily influenced by the layered character

---

[201] See CompuServe (1995).

[202] Section 2.4 shows how this drastically changed in the course of convergence when make or buy decision all of a sudden became a crucial part of the value creation and in fact the overall business strategy of on-line services. Case Study 2-6 illustrates this development with the example of integration of Internet standard technology into the on-line service infrastructure with the example web browsers, which kicked off "the browser war". However, to better understand proprietary nature of and incompatibility of the system, it is an interesting fact that CompuServe traditionally used 36bit technology, which was not compatible at all to most 32bit hard and software components. Furthermore, the majority of host computers where NEC machines, which NEC phased out in the 1970s and CompuServe bought the entire stock of the remaining hardware and experience the expected replacement problems at the end of the product life cycle with these machines. Hence, the company was locked into its own technology decisions from the early days. This technological background of CompuServe is one of the crucial factors, which diminished possibilities of surviving Internet based competition (according to interviews with Bob Horton, Vice President Technology CompuServe, 19th of April 1997, Columbus and 2nd of October 1997, London and Dave Bezair, Director Product Management CompuServe, March 26th 1997, Columbus).

[203] See Porter (1985). Section 2.4 describes how convergence opened up a firm's boundaries to suppliers, who then became competitors. It will be argued that the new constellation exhibits similar patterns in the value system structure as the formerly integrated structures although in a highly virtualized cohesion.

of the system architecture (see Figure 2-25). The **hardware** layer was the only pure external component, where on-line services achieved compatibility to standard, off the shelf, end user products, respectively in microcomputers and modems.[204] The other layers can be summarized as **content** as the central layer, which was supported by **software** technology, **telecommunications** technology, and a **hosting** technological layer. Each of these layers can be seen as a multi-layered system as it is analyzed for the telecommunications or software layers.[205] For example, in the software layer, particular layers for the usage of the software package and the production of middleware, and for the strategic commercial software can be distinguished. The distinction of different layers is shaped by one's standpoint. Of course, a pure software vendor would emphasis the granularity of the software layer and might perceive aspects of content as being less important. To put things in perspective from an on-line service stand-point, cohesion is dominated by the customer needs and the underlying technological system architecture as illustrated in Figure 2-26:

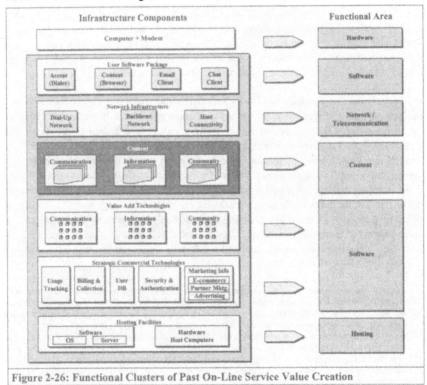

Figure 2-26: Functional Clusters of Past On-Line Service Value Creation

---

[204] Note that the French Minitel differs in this point as Minitel also incorporated proprietary usage of hardware. For additional information on the Minitel model see Derian (1999).

[205] See Bar / Borrus / Steinberg (1995), Gong / Srinagesh (1995) for the communications networks, Messerschmitt (1996) using the OSI model for the computer and software models and Werbach (1999) for the Internet.

Figure 2-26 shows how the **system infrastructure indicates clusters,** which describe very **different functional**[206] areas within an on-line service. This can be applied as a first indicator towards the goal of generating a general structure of distinct value chain components, which **explains the value creating logic of on-line services.** In addition to this technically driven derivation, the obvious **heterogeneity of the layers** exhibit a **strong internal homogeneity analytically supporting** the thesis **of this particular point.** Moreover, there are further business specific reasons, which foster the decision to differentiate the object in this way. **Each layer is distinct under five factors: the required skill sets and competencies; a key success measurement, which drives the business model; the underlying economics; a dominant industry on the supply side; and the underlying needs on the demand side.** Figure 2-27 outlines this for the different layers and factors:[207]

	REQUIRED COMPETENCY	KEY MEASURE	ECONOMICS	DOMINANT SUPPLIER	KEY NEEDS
Telecom. Network	• Network set up	**IP traffic** • Number of calls (average, peak) • Number of hours • Average throughput	• Economies of scale (supply side)	• Telecom industry • Hardware (modems)	• Agreed quality level regarding key measures
Hosting	• Load Management • Service responsiveness to application teams (e.g. webmasters)	**Processed data** • Throughput • Processes Requests	• Economies of scale (supply side)	• Telecom (connectivity) • Hardware (Host computers) • Software (OS, server software)	• Agreed quality level regarding key measures
Software	• SW Programming • Creativity • Development project management • Understanding complex needs	**Quality delivery in time** • Application performance and complexity • Update / development in time	• Economies of scale (supply and demand side) • Economies of scope (SW bundling)	• SW industry	• Agreed quality level regarding key measures
Content	• Content Programming • Creativity • Affinity • Community Management	**"Eyeball" traffic** • Number of users • Intensity of usage • Quality of user / usage	• Economies of scale (supply and demand side) • Economies of scope (demand and supply side)	• Media industry • Users itself	• Specificity • Actuality • Interaction
Devices [208]	• Ease of use • Hardware engineering; assembling	Units sold	• Economies of scale • Economies of scope (bundling)	Partner relation with PC and modem industry	• Easy assembling of hardware and on line service

Figure 2-27: Cross-Layer Analysis of Proprietary On-Line Service Layers

Figure 2-27 outlines the heterogeneity of the distinct layers. The table shows very significant heterogeneity in its comparison of the five layers. In other words, **the business of each layer differs at its fundamentals with different organizational cultures as the result.** The following example illustrates this high degree of diversity within an on-line service. If one con-

---

[206] Note that the "functional" does not refer to the traditional understanding of general functional areas in organization such as marketing, production, R & D etc. It refers to specific functions of the provision of an online service, which exhibit a clear distinct character.

[207] Note: The overview given in Figure 2-27 characterizes the view from an on-line service. Thus, obvious effects like the economies of scope in the telecommunications provider business are not mentioned and so forth. The reason is that on-line services could only capture scale effects by cost digression through increased traffic volumes.

[208] Devices were explicitly not part of past on-line services but they were a crucial component to deliver on-line services. Hence they appear in gray. In the course of the Internet the integration with the devices increasingly took place.

siders the content layer, one finds "content type of people," who understand aspects of certain contents. These people usually have a high community affinity and, hence, understand the underlying on-line needs of this community. For example, the announcement of a Nobel laureate may be good front content, which links into an academic community where users discuss the details. For business partner relationships, the content managers team up with content providers from the media industry. They need to build a business on top of a community by leveraging the strong supply side economies scale (e.g. flat rate inbound costs and variable outbound revenues) and the network effects of the community on the demand side. Thus, they mainly on increasing of the number of "eyeballs around".

Very different the requirements on the telecommunication side, serving the main need for connectivity, needs to provide extremely high quality levels where one tries to find the best telecommunications provider to handle a certain number of connections with a certain aggregate connect time with an average throughput. A typical business-to-business environment as compared to the consumer environment of the content layer.

People working in the software layer experience a very different kind of environment as well. It is required to specify complex user needs and to translate them into software programming. Technological issues dominate where software programming is the main activity and where creativity needs to be managed in projects under a high discipline in respects to quality, cost and time.

People serving in the hosting layer of the on-line industry monitor the inbound and outbound traffic of "their" computers and try to handle the load on these machines. It is rather secondary as it is content or applications that creates the heavy load on the host computers. Operators usually do not know if increased download activity is caused by a new software release or a chat event with Michael Jackson, especially if at the same time representatives of the content or software layer request the installation of a chat tool upgrade to make sure that Michael Jackson can include hyperlinks in his chat.

This short illustration basically illustrates what is expressed in Figure 2-27: Each layer is a different environment with a very different underlying logic, which leads to a different logic of value creation. Due to the high level of integration of the value chain, most of the exchange relationships were part of the internal value chain, whereas Case Study 2-4 will show that these internal markets[209] did not work efficiently at all in the case of CompuServe.

This analysis enables one to work out an **alternative view about the value creation of on-line services, which is able to consider the power of network effects (see 2.2.1). This view is different from the classical view of value chains from traditional media or telecommunications industries, which does not show the various horizontal and especially vertical network effects caused by the multi-layered constitution of this environment. Moreover, this does not consider the influence of the converging industries and their particularities. This factor becomes mission critical in a situation were convergence creates such a multi-layered environment and exhibits the network effects, which determine**

---

[209] See Miles / Snow (1993) for a discussion on internal markets and networked organizations.

the competitive position of involved players. 2.4 will show how convergence created such a situation and which structural implications occurred thereafter.

Figure 2-28 shows that the majority of the value creation resided within the firm value chain before convergence forces started to affect the industry. It is crucial to assume that **each layer includes traditional functional value chain components**, such as production, marketing or customer services as primary activities and administration as a supporting secondary activity, just as a generic value chain view would include them. This traditional understanding is implicitly assumed within each layer of the suggested value creation structure. At this time, the hardware layer was in fact not yet part of a firm's value chain. However, for consistency purposes, with the later framework it is reasonable to include this layer. As per definitionem (see above) a complete on-line service bundle includes this layer, which can be seen as virtual part of the on-line service system.

One the one hand, this analysis prepares one for understanding the impact on on-line services in the course of convergence and why this thesis suggest some similarities in the value creating layers of the on-line industry for the future Internet-based development. On the other hand, the structure is rich enough to comprehensively explain the direct value adding activities and network effects for the provision of a complete on-line service bundling. Figure 2-28 summarizes these findings and presents the complementary value chain layers and their exchange relationship:

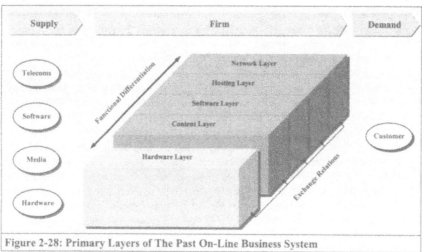

Figure 2-28: Primary Layers of The Past On-Line Business System

In this constellation the **player from the converging industries were the main suppliers.** From their standpoint **on-line services were just another channel to distribute their products and services** and as mentioned above **on-line services could capitalize on their gate keeper position in this channel. Both sides enjoyed their complementary positions and experienced mostly indirect supply chain network effects.**[210] Growth of the on-line services

---

[210] See Figure 2-13 and Economides (1996) who derives the phenomenon of indirect network effects in a typical supply chain, which he regards as a one-way network.

motivated the media companies to provide more content in an interactive format and tele-communication providers to enhance availability of a dial-in infrastructure, which was sup-plied to the network divisions of on-line service providers. In return consumers benefited from better content and higher density of dial-in POP's. These examples show the indirect network effects over vertical layers as outlined above. As long as the on-line service custom-ers were not considered direct customers by the converging industries, on-line services could maintain their strong bottleneck position. **2.4 will show how open standards opened the market for the former suppliers, which then changed their role to become competitors in their specific segments. Depending on their relative positioning, they became either competitors or partners. In any case, the compatibility and complementarity of compo-nents and the bundling of singular, contingent, components created two-way network relationships, which caused much larger direct network effects.**

The figure also shows that most of the **layers relevant for the creation of network effects were internalized in a vertically integrated structure.** Proprietary technology was identi-fied as the reason for it. With the presence of open Internet standards, growing connectivity and digitalization (see Figure 2-6) this space was opened up to competition and players from the respective supplier industries were able to enter this value creation area. This had far reaching effects on the entire setting because the forces behind these industries as well the logic of the converging environment were internalized in the competition of the on-line in-dustry. In this respect 2.4 will analyze the adjustments that accommodated with these changes, which resulted in a new setting for the on-line industry in the Internet environment. In order to provide the reader with an understanding regarding the economics and the struc-ture in this layered cohesion during this time of transition, Case Study 2-4 outlines data relat-ing to the German and United States business of CompuServe.

This case study highlights some figures of the CompuServe on-line service between early 1997 and the middle of 1999. It provides a good representation of the direct activities and value creation across the multiple layers of the business system. The insights will be derived from figures of the German and the United States holdings, which are summarized in Figure 2-29. The relative numbers represent the finan-cial resources allocated for direct activities in the respective layers. The remaining percentage was allo-cated for indirect activities. The first line shows the contribution of the on-line service properties to the overall CompuServe business in the given periods. The overall revenue / volume sold (subscriptions and usage hours based on several pricing plans) stayed constant over the analyzed period. The overhead costs are deducted in order to focus the primary levers of profits. The marketing and customer service expen-ditures were spent for the overall bundle and it is impossible to determine their contribution to the singu-lar layers. The necessary conjoint analysis, which could explain it, is not available. Therefore, it is impossible to allocate them to the distinct layers in a meaningful way. Instead they are outlined in an in-dependent line, although they implicitly contributed to each layer. The given data basically shows "how much was done" or "how many resources do we dedicate to" the respective layers.[211] The following will ask and answer questions about significant aspects of the data shown in Figure 2-29. This will illustrate economics, structure, and conduct of the industry and will ultimately give an impression for the business situation.

---

[211] See Esser / Ringlstetter (1991), pp. 523-525 for qualitative and quantitative ways of showing "how much is done" on distinct value chain areas and the according conceptual framework of the value chain.

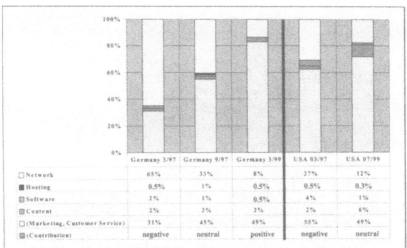

	Germany 3/97	Germany 9/97	Germany 3/99	USA 03/97	USA 07/99
☐ Network	65%	33%	8%	27%	12%
■ Hosting	0.5%	1%	0.5%	0.5%	0.3%
☐ Software	2%	1%	0.5%	4%	1%
☐ Content	2%	2%	2%	2%	6%
☐ (Marketing, Customer Service)	31%	45%	49%	55%	49%
☐ (Contribution)	negative	neutral	positive	negative	neutral

Figure 2-29: CompuServe's Direct Activities and Allocation of Value Along the Layers[212]

➔ What are the main activities?

The table shows that over the time direct activities in the functional area of **marketing and customer service**, basically acquiring and retaining customers, consumed more and more of the resources. This can be explained with one external factor and one internal factor: (a) the accelerated growth and competition of the market made it more resource consuming to compete[213] and (b) the increased technological complexity and instability of the product made it more difficult to gain and retain customers.[214] Obviously the **ownership of and / or access to customers was an increasingly crucial factor of the business model** and, furthermore, the **product quality directly influences the economics of the business.**

➔ In which layer does the value lie?

---

[212] Data according to CompuServe Germany internal data and interviews with Dave Bezair, Director of Product Management CompuServe, March 26th 1999, and Oscar Turner, Director Strategic Planning CompuServe, 27th of March 1997, Columbus. Usage devices were not a part of the product bundling integrated by the on-line services at this time. Hence, they are not shown in the data. Different attempts to integrate the device emerged in 1998 /1999. e.g. Alcatel shipping subsidized devices trying to capitalize the device desktop (1998, see interview with Benoit Raimbault, Marketing Manager Alcatel, 24th of July 1999, Paris and Case Study 1-1), Dell integrating the free "Dell Online" service into machines in the UK and Germany in 1999, AOL acquiring a manufacturer of a $200 PC and offering AOL including the PC in 1999 and finally the FREE PC model in 1999. At the same time CompuServe and MSN sponsor every purchase of a Gateway 2000 computer with $400, if the customers agrees to sign up for a three year subscription.

[213] See Allensbach 1997, CompuServe / W3B 1996, Datamonitor (1998), Yankee Group (1997), W3B (1996, 1997, 1998), KMPG / Yahoo! (1998) for an extensive overview of the competitive situation at this time.

[214] In late 1996 CompuServe rolled out the CompuServe 3.X client software generation. This technology incorporated the Microsoft Windows 95/NT Dial-Up Networking (DUN) and Internet Explorer 3.02 instead of CompuServe's old proprietary dialer (Cid) and Netscape 2.04. In particular the Windows DUN was an extremely unstable technological component, which failed to work even during installation processes. For these reasons, a higher percentage of the acquired customers failed to become a member during the on-line sign-up process – because they could not get on-line. As the dialer did not work reliably and stably, many customers left the service. This increased outlay for acquisition / retention, marketing, and customer service. See CompuServe (1997), CompuServe / Teleperformance (1997), CompuServe / Gartner Group (1997), (1998), and CompuServe (1998).

If one analyzes the dimension of the layers, one finds a surprising fact: that the telecommunications part of the business, based in the network layer, was by far the dominant part. Although on-line services used to be marketed with a rationale focusing on the content, the actual value added by this area is surprisingly small, it is similar to the hosting and software activities. This is the first key lesson from an economic standpoint. In the late 1990s, the value created was allocated by-and-large to the network layer. **Obviously in the late 1990s, telecommunication is the dominant factor in the economics of an on-line service bundling.** Therefore, the following will further analyze the network layer as it seems to be the strongest economic driver in the business of an on-line service bundling.

→ Why did the network layer decrease so much?

If one analyzes the difference in network spending between 1997 and 1999, a significant decrease becomes apparent. There are two main reasons for this. First is the general market trend of decreasing prices for network connectivity. New technologies in combination with rapidly increasing volumes in a scale driven business (see 2.4.2) drove down the costs for the overall market of network connectivity. As a consequence **the market rates for data telecommunications were constantly and drastically falling** as shown below in Figure 2-30:

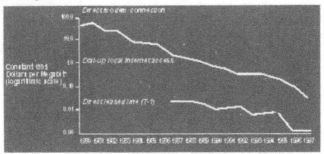

Figure 2-30: Decrease of Data Transmission Costs 1980-1997[215]

But the second aspect is specific for the vertical integration of CompuServe which is analyzed below.

→ Why are the resources spent on the network layer so extremely high in 1997 ?

CompuServe had a network division (CNS) and a on-line service division (CIS). Until the takeover of Worldcom and AOL in February 1998 CNS was the exclusive supplier of network capacity to CIS. Thus CNS was able to charge CIS high rates, as **the on-line service was completely locked-in to the internal, overpriced supply relationship.**[216] Furthermore, the data network business is driven by strong scale effects, which was constrained by the number of subscribers in the integrated bundle. Hence, as an integrated system **CompuServe could not realize scale effects** in the network business, such as the large telecommunication players could. An analysis of the rate structures reveals two reasons: While CIS charged the end customer $2.95 per minute for the service bundle it had to pay $2.40 just for the provision of the network by CNS in March 1997. At the same time, the market price was at $0.95, which shows the rent CNS captured with this specific lock-in. In fact, these distorted internal prices resulted in CNS being very profitable and CIS experiencing a large deficit. On the other hand, in March 1997 these

---

[215] Data based on a New York to Los Angeles connection shown in a logarithmic scale. Chart taken from the closing presentation of Regis McKenna at the BRIE conference "The Digital Economy in International Perspective - Common Construction or Regional Rivalry" held in Washington D.C. May 25th 1999.

[216] See Freese (1995) on internal pricing.

internal prices were the best leverage to improve the economics of CIS particularly in Germany and the other European properties. In September 1997 the prices were adjusted to $1.40 per minute in Germany, although, this still did not match the market price. However, at least CIS could attain a neutral financial result, which was the main goal at this time because a takeover was expected. For these reasons, the company tried to solve the internal disparities and set prices to result in a balance of sorts. This measurement dramatically shifted the distribution of value creation from CNS to CIS. The on-line service needed to allocate only 33% compared to 65% of its resources for primary activities to the network. While the prices and volumes to the end customer stayed constant the economics were significantly improved for CIS.[217]

➔ Why did the German network layer change so rapidly when compared to the US?

The comparison between the German and US data shows that the network layer exhibited much larger adjustments in the German market than in the US market. There are three main reasons:

First the **US market was already at a higher maturity stage**. The US market is by-and-large the leading market regarding overall development and stability of the Internet. The following key data regarding prices and volumes highlights this fact: The adoption rates of Internet access in late 1998 reached 18 % in the US and only 8% in Germany.[218] This shows that the German market was in a stage of the early adopters while the US market had already reached the early majority.[219] Even more drastic is the disparity with respect to usage rates illustrated with the example of the world's leading web site: in early 1999, www.yahoo.de had 2.5 million page views per day while the US property www.yahoo.com had 100 times more with 250 million page views per day.[220] Furthermore, the OECD (1999) puts this into perspective by pointing out that the overall monthly end customer usage costs for the Internet in the US is $41, which puts it at number ten of all OECD countries, while Germany ends up at place 28 with monthly costs of $70.

Second is the fact that CSI in the US managed a stable number of over 1 million customers at the time of this analysis, while Germany was managing approximately 250,000 customers. The US service had been growing since 1969 while the German property started its operations in 1993. The US supply relationship of CNS to CSI was simply more stabilized and **the US on-line service historically had a stronger bargaining position**.[221]

Third is the overall background of the underlying telecommunications industry. The US has had relatively stable competition for long time. The **FCC regulated the US interconnection rates and conditions** to the local loop and the local call pricing was set at a monthly flat rate. The telephone connection and data connection was provided in an environment of a stable and regulated competition, while all other markets were dominated by local telephone monopolies. The **WTO telecommunications negotiations** resulted in a global agreement to privatize this sector and to allow competition. Consequently, all other

---

[217] See also Case Study 2-5 for the unbundling of the two divisions.

[218] See KMPG / Yahoo (1998), GFK (1998), Allensbach (1998)., Margherio et. al (1997).

[219] See Kotler / Armstrong (1998).

[220] According to interviews with Matt Rightmire, Director Strategic Planning Yahoo!, 28th of April 1999, Santa Clara, Ned Taylor, Director Business Development Yahoo!, 6th of April 1999, Santa Clara, Peter Würtenberger, Managing Director Yahoo! Germany, 2nd of June 1999, Munich and Fabiola Aredondo, Vice President Yahoo! Europe, 4th of June 1999, London.

[221] According to interview with Dave Bezair, Director Product Management CompuServe, March 26th 1997, Columbus and internal insight of the author.

WTO countries introduced regulated competition in the late 1990s. Regulatory expertise for this sector did not exist and competition needed to be introduced quickly. Thus, voice and data network markets experienced turmoil. The on-line service network layer was hard hit by this new regulatory regime.[222] This is a powerful example of how the exogenous environment translates into the endogenous variables and shapes the size and structure of the on-line industry. While the regulatory regime in the US remained constant during the timeframe under analysis, the German market experienced deregulation and privatization in 1998, which resulted in an even more favorable condition for the German CompuServe unit than for the US unit. The Δ from 3/1997 to 3/1999 reveals a dramatic shift of the value creation in the German market. It exhibits the aggregation of consumer network traffic as an on-line service changed its role: **A cost driver in fact become a value driver.** This begs the question of how players with different positioning can capture the value created. The data shows how the positioning of consumer on-line services improved between 1997 and 1999. At the end of 1999 this position seems to erode again caused by new regulatory and competitive constellations. Therefore, the question for the upcoming decade of ubiquitous multimedia is which players from the media, telecommunications, hardware, software or finally the service packager area will be better off. Part III will lay out a host of scenarios in this respect.

→ Why did the US shift resources so rapidly in the content area?

In 1997 CompuServe had decided to implement a **new strategy for the on-line service division.** The strategy was code-named "CSi97". Its goal was to develop a pure content offering on a BYOA (bring your own access) strategy. Users had their own ISP and used solely the CompuServe content produced on Internet technology (html). This strategic shift has to be seen in the context of an upcoming acquisition. CompuServe at this time needed to develop a content based strategy detached from the network business because both units were expected to be separated (see Case Study 2-5). This shift was accelerated after the acquisition of the on-line service division by AOL, which shifted CompuServe onto the AOL technology platform (see below) and focused on CompuServe as an offering which was differentiated by content and branding. Therefore, resources for content programming needed to be increased.[223]

→ Why did the software and hosting resource shift so rapidly?

In the past CompuServe was a completely vertically integrated firm. As more and more of the business was shifted to the Internet and while Software companies tried to capture Internet client software markets **CompuServe could apply Microsoft technology** (browser, dialer) **for free** (Case Study 2-6). After the acquisition through AOL, the **technology platform shifted to AOL technologies, which left very little software activities in the CompuServe operations.** The platform shift to AOL also incorporated the hosting layer, which explains the decrease in this area (see also Case Study 2-5). The reason why the hosting activities increased in Germany (9/1997) was an attempt by the German subsidiary to develop some independent hosting operations.

→ What will happen to the layers?

This is a crucial question. The analysis above puts the network layer in the foreground. If the analysis focused on the early 199s, then the content layer would be much stronger. At that time business models for

---

[222] According to interviews with Peter Cowhey of UC San Diego, former advisor to the FCC WTO negotiations, 20th of April 1999, Berkeley and Konrad Hilbers, CEO CompuServe Europe and COO AOL Europe, 9th of February 1999, Munich. See also Case Study 2-1 for an example how regulation can rapidly increase market volumes, market structures and change business models.

[223] According to interview with Bob Kington, Vice President Content CompuServe, 18th of August 1997, Columbus.

content were generating larger contributions with different pricing schemes (see Figure 2-22) than was the case in the latter half of the 1990s. The content erosion was due to the ubiquitous availability of free content on the wold wide web. Media players in the future need to build new business models around the content in the world wide web and need to position themselves in a way to capture the value that is created around content. In the late 1990s, the value was captured by service providers (ISP's and OSP's) and telecommunication carriers. Free content and advertising revenues are not the sole solution for media players in the web. An analysis of the early 1990s would have also shown stronger value creation in the software layer as CompuServe was still able to sell its software for $29.99. Increasing on-line service competition in the mid 1990s terminated this business model. By the time under analysis, all services gave their software away for free as an acquisition tool. With the emergence of the world wide web, free browser and email software, the software layer shifted into value creation even more. It moved into a rather strategic position as the browser war (see Case Study 2-6) between Microsoft and Netscape showed drastically. The acquisition of Netscape by AOL and its strategic alliance with SUN supports this thesis. If the software layer is directly capitalized through the software itself or indirectly through their strategic application in business models leveraging the software ownership are issues for the future. Part III will discuss possible scenarios in this regard. Broadband deployment, mass market adoption, a variety of services, a variety access devices, and the positioning of the converging industrial sectors will be the central factors in this transition.

Case Study 2-4: Economics in the On-Line Service Industry Structure 1997-1999

Overall this case study provides an understanding for the **distribution of value creation** in the on-line service industry in the late 1990s. It shows how **internal and external markets, supply side scale effects, competitive bargaining, influences of national telecommunication deregulation, development cycles of different regional markets** and **industrial positioning** change the economics of the business. Furthermore, the underlying reasons generated understanding regarding how the economics can change in the future. An obvious intermediate result is that **strategic positioning within these layers will determine who captures the value**. Part III will use the model of the industry developed in part II and will derive an related set to equip players with the strategic tools to successfully play in the future on-line industry. The following will continue to analyze the structure of the industry in the late 1990s in order to generate a consistent and sustainable model of the industry.

Case Study 2-4 illustrates the friction within the industry, created by the effects of the first wave of convergence, caused by the emergence of the Internet, which is further analyzed in 2.4. [224]

2.4. The Shock of Convergence – Disintegration and Transition into the Internet Paradigm

The **effects that are currently discussed under the common headline of convergence mainly cause the adjustments in the institutional framework of on-line services.** Convergence affected the on-line industry at its very fundaments. **The explosive growth** of multimedia and e-commerce are the obvious results of it. **As a result, a small niche industry shifted**

---

[224] Similar friction affecting key business data can be expected for the broadband world as next major discontinuity of the on-line industry (see also part III and Case Study 3-6).

into the spotlight as one of the builders of the Internet, one of the most discussed in the second half of the 1990s. This shifted the competitive environment of the on-line industry:

> "In mid-1996, the environment for consumer on-line services (OSP's) was experiencing rapid change. In 1996 the on-line service companies were not only more competitors, but also more substitutes. The Internet and the World Wide Web had gained tremendous momentum and were threatening to steal much of the growth in the number of on-line users."(Murphy 1996:1)

> "The Internet had changed the competitive landscape and the on-line services found themselves in a battle on all fronts. The new competitors consisted of telephone and cable companies, content companies, Internet Service Providers (ISP's) and even Internet browser and search engine companies. The battle was emerging as one for control of the millions of potential customers' 'eyeballs' " (Murphy 1996:3)

In other words, the Internet as a new framework for on-line based business and not on-line business itself has to be considered as the truly new phenomenon, which needs to be analyzed. In this context 2.3 explains he past traditions of on-line services and analyzed the deeper structures. Section 2.4 is combines this understanding with the analysis of the current framework surrounding the industry, which was analyzed in 2.1. Particularly the analysis of the industrial environment discovered three crucial factors. Increasing **digitalization** and **connectivity** pulled the converging industries together and established the ICT constellation. The third factor is the emergence of **enhanced Internet standards**, which placed the on-line industry in the center of this **rapidly growing and changing environment** and resulted in the overwhelming **complexity and uncertainty as challenges for business strategy**. In this context, the next citation pinpoints that after 1996, it was clear that the Internet was the new basic platform for a new on-line service infrastructure.

> "Part of the technology debate seems already to be over. De facto standards have clearly emerged around such basic technologies as connectivity protocols. Most players recognize that these standard foundation technologies offer far more flexibility at lower cost than comparable non-standard options. After initially pursuing a nonstandard strategy, late entrants into the on-line services business such as Microsoft and AT&T have now performed a U-turn and endorsed standards. Similarly, Prodigy is currently migrating to a completely standard set of foundation technologies, while America Online is shifting its core network platform to a TCP/IP foundation." (Hagel / Bergsma / Dheer 1996:63)

Due to inferior forces of the on-line players, the laws of the large industries underpinning the Internet came to dominate the on-line area which ultimately resulted in an internalization of their laws of the market place as derived in 2.1.3. These laws of the market place can be summarized under four main categories. First it is a general trend of **virtualization of the value chain** (2.4.1) induced by the ICT area which particularly affects the on-line industry as it is obviously an information intense business. In addition to this general trend, which affects almost any industry to a certain degree, there are three specific factors induced by the converging industries. Their dominance as players in the on-line environment caused a transfer of their **economics of scale and scope** (2.4.2) into the on-line area. This growing competition leads to a growing **competitive advantage derived from specialized competencies** as the business becomes increasingly specialized (2.4.3). The fundamental inclusion of these factors now heavily determines the economic logic of the on-line industry and results in the accompanying structural changes in the respective market (2.4.4).[225]

2.4.1. Deconstruction of the Value Chain

The first – general - trend, which hit the on-line industry, was the virtualization of the value chain due to enhanced **information and communication technology** (ICT) and especially the particular effects of **open Internet technology standards,** which in turn drastically increased the possibilities to disintermediate the business system. In general, the following factors can be used to understand to which extent a business is affected by this **trend to virtualize the value chain:**[226]

- Degree of globalization and internationalization
- Time and costs intensity
- Flexibility and quality
- Speed of innovation, development life cycles
- Detachability of physical goods flow and according information flow

All the above factors significantly figure in on-line industry and hence exposed the value chain of the industry to the accompanying deconstructing forces. Concerning the fifth factor, the on-line industry deals with information goods[227] and causes the business system to be vulnerable to the virtualizing forces. In general the separation of the physical part from the information part of the value chain leads to the possibility to disconnect components of the value chain and has:

> "Implications for Competitive Advantage. Deconstructing a vertically integrated value chain does more than transform the structure of a business or an industry -- it alters the sources of competitive advantage. The new economics of information therefore not only present threats to established businesses but also represent a new set of opportunities. Every industry will shift according to its own dynamics, and those shifts will occur at different speeds and with varying intensity. No single set of predictions can be applied across the board, but some fundamental strategic implications of the changing economics of information can be drawn: Existing value chains will fragment into multiple businesses, each of which will have its own sources of competitive advantage. When individual functions having different economies of scale or scope are bundled together, the result is a compromise of each -- an averaging of the effects. When the bundles of functions are free to re-form as separate businesses, however, each can exploit its own sources of competitive advantage to the fullest." (Evans / Wurster 1997:78)

---

[225] See Dempsey et. al. (1998) who are discussing the new logic of the on-line environment. See also Wössner (1999b) who illustrates the trend from a standpoint of a player representing the media industry.

[226] See Wüthrich (1997), pp. 214-215 and Evans / Wurster (1997) who found the last aspect of disintermediation of physical goods and information goods which desegregates the physical and the virtual value chain.

[227] See Varian / Shapiro (1998) for a comprehensive discussion of the particularities of information goods.

Evans / Wurster discuss the deconstruction of disintermediated value chain components and **highlight the impact of information**. Their notion of industry specific economies of scale and scope with specific components clarifies the remaining significance of these traditional economic concepts and serves to connect it to notion of network economists and their thinking on network effects in value chains. In additional to the classical effects described in Industrial Economics, **bundling with superior economics exhibit competitive advantage because the complementarity of compatible components provides these bundling with network effects**:

> "Some new businesses will benefit from network economies of scale, which can give
> rise to monopolies (...) [by , C. G.] creating network economies of scale." (ibid.:80)

In this context, it needs to be added that ICT enables this desegregation and ubiquitous Internet standards take advantage of it in the case of the on-line industry. **Decreasing transaction costs** change the economics of institutional arrangements in a way which favors an organization of value adding processes in a market than in a hierarchical arrangement. Hence, technology, on the one hand, enables the change and, on the other hand, drives the change by affecting the logic of the economics.

Evans / Wurster (ibid.) note that the forces of deconstruction are industry specific. **In the case of the on-line industry, the primary good was information and the singular components of this information bundling could be easily unbundled in the presence of standards. Furthermore, the majority of the business processes are based on the organization of information.** One example of this is customer service data connected to the usage tracking and billing databases, which tracked the customer activities. Handling customer requests and supporting their issues created secondary value. The required product for this activity was information available in digital format and accessible with standard ICT. In fact, the customer support centers of both AOL and CompuServe in Europe are run by Bertelsmann units, which leveraged their database management and customer service know-how into the on-line service support area by interconnecting the connecting information systems. The units were able to learn the specifics of the product, during the general process of handling customer service requests, which is similar to frequent flyer programs and bookclubs handled in similar Bertelsmann units. Another example is telecommunications connections. The commercial interconnection between opening a data connection and billing on top of this activity was the tracking of this connection in the billing structure of a service provider. If one party connects the customer and maintains the technology to identify the customer (i.e. authentication technology) and to transfer the usage data into a third party billing structure, the third party can bill the service. In this case the "face the customer" can be either the network provider with a privately labeled bill of the service provider or it can also be the service provider billing the third party network sold under private label of the service provider. This is just one example of how the billing and the customer service processes can be deconstructed. In fact, more components that are analytic are in this process and, depending on the transaction costs, many of these components could be, and are, deconstructed into a virtual value creating process. The transaction costs are the parameter, which determines how many process components shall be disintermediated. The transaction costs are driven down by ICT.[228] In the cases of old legacy systems and proprietary EDI technology, transaction costs are much higher as these technological solutions have to be developed for a particular problem. This lead to the second factor, which specifically drove the virtualization in the on-line industry.

The **availability of open standard technology** creates a space for new players to organize the information of a single business process **for an increasing number of components in the system's infrastructure** and is required to establish on-line services (see Figure 2-25). The standardization of these components enables companies to **focus on their core competence and develop technology around this focus and interconnect the process, which is based on this competency, to business processes of other complementary components in a complete on-line service business system.** A dial-up network provider able to open its network to many parties who are able to interconnect their system infrastructure components is just such an example of this. By this, it is meant that most of the Internet service providers, who offer a global network, are just responsible for the billing, consumer marketing and customer service part of the business. The vast majority of them resell the global UUNet network as a wholesale service to smaller players who manage the end customer and collect the usage fees. The delta between their retail prices and UUNet wholesale conditions defines the margin for the billing, marketing, and customer service components for this virtual value chain. The availability of these open standards enables competitors to deconstruct the value chain underlying the proprietary on-line services to rebuild it in a virtual way.[229] An analysis of the particular system infrastructure components reveals that components in some areas are available on open standard technology, such as web server, site programming language (html), email and so forth. Others are not yet available in open technology, such as the commercially crucial components of billing and consistent user management. In all the areas where often superior open standard technology is available the vertically integrated, proprietary processes can be easily virtualized by external vendors. This availability of standard technology components to interconnect business processes explains why the on-line industry was so deeply affected by virtualization processes.

Next to these general effects of virtualization of the business processes, particularly driven by **Internet standard technology**, this virtualization **invited new competitors to enter the competition in the business process areas of their respective competencies.** Figure 2-28 shows that the converging industries are the main suppliers of on-line services. Enabled by available "off the shelf" technology and attracted by the outrageous growth rates **players from the convergence industries entered the on-line business with their own business operations. This occurred in a competitive and sometimes in a cooperative way combining existing complementarities.** In both cases, the entrance into the industry internalized the underlying economic logic of their respective industry and resulted in economies of scale and scope. Finally, the specialized competencies became a stronger source for competitive advantage.

---

[228] Picot / Reichwald (1994).

[229] See Case Study 2-5 which highlights a prominent showcase with AOL, CompuServe and Worldcom. The interoperability of the technology enabled the players to unbundle parts of the value creating layers and to assemble these components to larger aggregates to achieve better economies of scale while focusing on the core processes.

2.4.2. Economies of Scale and Scope

The economics of proprietary on-line services were driven by the size of their subscriber base. Potential economies of scale were aligned to this measure. **Especially the network externalities,** which create the network industry particular demand side economies of scale, were constrained by the growth measure. **Demand side economies of scope could be captured through the vertical value layers,** while they could not realize scope effects in other horizontal business as they operated solely in the on-line service business. **Due to their high vertical integration, they had to maintain value-adding processes in the areas of telecommunications, hosting, software, and content programming.** In order to provide, for example the network component, proprietary services had to purchase network capacity and build their own dial-up networks. Due to their proprietary technology they could not rely on open standard "off the shelf" software for their servers, value-adding back-end technologies, client software for content, email, chat, dialing and so forth. Part of their content was purchased from media companies, parts were their own productions, and a large portion was user-generated content within their communities.[230] The legacy systems of CompuServe relied on proprietary 36bit hardware technology, which was not compatible to state of the art standard computer technology.

In the presence of the openness of technology in the converging Internet arena, **new entrants can use superior supply side economies of scale by leveraging off their existing business structures.** They are able to horizontally enhance their value creating structures with on-line based business. This is a powerful aspect because all of the four **converging industries exhibit strong scale effects in their underlying economics.**[231] In fact media, telecommunications and software industries all exhibit enormous effects of economies of scale. they are faced with high initial fixed costs (for content creation, e. g. a Hollywood movie, a telecommunications network or the research and development of an operating system) and low marginal costs. This creates economics, which make businesses increasingly profitable with increasing volumes.[232] **Traditional on-line services could not capture these high volumes as the growth of each of the components was bound exclusively to number of subscribers.**

Telecom carriers face **large up front investments** in their technical infrastructure[233] and very **low variable costs** for the data and voice traffic, which they transport over this infrastructure. Therefore, with each additional unit sold, the business captures **increasing incremental contributions.**[234] The ownership of this infrastructure causes these economics.

---

[230] See Hagel Armstrong (1996, 1997).

[231] After the break-even is reached, these economics provide extremely high incremental profit margins (see e.g. Varian / Shapiro 1998, pp. 3-4 outlining the media industry standpoint).

[232] See Varian / Shapiro (1998).

[233] See Margherio et. al. (1997), p. A1 – 8 for an analysis.

[234] See Varian / MacKie-Mason (1994a, 1994b, 1994c) for the economics of provision of data networks and Varian / MacKie-Mason / Shenker (1996) for the perspective of network providers entering content editing function in their networks.

Renting this infrastructure is usually based on volume based variable prices for the renter.[235] Consequently, with decreasing incremental costs the owner of the infrastructure can better capture the profit than the renter, once a certain break-even point is reached.[236] Therefore, telecommunication firms, which own the network infrastructure, already operate a high level of voice and data traffic. For these players, Internet traffic is just a horizontal enhancement of the existing value chain (see 1.1.2). From their standpoint, additional usage created by on-line connections generates incremental revenues with a high contribution margin because their high volume telephone business already covers the enormous fixed costs and the variable costs for additional usage are small. An on-line service, which has to purchase or rent the telecommunications capacities, has to pay prices based on usage and experiences a linear increase of costs aligned to the usage increase. Therefore, the fixed costs are lower but the variable costs are higher for the renter. A network owner experiences heavily degreasing allocated costs for additional units. The renters economics are inferior over certain critical volumes. While traditional on-line services are only offering the Internet access to their subscriber base they are not able to compete on the network side with telecom carriers which utilize their existing business.[237] This explains why **economies of scale were driving unbundling forces of the network layer** for of on-line services. The following Case Study 2-5 will illustrate this unbundling and specialization process of the network and telecommunications layer.

In the past on-line services needed to establish their own data network infrastructure as part of the system infrastructure as it was described above. The market was an extremely specialized and global network without standardized products from telecommunications providers. Hence, the on-line services needed to set up their own POP's, the formation of which depended on the distribution of their subscriber base in order to make the applications available at local telecommunication rates. **The business was not the provision of a network but the provision of interactive on-line services**. A preliminary system infrastructure component was the provision of a network infrastructure with a sufficient number of POP's which resulted in a leading player like CompuServe offering more than 2.000 POP's spread all over the world with an emphasis on the main markets of North America and Europe. This network was almost exclusively established for the 5 million subscribers of the on-line service. Only one-third of the traffic was generated with cross-selling of the dial-up network to global firms. **In the course of convergence, data traffic on the global telecommunications networks was increasing at far higher rates than the voice traffic**. The strategic relevance of a strong position in the data business grew rapidly for large telecommunications carriers. The prices to provide data connectivity do follow strong cost digression. Hence, in order to be successful in the telecommunications business, it was crucial to be a big player. At the same time on-line services still had to maintain their own network infrastructure in the absence of global dial-up networks. In 1997 Worldcom was still a second tier telecommunications carrier but it planned to become a leading global player by rapidly entering and dominating the data traffic business. Its analysis revealed that the data traffic would grow by a factor 1.000 per year in the late 1990s. To become a leading

---

[235] See Gong / Srinagesh (1995). In order to give a quantitative impression about the massive cost digression for the network business the following list provides monthly charges for leased lines depending on the bandwidth: 0.0096 Mbps cost $1.150, 0.056 Mbps cost $1.300, 1.5 Mbps (T1) cost $7.000 and 45 Mbps (T2) cost $ 66.000 (data for the US long distance market in late 1997 according to Coffman / Odlyzko 1998, p. 23).

[236] See Economides / Himmelberg (1995), Varian / Shapiro (1998) and the further discussion of the economics of networks in 2.2.1.

[237] See also Zerdick (1999, eds.) pp. 94-96.

137

up networks. In 1997 Worldcom was still a second tier telecommunications carrier but it planned to become a leading global player by rapidly entering and dominating the data traffic business. Its analysis revealed that the data traffic would grow by a factor 1.000 per year in the late 1990s. To become a leading player would require the establishment of the needed infrastructure to dominate this market. At this time, the largest global networks were owned by UUNet, CompuServe and AOL. While UUNet was a pure business-to-business player CompuServe and AOL were mainly in the consumer business and maintained their network divisions CNS and ANS as necessary parts of the system infrastructure. The traffic in these networks was mainly constrained by the growth of the subscriber base of the on-line services. Thus, the cost digression effects were determined by and aligned to the consumer growth figures. In order to grow quickly and acquire the needed organization, Worldcom decided to buy UUNet. At the same time H & R Block, a large tax accounting firm, who owned CompuServe decided to sell it. Worldcom was interested in the network infrastructure and offered $ 1.2 billion for CompuServe. However, **Worldcom** considered itself primarily a **telecommunications carrier driven by carrying traffic and its supply side economies of scale**. It was clearly **positioned in the business market**. Hence, it was not interested in the on-line service, which is a pure consumer business. At the same time, AOL had massive network problems due to explosive growth of the subscriber base, which was not supported by its own network infrastructure. Furthermore, **AOL was clearly positioned as a firm playing in the consumer market, which was driven by the growth of the subscriber base and the demand side economies of scale**. It seemed logical that Worldcom would handle the traffic for AOL and CompuServe on its global network at agreed quality levels, which would then unbundle the network layer from the formerly integrated on-line service bundle as it is illustrated in Figure 2-31:

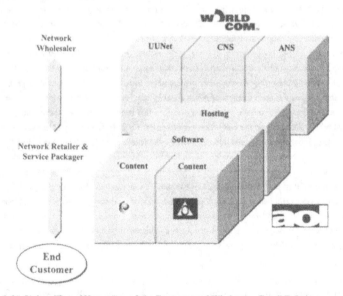

Figure 2-31: Unbundling of Networks and the Emergence of Wholesale - Retail Relations

As Worldcom would generate additional traffic through these other channels, it consequently could realize large economies of scale. Therefore, Worldcom offered AOL the CompuServe on-line service plus $250 million in exchange for the AOL network. Using this unified network infrastructure of UUNet, ANS and CNS could achieve their goal to grow in the data network business and generate a growth business

Worldcom at lower prices than before. Furthermore, the move of the CompuServe on-line service to the AOL technology platform gained stronger scale effects on the software and hosting layer as well. For these reasons, AOL released a new version – CompuServe 2000, which is completely based on AOL 4.0 technology. The brand and the content differentiate the two offerings. Hence, both players gain economies of scale and are able to focus on their business. Worldcom gains through aggregation of data traffic in the telecom business and AOL gains through the aggregation of "eyeball" traffic in the consumer media business. AOL manages its large subscriber base with its marketing competencies and strong commercial software in robust legacy systems. A three-way deal was designed and signed in December 1997. **As a result the network layer of the largest two on-line services was unbundled by the forces of convergence and since then consumers have been buying a virtual network bundling under the well-known consumer brands of AOL and CompuServe, both of which use the Worldcom network.**

Case Study 2-5: Unbundling of Networks into Wholesale and Retail Layers

The **hosting layer exhibits strong economies of scale as well.** This is also a valid statement for each singular component containing host connectivity, computer and server technology and for the labor costs of monitoring the load on the host computers. These factors favor the on-line services as they are in fact leading players with regards to the size of hosting operations. A large majority of the content and community functions, which are used by the players, are hosted within the on-line service hosting farms. As the on-line services control a large number of on-line users, they are able to consolidate an enormous part of data traffic within their host structures. Accessibility of servers for upgrades, enhancements, and adjustments is a crucial offering in this layer. This favors the internal creation of the components in the hosting layer and, therefore, the unbundling effects did not hit the traditional on-line industry significantly. Furthermore, many of the future business models will be built upon commercial applications. Powerful analysis of usage data will deliver customer profiles and patterns which will enable these models.[238] The respective data will be generated on this hosting level. Hence, in addition to scale effects it has high strategic relevance to retain this layer within internal structures.

Similar economics, as found in the telecommunications layer, are exhibited in content of the **media industries.** High fixed costs are attached to content creation and the incremental costs for additional copies are very low – in the case of digital transmission often almost zero. For example, the creation of a detailed analysis of certain stocks is expensive to create and once available in a digital format very inexpensive to reproduce. A Hollywood movie is an extreme example of this. The first copy carries costs of many millions. These costs are primarily sunk costs because they are largely irreversible . The owner of intellectual property rights to this content need to increase the usage volume to the maximum volume – the business model is driven by the volume. On-line services could generate variable revenues from external content at variable costs. The intellectual property right holder could capture a linear increase in revenues with a digressive costs for the product. With the content companies entering the business, the economics of the supplier were better than the economics of the on-line services, acting as the renters. This supported the **unbundling of large portions of external content.** An example is the Pathfinder package (Time, Sports Illustrated, People etc.) of Time Warner. This is a large cost driver at the content layer for CompuServe. This drove the on-line service

---

[238] See Hagel / Armstrong (1995, 1997a), Hagel / Rayport (1997b) and Hagel / Sacconaghi (1996).

to cancel the agreement and to link to the web-based Pathfinder domain. Whereas the former arrangement included royalties of $2.4 million per year, the later agreement leveraged the traffic going through the CompuServe network and the ability to link to the advertising supported the free Pathfinder.com site. This drove down the cost for content but also unbundled the content from the internal structures of the service and virtually added it to the overall package. These economics explain why on-line services emphasize the business around user generated content such as chats, personal homepages and forum messages, which are content generated at no costs.[239]

Software is commercially and legally **defined as content and it exhibits similar economics.**[240] The industry faces high research and development costs with low cost of reproduction and distribution.[241] For example, the costs for the first copy of a browser consume millions of dollars in development costs. The incremental costs for additional copies – for example via download distribution – are in the range of a few cents and are almost negligible. In the past, on-line services needed to develop their own software components because there no open standard technology was available. With the rise of the World Wide Web more and more components became available in compelling Internet technology. Website content of the WWW is only the most prominent one, email or dialing software and the communities of the Usenet newsgroups are other crucial components. **As a reaction to these functionally equivalent components based on Internet technology, on-line services either needed to enhance their proprietary software to integrate these Internet components into their services or need to bundle standard Internet software.** Some of the components, like strategic commercial software for billing and collection, were based on legacy systems and a **technology shift endangered mission critical business processes.** Hence, these components remained largely based on old technology. As software development was not the core business, other components of the software layer were likely to be replaced by standard components in order to **capture complementary synergies between on-line services and players from the software industry.** These bundlings could be captured by **acquisition** of players or **partnership** contracts or **purchases** at prices per software unit. The following Case Study 2-6 shows these different coordination mechanisms between market and hierarchy[242]:

In late 1994, CompuServe added an Internet gateway to its portfolio of content applications. In order to implement this, a network gateway needed to be set up and the user client software needed an upgrade with a web content client, a.k.a. browser. In early 1994 a company called Spyglass, which was a NCSA spin-off, offered commercial licenses of the first browser, branded "Mosaic", for an up front fee of $100,000 plus $5 per copy. The first commercial player marketing the Mosaic software was a Seattle

---

[239] For additional analysis of the economics of content see Varian (1995, 1997, 1998c, 1999a) and Varian / Shapiro (1998b).

[240] See Varian (1993) and Varian / Shapiro (1998b) for the economic perspective. See Haynes (1999) and Samuelson (1999) for the legal background analyzing the intellectual property rights and corresponding institutional aspects.

[241] This is different from the telecommunications industry, as the high initial costs of the media and software industry are sunk costs to an even greater extent. It is very hard to sell a half-done stock report or a third of the development of a browser whereas the physical assets of a tangible telecom network infrastructure carry tangible assets.

[242] See Williamson (1975, 1986, 1999, eds.).

based company called Spry, which was also developing ISP at this time. Spry offered Mosaic with a set of other Internet tools for email, newsgroups, and dial-up as "Internet in a Box" for $29.95. By the end of 1994, approximately. 10 browsers were available on the market [243] Netscape and Spry were early players in this market. Both companies were potential allies or takeover targets of the on-line services, since the services needed to gain access to Internet software components and competencies. After negotiations with several players, including Netscape, CompuServe decided to acquire Spry in March 1995. CompuServe did not further develop this business but used the browser component for the client software version 1.4, which enabled users to view WWW content in addition to proprietary CompuServe content. Besides integrating the software, CompuServe did not intend to allocate further resources in the development of the browser and ISP business of Spry. As CompuServe did not fuel the development of the Spry browser it became an inferior product after the competing Netscape browser was upgraded to Netscape version 2 in October 1995. In 1996, CompuServe included Netscape 2.0 into the CompuServe version 2.1. Netscape was paid on a royalty basis per CompuServe subscriber. The institutional arrangement for the browser shifted from a hierarchical model to a market based model. Netscape could capture better economies of scale by distributing a browser to a wide audience of Internet users than CompuServe could, as it was was developing the content software for just its the own limited user base. In addition, the specific competencies and focus of Netscape resulted in a better product compared to the software of a typical on-line service with diversified operations in functionally different layers (see Figure 2-26). CompuServe did not plan to further develop their own Mosaic software, as the company decided that it was not in the software business – it should keep its focus on supplying on-line services in a complete package. The browser part of this package was not developed internally anymore in the presence of available standard technology. This was a crucial milestone for the unbundling of a proprietary product. When Microsoft decided to enter the browser software market in 1995, Netscape suddenly experienced fierce competition. "In early 1996, Microsoft had developed a number of strange bedfellows. While still considering itself a competitor to on-line services [though its MSN on-line service, C. G.], it has also become collaborator with AOL and CompuServe. (...) As a result Microsoft had agreed to place their icons on the windows screen. In return, AOL and CompuServe made Microsoft's browser the standard browser from their proprietary services, relegating Netscape and their own browsers to optional." (Murphy 1996:13) As indicated by Murphy, CompuServe could leverage off this competition, with Microsoft as powerful and determined later comer. Microsoft is in a complementary vertical layer, so CompuServe signed a contract with it to include its Internet Explorer software IE 3, and later IE 4, into the next CompuServe 3.X versions, which were to be shipped from the second half of 1996 until early 1999. CompuServe did not pay any money for this software component but automatically opened market access to on-line users of browser software. In exchange, it received Microsoft's commitment to integrate CompuServe in the OEM (OSR) version of Windows, which meant that almost any personal computer had a pre-installed CompuServe client software bundled with the operating system. Both players had to combine, in order to capture the vertical network externalities. Microsoft connected the CompuServe client software with virtually every client device, which represents the potential market volume. CompuServe exclusively connected Microsoft's client software to the largest on-line user base at this time. The actual agreements were made in late 1995 and over the course of 1996. At this time, CompuServe was still the leading player in the Internet industry and the deal with Microsoft was a significant signal to the entire Internet community.[244] AOL switched to

---

[243] See Kwak (1998), p.3.

[244] In fact, CompuServe agreed to use more than just the client software component as part of the new system infrastructure for Internet based on-line services such as server technology, content management, email

MS for the same reasons in March 1996. Consequently, the two leading players chose cooperation based on the exchange of complementary assets over internal development and purchase of market penetration. Over time the deal proved to be successful. The bundling with the PC operating system was the by far largest distribution channel for CompuServe and contributed far above 10% of new subscriber acquisitions. Microsoft could cut its competitors off from the largest two distribution channels for browsers. In addition, Microsoft was a able to cut distribution deals with a host of ISP's[245] and to bundle the Internet Explorer browser to the windows operating system. By dominating the sole usage device and the majority of access providers, Microsoft was able to control the crucial market channel for browser software. Microsoft was able to break the dominant position of Netscape and become leader in this market or as analyst Oliver Seidman (1997) stated already in March 1997: "The browser wars are over. Microsoft won."

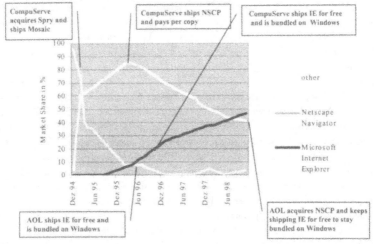

Figure 2-32: Browser Market Share and the Conduct of On-Line Services in the Browser War[246]
This example has several implications, which are rooted in the underlying industry structure. First it shows the superior economies of scale of a specialized and focused software player like Netscape compared to a packager like CompuServe. Second it shows the example of Microsoft and their PC desktop operating system monopoly have powerful vertical network effects, or in other words – scope effects, which dominate the multi-layered industry. Third, it shows how a vertically integrated player has to compete with the competencies of specialized players on the singular components of horizontal layers. It also shows the rapid changes in the coordination of the value creation between different institutional arrangements necessitated by the rapidly changing environment.

Epilog: In early 1999 AOL took over Netscape in an attempt to challenge Microsoft and the Wintel paradigm in an alliance with Sun Microsystems (see Zaret / Meeks 1999). In an autoreply Oliver Seidman notes: "Almost exactly two years ago I wrote: "The so-called browser wars are over. Microsoft won." I got quite a bit of venomous e-mail over that! But being right is often the best revenge. But while Micro-

---

boxes, dialer and many others. These aspects are left out at this case in order to show the significant aspects for the browser market.

[245] See Netaction (1997).

[246] Study by the author with additional information from Murphy (1996), Kwak (1998), Bamford (1997) and Gartner Group (1997l).

soft is winning the browser war, and while I find IE 5 superior to Netscape's latest Navigator browser, I'm pleased to say that the browser wars are back on." (Seidman 1999b).

Case Study 2-6: Scale & Scope Effects, Competencies, Make or Buy Decisions and the Role of On-Line Services in the Browser War

This example shows several implications which are rooted in the underlying industry structure from the perspective of the centrally located software layer of the industry. First it showed the **superior economies of scale of a specialized players in respect to the different vertical layers** with the example of the software player Netscape who was compared to a vertical packager like CompuServe. Second **the example of Microsoft showed how powerful vertical network effects, or in other words scope effects, dominate the multi-layered industry.** Third it showed how **a vertically integrated player has to compete with the competencies of specialized players regarding singular components on each horizontal layer.** It also showed the **rapid changes** in the coordination of the value creation between different institutional arrangements caused by the rapidly changing environment. The following will further analyze these effects while Case Study 2-6 is a good illustrative example of many of the effects.

Case Study 2-6 shows how Microsoft used its **economies of scope** and respectively the vertical network effect to **leverage the dominance** of their the PC operating system monopoly in a way to generate competitive advantage in vertically related markets. The **multi-layered environment fosters these scope effects** but due to the nature of the new types of players in the on-line industries, which usually have widespread activities, economies scope are becoming a crucial factor to an even greater extent. As described above the **convergence of technologies** was accompanied by a **convergence of needs** as well. Therefore, a source for competitive advantage is the potential and the ability to **leverage synergies** between different business activities. An analysis of the products as well as the needs reveals that many of on-line based business activities are in a highly complementary relationship to other businesses of the converging industries and ideal to use scope effects. Consequently, **bundling strategies for these complementary components become a main source for competitive advantages.**[247] For example, telecommunication providers can complement their telephony business by cross selling Internet access to existing customers on the monthly bill or with the existing customer service hotlines. This expands the revenues and general retention rates of the networked businesses. This new business in return generates additional traffic for the backbone networks and causes low variable costs and high incremental contributions as described above. Media companies promote their virtual entities on the web within their traditional platforms such as print products or TV and radio shows and vice versa, which keeps the users within their networks. The software industry has an especially strong tradition of bundling different products together. It is clear fact most of the web software components owe a significant portion of their adoption rates by being bundled with complementary software. The Windows operating system and the bundled add-ons, like the browser described in the example above, are a prominent example for this strategy.[248] Consequently, it is a crucial part of the logic of the on-line

---

[247] See also Zerdick (1999, eds.), 179, 206-213 who emphasizes the importance to develop complementary components system bundlings in the Internet economy.

[248] See SPA (1999).

area to be able to **benefit from these complex connections of the multi-layered industry constellation.** These composite goods bundle components into a joint system and result in strong direct network effects. Some players can also generate indirect network effects by utilizing existing primary and secondary value chain processes in lateral areas of their business and generate indirect network effects by creating higher demand of these value chain components. Examples are the mutual use of customer support processes as primary activity or individual business units using the standard accounting services delivered by corporate headquarters.

On-line services were not able to capture scope effects due to low horizontal integration and a non-existing portfolio of horizontal markets as the players from the converging industries. Their scope effects could have been generated by the high vertical integration but on each of these vertical layers, they were playing in fields where they needed to compete with the scale economics of large players. This supported the **unbundling forces of the vertical layers.** Moreover, they had to compete with the particular competencies of the respective vertical players, which will be analyzed in subsection 2.4.3.

2.4.3. Competency based Competition

Past on-line services closed their entire value system through their proprietary technology. In such a strategy, the competing players needed to internally develop skills in all areas of value creation of on-line services. These particular areas required a heterogeneous set of skills as discussed above (see Figure 2-27). Proprietary on-line services were running their own telecommunications dial up and backbone networks, data hosting center with operations units, software development teams[249], huge call centers for customer service, as well as content acquisition and content editing groups. This implies the requirement of a **wide spectrum of competencies** for the different necessary practices and the **ability to bundle** them to a value system in order **to provide successfully an on-line service.**

With the presence of a growing number of entrants into the market, the players have had to become more competitive and have needed to master their business at higher professional levels with increasing specialization in the mission critical processes. The development of specialized competencies becomes of growing importance. This basic principle was true for the on-line industry.

2.3 shows the **complexity and heterogeneity of components and underlying skillsets,** which are required to package a complete on-line service bundling. Open Internet standards breached the boundaries of proprietary on-line services and consequently initiated competition with new players with a more focused set of competencies. Considering the components, which are required to establish a complete on-line service experience (see Figure 2-25), each of them defined a potential market place for new entrants. In fact a **rapidly growing number of players entered the competition.**

New competitors could either tap the scale driven experience curve effects of large players or focus their resources on a niche and quickly develop specialized competencies, often by

---

[249] e. g. for client software, server software, content management systems, MIS etc.

imitating proprietary on-line service components like chat, message threads, or file up-load/download area. In contrast, the on-line services lacked the need to develop excellent skills in the all areas, as this was not required in the absence of competition in the proprietary past. They were rather focusing on supplying a package, the goal of which was to provide an encompassing, compelling user experience. As convergence and the Internet standards created this new competitive environment, on-line services were vulnerable to entrants with virtually any system component available in standard technology. In the majority of processes under-lying the system components, on-line services maintained operations but on much smaller scale than players from the respective vertical layer. They could not go as far down the learn-ing curve and experienced inferior competencies. In the presence of growing competition, much of their skill set turned out not to be competitive. This was a potential threat to virtually any component where competitors were able to enter the competition due to standardization.

With respect to superior competencies, **two types of players** have to be distinguished. **Large players from converging industries** could attack them with components following the eco-nomics supporting large aggregates such as content clients, email clients, and dialer client software, dial-up networks, news content. Equally, they have problems of keeping track of competition in specialized components, which are supplied by relatively small players to smaller and focused markets such as computing communities, email, spell check software and so forth. These **small, mostly start up players were usually based on entrepreneurial con-cepts,** which have small up front investments and which exhibit demand side economies of scale like the prominent network driven example of the ICQ community. Focused, flexible, and specialized players have better opportunities to deliver superior value to the customer in these markets. In addition to the availability of alternative standard technology components, **consumers suddenly had choices** between competing products. Consequently, each of the new players was taking a piece of pie away from the on-line services. Providing excellent quality and being competitive in pricing in each component became crucial to remain success-ful for the on-line services. However, the activities of on-line services were so widespread and heterogeneous they had to withstand fierce competition of players with further developed spe-cific competencies. This is true for the rather mass market oriented components as well as specialized components for small niche segments. Overall, it can be concluded that **large players from the converging industries and the enormous underlying forces pushing this convergence, account for the vertical unbundling, while the small niche players fostered the unbundling processes of singular components in the horizontal layers.**

On-line services not only exhibit patterns, which resulted in weaknesses caused by their skill set. As it was stated above, **Internet technology is still lacks crucial components of a strategic commercial system infrastructure, such** as billing, tracking, security, and authen-tication. In this area, on-line services can protect their business models and explains why they are able to maintain subscription based and transaction based revenue streams –still a major difference from pure Internet players. The other unique and difficult to imitate aspect of on-line services is their **ability to bundle a package of extremely heterogeneous and complex components,** such as data telecommunications networks, hosting facilities, client technology and multimedia content production into a viable commercial package. They were not excel-lent in any single component but they knew how to assemble all of them to a complex bundle of heterogeneous components in a way, which is able to generate an overall positive user experience as opposed to just offering "the fastest and cheapest email". The strong position of AOL is based on an easy-to-use, consistent and integrated user experience of the dominant on-line applications: dial-in connecting, email, chat, community organization and browsing. AOL is able to provide this, billed on one account and delivered on a single installation CD – the one stop shop for mass consumers who are not technically savvy. The reduction of technical complexity into a consistent intuitive mass market product is the real value driver of AOL. This asset combined with the large community as a market driven asset results in a solid market position, which can be translated into bargaining power with most market participants. **On-line services derive these competencies from a significant learning curve of almost two decades invested in understanding what makes a complete on-line user experience superior.** This requires an understanding of system infrastructure components at all layers. The completeness of this competency can only be generated with a high degree of vertical integration, which is hard to imitate. As a result, the most sustainable differentiating competency is the integration of all layers and the bundling competence combined with a clear understanding of the complex set of user needs. Most of the large entrants did not succeed in offering consumer bundles with a complex set of components. AT&T was not able to grow its consumer ISP Worldnet to a leadership position, neither did Microsoft succeed with MSN and MSN.com, or as analyst Oliver Seidman noted in respect to the threat of these players to AOL regarding their insufficient competencies:

> "Yes, I know AT&T is marketing WorldNet a little more now, but it's too little too late. Sure, they'll attract some customers, but they missed the window. To put this into some perspective, at the end of September 1997, WorldNet had 963,000 subscribers, a year later at the end of September 1998, it had added only 20% (or 220,000) to come in at around 1.2 million subscribers. Over the same period, AOL added an additional FOUR MILLION accounts, or more than 18 times as many subscribers as WorldNet added.
>
> Even if AT&T were to acquire Microsoft's MSN dial-up subscriber base (which is anywhere from 1 million to 2.5 million subscribers, depending on who you talk to) it would not have significant momentum to stem the tide of AOL." (Seidman 1999a)

A media player like Time Warner with "Pathfinder" exhibits the same inability. Bertelsmann could only grow successful units in joint ventures of original players with AOL and Lycos. Independently developed ventures positioned in the content layer could not break though in the late 1990s. A lack of **understanding of the particularities of the interactive on-line medium, the complex technological prerequisites and the underlying needs structures** are the obvious reasons. **These competencies are not easy to imitate** in a large scale. Different from the large players, who try to transfer their traditional competencies to the on-line area and fail with this strategy, **small niche players with a clear customer focus and a precisely defined need are able to develop components with a higher excellence.** The large on-line services have to spread their attention among many needs and components. Specialized chat and community services like (now AOL's) ICQ and the (now AOL) Instant Messenger's buddy list represent these type of small players.

Furthermore, **on-line services were acting under stable business models, which provide solid revenue streams. This is a strategic advantage which many small Internet start ups** do not enjoy. Venture capital and the stock market are hedging against this disadvantage in many cases but the lack of a solid business model is a fundamental problem to creating an enduring business. For this reason, many start ups fail or in case of success are acquired by large players either from the converging industries or AOL, which has to be seen as a very unique type of on-line service that can leverage their dominant market position. Further discussion of the strategic position of players within the market structure modeled in this second part and the according implications will be conducted in the third part.

This characterizes the situation, which was created by convergence and the World Wide Web. The environment was growing but overall the on-line services were fated to loose parts of their service bundling which were broken out of the formerly vertically and horizontally integrated service bundling by a host of competitors. Depending on the competitive behavior these external components may be integrated through a market mechanism. This is the case with an access network which is purchased from wholesale ISP's. Alternatively, strategic cooperation may be the integrator, such as the bundling of web browsers with the client software package. Finally, strategic acquisitions may be the integrator, such as with the community tool of the instant messenger / buddy list by AOL. Subsection 2.4.4 is summarizes these effects

2.4.4. The Results: Unbundling, Differentiation and Explosive Growth

To summarize, the exogenous parameters translated into the internal structure and shaped the laws and mechanisms of the industry. In addition to the analysis of the exogenous parameters conducted in 2.1 the following summarizes the internal aspects of the black box (see Figure 2-1). The **main drivers in the exogenous environment** were the growing connectivity and digitalization, which created the new information and communication technology sector (ICT). The rise of open Internet standards enabled players from the ICT area to contribute components of on-line services. The overwhelming forces driving these players pulled the on-line industry into the center of this new sector as described in the following thesis:

> The digital convergence and increasing connectivity combined with the emergence of Internet standard technology pulled the on-line industry into the **Internet paradigm** of on-line services. This implies that the actual new phenomenon is not the existence of on-line services but is the existence of on-line services in a standardized and rapidly growing open system which is based on the ICT area as new industrial sector.

As the industry shifted, the respective **laws of the convergence industries** playing in the ICT sector **were internalized** as new underlying laws of the marketplace. Their **economies of scale** defined the new cost structures. The network character of the services in addition created demand side economies of scale, or in other terms, network externalities as introduced in 2.2.1. Considering the multi-layered environment additional **network effects** were created between the vertically related value layers. These effects can also referred to as **economies of scope** as it is defined in Figure 2-33. They were at first created between the vertically related telecommunications networks, media content, software, hardware and hosting layers. These were then bundled into a system serving one customer with a composite system, which resulted in direct network effects. In addition, some players could realize scope effects with between the vertically related value layers. These effects can also referred to as **economies of scope** as it is defined in Figure 2-33. They were at first created between the vertically related telecommunications networks, media content, software, hardware and hosting layers. These were then bundled into a system serving one customer with a composite system, which resulted in direct network effects. In addition, some players could realize scope effects with lateral functions on primary and secondary value chain activities creating indirect network effects. The growing competition created by large and small entrants forces players to master their processes on a higher level of excellence, which in turn requires the cultivation of special competencies. Players need to be focused. The overall competitiveness results in higher degrees of professionalization and specialization. Aside from these three specific trends, the general trend of **virtualization of the value chain,** which is enabled by the ICT area and specifically the Internet standards, influences the information intense on-line industry strongly. Figure 2-33 illustrates how the changed external setting affected the on-line industry in such a way so that these new factors were internalized as endogenous variables of the industry system which is heavily influenced by network externalities. The large cube at the bottom represents the industry system.

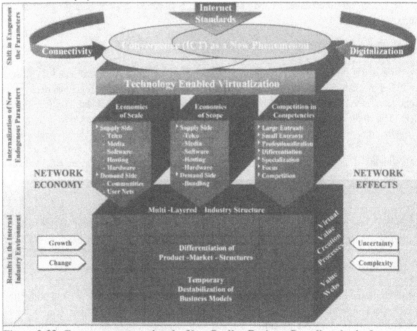

Figure 2-33: Convergence translated a New On-line Business Paradigm in the Internet

The following effects on the industry become evident if one examines the on-line industry from the suggested genuine perspective. This new setting causes them. First among the effects is the **enormous growth and speed of change as well as increased complexity and uncertainty** caused by the large number of new players. This affects the entire cohesion as well as the singular components, which are virtually hidden in the large cube representing the on-line industry. This will be further analyzed with its microstructures in 2.5. These general charac-

Second is the **unbundling** of formerly joint components. Large players from the convergence industries were dominating the economic laws of the market place which was massively adjusting the economies in respect to the entrants scale advantages and further developed competencies as illustrated in Case Study 2-5. In addition, singular superior components of focused start up players had the same effect in niche components. Large aggregates were unbundled from the pressure of the forces typical of economies of scale and small components were unbundled by the focused competencies of specialized players who could access demand side economies of scale after the break even of a certain critical mass. The structure of the on-line area has to be seen as a **multi-layered industry**. Although open standards and ICT enable this trend, it certainly has to be seen as a different trend than the virtualization of the value chain. It was much more an effect described in typical industrial economics rather than a virtualization trend driven by decreased transaction costs. The **network effect** unfolds its power under to the open standard of all components and results in the interoperability of network components. For these reasons, it seems sensible to define this process as an unbundling process or deconstruction of the value system and the assemblage of a new cohesion. The area largely follows the requirements of a **network industry**. This multi-layered aspect of the industry is represented in the topside of the industry system.

Third, the technology and decreasing transaction costs enabled players to organize **business processes at higher levels of virtualization** and focus on the core competencies by establishing **value webs**. This has to be seen as a different aspect than the unbundling process described above. The unbundling process was driven by economies of scale and network effects, whereas the virtualization of certain business processes detaches formerly joint business process components into several components, which are organized by more focused units, while the ICT minimizes the transaction costs between these organizational units. The examples given were (a) the organization of accounting as an overhead function, which focused an accounting unit at headquarters or (b) the organization of customer support by a specialized customer service unit. These virtualization aspects are represented in the right side of the industry system.

Fourth, overall **competitive behavior changed fundamentally**. Additional players entered the field. **Former suppliers** from converging industries changed roles and **became competitors or partners** of the on-line services in the area of their respective components. This resulted in the **destabilization of formerly solid business models and role definitions among the players**. Business guidelines like the ROI temporary lost their strength as valid parameters as Andy Grove casually highlighted in August 1997:

> "What's my return on investment in e-commerce? Are you crazy? This is Columbus in the New World. What was his ROI?" (Andy Grove)[250]

This new structure has widespread implications for the definition of the industry. The **deconstructed industry structure** creates enormous **difficulties for singular players to integrate larger chunks of the industry system**. Consequently, the players need to **rebuild complete value chains with complementary components**. The host of new players creates a large

---

[250] Andy Grove (Chairman of Intel) cited after Zenith (1999).

portfolio of interconnected markets within this new setting, which translates into a **differenti-ated product-market structure** on each layer. Many of these markets are transforming into mass markets while others become niche markets. Due to the fundamentally different charac-ters of each layer, players are not able to participate in all fields but must concentrate on areas of their respective competencies. Consequently, they have to **interconnect businesses with other players to integrated systems**. The rapid speed of change forces the redefinition of the marketplaces and is not stable over time. This is a fundamental difference to the other niche markets with highly integrated players and very stable laws and structures. The singular com-ponents exchanged over these markets are needed to assemble a complete on-line service. As opposed to the past, the on-line industry is no longer a closed system. The interconnection of these markets establishes the on-line industry as a virtual system of other industries, which leads to the following thesis:

> The on-line industry is a virtual industry, which is constituted of a networked system of composite components supplied by players from several industries with the conver-gence industries accounting for a majority of components.

This thesis becomes crucial if one is to understand that the on-line industry itself follows dif-ferent rules than the industries, which constitute the on-line industry. While analysis of the past on-line service traditions revealed unique particularities, the analysis of the on-line in-dustry in the Internet paradigm (2.5) shows that these particularities were retained to a large extent and even extended in some aspects.

Overall, one can summarize that all of these structural aspects of the industry indicate rapid change and instability. Therefore it seems reasonable to conclude that the **industry is not yet in equilibrium** . With the presence of network externalities in numerous of the industry com-ponents, the theory of **network economics predicts system immanent instability**. This leads to the conclusion that temporal stability in some areas of components does not lead to a sus-tainable stability, and indicates the general aspects of **change and uncertainty as fundamen-tal characteristics of the on-line industry**.

2.5. On-Line Industry in the Internet Paradigm – Reinvention of the Past

Why is this section called the reinvention of the past? The fundamental point argued in this work is that the current discussions examining the Internet overlook the real business concept of on-line services as they are not able to see the forest, while looking at the trees of techno-logical clutter. Although this business can be described in a simple manner: hook up people on-line and provide them with interactive services that they request. No installation and as-sembly hassle of compatible – and tested and mature – open standard components. Everyone knows that this is not the case and everyone complains about it. For these reasons 2.3 outlined the "good old days of on-line services". This picture will guide the direction.

The current common perception seems able to see the distinct competitions in the Inter-net framework and although nobody refutes that they are all somehow interconnected, observers fail to see the overall cohesion of components that ultimately shape the com-plete system.

In order to clarify this point, an analogy helps. One can imagine the "good old days" of telephone. There was one firm horizontally and vertically integrated in a giant natural monopoly. In the absence of open standards and shared resources, the investment in development and deployment of a telephone system where simply too large to lead to a competitive market. On these grounds AT&T developed a closed system architecture with hardware components for the end user (telephones), networks with switches and pipes and a large "back-end" for the provision of service, pricing and billing. After the decision to break-up this "industrial monster" and allow competition, the system became unbundled. Lucent was the supplier of hardware, the RBOC's managed the customer and handled the local calls, AT&T handled the long distance calls and still sold some end user hardware and so forth. The former suppliers could forward-integrate into former monopoly areas, new start-up player could provide long distance service (Sprint, MCI) and data services (CompuServe or IBM-net) or provide all sorts of other components. People still pick up their phone to call grandma on her birthday, however the difference today is that it is probably not one but several dozen companies involved in getting this call through.

Structurally this is exactly what happened to the on-line industry as it was described in 2.4. People still dial a service provider number with a device to get on-line and check their email, chat with others, read the latest Reuters news, or place their holiday pictures on their personal homepage. From an industrial perspective the product system became unbundled and former suppliers became competitors and a host of new competitors entered the arena. Users get their computer, modem, access connectivity, software, communications services, content, communities, and commercial offerings from a large variety of vendors.

Different from the telephone industry where public policy caused this shift, the on-line industry was shifted by technological discontinuity. However, the structural results are the same. On the other hand, different from the telephone industry the on-line services exhibit larger complexity and involve players from distinctly separate industries. In the past users received their products and services in a consistent bundle from a single source vendor such as CompuServe, just adding a standard PC and modem. Because of convergence, today there are unbundled components so customers have the pain of choice with respect to the components, and then the pain of assembling them. Unfortunately the technology is by-and-large immature and not a turnkey solution. Assembling these components tends to be difficult for the users. The quality and stability of services is not as high as it used to be, but because of much nicer user interfaces and a much larger variety of offerings customers bear with it.

However, common sense tells us that this is not a natural state and just a symptom of the immaturity of the industry. Would a mass market accept purchasing a complex product, like a car with components that need to be assembled? Would there be a business for standard car parts such as engines, bodies, brakes and a service industry for assembly and customization to reduce the complexity for the customer. The turnkey solution of cars has great value. Although turnkey solutions have been promised, so far the compatibility of the components is not sufficient.

Along these line part III will outline the forces in the industry which will lead to in increasing concentration of product components and firms and hence to an integrated solution as in the past – just on a new technological paradigm. The forces of economics, customer needs and innovation of entrepreneurs will bring this market to a higher level of maturity.

Arguing from this standpoint, the following will present the constitution of the on-line industry in the Internet paradigm. Subsection 2.5.1 will describe how the openness of the new technological paradigm of Internet technology establishes an industry consisting of vertically located horizontal layers. In this structure, a host of players bundle components to a virtually established on-line service offering. This lays out the structures, which establish a virtual business system provide a variety of on-line service offerings in a shared business network. Based on these findings subsection 2.5.2 derives a multi-layered model for the application in the on-line industry.

2.5.1. The Multi Layer Business System – The New On-Line Business Paradigm

The following discourse analyzes the structure of the on-line industry in the framework of the Internet. The analysis reveals the structural shift exhibited by the Internet. **Aspects of "openness" in market conduct and technology, mass market, capital resources** and so forth are quite novel factors for players in the on-line business. From the standpoint of past on-line services, as described in 2.3,

> "(...) a new computing paradigm – "Internet Computing" – was rapidly taking shape. This new paradigm was the result of the confluence of several independent technological developments: the emergence of the Internet and the World Wide Web, client/server based computing, web browsers and web servers, and a new computer language called Java." (Bamford 1997:1)

Yet, this work argues that the fundamental structure exhibits **strong similarities with the past structure, yet in an open, unbundled, and hence virtualized manner.** In this setting, a number of players use open standards as basis for product development and finally establish a complementary set of components in a virtually collaborative effort. In the new technological situation of converging computing and telecommunications systems, a large variety of solutions can be assembled by combining the singular open system components to a complete offering.

> „In the environment of converged telecommunications and computing, the old-style design problem embodied in one organization presenting a complete end-to-end turnkey solution is gone. Rather, many vendors are participating, in effect, in the collective design of the infrastructure of the future. Such designs must take in account numerous external considerations, such as network externality, standards (or lack thereof), interoperability, adaptability and etiquette, etc." (Messerschmitt 1996:34)

Various authors emphasize the **technological shift from vertical systems** (e.g. vertically integrated IBM mainframe solutions with software and services for vertical industries) **to horizontally layered systems** such as in the Internet. Messerschmitt points out this shift[251] where:

---

[251] See Messerschmitt (1996), pp. 10-13.

"An important feature of horizontal integration is the *open interface*, which has several properties: It has a freely available specification, wide acceptance, and allows a diversity of implementations that are separated from the specification. Another desirable property is the ability to add new or closed functionality.[252] Open interfaces enforce modularity and thus allow a diversity of implementations and approaches to coexist and evolve on both sides of the interface." (Messerschmitt (1996:11)

This describes the technological structure of the Internet, where open technologies enable virtually every player to interconnect its components with the components of other players who apply open standards. The nature of this technological structure deeply affects the industry structure. For these reasons it is incrementally becoming a mainstream standpoint in the late 1990s that **the Internet industry structure exhibits horizontal layers.**[253] **Their vertical interconnection virtually establishes the industry,** hence a similar structure to the old style proprietary on-line services, yet in an open structure.

With this new technological and industrial infrastructure based on open standard systems on-line services represents the fundamental shift for the on-line industry compared to proprietary legacy as described in 2.3. Considering the similarities, insights of the Old World can be leveraged into the new Internet paradigm. If one assumes a layered cohesion the **key question becomes, where are the boundaries of the layers set and how are the layers interrelated.**

This thesis holds that the **predominant influence of technology on industry structures is supreme.**[254] The reason is that new technology enables new business based on technologies. The business models and industrial structures, which are built on these open technological structures, in return virtually reflect the underlying layered technology.

"The lowered barriers to application development embodied in the migration from vertical to horizontal architectures have and will play an important role in industrial organization.." (Messerschmitt 1996:34)

In this sense the new technologies create a virtual industry as expressed above. Figure 2-34 highlights almost the same components structure as it was derived from proprietary on-line services. The only enhancement is that the variety of components results in a more differentiated sub-layering. In the past this sub-layering was organized in internal markets in the respective functional areas of on-line services,[255] whereas in the open Internet framework this is organized in an open market structure, which is be characterized with layers as well. The large difference is that each of these components is available from different vendors and is compatible with other horizontally or vertically positioned components of other vendors. Com-

---

[252] We define *closed* functionality as not published or extensible by other parties. *Proprietary* functionality may be published and extensible, but is subject to intellectual-property protection.

[253] See Messerschmitt (1996). Yoffie (1997), Bane / Bradley / Collis (1996), Nolan / Bradley (1998), Bar / Borrus / Coriat (1989) and Gomez et. al. (1999).

[254] See also Booz Allen Hamilton (1998c).

[255] See Miles / Snow (1993), and Miles / Snow / Coleman (1992) for a comprehensive discussion on internal markets and market mechanisms in hierarchies. See Case Study 2-5 for an example of the internal market within the CompuServe network and on-line services divisions.

posite systems can then be established by combining or assembling several components into a greater product bundling. Ultimately each of the components can be seen as a distinct – but interdependent competition – in the Internet arena.

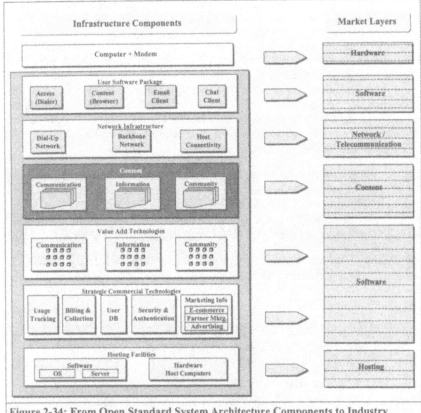

Figure 2-34: From Open Standard System Architecture Components to Industry Structure

Figure 2-34 shows the constellations of technological infrastructure components on the left side and the resulting horizontal market layering on the right side. There are clusters for networks, hosting (end user and back end), software, content and hardware, which are the same layers that were relevant for proprietary on-line services. When these components work together, they provide a complete on-line service offering and establish the currently highly virtual, business system[256]. In this, the players combine their activities to form a "production chain", which combines the individual activities.[257] On these grounds, one can derive the following layered production system as shown in Figure 2-35. It shows five layers, which are all interconnected in reciprocal relationships. A switch from one layer to another layer results in

---

[256] Ketelhöhn (1993:29) describes the business system as a "(...) sequence of activities, used to deliver the product/service, between the supplier of raw materials and the final consumer of the product/service."

[257] See Borrus / Zysman (1997) for an analysis on production chains focusing on the "Wintel" paradigm.

a fundamental shift in the paradigm, which will be further elaborated below. Depending on the granularity of the underlying component structure each layer has corresponding sub-layers.

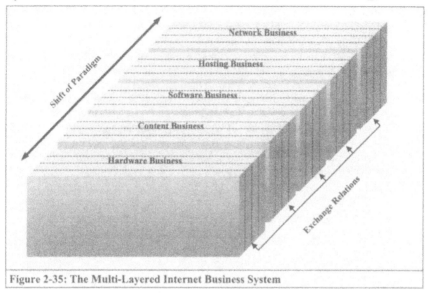

Figure 2-35: The Multi-Layered Internet Business System

One distinguishes among these five main layers and considers the sub-layers. This view is specific to the players competing in the direct on-line industry. The reason why one should distinguish these five main layers and only these five is that the sub-layers are **caused by alternating levels of heterogeneity / homogeneity** depending on the definition of layers.

Although being interconnected and interdependent, in fact **the five main layers exhibit a significant heterogeneity with respect to the other ones**. The reason for this distinction in fact follows the same rationale argued in 2.3.4 and the same data as shown in Figure 2-27 remains valid within this Internet framework.

The reasons for the five layer distinction are heterogeneity / divergence of the layers with respect to:
- Corresponding tasks and competency requirements [258]
- Key measures
- Supply side
- Customer needs and demand side
- Laws of the market place
- Economics are not following the same parameters

---

[258] The abilities required to perform the tasks in the competition of each layer vary fundamentally. This will be put into perspective with the resource-based view in part III, which will compare the competence configuration (Krogh / Roos 1992) of firms with these requirements. The fundamental key measure drives the business in the respective layer.

Different sub-layers also provide for different components. An examination of the factors – demand, supply, economics, key measure of the business, laws of the market place and competency requirements – shows that they in fact follow very similar patterns. Thus, one can state that **the sub-layers of each main layer are very homogenous**. It is, for example, easy for a player in the software layer to roll out another software product, or for a news site to also provide a sports site. Their environments are very homogeneous. But if a software company, e. g. Microsoft, wants to enter the content business, e.g. with MSN and MSNBC it has to set up independent new organizations which do not follow the rules of the core business.

This indicates that **firms with divergent industrial and cultural backgrounds need to come together and cooperate in the on-line environment.**[259] This leads to difficulties in the setup of network partnerships. In the case of vertical integration, these differences have to be organized within the boundaries of one firm. This thesis argues that due to the paradigmatic shift from one layer to another layer, vertical integration is hard to accomplish. In the case of a complete **vertical integration the firm's resource base is over stretched and the competencies are too much** to be managed successfully.[260]

The inherent homogeneity exhibited in the sub-layers and the heterogeneity exhibited in the main layers leads to an enduring structure of the identified five layers.

The empirical history of proprietary on-line services as well as the industrial evolution in the Internet framework in the second half of the 1990s developed along these lines.

Consequently one can state that complete successful vertical integration is not possible and **the overall system exhibits a virtual industry** and will do so in the future, as occurred during the unbundling processes of convergence. The industry is predominantly constituted by the converging overlap of the computer, software, telecommunications, media, and consumer electronics industries. Internet standards are the smallest common denominator connecting the layers. It exhibits a multi-layered cohesion, whereas singular players are unable to vertically integrate over all layers.

Each layer indirectly or directly affects the other layers. Vast interdependencies arise from this structure. The layers have to be seen as distinct but interconnected entities as shown in detail in Figure 2-35. **Overall, it can be stated that the layers are interdependent and have a two-way complementary exchange relationship but individually exhibit a paradigm shift**. Different from the proprietary past each of the layers and sub-layers establishes a competitive environment.

Figure 2-36 is a snapshot of the emergent layers, outlining the situation in 1999. The left column shows the layers and the sub-layers as they are emerged in 1999. The center column represents examples for supply side players and the right column for demand side players.

---

[259] See Booz Allen Hamilton (1995), p. 65 and Colombo / Nguyen / Perrucci (1997), pp. 209-223.

[260] These aspects will be further elaborated in the discussion on networking strategy (3.3.3).

Layer / Sublayers	Supply Side	Demand Side
Network Backbone Dial Up Gear	• MCI/Worldcom, ATT • Many niche players • Cisco, Lucent, Alcatel	• Telecom providers • Retail ISP's / OSP's • Enterprises
Hosting Professional ("dedicated") Consumer ("shared")	• UUNet (Wholesale) • ISP's / OSP's (branded retail) • Small providers (niche retail)	• Retail ISP's • OSP's • Enterprises • Consumer
Software / Technology Community Content Communication Billing Authentication / Security Subscriber Management other	• Microsoft • Oracle • Sun • Netscape • Broadvision • Portal • Sterling Commerce • Various small niche players	• OSP's (=AOL) • ISP's • Enterprises (Corp., SME,SOHO) • Consumer
Content Content Communication Community Ecommerce	• AOL.com • WSJ, CNet • JFAX , Efax, Hotmail • ICQ, AOL Instant Messenger, • Online Banking & Broking • EBay, Priceline, Buy.com	• Business • Consumer
Devices PC Web-Phones TV Set Top Boxes PDA's Wireless Phones Game Consoles	• Dell, Compaq, Apple • Alcatel, Samsung • Sony, Philips • 3Com • Nokia, Ericsson, Siemens, Qualcom • Nintendo	• Business • Consumer

Figure 2-36: Market Layering in Layer / Sublayers & Typical Players (Snapshot 1999)

The main layers outlined in this overview will stay constant. Nevertheless, the sublayers and characterization of demand side / supply side players will change during the process of technological innovation and market consolidation. Technological innovation enables new business models which in return will create new sublayers within a main layer. On the other side, many players shown in the center and right column will integrate and new start-ups will enter the arena. In the long run, consolidation will stabilize the constellation and concentration will significantly increase. This is due to the underlying industrial and network economics of these industries as discussed above. From a micro-perspective these change processes will be driven by the conduct of the players and the manner in which they arrange their exchange relationship. Figure 2-37 gives an overview about the situation in the industry in the late 1990ies.

Layer	Exchange relation	Conduct
Network	• Typical supplier – customer relationship • Exception: large customers like AOL. In this case a singular customer is mission critical because of aggregation of market power. In this case partner or acquisition.	• Aggressive negotiation about prices • Service levels crucial • Usually little competing and complementary relationships because of lateral industry positioning. **Intra and interlayer Market exchange** **Increasing M & A**
Hosting	• Typical supplier – customer relation • Exception: Large players operate use hosting for strategic reasons or economies of scale.	• Large players operate own units (cost, quality and strategic reasons) • Focus on service levels **Intra layer market exchange** **Inter layer competition)**
Software Technology	• Typical supplier – customer relation • Frequently complementary relations. Often leads to hybrid exchange relations	• Blurring enemy / friend definitions • Time based competition • Many collaborative efforts **Inter and intra layer co-opetition** **Increasing M & A** (depending on degree of competition)
Content	• Former supplier – customer relations decreasing • Bartering • Traffic (=market share) against services • "Eyeballs' as currency • Market access main goal	• Everybody plays with anybody • Suspicious cooperation • Partners due to necessity • Competitive partnerships • Blurring enemy / friend definitions • Time based competition **Inter and intra layer co-opetition** **Increasing M & A**
Devices	• Traditional supplier and distribution channel structures eroding, as do traditional business models • Cross subsidizing of old business models with on-line business models	• Cooperation with other convergence players to be not left out • Market participation as main goal **Intra layer competition** **Inter layer cooperation** **Increasing M & A**

Figure 2-37: Coordination & Strategic Conduct in the On-Line Industry, 1998

Overall, this overview shows that the industrial exchange relationships and conduct are exhibit **collaborative efforts**. This can be particularly traced back to the open system, non-profit past of the Internet and the **early start-up period** where players grew together rather than wasting resources in competitive battles. Players realized that there were enough growth opportunities for all players to grow big. **In the end of the 1990s a shift in strategic conduct increasingly emphasized merger and acquisition activities and lead to the first consolidation processes.**

With respect to the multi-layered constitution of the industry, the first consolidation processes occur at the boundaries of firms where they exhibit interfaces to other components and other layers.

For example, content players like Yahoo! or Lycos start their **first stage take-over activities in the sub-layers** by taking over complementary or substitutes in the content layer. Yahoo! purchase of Geocities and broadcast.com or Lycos buying Tripod and Wired are examples for this conduct.

In the second take-over stage, these players also integrate into the other main layers. For example Yahoo! is increasingly buying software players as firms for on-line set-up and dialer technology or software firms offering content converters for alternative devices. The former opens the way to a virtually bundled network, hardware, content, and commerce under the Yahoo! brand. The later pushes the Yahoo! brand into new customer segments, which are being tapped by non-PC devices like personal digital assistants, wireless phones, or set-top boxes.[261] At the same time AOL is buying low-end PC manufacturers after software and content companies were already overtaken.[262] This underpins the thesis stated at the beginning of this section where the openness of the industry and the variety of the players in this huge collaborative effort were described as a temporary phenomenon and where maturity processes were predicted as leading to constellations of higher integration.

These empirical findings will be further analyzed in part III where considerations with respect to networking strategies (3.3.3), adoption strategies (3.3.5), and the co-opetitive games (3.3.6) will explain these processes employing the underlying industrial and network economics as well as the strategic intentions of individual players.

On the grounds of the empirical findings and the theoretical insights of network economics worked out in part II 2.5.2 will model the industry for the later business strategy applications in part III.

2.5.2. The Applied Model

The following presents a multi-layered model which can be applied to analyze situations in the on-line industry in the Internet framework. This model combines the data of the field and the conceptual model (see Figure 2-20), which was developed in the theoretical framework of 2.2. It incorporates the **five main layers**: devices, content, software, hosting and networks, each with a **dynamically evolving number of sub-layers**.

To restate, the main layers can be assumed as constant due to their inherent heterogeneity and contingent roles in the provision of on-line services. Each layer has 'n'' sub-layers. The distinction of these sub-layers is foremost dependent on the competitive situation in the market, where new horizontal layers emerge steadily through start-ups and disappear through acquisitions, and secondly dependent on the particular perspective of a firm. For example, firms located in the content layer perceive this layer with a high level of granularity, while the network layer appears rather superficial. One must take into consideration that this **model exhibits a level of flexibility, which is required for application by firms with different positioning**. Moreover, it allows for adjustments for a particular strategic direction, such as marketing alliances, business development strategies, or merger and acquisition strategies. Depending on the specific issue being analyzed the model can be constructed with an emphasis on certain areas with an alternating number of sub-layers.

In order to consider the influences of **the exogenous parameters, the factors – technology, society, policy and industry – are assembled around the multi-layered** industry. Adjust-

---

[261] According to interviews with Yahoo! Executives Ned Taylor (Director Business Development), 6th of April 1999, Santa Clara, Matt Rightmire (Director Strategic Planning), 28th of April 1999, Santa Clara, and Peter Würtenberger (Managing Director Germany), 2nd of June 1999, Munich.

[262] According interview with Chris Hill, Executive Vice President Corporate Development AOL Europe, 23rd of June 1999, London.

ments in one factor result in adjustments in another factor. In other words, **the model assumes a dynamic structure**, with each factor influencing the other factors in a chain of multiple causes and effects. An example would be how new technologies affect society, policy and industry when faced with a new situation just as it will affect each layer. It is in this sense that the "exogenous parameters" of shape, size, and structure (the specific layering) are discussed in 2.1.5. Yet, on the other side, adjustments in the industrial structure will influence the external as well as other internal factors. Hence, the model assumes not a one-way deterministic constellation of the exogenous parameters influencing the industry, but also the opposite direction. The empirical findings of any given model must include both directions.

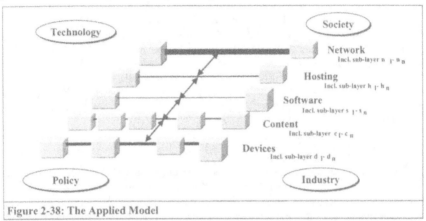

Figure 2-38: The Applied Model

The observations of causes and effects vary depending on the standpoint. For example, a player in the content layer reacts differently to software innovations than does a player in the network layer. According to the standpoint, the model can be constructed differently and can emphasize the factors, which exhibit the highest significance for the position and strategic intentions of a particular firm. Most likely the majority of the players will be located in the converging industries of telecommunications, media, computer hardware and software, or consumer electronics. Their respective "on-line", "Internet", "multimedia", or "interactive" units will observe the industry in a particular way and will emphasize different factors. In this sense, the model needs to be customized to specific situations as

> "We must choose an appropriate systemic view each time we change the industry under study, i.e.: the systemic view used in one industry may not provide useful insights in another industry." (Ketelhöhn 1995:450)

Just as Ketelhöhn points out, adjustments are needed in the systemic view which will change depending on the industry under study. Certain systemic adjustments occur in the model if on-line players with different position in the layers of the on-line industry analyze their competition. It is crucial to consider that the systemic view of the on-line industry fundamentally differs from the systemic view of each converging individually (see also 1.1.2 for the particular perspective discussed by the author).

Furthermore, **the model draws the industry in a virtualized constellation.** Although Part II argues that the industry will experience forces supporting horizontal and vertical integration, one can expect these forces will result in larger networks. In addition, one can expected that some players will integrate virtually in multi-firm value nets in order to capture virtual scale and scope with higher levels of flexibility. At the same time, other players will integrate singular components into larger units with one firm capturing increased scale and scope with higher levels of control.

The model does not explicitly draw the customer in this constellation, as there will be multiple customer relationships and not necessarily "the battle for customer ownership" (Hagel / Lansing 1994) as many argue. A customer needs a device and provision of content, software, hosting, and a network. This can be offered in a one-stop shop solution of an integrated player such as AOL, or in a virtual way as:

> "Some companies are likely to follow a systems integration approach, in which they
> (...) select optimal elements in terms of price and performance, package them to-
> gether, manage the bundles and offer it to the customers on a one stop basis" (Noam
> 1996:22)

Finally, the customer itself can select the needed bundle of components, which results in multiple customer ownership. In this sense, a hardware, software, content, network, and hosting player can share the customer, as the following citation of Mike Homer, Executive Vice President and General Manager of Netscape's Netcenter emphasizes:

> "A lot of people on the internet want to argue "ownership of the customer," and the
> truth is that we can all own the customer." (Goldman Sachs 1999:83 -84)

Therefore, the customer is virtually included in the model and depending on the product bundling and underlying organizational structures, it may be an exclusive relationship or a multiple faceted customer relationship shared between different complementary vendors.

On the grounds of this model, business strategies can be derived with the tool set which will be worked out in part III. Along these lines, one should reconsider the fact that the commercial advent of the Internet in 1995 there were quite a number of on-line services around, all based on proprietary technology.

> "While growth seemed to be a certainty, it was less clear which companies or type of
> company would emerge as winner in this industry. One thing, however, was clear:
> there would be a variety of players, strategies, and services competing for a piece of
> the on-line pie" (Murphy 1996:1)

Hence, many observers were critical about the future of the integrated on-line service model.

> "As the rise of the Internet's World Wide Web dealt a deathblow to commercial on-
> line services such as CompuServe, America Online, and Prodigy? Observers predict-
> ing the demise of the proprietary on-line model are certainly not hard to find. At the

same time, in the last year alone, America Online added more than 3 million subscribers and with only about 12 percent of American households actually signed on to an electronic network of any kind, it is too early to judge which of the competing networks will gain the upper hand. (Hagel / Bergsma / Dheer 1996:57)

In 1996 Hagel et. al. discussed this issue and noted the concurrent enormous growth rates of AOL. It was expected that the chosen strategies of these large players in this "high risk – high gain" situation would make the difference with respect to their future performance.

"In the light of the changes, the leaders in consumer on-line services – America Online (AOL), CompuServe, and Prodigy, were pondering their strategic alternatives and re-examining the viability of their current business models which were under significant pressure. Industry analysts wondered how the current players would protect their place in the industry value chain and if they would be able to adapt to changes in their environment" (Murphy 1996:1)

Five years later some of the old services no longer exist and some do, although they exhibit very different performance. Prodigy and MSN play a marginal role. CompuServe survives just as a brand of the larger AOL. AOL became the dominant player in the Internet space (see Figure 2-11), and still grows at a pace of 3 million customers per year, and is expected to exceed the 20 million subscriber base worldwide –larger than the other top 10 competitors combined. **The conduct of players in network markets results in drastic differences in the according performance of firms**.

This leads to the conclusion that consideration of industry structure and technological shifts does not capture everything. Business strategy and strategic conduct has salient influences on the performance of players in the on-line industry.

Part III translates the insights from the structural framework of the Internet into a strategic framework by reducing the complexity of the filed, and explaining the forces of cause and effect in order to make strategically manageable decision in this marketspace:

"All frameworks are created to simplify complexity in a way that help the thinking process of decision makers. The goal is to understand reality and then shape it" (Ketelhöhn 1993:3)

This paper will develop a tool set for business strategy. This will highlight the factors, which take into account the divergent performance of players in the on-line industry. This tool set will also explain why comparatively similar players like AOL, MSN, CompuServe, and Prodigy started from the same point but why different conduct resulted in such different performance. Furthermore, this set of tools works for players, which are offspring from the commercial Internet era and which created a host of diverse players such as Yahoo!, Tripod, Broadvision, Portal, Palm, and Freesurf.

Part III: On-line Business Strategy - Analysis & Tools

3. Navigating in the On-Line Industry - Firm Strategy

Part III **analyzes strategic implications in the on-line industry** and develops **a tool set as a framework for business strategy**. It proceeds from the individual company perspective. This complements the considerations of structure, conducted in part II, with this strategic perspective. It also lays out the particularities for firm strategy given in the industry structure and develops a **strategic framework (tool set)** and the accompanying **individual tools to analyze, generate and conduct a business strategy in the multi-layered on-line industry**.

Section 3.1 outlines the particular **challenges for business strategy** present in the industry environment. These factors indicate the required issues needing to be solved with the accompanying theoretical components in order to work out a business strategy tool set.

Section 3.2 discusses the insights of **mainstream business strategy** approaches by analyzing the appropriate elements of the market-based view and the resource-based view. The analysis and application of the mainstream strategy theory provides the **conceptual framework of the tool set needed to derive a strategy** with respect to the industry model.

Section 3.3 develops the **individual strategic tools to conduct a strategy** according to the framework of the tool set. For these purposes, it applies the strategic implications of two **net-centric approaches of business strategy**, specifically business strategy in the context of network economics and the game theoretic co-opetition concept. The author will deliver product, networking, pricing and adoption strategy tools, which are designed to create and leverage network externalities with complementors in the standard co-opetition constellations.

Section 3.4 **summarizes the business strategy instruments** developed during the course of this and puts model, tool set and individual tools into perspective.

The structural framework of the applied model (see Figure 2-38) serves as the object upon which the business strategy focuses. In this sense the industry structure provides the data of the field, which can then be processed within the strategic framework of the tool set, in order to generate a strategy. Once a strategy is formulated, the individual tools can be applied to orchestrate the strategic conduct, which effects the industry structure (see 3.4).

3.1. Challenges for Business Strategy

The analysis of the on-line industry conducted in part II reveals that the industry is a highly attractive environment, given current growth rates and the future market potential. Techno-logical innovation will substantially take place in this industry and will enable additional op-portunities for commercial players, which are not even imagined today. On the other hand it becomes evident that the area is highly complex and development paths are uncertain. This results in demanding challenges for business strategy. Part II approached the on-line industry as a black box. It discusses a set of exogenous parameters, which determine the size and the structure of this black box. The following sections analyze the endogenous aspects of the system. This conceptual analysis as well as the empirical analysis reveal the current state of the endogenous variables and the mechanism and laws of this multi-layered industry structure. The analytical sections result in a model of the on-line industry as summarized in the applied model (see 2.5.2). The following will discuss the challenges for business strategy, which are caused by the particularities of this business environment. First 3.1.1 will discuss the issues within the **exogenous parameters,** which translate into the endogenous factors and hence become a major strategic planning issues. Within the industry system one can distinguish issues of the **product – market aspects** (3.1.2) and the particular **network aspects,** which are caused by multiple interdependencies of the multi-layered industry (3.1.3). Section 3.1.4 summarizes these issues and puts them into perspective through the course of chapter 3.

3.1.1. Challenges Caused by the Exogenous & General Field Parameters

The analysis of the exogenous framework in 2.1 revealed that the exogenous parameters exhibit significant **immaturity**. In many aspects they lag behind the development of the endogenous parameters because significant business occurs despite the absence of stable framework parameters. This is shown with examples such as privacy protection, taxation, tariffs, and commercial technology. Therefore the planning of a business strategy must take into account the exogenous parameters affecting the business model as variables rather than as fixed external factors, which can help to frame the strategic scenario of a certain case.

The conduct of the **political sector,** demand and supply side factors of the **social environment,** and the **technological developments influence the size and structure of the industry.**[263] Adjustments among these factors influence how boundaries between horizontal markets are drawn and which size affects particular competitions. This results in opportunities and threats for players in this field. Hence, a business strategy tool set needs to consider these influences in a way that an adjustment of specific factors can be **translated into particular effects for individual players** and their competition.

Overall it has to be stated that the development of the exogenous parameters translates not just attractive **growth** as a challenge but also the general characteristics of **rapid speed of change, enormous complexity** and **uncertainty** into the industry system.

This results in certain structural challenges for business strategy as discussed below. But besides these aspects, the immaturity of the field also results in a troublesome **methodological issue**. The problem being that data about the field is either not available, not precise, or ambiguous. In-depth detailed analysis suffers from **poor quality of quantitative data,** which is required for the modeling of specific scenarios and cases. Quantitative statements of market researchers, analysts and consultants often have the quality of rough plausibility assumptions based on scenario techniques. It is especially troublesome that the quantitative data about mission critical and strategically crucial factors[264] is unreliable. It is still a common phenomenon

---

[263] The industrial aspects are mostly internalized and can be regarded as endogenous parameters (see 2.1.5).

[264] Strategic data of interest are, e. g.: number of on-line users, current and future penetration of enabled access devices (see 2.1.2), market shares of operating systems and browsers, price elasticity and aggregated demand, conjoint analysis about singular applications an pricing models, actual and potential revenue of market segments such as Internet access, Email, content, ecommerce, advertising, services, deployment of access network technology.

that one is exposed to a "menu of choices" about a singular business planning factor as Stuart Feldman observed:

"The Internet will grow. Pick your forecast!"[265]

Overall the industry does not yet exhibit stability of the parameters, which would be required to apply certain common business strategy tools. As a result, many tools are not applicable. This methodological issue needs to be considered, when choosing tools.

This leaves business strategy in a high gain-high risk situation as the opportunities are enormous yet planning parameters are very unstable. This unstable situation is translated into the endogenous factors of the product-market area as 3.1.2 analyzes.

3.1.2. Challenges Based in the Product-Market Area

In general it can be stated that the majority of the challenges arising for business strategy in the product-market area can be traced back to the **fundamental immaturity of the industry and the early stage of the market development process**. Adoption rates of the different markets are either in the stage of barely having penetrated the early adopters (Europe) or in some markets or at most – the early majority (USA). In the latter adoption rates are slowing down slightly whereas the former markets exhibit an increasing adoption rate of Internet usage. This development stage challenges players with enormous growth and the issues of continuous change in the external and internal environment of the firm.

2.4 reveals that the business suffers from an – as yet limited – portfolio of **premature business models**. The existing revenue streams are neither stable, nor sufficient, and new revenue streams are under discussion but have not hit the market yet. As a result, solid financial planning is not possible. Firm strategy reacts to this situation by focusing on the increasing market share and assumes – or better said, hopes for – the emergence of solid business models in the future. This increases the risk that any business strategy will be unable to deliver sufficient business direction.

Moreover convergence (see 2.1, 2.2.2, 2.5) leads to **blurring boundaries of competition,** which creates the difficulty of defining clear and enduring product-market structures as well as clear lines of competition. Business strategy tools loose their power as planning tools.

Virtuality challenges business strategy to understand a **virtual marketspace** with definitions of time and space different than in the real world. Processes appear to run faster, barriers seem to be lower, regional boundaries seem to be redefined. Business strategy has to discover how to grapple with these phenomena.

---

[265] Stuart Feldman at his keynote speech at the conference on the legal and policy framework for global electronic commerce at UC Berkeley, March 5, 1999. He stated in the context about the growth and economic contribution of the digital e-conomy that forecasts vary drastically, sometimes even with a five-fold difference. He concluded that the only mutual insight are the rapid growth predictions, while concrete quantitative statements appear divergent and ultimately worthless.

The discussion of **network externalities in horizontal network markets** (2.2.1) explains positive feedback effects as market forces, which support a typically low number of players in horizontal competitions. The resulting market patterns imply specific strategic decisions, which are different from other markets.

Furthermore, the analysis in 2.1.2, 2.4 and 2.5 reveals the **immaturity of products and underlying technology**. Technological complexity of available products and limited interoperability of components renders product not yet mass market compliant. Products and their technology are immature and often far away from being at a satisfactory quality level. The rapid and still infant development stage results in insufficient technology for the end users.[266] The non-commercial past of the Internet leads to insufficient commercial technology for vendors. Furthermore it is unclear which network platform technologies will dominate in the future. Business strategy cannot rely on stable technological parameters and product qualities, which adds additional risk to the business planning. In general one can still agree with the absence of a "dominant design" (Utterback 1994) for the on-line services.[267]

These issues are located in the product-market arena and taken as a whole lead back to the immaturity of the business environment. But due to the multi-layered nature of the on-line industry complex interdependencies arise, which create additional challenges for business strategy.

3.1.3. Challenges Caused by the Interdependencies of the Multiple Layers

The particular constitution of the on-line industry environment connects a host of horizontal market layers in a way that each of them can be seen as a distinct but not interdependent layer. This causes additional complexity and particularities which create specific challenges for business strategy.

First, the aspect of **vertical network externalities** as described in part II is a dominant factor determining success or failure. Parameters need to be identified and conceptualized as to how to set up a vertical network. Issues ranging from the right type of connections to the right kind of components, with respect to products and players, need to be solved for a sufficient business strategy tool set to emerge. For these, the role of **complementors** in the industry needs to be further analyzed.

As many relations in vertical – and in some cases horizontal – networks are not clearly competitive or cooperative, the aspect of **hybrid co-opetitive relations** of players has to be analyzed. This needs to be conceptually integrated into a strategy tool set

---

[266] The overwhelming success of Apple's iMac is an obvious indicator that people are willing to pay an extra premium in order to have a stable and user friendly computing product. Future web-enabled consumer electronics devices promise improvements in the same direction. The micro computer is a product, which carries enormous complexity and has so far failed to offer stable technology serving invisible in the background and is consequently devoted to user friendly focus. It seems to be common sense that future mass market products have a much more user friendly design than current computing devices which have failed to exceed a 30%-50% adoption rate.

[267] See Utterback (1994), pp. 23-26 for the notion on dominant designs. He points out that a dominant product design generally goes along with dominant market structures as well (ibid.), pp. 32-35, which is caused by positive returns to scale. This effect is particularly strong in network markets.

Last but not least each of the horizontal layers in the virtual industry system exhibits a powerful dynamic. The unstable state of the exogenous parameters adds change as well. These are two strong drivers of change. As a third factor, one must consider the interconnection of rapidly changing layers and components, which leads to a multiplied dynamic for the overall framework. Therefore the **dynamics of the interdependencies** challenges the rational reasoning of the according planning processes.

Overall this results in a complex set of challenges as summarized in 3.1.4, which also provides an overview on how part III of this work intends to apply business theory to solve these issues.

3.1.4. Summary and Structure of the Strategic Challenges

The above analysis has shown that business strategy is confronted with a number of particular challenges typical for the on-line industry. They are rooted in the exogenous environment, which are translated into the general field parameters as well as in the product-market area. The technological and industrial structure of the industry creates multiple interdependencies of interconnected layers. But there is also a feedback trend from the industry influencing the exogenous environment because its entire cohesion is still in a very fluid stage. Constant motion and fuzziness are issues with which the business strategy must grapple.

Application of business strategy tools needs to employ current data as well as predictions regarding future developments. As the exogenous and endogenous parameters create this opaque situation, business strategy must apply tools which are capable of comprehending **complexity, uncertainty, growth and change,** while the available data leaves significant uncertainty and ambiguity. The cohesion of the on-line industry and the whole Internet framework are fluid and inconstant. In this unstable situation, Stuart Feldman has identified **the most fundamental strategic question:**

> **"What are the fixed factors?"** (Stuart Feldman 1999)[268]

Failure to identify a sufficient number of stable parameters, exposes one to a floating framework with all factors being variables and – to use analytical terminology – more equations than fixed parameters, which results in an incomplete system. Results produced by this system are ambiguous. Therefore, the process of generating a strategy must identify the fixed factors, which can serve as solid planning foundation. Without identification of the fixed factors, each modeled scenario will be based on a set of completely ambiguous input and will result in ambiguous output. This implies that the business strategy as an analytical approach generates no added-value to the business direction and leaves only intuitive management as a way out.[269]

---

[268] Stuart Feldman in his keynote speech at the Conference on the Legal and Policy Issues on Global Electronic Commerce. See furthermore BCLT (1999) and Cioffi (1999a).

[269] See Agor (1986) and Wiesman (1989), Welsch (1993), Kahneman / Tversky (1974) for a soft-fact, intuitive management approach. Nevertheless, Schoemaker (1994) points out empirical evidence for the unreliability of intuitive decision making in strategic management.

This work argues that the identified challenges can be mastered to a certain extent and that the market structure, as analyzed in part II, incorporates enough perceivable patterns, structures, and mechanisms that a **conceptual approach** can be translated into a business strategy tool set. The critical position of the author regarding a quantitative approach, due to poor quality of data, was discussed above.

The corresponding tool set for business strategy, which covers concerns of the product-market and value network area, must acknowledge these challenges. Relevant components of strategic theory need to be identified and applied. The introduction of business strategy theory needs to discuss which tools are applicable and how they can be integrated into a tool set, which can cope with the strategic problems of the product-market and value network aspects of the on-line business. In the light of the current debate it is nevertheless a relevant question: **Is the Internet a new e-conomy or do old principles still apply?**

The Internet is a rapidly moving environment, which appears, especially from short-term perspectives, as chaotic. Such a short-term view perceives Internet economics as following different or new principles. Sky rocketing market capitalization of medium sized companies[270] and emphatic and inspiring statements highlighting particularities of the Internet as a business environment support this perception. For example Netscape's chairman and founder, Jim Clark, spread such a position in 1995:

> "The Internet is low cost. We proved that by using the Internet to distribute our first product, and we were able to build a customer base of 10 million users in just about nine months. Our only expense was the engineering cost of making the program (...) So we see this potential for low cost distribution of any kind of intellectual property (...) that can be represented as bits." (Clark 1995: 70)

This perspective which fosters entrepreneurial wishful thinking fuels the perception of the web as a "brave new economic world". This standpoint is particularly supported by many consultants, who want to sell their fashionable management concepts, in order to be the "Digital Pioneers" (AT Kearney 1998a) in the new "eEconomy" (Andersen 1998b). Obviously developing the foundation for a host of consulting projects they hold the position that

> "In the digital frontier of this economy, the players, dynamics, rules, and requirements for survival and success are all changing." (Tapscott 1996:xiii)[271]

Varian / Shapiro critically add that

> "Visionaries tell us that the Internet will soon deliver us into that most glorious form of capitalism, the 'friction-free' economy. How ironic, then, (...) the enormous rigidities that plague the information economy.
>
> We agree that the Internet will make shopping easier than ever, but much of the talk about friction is fiction." (Varian / Shapiro 1998a):103

---

[270] See Goldman Sachs (1999a, 1999b, 1999c).

[271] See furthermore Kelly (1997, 1998) and Bernstein (1998) describing the novel economy.

Along these lines the author argues, that although organizational boundaries and processes will change, most of the rest is a **hyperbolic view of fashionable arguments**. It considers today's short-run phenomena and does not put the current constellation into a long term perspective. The academic discussion regarding borderless enterprises and virtualized corporations anticipated this trend a long time ago.[272] It is now finally arriving in business practice in a larger scale. Low costs, ubiquity and openness of components will drive the virtualization of business to a larger scale and add velocity. But these are just effects of causes, which were discussed in the economic and business theory a significant time ago.[273] It is now finally arriving in business practice in a larger scale. Low costs, ubiquity and openness of components will drive the virtualization of business in a larger scale and much higher velocity. But these are just effects of causes, which were discussed in the economic and business theory since a significant time.[274] This work argues that the digital e-conomy does not produce fundamentally new economic principles. Or to apply the motivation, which drove Varian / Shapiro (1998) **to repackage and translate old microeconomic business strategy** for "A Strategic Guide to the Network Economy"[275]:

---

[272] See Williamson (1990, eds.), Nohria / Eccles (1992, eds.), Davidow / Malone (1992), Jarillio (1993), Picot / Reichwald / Wigand (1996) and Wüthrich (1997). Past EDI systems were already enabling processes and trends. But high costs and proprietary nature of these systems constrained them to relatively small scale and longer roll-out cycles. This is different since the widespread deployment of low-cost, open standard Internet technology, which will replace the EDI technologies as ecommerce platform (see Schutzer 1997, pp. 521-523). "[But finally] E-commerce comes of age. Electronic commerce used to be the preserve of large companies that could afford to build or lease the necessary proprietary networks. Applications were mostly limited to EDI (electronic data interchange) and EFT (electronic funds transfer). The computer systems required were generally mainframes, with complex, purpose-specific software and massive systems integration requirements. Today, [because of the Internet, C. G.] however, users of all stripes need only a PC and a phone line to take advantage of the growing number of public and private networks that use standard protocols such as TCP/IP. This scalability puts small businesses on an equal footing with large corporations." (Harrington / Reed 1996:70).

[273] See Williamson (1990, eds.), Nohria / Eccles (1992, eds.), Davidow / Malone (1992), Jarillio (1993), Picot / Reichwald / Wigand (1996) and Wüthrich (1997). Past EDI systems were already enabling according processes and trends. But high costs and proprietary nature of these systems constraint them to a relatively small scale and longer roll-out cycles. This is different since the widespread deployment of low-cost, open standard Internet technology, which will replace the EDI technologies as ecommerce platform (see Schutzer 1997, pp. 521-523). "[But finally] E-commerce comes of age. Electronic commerce used to be the preserve of large companies that could afford to build or lease the necessary proprietary networks. Applications were mostly limited to EDI (electronic data interchange) and EFT (electronic funds transfer). The computer systems required were generally mainframes, with complex, purpose-specific software and massive systems integration requirements. Today, [because of the Internet, C. G.] however, users of all stripes need only a PC and a phone line to take advantage of the growing number of public and private networks that use standard protocols such as TCP/IP. This scalability puts small businesses on an equal footing with large corporations." (Harrington / Reed 1996:70).

[274] Wüthrich et. al (1997:43) discusses this cohesion of lower transaction costs in the presence of ICT and firms focusing on their core competencies. He points out that it results in the emergence of virtual network organizations: „Der von vielen Firmen verfolgte strategische Ansatz einer **Konzentration auf die Kernkompetenzen** und die damit verbundene Neugestaltung der Geschäftsprozesse, führt zwangsläufig zu firmenübergreifenden Kooperationen (...) In virtuellen Netzen (...). Die höheren Transaktionskosten, die in diesen losen Netzwerken entstehen, bleiben dank der Möglichkeiten, die uns die heutigen **Informations- und Kommunikationstechnologien** zur Verfügung stellen, beherrschbar.".

[275] Subtitle of their book "Information Rules" (Varian / Shapiro 1998). See also Varian (1989) arguing for the use of neo-classical economics, which he obviously considers as his home base.

"The thesis of this book is that durable economic principles can guide you in today's frenetic business environment. Technology changes. Economic laws do not. If you are struggling to comprehend what the Internet means (...) you can learn a great deal (from economics, C. G.). (...) many of today's managers are so focused on the trees of technological change that they fail to see the forest: the underlying economic forces that determine success and failure." (Varian / Shapiro 1998:1-2)

The author concurs with this position. **Particularly in the messy Internet environment fundamental approaches shine with a certain charm, when compared to the short term hyperbolic trends, which frequently dominate the debate in the industry.** To this end, some very old concepts from the market-based view will be introduced and discussed. **Early insights regarding economies, systems and societies of scholars, such as those, which emerge from Hayek or Schumpeter, seem to be more relevant than ever.**[276] Who is talking about "push-technology" today, who will talk about "Portal Sites" in a few years? A closer analysis of the work of many network economists will also disclose that they primarily rest on old concepts of microeconomic business strategy and combine these insights with a new terminology.

Referring back to Jim Clarks statement regarding the opportunities of the new Internet era, it is worthwhile pointing out that the competitive behavior of Netscape's browser (and other client software) business against Microsoft drove prices to zero and, that the large competitor was able to use the same low cost distribution channels, which Jim Clark mentions above. In addition, Microsoft was able to utilize scale and scope effects of a large, and competent firm. At the end of this mass-market competition, Microsoft had more than a 50% of the market share and Netscape could not remain independent.[277] In early 1999, Netscape was divided into a back-end business (the units going to SUN) and a front-end business (the units going to AOL). This strategic scenario may be explained in terms of industrial economics, framing the discussion in the following manner: Microsoft was the cost leader in a mass market, had control of market access, access to capital, and finally executed well the orchestration of economies of scale and scope resident within Microsoft. Obviously competencies to develop and to market software played a role. Moreover, the terms of network economics can explain forces driving market developments in this network market with horizontal network externalities (Microsoft heavily sponsoring Internet Explorer and finally enjoying positive feedback after reaching critical mass). Last but not least, is the virtuous game of Microsoft bundling product components with other components (e.g. bundling the browser with Windows) and partners in a co-opetitive way, which created vertical network externalities.

---

[276] One of the associated research fellows analyzed the virtual value creation in "value webs" and market places and ultimately found the power of Adam Smith and the concept of the "invisible hand" as one of the most compelling arguments. Evidently, the power of these old ideas still provides enduring enlightenment. See furthermore Selz (1999).

[277] In addition it must be stated that Netscape by-and-large derived its revenues from the enterprise businesses with server software (enterprise server, merchant server etc.) while the browser business played the strategic role: to "own" the user interface to the web. However Netscape experienced a comparable loss of market share in the "back-end" business. For further details see SPA (1999).

In particular compared to past experience, it is rather the **velocity of processes and a redefinition of space**, which makes the Internet environment appear different to human perceptions.

> "Our perceptions of time and space are transformed by real-time (interactive, C. G.)
> information technologies" (Cioffi 1999b)[278]

Hence the enormous speed of internal and external change and an understanding for *"marketspaces"*, as intelligently coined by Rayport / Sviokla (1994), **are the environmental factors which need to be handled – not new economic principles.**[279]

For these purposes business strategy mainstream approaches will be discussed as well as more current, net-centric approaches. The author argues that one can derive insight from both sides and thus should combine them in an applied conceptual framework. On the one hand, the **market-based view** and the **resource-based view** can contribute insight from a general standpoint but leave open some field specific issues, especially with respect to the network aspects. On the other hand **net-centric approaches of network economics and co-opetition** are partial approaches but provide insight with regards to the particularities of the network industry. Figure 3-1 outlines how the findings in the wider **market structure create business strategy challenges which need to be translated into issues for business strategy in order to derive a strategy tool set for individual firms to work with the suggested model.**

---

[278] Cioffi is citing Regis McKenna in his closing remarks at the conference "The Digital Economy in International Perspective: Common Construction or Regional Rivalry", Washington D.C., May 27, 1999.

[279] This is one of the convictions, which was generated in various discussions with other scholars in this area. This is particularly true during the workshops with the fellow researchers at the MCM in St. Gallen, Switzerland. While this "new information economy" was initially perceived as a fundamentally new business environment the ongoing research and discussion shaped the mutual position that this new economy is not all that new. The key factor is that human perception tends to perceive things in real time. As the processes in the Internet environment happen with enormous velocity, human perception does not realize that it is the factor time, which is the genuinely different aspect. From a little distance things appear not as distorted. New markets and business models were created all the time. Competitive borders are blurring and shifting all the time. Varian / Shapiro (1998:1) start their book with a story, which underpins this statement: "As the century closed, the world became smaller. The public rapidly gained access to new dramatically faster communication technologies. Entrepreneurs, able to draw on unprecedented scale economies, built vast empires. Great fortunes were made. The government demanded that these powerful new monopolists be held accountable under the anti-trust law. Every day brought forth new technological advances to which old business models seemed to no longer apply. Yet, somehow the basic laws of economics asserted themselves. Those who mastered these laws survived in the new environment. Those who did not, failed.".
A prophecy for the next decade? No. You have just read a description of what happened a hundred years ago when the twentieth-century industrial giants emerged. Using the infrastructure of the emerging electricity and telephone networks, these industrialists transformed the U.S. economy, just as today's Silicon Valley entrepreneurs are drawing on computer and communications infrastructure to transform the world's economy".
Furthermore, globalization of markets continued apace before the World Wide Web was around (see Ghoshal / Bartlett 1990, and Ghoshal / Westney 1993, eds.). At the end of the day, the most fundamental shift for strategic management theory is the discussion of how one has to react to "hyper-competitive" environments with accelerated change of structures, increased complexity and uncertainty where sustainable competitive advantage does not exist (see D'Aveni 1995). Bounded rationality (Simon 1957) of underlying decision making processes in organizations (March / Simon 1958) points out the natural limitations.

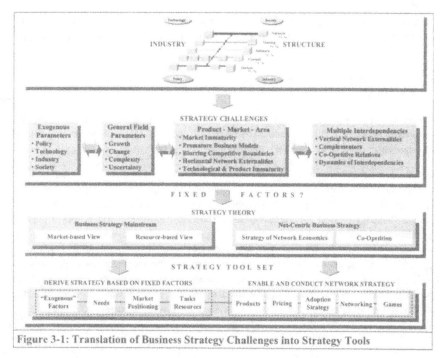

Figure 3-1: Translation of Business Strategy Challenges into Strategy Tools

The following section will discuss the appropriateness and insights from the corresponding theory of business strategy. These elements will be worked out below and are required to assemble a tool set for the product-market and the value network strategy in the on-line industry. This tool set needs to provide an abstract framework to process data according to the empirical findings of the field. Moreover, it has to apply existing theoretical frameworks and models in a manner tailored to the specific issues discussed above. Overall, one can state that the main challenge is to define the level of abstraction for the tool set in a way, which is applicable for concrete business situations on the one hand, and which generates general and enduring instruments and a model for the on-line industry comprehending mechanisms, laws, logic and strategic implications on the other hand. This proceeding will solve the applied research problem defined for this thesis. Along these lines Cusumano / Yoffie point out

> "(...) that some of the strategic precepts of the pre-Internet world continue to ring true. Several core elements of competitive advantage – vision, leadership, innovation, quality, barriers to entry, customer lock-in, switching costs, and partner relationships remain critical to the overall equation for creating a successful company, even in the most turbulent of environment." Cusumano / Yoffie (1999:81)

For these purposes 3.2 will discuss the aspects of the business strategy mainstream.

3.2. Business Strategy Mainstream

Mainstream business strategy theory is dominated by two fundamental approaches: the market-based view and the resource-based view. In order to put these two views into perspective one can apply the idea of the SWOT-Analysis.[280] It distinguishes between opportunities and threats of the external market environment, and strengths and weaknesses inside of the firm as initial point to derive a strategy. Whereas the market-based view focused on the former to derive a strategy, the resource-based view emphasizes the later. Consequently, both views are based on divergent premises as compared in Figure 3-2.

| PREMISES | |
MARKET-BASED VIEW	RESOURCE-BASED VIEW
• Players within a strategic group are identical regarding firm resources	• Players within one strategic group can diverge with regards to their firm resources
• Allocation asymmetries are not sustainable because resources are mobile and available over the factor markets	• Transaction cost of intangible resources cause heterogeneity between firms can be sustainable
Unit of the Analysis	
• Business units	• Firm as an entity
Scope of the Analysis	
• Industry	• Single firm
Locus of Competitive Advantage	
• Outside the firm	• Inside the firm

Figure 3-2: Overview Market-Based and the Resource-Based View

Whereas the market-based view follows an outside-in mindset of strategy making, the resource based view follows the opposite inside-out mindset. It focuses on the particular resources, which create strengths and weaknesses inside a firm as the locus from which to generate competitive advantages.[282] One can argue that both approaches have a complementary relationship.[283] Whereas one approach focuses on the market as a source to derive a strategy, the other approach focuses on the internal aspects of a firm. A combined perspective covers a wider area of information and provides a more complete picture. This is the underlying concept of the SWOT-Analysis. Section 3.2 discusses the insights and added-value of both approaches for a business strategy tool set for the on-line industry.

3.2.1. Market-Based View

The market-based view is the oldest of the approaches introduced here. In it, one can trace back to the microeconomic roots of business administration. It was developed in the 1930s as part of industrial economics. It was initially intended as a means to analyze industrial structures in order to provide economic and public policy makers with insights to control effi-

---

[280] The SWOT-Analysis was developed by Andrews and refers to the dimensions strength, weaknesses, opportunities and threats (see Barney 1991, p. 100).

[281] See Barney (1991), pp. 100-102.

[282] See Rasche (1993), p. 423, Binder / Kantowsky (1996), p. 29 and Verdin / Williamson (1994) p. 10. In this context Wernerfelt (1984:172) defines resources very broadly as "Anything which could be thought of as a strength and a weakness of a given firm.".

[283] See Mahoney / Pandian (1992), p. 363.

ciency and ensure competitiveness within industries.[284] Later the theory was extended into business strategy. Bain (1956) developed the **Structure – Conduct – Performance (SCP) Paradigm**. Its basic version assumes a deterministic relationship between the variables. The performance of an industry is a function of the conduct of the players on the demand and supply side, which in turn depends on the structure of the industry. The reference points for industry structure are the two extreme market constellations of monopoly and perfect competition – elements of the neoclassical **theory of markets**. Production factors are assumed to be perfect substitutes and mobile, and thus defines resources as a strategically nonrelevant parameter.[285]

In this framework, markets naturally emerge as perfectly competitive over time. The reason for other market constellations is market imperfections and information pathologies. **Friction and imperfections in the market structure provide firms with the potential to capture economic rents.** This basically represents a view of business strategy typical from the microeconomic standpoint. It analyzes the structure of a market and assumes perfect information and low or no friction in the long run, which gives firms little space for sustainable differentiation:

> "In the long run, the rate of return available from competing in an industry is a function of the underlying structure" (Porter cited after Lado / Boyd / Wright 1992:79)

The market-based approach is a consistent and renowned framework used in order to analyze the competition and profitability of an industry and to derive strategic advice based on the model. The underlying theory of markets tells a lesson on a high level of abstraction, which should work in the Internet age as an emerging economic environment as well, as pointed out above by Yoffie / Cusumano (1999). The analysis below will prove this in a simple way. Moreover the theory of network economics, which was introduced in 2.2.1, is a concept developed in the tradition of microeconomics. This work demonstrates in 2.2.1 that lessons regarding the mechanisms of network industries can be outlined in a SCP – Paradigm. Last but not least, Varian / Shapiro (1998) deliver fundamental strategic advice for players in network industries: the creation of **switching costs** is desirable in order to lock-in customers. These switching costs are just another term for **friction** in a market, or in Porter's terms they are **mobility and entrance barriers**, which allow firms to capture an **economic rent** based on the business with their **locked-in customers**.[286] Hence, these are obviously consistent approaches based on the same microeconomic traditions. Therefore, their strategic implications contain logical interfaces to the underlying theory of the industry model (see part II), which was worked out based on the analytical framework of these approaches.

In the market-based mindset the players who select the most attractive industries and are able to adapt to the market structure in the best way gain competitive advantage. Firms can protect their competitive position with the creation of entrance barriers against potential new competitors and mobility barriers against existing competitors to constrain them from moving

---

[284] See Osterloh / Grand (1994), p. 278 and Wolfsteiner (1995), p. 34.

[285] See Grant (1992), p. 40, Knyphausen (1993), p. 775.

[286] See Porter (1980), p. 10, Antonelli (1997), p. 644 and Caves / Porter (1977).

from one strategic group to another.[287] This is basically the **ability of firms to create friction based on the strategic use of information and know-how**. The success of a firm is dependent on the ability to find, use, protect and develop entrance and mobility barriers. The barriers decrease the competitive force (Porter 1980), which would drive down profits.[288] According to Porter, barriers can be created by:[289]

* Scale advantages
* Product differentiation[290]
* Capital requirements[291]
* Adaptation costs of customers[292]
* Market access

Porter (1981) originally states that:

* Technology,
* Product design and
* Restrictions on entrepreneurial conduct

are given factors in the market. This represents rather mature and static industries. In the case of the Internet, these factors seem to be particularly dynamic and under the control of firms. Strategy can explicitly formulate and create barriers by technological standards setting, product design, and creation of new products. The creation of new business models and their entrepreneurial implementation in the presence of ubiquitous venture capital renders the last factor much less of a given than it used to be in traditional industries. Thus, they **have to be considered as additional factors to create barriers.**

To create barriers describes interference by firms in the market structure. As it was stated above, the initial version of the SCP Paradigm modeled a deterministic relationship. If one knows the market structure and the performance of the industry, then one can compute the respective returns for the company according to the conduct of players in the game. This would assume – consistent with the neoclassical theory of markets – that the market structure is exogenously determined. Krogh / Roos argue that in reality the market structure is endogenous and is created by the conduct of firms and the interaction between competitors.[293] One could argue that with increasing dimensions in an industry, the SCP patterns increasingly un-

---

[287] Industrial Economics initially assumed that firms are homogenous. Porter enhanced this rigid definition by introducing the concept of the strategic group, which defines a group of firms within one industry which pursue the same strategic patterns. See Porter (1987), pp. 177-180.

[288] See McWilliams / Smart (1993).

[289] See Porter (1987), pp. 33-34.

[290] This term is comparable with the term "versioning" discussed in the context of network economics (see 2.2.1).

[291] This factor has to be seen under the particular conditions of the Internet where presence of a virtually infinite capital flow via venture capital and the stock market actually lowers barriers routed in capital requirements (see Cohen / Fields (1999). The differentiating aspects seem to be rather the specific capability of firms to deal with investors and the stock markets.

[292] These costs are the switching costs referred to in network economics. These artificially created frictions result in lock-in effects of customers to a certain product, which exhibits inferior economics. But lock-in appears if switching costs are larger than the competitive advantage of an alternative product.

[293] See Krogh / Roos (1996a), pp. 8-12 and Grant (1992, pp. 61-64.

derestimates the dynamics of competition and market structure. For exactly these reasons Porter developed a **dynamic version of the SCP-Paradigm**, in order to render comprehensible the market dynamics.[294] It considers feedback effects from performance to conduct and from conduct to structure. As a consequence the market structure is not considered a fixed parameter from which to derive a strategy. It can be also seen as a variable to conduct a strategy.[295] In this way it is a more sophisticated framework to model a market constellation. Ultimately the SCP-Paradigm is an analytical component of the market based view. It models mechanisms in market cohesion but does not directly deliver a business strategy.

When applied to the on-line industry, this means that the industry is modeled in a way that players can influence the underlying parameters of the market structure and that the market structure influences the performance of firm's conduct. Furthermore, this implies that the performance of markets in return is a cause for effects felt on exogenous parameters of the market structure and the conduct of players. In fact the analysis in 2.1 reveals that the exogenous parameters influence the structure and size of markets. In the opposite direction, players can also influence these factors with their conduct. Moreover it becomes evident that the exogenous parameters are in a premature stage and are closer to variable than fixed parameters (see also 2.1. Particularly during **the premature stage** of policy, social, technology and industrial sector development, with respect to positions in the Internet, **this space is opened for proactive business strategy.**[296]

This may occur in two situations. **First, firms can interfere with the exogenous parameters in existing markets.** This occurs when a software company like Microsoft proactively drives Internet standardization processes at the WWW Consortium (W3C) in a manner, which will support Microsoft's technologies.[297] In this case technology standardization predominantly influences entrance barriers. One can also imagine an incumbent telecommunications provider lobbying for certain interconnection rates, which are set by regulators. In this case interconnection rates directly influence the economics of the business models of telecommunication competitors.[298] Another prominent example is how Microsoft, Sun and Netscape are using the large anti trust trial of the US Department of Justice against Microsoft's (mis)use of the Win-

---

[294] Porter (1981), p. 616 enhanced the SCP-Paradigm in the 1980s in the course of his work on competitive strategy (Porter 1980) and the creation and protection of competitive advantage (Porter 1985). He modified the formerly rigid assumptions and stated that only some fundamental market parameters such as product characteristics and available technologies would be given and possibilities for entrepreneurial conduct and influence on markets would exist (see Porter 1981).

[295] The discussion below explains Hayek's ideas on how the use of knowledge creates this market dynamic.

[296] Policy has by-and-large recognized this current state and therefore pleads for self-regulation, which is preferable to premature external regulation (see Cioffi 1999b).

[297] According to interviews with Josef Dietel, Senior Consultant W3C, 17th of March 1998, Hannover and Wolfgang Schneider, Business Development Manager Microsoft, 16th of June 1998, Munich.

[298] See Economides (1995a) and Economides / Woroch (1992), Economides / Woroch / Lopomo (1997) for the economic principles of interconnection, Teletalk (1998, 1999b) for a regulators view, Teletalk (1999a) for an incumbent position. See also Case Study 2-1 for an example with direct on-line business implications. It shows how – asymmetrically distributed – expert knowledge about industry specific technological and business management practices, in this case the provision of an Internet access service, enables players to capture a margin. Furthermore, it illustrates how an open standard technology lowers entrance barriers for new players. Finally, it shows how market know-how of all players drives the market dynamics in a Hayekian sense.

dows desktop operating system monopoly.[299] Considering these examples reveals an additional business strategy dimension. Netscape CEO Jim Barksdale summarizes the essential of this strategy:

> "(...) working with the government is far more product than trying to ignore it" (Jim Barksdale)[300]

These cases show how the competitive arena becomes extended to the court rooms and lobbying in Washington or other governmental seats. Regulatory policy, legislation / jurisdiction, standardization as well as the other "exogenous" factors identified in 2.1.5 will determine competitive lines and laws. Industrial players obviously conduct proactive policy in this arena to influence the game in their favor.

Second, firms can create new markets from the scratch. Particularly by defining new markets, or considering the multi-layered industry constitution – one should say market layers – a player can invent a new market layer, and hence initially create a monopoly. The "laws of the marketplace" (Porter 1989:273), which ultimately explain the context of strategic conduct, can be defined by the first mover, as also Prahalad / Hamel point out:

> "Yet in emerging opportunity arenas (...) the rules are waiting to be written" (Prahalad / Hamel 1994:31)

In this case not only internal aspects (e. g. know-how, scale effects) but also external aspects (standardization, copyrights, patents) can be used as entrance or mobility barriers prohibiting other players from entering or moving within the competition.

In both cases, industrial players do obviously not exhibit purely adaptive behavior. The examples show how exogenous parameters can be internalized by the strategic conduct of players, which certainly influences the exogenous parameters. Applied accordingly, the dynamic version of the SCP-Paradigm is able to model the strategic constellation of the dynamic on-line industry. Consequently **the "exogenous" parameters need to be internalized in a strategy tool set as part of the endogenous variables a given business strategy is moderating**.

However, in the light of the strategic challenges described in 3.1.4, **the market-based view exposes a fundamental problem for the on-line industry: it derives strategies from the market environment, which is assumed to be constant in its structure. In the case of the on-line industry, market structures are constantly changing and exhibit unclear boundaries. This raises questions: what are the fixed factors on the market side and to which extent can market-based strategy be applied for the rapidly changing and fuzzy on-line industry?**

---

[299] See DOJ (1999) and Microsoft (1999) for the arguments of both sides in this legal dispute and SPA (1999) for a comprehensive discussion.

[300] Cited after Varian (1998b:chart 2). Additional information about Netscape dealing with the political sector from the interview with Peter Harter, Global Public Policy Counsel of Netscape Corp., 5th of March 1999, Berkeley.

This work takes the position that although the Internet is a rapidly moving business environment, the basic theory of markets does apply. This general theory provides good advice for the strategic challenge of missing or premature business models in immature markets (see 3.1). In microeconomic theory, market imperfections – friction – are the fundamental explanations for the economic profit of firms. These imperfections result in market structures, where firms can earn rents. **Hence in the absence of stable business models in immature markets, the microeconomic theory of markets should point to the fundamental means for firms to generate economic profits.** The following will walk through the different market types and their fundamentals.

If a firm creates a new market it will be a monopoly player. This is a comfortable position for a firm. The – static – neoclassical theory of markets points out that **in a monopoly situation the firm captures rent.**[301] The Internet is an environment where markets based on new business ideas are constantly emerging, which in return constantly create temporary monopolies. The challenge for firms is to protect this market structure. A great example is Microsoft's PC operating system monopoly or the domain name registration monopoly[302] of Network Solutions.

If, on the other hand, a firm enters an existing market in which a high number of firms compete, **perfect competition** will drive down profits and the **consumer captures the economic rent.**[303]

This is ultimately rooted in economic basics and does not sound all that new. On the other hand, one can argue that it is better to point towards the direction of significant insights rather than marginal aspects, particularly as firms conducting business on the Internet frequently neglect these insights – these fundamental laws contribute the largest added value. Moreover, the recent work of economists like Varian, Economides, Katz et. al. argues along these lines.

A start up with a business idea of a general news site will find that there is incredible competition, which does not make it an attractive choice. Developing a new operating system, such as Sun's Java, seems to be a much better business idea as there is only one monopolized paradigm. Creating the next generation's paradigm is certainly an attractive position. Therefore, creating monopolies – particularly by creating new markets and protecting them – is a more tenable strategy than entering an existing dog-fight. This is not a new insight, but in the fuzzy Internet environment, it is worth pointing out, particularly as windows of opportunities are still open in the late 1990s..[304] Applying a business model in a market where entrepreneurial creativity can still invent new ones is obviously not the most efficient way to go. Start-up

---

[301] See Varian (1978), p.81.

[302] With the privatization of the Internet the US government was also privatizing the domain name system. It created a monopoly by giving the licensee to one company, Network Solutions. In 1999/2000 the non-profit organization ICANN is sorting out solutions how to create a more efficient system for the provision and management of domain names (see ICANN 1999).

[303] See Varian (1978), p. 84.

[304] See Wäsche (1999), pp. 1-2, who is comparing the current "windows of opportunities" (ibid.:1) in the Internet with the 1870s in Germany when new investment banks were rapidly emerging.

companies are constantly proving that innovative business models are possible in the Internet framework. Venture capitalist, Ann Winblad, expresses this in the following manner:

> "By the end of the day the Internet is still basically a competition of business models. Trial and error of new models will show which models are the most competitive ones in the long run."[305]

Traditional publishing companies are in the midst of experiencing this phenomenon: the new multimedia markets on the web host a large number of – often new – players. When a traditional publisher enters this New World, it finds that the new business does not generate the profit experienced in the old print world. Therefore, it needs to redefine or reinvent the markets with new business models.[306]

The theory of markets and microeconomics answer more questions. Varian / Shapiro[307] comprehensively discuss product and pricing strategies for network markets. They refer to this as a **versioning** of products with **differentiated pricing** for different customers. In terms of traditional microeconomics this is basically the idea of **product differentiation** combined with the idea **discriminatory pricing**, where the rent goes to the producer.[308] Obviously not a fundamentally new idea, but "versioning" is just a more technological and web-centric terminology. In terms of Internet business this foregoing would be called **mass customization and personalization**.[309]

If one translates this example into microeconomics, it leads full circle to discriminatory pricing according to product differentiation. Each personalized product serves one customer. At first glance, the market for each combination would be a bilateral monopoly.[310] However, with respect to Internet goods, each of the product versions is based on

---

[305] Ann Winblad, partner of Hummer Winblad Ventures, in her lunch speech at the conference on The Legal and Policy Framework for Global Electronic Commerce, International House UC Berkeley, March 5, 1999. Winblad statement points in the direction of creativity, information advantage and protection, which are fundamental parameters of market-based business strategy. Their role in the competitive dynamics of markets will be discussed below. For a discussion on business models see also 3.3.4.

[306] According to interview with Martin Stahel, Chief Strategy Officer and Member of the Executive Board Gruner+Jahr, 19th of June 1999, Hamburg. See also Varian / Shapiro (1998), pp. 83-102 for an elaboration on new business models for traditional media content on the Internet platform.

[307] See Varian / Shapiro (1998), pp. 53-82.

[308] See Katz / Rosen (1991), pp. 469-486. Although it has to be pointed out that that this constellation is welfare optimal in network markets, due to the discriminatory pricing (see Varian 1998a and Economides / Wildman 1995 for further analysis).

[309] This would be an example for a hybrid strategy, following the patterns of a mass market cost leader and a differentiated strategy. Pine (1993) introduces this concept and points out that situation with low change in processes and high change in products allows for mass customization as a superior strategy. Obviously Internet technology provides the right parameters for such **hybrid strategies,** which are "stuck in the middle". This is one of the reasons why the author declines to apply some of the instruments of the market based view: in particular, Porters concept of generic strategies (see below).

[310] See also Case Study 3-5.

"technologies (which, C. G.) involve high fixed costs, significant joint costs and low, or even zero, marginal costs.[311]" (Varian 1998a)

Hence, production functions of product versions for differentiated products involve no or low incremental cost. Frequently all versions can be subsumed under the same production function. Under these conditions one can treat it as one product serving many customers. Therefore, it can be modeled as a monopoly with discriminatory pricing. Although this market type at first looks like a bilateral monopoly, it is a supply side monopoly. In this case, the **rent goes to the producer**,[312] but exhibits the welfare benefits mentioned in 2.2.1. It is the technological possibilities of the Internet, which provide the options to implement such models exhibiting highly efficient economics.

The theory of markets also discusses **oligopoly situations**. The traditional approach is to discuss a duopoly, modeling different patterns of strategic conduct. The classical cases are: two players coordinating themselves and sharing the rent equally (Bertrand), or one assuming the leader role and the other one becoming the follower. In this case, the leader gets a bigger portion of the rent (Stackelberg). In both cases the rent for all firms is lower than in a monopoly.[313] If both players initiate fierce competition, a duopoly can simulate perfect competition. In this case, the consumer captures the rent. In this context, the example of the browser market shows how the highly competitive behavior of two players in an oligopoly situation drove down the rents for both players over the game period and resulted in a free product offering for the consumer. In other cases, like the competition for server technology (which is also a narrow oligopoly) the players do not operate in such a competitive environment and are able to earn comfortable rents. The lesson here is that it is better to be the sole supplier of a product or service or if there is one competitor it is the better strategy to be the first mover, which is particularly crucial in network markets for information goods as 3.3 will further elaborate. **In the presence of network externalities the sole or first mover is supported by stronger positive feedback which frequently makes this lesson mission critical**. Along these lines Yoffie / Cusumano (1999) conclude that players in fast moving and growing technology environments – in their case Netscape and Microsoft – should **avoid fierce competition and rather grow into a free and uncaptured marketspace**:

"Move rapidly to uncontested ground to avoid head-to-head conflict" (ibid.:73)

Yoffie / Cusumano explain how Netscape was able to withstand Microsoft's scale and scope effects, fueled by its tremendous underlying economic power, for such along time. Netscape was moving into new markets, defined the structure and was able initially to shape the rules of competition:

---

[311] "By "joint costs" I mean the cost of those factors of production that are used to produce more than one output. (...) " (ibid.).

[312] See Katz / Rosen (1991), pp. 469-486.

[313] See Varian (1978), pp. 101-102 and Katz / Rosen 1991, pp. 552-556. See Economides (1993) for an analysis of composite products in duopoly situations, Economides (1992) for examples of former telecommunication monopolists who invite further competition. Economides / Wildman (1995) point out that discriminatory pricing in the transition from monopolies to more competitive structures (monopolistic competition) is welfare optimal.

"Moving to uncontested markets allowed Netscape to define the terms of competition" (ibid.:75)

Nevertheless, ultimately Netscape was not able to escape the head-to-head competition of a duopoly situation. Microsoft followed Netscape, adapted its strategic behavior, and overtook browser market leadership by flexing its economic muscle against the smaller competitor. The better economics succeeded.[314] But this short duopoly example demonstrates the dynamics involved in markets over time, which cannot be explained in a static equilibrium model. The neo-classical theory of markets and the underlying SCP – Paradigm provide only **static models** and assume mature markets in an equilibrium state. In this context competition is perceived as a state and not as a process.[315]

"The assumption of a perfect market in this sense is just another way of saying that equilibrium exists but does not get us any nearer to an explanation of when and how such a state will come about." (Hayek 1937:33)

This modeling does not sufficiently explain the **dynamic of change** in market constellations, demonstrated using the Netscape / Microsoft duopoly example. In high technology areas like the Internet the role of **technological innovation should be seen as enabling dynamic, with entrepreneurial firms in the driver seat, controlling speed and direction.** This refers to Schumpeter's idea of entrepreneurs driving a constant process of "creative destruction" (Schumpeter 1943:81). The creation of new concepts results in new or alternative market settings. He postulated that firms not only compete over price but also over innovative technologies and improved product characteristics.[316] Kenney / Burg point out this powerful contribution of Schumpeter's understanding of the role of technological innovation:[317]

"(...) Schumpeter (1964) recognized the role of technical innovation as a powerful trigger for new firm formation and, in some cases, entire new industries." (Kenney / Burg 1999:4)

---

[314] See Yoffie / Cusumano (1999).

[315] See Knyphausen (1993), p. 782 and McWilliams / Smart (1993), p. 70. But Hayek (1937:33) criticized the static equilibrium mind set of economists already much earlier advising "to push theoretical investigation beyond the limits of traditional equilibrium analysis." He (ibid.) pointed to dynamic application of knowledge as "(...) foresight proved to be of fundamental importance for the solution of the puzzles of the theory of imperfect competition, the questions of duopoly and oligopoly (...), in the treatment of the more "dynamic" questions (...).".

[316] See Schumpeter (1943), pp. 81-85 and Schumpeter (1952). See Köster (1983), p. 163 for the scientific and historical context. See Abernathy / Clark (1985) and Abernathy / Utterback (1978) for a discussion of Schumpeter's ideas in the context of innovation and technology and Utterback (1994) for the aspect of technological innovation and market dynamics and Kavassalis, / Solomon (1997) for a perspective to telecommunications after the emergence of the Internet.

[317] Whereas innovation in this context can be understood as "(...) the market introduction based on invention, research, and development of a new product or process." (Wienandt 1994:18) [translation, C. G.]. Drucker (1985:67) defines innovation from a firm standpoint as "(...) the effort to create purposeful, focused changed in an enterprise's economic or social potential.", whereas comprehensive innovation frequently emerges in a process which involves existing and new firms (see Utterback 1994, pp. 29-33).

When one strives to understand market dynamics, one should recall Hayek's ideas within the **market process theory.**[318] His concepts explain the development of markets in a general way. They specifically include the constant dynamic change such as exhibited by the structure of **"emerging markets"** (Krogh / Roos 1996a) such as the on-line industry. These markets do not yet exhibit a high level of stability and maturity to approach a state of equilibrium.

> "It is clear that, if we want to make the assertion that, under certain conditions, people will approach that (equilibrium) state, we must explain by what process they will acquire the necessary knowledge." (Hayek 1937:46)

The **asymmetrical distribution of knowledge** (Hayek's informational resources) in a market creates opportunities for firms to invent new concepts and to earn rents.[319] But ultimately

> "The economic problem (...) is not merely a problem of how to allocate "given" resources (...). It is rather a problem of how to secure the best use of resources known to any of the members of (... a firm, C. G.). Or, to put it briefly, it is a problem of the utilization of knowledge (...)." (Hayek 1945:519)

Hence, next to the asymmetrical distribution of information, **the use of knowledge is the fundamental source of market dynamics.** A temporary equilibrium is created by the price mechanism.

> "Fundamentally, in a system in which the knowledge of the relevant facts is dispersed (...), prices can act to co-ordinate the separate actions." (Hayek 1945:524).

This does not sound like the most recent news to academia, but in the hyperbolic discussions of the information economy old facts evidently need to be rediscovered, as Varian / Shapiro point out in their discussions regarding strategies for the Internet:

---

[318] A different idea of monopolistic competition is the dynamic market theory: It assumes that markets have development cycles. An innovative entrepreneur creates a new market as a first mover. He initially enjoys a monopoly position and can capture rent. Other players are attracted by this opportunity and enter the competition. The competition increases over time and players drive down their profits. The final stage is a perfect competition. See Katz / Rosen (1991), pp. 506-508. This model basically assumes only temporary friction, in this case, scarce creativity of risk taking entrepreneurs, and over time the market tends to the equilibrium in a perfect competition. This model is not compliant with the findings about network markets in 2.2.1, which highlight markets with a trend towards concentrated structures with one or few dominant players. Economides / Flyer (1997) point out that these non-perfect competitions are welfare optimal due to the demand side economies of scale. Hence the basic idea of monopolistic competition seems not to model the industry appropriately. Therefore, it could advocate potentially incorrect lessons for the dominant players.

[319] Eye opening in this context is the following citation of Varian regarding: "little mention of the topic of information (...) [which, C. G.] is not unusual for an economics text; until 1960, virtually no discussion of the economics of information was available in any explicit form." (Varian 1978:290). He highlights "asymmetry of information" (ibid.:291) as a crucial parameter in the dynamics of economies and an area in which firms can earn rents. This notion demonstrates the tremendous insights of Hayek in the 1930s and 1940s. The early work of Varian in a context of neo-classical microeconomic analysis displays his early interest in the "economics of information" (Varian 1978, pp. 290-305), which developed into his main interest in the early and late 1990s, which is great timing considering the rise of the "information age" during the course of the network economy and the Internet, where "information rules" (Varian / Shapiro 1998).

Focusing on the knowledge resources, the dynamics of this market constellation are created by the diffusion of new ideas – usually triggered by information – in a social system and the means by which entrepreneurs use their informational advantage. Rogers (1995) analyzes the patterns of diffusion of information and innovation in a social system and describes it as

"(...) the process by which an innovation is communicated through certain channels over the time among the members of a social system" (Rogers 1995:35)

whereas firms need to be more innovative than others which is exhibited by

" (...) the degree to which an individual or other unit (e.g. a firm, C. G.) of adoption is relatively earlier in adopting new ideas than other members of a system." (ibid.:22)

In other words: **Firms need to know more, better, earlier, and use this to their advantage.** Again, this does not sound like the latest news, but in the particular situation of the Internet, this statement is highly significant and makes this lesson is particularly strong.

Different from neoclassical market theory, individual firms are not modeled as reactive players who are price-takers adjusting their volumes. Instead, firms are seen as proactive players who define markets and laws of the marketplace. The better provision of information places a firm in the position to create a favorable market. The distribution of information over time will determine the probability of players to be successful. Their conduct dynamically adjusts market structures. In each period, the market exhibits a constellation, which can be described with the basic theory of markets. This has two interesting implications for this work. First, it points to the importance of knowledge, or in other business terms, firm resources, as a reason behind both firm performance and changes in the market structure. Hence, it is a market based tradition, which considers aspects which are contained in the resource-based view (3.2.2). Second, the power of information is underlying the innovative forces of the on-line industry, which drive constant change, as Netscape discovered in the emerging browser arena in 1994-1998. This enhancement to the neoclassical theory of markets allows the observer to view the knowledge factor as a fundamental driver of the market structure. **Firms, which are able to manage knowledge resources and use this in their business strategy can play an active role in creating and controlling the market.** The subsequent strategic issue from a firm's standpoint is to identify positioning and means to use the informational asymmetries to create and enhance friction in a market to maintain that position. Although this might sound abstract and theoretical, the history of Netscape and the browser market can serve again as a prominent example as illustrated in Case Study 3-1:

A 22 year old Marc Andreessen, one of the leading developers of the first – still non-commercial – NCSA Mosaic browser. Together with Jim Clark, a 49 year old Silicon Valley executive and entrepreneur, they understood the emergence of the World Wide Web and the role of the browser. They recognized it as THE user interface of the future media and computing paradigm. Andreessen understood the technology and the user, Clark the laws of market place and how to start-up a company. This equipped the team with exclusive informational advantages and abilities to capture this opportunity.[320] On the other hand, Microsoft was a late comer to on-line business and the Internet. A first attempt to gain experience was the introduction of the proprietary on-line service platform MSN in August 1995.[321] It was rather traditional approach. By gaining experiences with MSN and observing the rise of the web Microsoft learned about the rules and the critical components of the on-line business in the presence of the Internet. In 1995 he finally decided to fully embrace the web with all Microsoft products.[322] The browser as the common interface to this world was the strategically critical component and therefore in the center of Microsoft's Internet strategy for the coming two years.[323] It took Microsoft two software generations to be able to produce a product comparable to Netscape. In August 1996, Microsoft introduced Internet Explorer 3.0 which was the first really competitive Microsoft browser.[324] By then, Netscape had a market share of almost 90%.

This shows how the diffusion of information and the generation of know-how in firms at first generated a competitive advantage for Netscape. But later, as another player generated comparable know-how, fierce competition rapidly emerged in Netscape's former monopoly market, which was dominated by the economic power of Microsoft (see above). Along these lines Jim Barksdale, CEO of Netscape, illustrates this entrepreneurial pursuit for the information and the aligned market dynamics: "Where is the market, and what products can we build to grow into that market? (...) This is the most competitive business on the planet. And honey attracts flies. If we find something that looks attractive, our competitors will be after it as well." (Bamford 1997:1) (see Case Study 2-6).

Case Study 3-1: Netscape, Microsoft, The Use of Knowledge & Market Dynamics

Figure 3-3 summarizes the insights from the theory of markets and highlights two fundamental lessons. First, it is the **strategic decision as to how one positions a business**. This position determines the initial potential to earn a rent. Second, the dynamics of markets depend on the **asymmetrical distribution and strategic use of knowledge**. The informational asymmetries are the resource firms use to create mobility and entrance barriers, which influence the market structure.

---

[320] See Bamford (1997) and Kwak (1998).

[321] See Yoffie (1996, 1998).

[322] See Gates et. al. (1996).

[323] See interview with Wolfgang Schneider, Business Development Manager Microsoft, 16th of June 1998, Munich.

[324] See Kwak (1998).

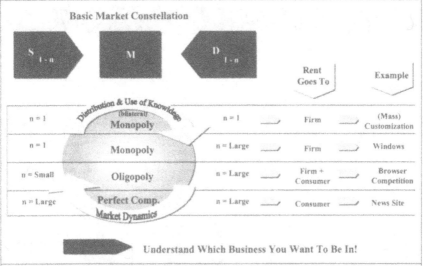

Figure 3-3: Market Dynamics & Distribution of Rent in Basic Market Constellations

An analysis of basic market constellation (neo-classical market theory) offers a favorable potential strategic positioning in the fuzzy on-line industry. The distribution,
acquisition, use, and protection of knowledge (market process theory) explains the
dynamics of markets, which is created by the players. A strong strategic position,
followed by rigorous protection of this position demonstrates a firms' ability to utilize knowledge.

Considering the analytical background of this work it is sensible to compare it with empirical
data of the field. Therefore, Figure 3-4 analyzes the network, hosting, software and content
layer of the on-line industry and proves that the market theory is a great strategic tool to point
towards potential rents in the infant on-line industry. It shows the demand and supply side and
the according market structure. Moreover **the most scarce resource / limiting factor and
know-how requirements indicate the key drivers of the economics of this layer**. The right
column describes prices, costs, investments and know-how as parameters for the current patterns of value creation in this layer.[325]

---

[325] The device layer is not analyzed as players from the PC (e.g. Dell), telephone console (e.g. Alcatel), PDA
(3Com) and cellular phone (e.g. Nokia) are just entering the on-line arena and solid data is not available yet.

Layer	Number of Suppliers	Customers Demand	Market Structure (limiting factor)	Value Creation (prices, costs, investments, know-how)
Network	• Few owners of infrastructure • Many wholesale layers	• Very large demand • Few large players • Many small players	• Narrow oligopoly • Telecom deregulation creates new value creation potentials • **Bandwidth is scare** • **Traffic aggregation is scare**	• Clear pricing structures • Rates decreasing • Investment intensive • **System integration know-how** • Attractive value creating potentials
Hosting	• Few big players • Many small players	• Very large demand • Few large players • Many small players	• Strong competition • Large players (AOL) operate hosting vertically integrated • **Service quality is scare**	• Clear pricing structures • Rates decreasing • High investments for infrastructure • **Operations know-how** crucial • **Datamining know-how** provides an additional value creation potential
Software	• Few dominant players (MS, Sun) • Many niche players	• Very large demand	• Trend for monopolies in mass markets area • "Go niche" for small players • Messy situation in strategic areas (->standardization) • **Delivery of complex quality solutions in time is scare**	• Extreme variation in prices • **Know-how intensive (complex know-how about customer, needs, technologies, vertical markets)** • High R&D costs, low production and distribution costs • Very good value creation potentials as SW connects hardware and value added applications
Content	• Many • Many similar players	• Many (very fragmented) • Demand is the limiting factor	• Perfect competition • Strong bargaining power on the demand side • **Demand "traffic/eyeballs" is the limiting factor while "content is there"**	• Value creation problematic • Prices towards zero • **Content and customer know-how** • Focus on market share as long term value driver

Figure 3-4: Market Structure & Market Situation in the On-Line Industry, 1999[326]

The analysis of the four layers shown in Figure 3-4 implies that in 1999 it is much better positioning to be in the software layer where the supply side is the limiting factor of growth rather than to be in the content layer where the demand side ("eyeballs") are the limiting factor. Every website could easily multiply its volume but a software company is not easily able to release a more stable and more complex version ahead of schedule, despite strong demand. While the content business is fragmented with an almost unlimited number of sites offering similar content the software business is " owned" by a few large players in the high volume segments / mass markets (e. g. operating systems, server, client software) and specialized players usually catering to the niches (e.g. content management systems, datamining / analysis software). This explains why players such as Microsoft, Doubleclick, or Broadvision earn large profits with their Internet offerings and content networks such as Time Warner's Pathfinder or Microsoft's Interactive Media Group fail to realize profits in a "commoditized" (Colombo / Nguyen / Perrucci 1997:214) content business. The positioning in the respective market environments makes the difference as who captures value. An analysis of the market structures is plainly able to provide this lesson. Moreover, at a time where narrow bandwidth is the reality, it seems to be a valuable position to own the pipes where this bottleneck occurs. Therefore, telecommunications players can capitalize on their networks, while demand for data traffic is growing by a factor 1000% per year according to UUNet.[327] Players who aggregate traffic, be data traffic or "eyeball" traffic, can leverage off the control of these limiting factors. This explains why the integrated bundle of AOL is an attractive business. "Owning "

---

[326] See IDATE (1999a), Deloitte (1998), Datamonitor 1998, Booz Allen Hamilton (1998b), OECD (1998b, 1998d), Gartner Group (1997c, 1997d, 1997f, 1997g, 1997h, 1997i, 1997k), Jupiter Communications (1998), KPMG (1998a), SPA (1999), Spectrum (1998), Goldman Sachs (1999b).

[327] See also Baack (1999), p.8.

the traffic of 20 million subscribers puts AOL in a position to negotiate good deals with content players as well as data network players. Content can be acquired under positive terms and scale effects drive down network rates. The breakeven of critical mass created these network effects for the network and content layer for AOL.

So far the analysis and discussion of the market-based view has delivered insight regarding the role of market structures, the market-based choice of positioning and protection of this position. Moreover, it discusses the role of information asymmetries driving dynamics in this constellation. This insight can explain in which part of the multi-layered industry a positioning of a business is favorable and which general market mechanisms apply. It laid out that frictions are desirable from a firm's standpoint and that the management of knowledge is a crucial parameter. This advice is based on the general and **fundamental insights of microeconomic business strategy**, which **provide stable economic principles. Therefore, firms can identify these principles as fixed points in the – somewhat chaotic – Internet.**

> "The bewildering pace of the Internet may even put a premium on these old fashioned
> virtues (...) for this 'new, but not new world'." Cusumano / Yoffie (1999:81)

The author argues that these economic principles, applied in a virtuous way, are one of the few fixed points in the Internet scenario.

Furthermore the author argues that **although** the microeconomic business strategy can contribute tremendous analytical clarity, **the corresponding strategy tools and instruments**[328]

---

[328] The most common instruments are Porter's (1985) five forces framework, which starts with industry analysis. This basically extends the theory of markets as discussed above. It reveals the attractiveness of an industry and the corresponding potential returns a firm can realize in this industry lead to generic strategies, which in return can be broken down into functional strategies using the value chain. The overall goal is to position oneself within an industry where a firm can protect itself best against the market forces and where the company is in best position to influence the market forces. The **five forces framework** is his fundamental component for the analysis of an industry structure (see Porter 1987, pp. 25- 32 and 2.2.2 for enhancements to the analytical aspects in multi-layered industries.) This tool has two sides to it. It has an analytical side, which helps to structure a market constellation with its underlying forces, which can drive down firm profits. This explains the general attraction and the competitive situation of an industry. This analytical side can certainly support understanding of a market constellation in a very structured way, although it is not designed to explain constant change and fundamental shifts in the laws of the marketplace. The other side is to conceptually translate these forces into a firm's profit equation. These in return lead to the core strategy: The translation into **generic strategies**, is in fact the quintessential component of the market-based view in business strategy. Porter postulates three generic strategies: cost leadership, differentiation, and focus. Players, who pursue one strategy, will have the highest return on investment. Players, who are stuck in the middle between strategies, will have a lower performance. First of all, this provides no advice regarding technological aspects or a firm's resources and furthermore the low / no cost possibilities for mass customization / personalization on the Internet might turn the "stuck in the middle", "hybrid strategies" (see Kirsch 1991, eds., pp. 539-557) into a winning path (see also footnote 309). The current trend of one-to-one personalized products (frequently coined: "My ......") might result in the victory of cost leaders in mass markets who deliver differentiated products. The strategic move of Amazon from a mass market cost leader for books into a differentiated one stop shop for a host of products can be seen as a prominent trial. "The long run" will tell if the economics of this model are superior.
The **value chain** is the tool, which can be applied to structure strategically relevant processes / components within a firm, and used to develop competitive advantages according to the chosen generic strategy (see also footnote (see also footnote 11). The application of this tool for this thesis would require a consistent value chain applicable for the entire industry and all players. This work argues that there is not consistent process structure, which is valid for the entire industry. Of course each individual firm can be analyzed with the gen-

of the market-based view do not deliver great value. The main reason is that they were designed on the basis of rather stable, clearly defined, and mature industries. Hence, the lessons provided by **these instruments**, such as the generic strategies, **prove to be correct in the long run, when industries have reached the maximum adoption rate and consolidation processes have led to a state closer to equilibrium. This is certainly not the case for the Internet environment.** The analysis has shown that the fundamental market parameters in the layers of the Internet framework are constantly adjusting. Uncertainty is too high to generate ex-ante scenarios, which are certain enough to provide the foundation for a strategy. In addition, the blurring of boundaries between competitors removes a lot of the clarity from the process of applying Porter's framework.[329] The technology adoption life cycle (Moore 1995) of the Internet (see Figure 1-5) has still not reached the majority by the late 1990s. An application of the Porter's instruments would analyze blurry and unstable market structures of the past and present , although they are possibly fundamentally different in the near future. This would underestimate the "Competitive Dynamics of Internet Time" (Yoffie / Cusumano 1999). The market-based tools – in particular the generic strategies – would use ex-post data and would derive strategy from this data.

> "It is important to remember that the so-called "data" from which we set out in this
> sort of analysis, are (..) the things as they are known to (or believed) (...). It is only
> because of this that the propositions (i.e. a strategy, C. G.) we deduce are necessarily
> a priori valid" (Hayek 1937:36)

Although of course not directly referring to the later instruments of the market-based view, Hayek (1937) analyzed the core of the dynamics in economics and pointed out a potential path for economists to work out their insights. He concluded that a given set of data from the field used for *a priori* propositions involves expectation or "foresight" (ibid.) about future actions. If expectations fail to be correct because other players conduct is different from expectations, the market definitions or rules of the marketplace underlying a strategy are no longer valid. Considering that rapid growth, change, complexity and uncertainty are strategic challenges (3.1.4) in the "hyper-competitive environment" (D'Aveni 1995), it does not appear a wise approach to derive a strategy predominantly based on the typical instruments found in

---

eral pattern of the value chain, but this would lead to insights for functional strategies, such as on-line service customer service outsourcing or Internet marketing, which is not the focus of this thesis.

[329] See 2.2.2, Dowling / Lechner / Thielmann (1998a), p. 5 and Grant (1992), p. 60. Furthermore, with respect to Porter's five forces and the seemingly clear definition of industry boundaries (as Porter 1980:27 explicitly defined as one of his assumptions) Kirsch states in general: "This is certainly an oversimplification as it is not explicitly considered that many firms are simultaneously active in several industries with partially very different market structures." (Kirsch 1988:224) [translation C. G.]. Kirsch refers to the application of Porter's framework of one firm being active in several distinct industries with different underlying market structures. This results in divergent strategic implications being derived from the market structures. This practical difficulty of the five forces created by the definition of an industry is precisely the case in the on-line industry. Because of its multi-layered constitution with each layer following individual laws of the market place, players are challenged to understand distinct market layers, which follow independent rules but which are interdependent due to the vertical network connections. This leads to the practical challenge of how to apply this approach. Boundaries of competition need to be defined. The strategies, which can be derived with this approach, are fundamentally influenced by how one defines competition. This is a crucial component of this approach. Nevertheless, one can argue that for analytical purposes the five forces framework still offers great value to perceive competitive structures and their relation in a multi-layered industry as shown in 2.2.2.

the market-based view. These instruments are ultimately rooted in static equilibrium models of microeconomic business strategy – a state the immature on-line industry is not even close to. Therefore, a rather static and retrospective view of market structures leading to the ability to derive strategies seems inappropriate as it would automatically address yesterday's situation and not the competitive challenges in future periods. Nevertheless, the market-based view delivers great analytical clarity and explains underlying economic fundamentals in a highly consistent way as discussed above. This provides economic orientation in "the forest of technological clutter".

However, there is more to be found on the market side than the underlying economics. This work argues that any market structure has one main underlying cause: scarcity[330] - of a good or service, which is demanded by customers and firms which are able to supply this good or service. The price defines the added value in this exchange relationship. This basic cohesion provides the outline for the following argumentation. The aspect of how firms are able to deliver a good, which is demanded, is analyzed with the resource based view in 3.2.2. The question of the **demand side of a market**, or if one will, **an industry, is ultimately rooted in the customer needs** and underlying purchasing power.[331] By the end of the day each competitor aims to fulfill the customers' needs. Each market structure has a fundamental root in the needs of people. This factor heavily influences the market structures, which develop on top of it. As the on-line industry does not provide stable market structures yet, it seems reasonable to look at the needs as a more fundamental layer. If these needs exhibit a constant character they should hence be applied as another fixed factor. Considering the fundamental needs information, communication, community and commerce (see Figure 2-23), one can assume that they are rather stable. These needs have stayed constant in the on-line service world for the past 20 years and if one takes into account traditional media, it becomes self-evident that they stayed constant for a much longer time. They have not changed with the emergence of the World Wide Web either.[332] There are no reasons why these fundamental needs should change. People want information, want to exchange information and want to build relationships for exchange, which go beyond the pure information exchange and embrace the simple fundamentals of social life.

The Internet as an inexpensive and increasingly ubiquitous interactive medium serves these needs. The dynamic aspect regarding how these needs are served is by-and-large determined by technology and its applications. But this does not alter the fact that the **needs are a constant and a fixed factor in the complex Internet framework**. Or as Jeff Bezos, CEO and founder of Amazon puts it:

> "Our strategy is always customer obsession rather than competitor obsession" (Jeff
> Bezos cited after Hansch 1998:C2)

This recommendation from a player with a proven track record is strong evidence that customer needs are a good fixed point for an analytical approach. Amazon wants to remain mar-

---

[330] Coase (1937), Williamson (1975, 1986, 1999, eds.).

[331] See Leitherer (1985).

[332] See America Online (1996), CompuServe (1996), Allensbach (1997, 1998), GFK (1998).

ket leader not by stressing the competition and the structures as they all seem to be quite fluid. Ultimately market structures are just an effect of an underlying cause. Customer needs are a driving cause rather than effect and, overall, are rather constant.[333] The same argument is advanced by Dowling / Lechner / Thielmann:

> "The complexity of the structure and dynamics of influencing variables in converging markets makes the problem of identifying relevant competitive forces and their relationships very difficult. However the analysis above suggest that for converging markets the starting point for industry analysis should be the customer and his/her needs (...). From this customer focus perspective it then becomes possible to analyze the structure of the industry" Dowling / Lechner / Thielmann (1998a:17)

Of course, the interpretation of how these needs are meet, is adjusted over time (phone calls will become video conferences, calls and emails will become multimedia messages sent to video boxes instead of voice boxes or mail boxes). However, it does not require outrageous fantasy to understand the current actualization and application of rather stable needs at any given time. Profound and continuously updated knowledge about available and upcoming technology can explain this easily. In order to derive a business model from these general needs, one needs to break down the needs to more specific dimensions. One could call them sub-needs like temporal aspects (synchronous, asynchronous), relational aspects (one-to-one, one-to-many, many-to-many), technological aspects (bandwidth, stability, feasibility, security, convenience). But all these sub-dimension can be traced back to the fundamental needs mentioned above.

Being able to understand this needs factor not only create a better planning foundation for business strategy, but it will be a particular **source to generate a competitive advantage,** not yet understood by many firms. As pointed out by Booz Allen & Hamilton:[334]

> "(...) companies still have not recognized the degree to which particular customer demands are driving market developments; these companies continue to compete primarily on the basis of technological innovation." (Booz Allen Hamilton 1998)

On these grounds, one can state the following hypothesis:

The structure of fundamental needs (see Figure 2-23) driving the Internet determines market-driven strategy implications rather than the actual market structures, which are results of these needs structures.

Furthermore, 2.2.2 shows how bundling of complementary needs creates complementary product bundlings which in return creates horizontal and vertical network effects. Therefore needs are not only a fixed factor. **Needs are a strategic factor when it comes to enabling network effects in a business network or product bundle to occur.**

---

[333] See also Case (1998) who points out AOL's emphasis on customers and to focus on serving the customers needs in the most immediate way.

[334] See also Bruck / Selhofer (1997).

Overall, the following implications for the on-line industry can be summarized from the market-based view:

- **The theory of markets helps to understand potential profits inherent in business models and depends on their positioning in a more or less competitive market environment.**[335] These fundamental lessons of the market-based view explain the economics and the logic of the on-line business. Empirical verification ultimately reveals that Internet economics and underlying economic principles are not all that new.

- **The strategic creation of friction in a market creates the potentials to earn profits.** This can be accomplished by scale advantages, product differentiation, management of capital and investors, customer adoption costs, market access, technology and standards, product design, and entrepreneurial conduct in new markets.

- **The dynamic SCP-Paradigm can be applied to model the complex interplay and mechanisms between factors in a market constellation.** The other classical instruments of the market-based view do not apply at this early stage of the fuzzy Internet framework. The application of a dynamic SCP-Paradigm enables seamless integration of the structural insights (2.2.1) and strategic insights (3.3) from network economics.

- **The internalization of the exogenous parameters (2.1) as strategic variables opens space for business strategy.** Thus, firms need to understand how exogenous parameters influence their competition and their business models. The respective factors of the political, technological, social, and industrial environment need to be analyzed for their effects upon the market.

- **First movers have the opportunity to define the rules and create the environment for all following players.** This area provides windows of opportunities, which are waiting to be captured.

- **Firms need to generate, utilize, and protect knowledge to define, create, and maintain market structures, which provide them with the possibility to generate sustainable profit.** This is the key to proactive conduct and an implicit formulation to the resource-based view.

- **Market dynamics follow the distribution and use of knowledge.** Hayek's basic law has held true since the 1930s and is potentially more relevant in the information economy of the Internet.

- **Needs are the only fixed parameter on the market side of a competitive arena.** Firms can use this fundamental "hook" as a guiding anchor for business strategy.

Overall it has to be stated that the market based view is a highly consistent framework able to generate insights regarding business strategy in an outside-in manner. However, this begs the question, is the discussion of a (dynamic) market structure, where firms create switching costs sufficient framework for business strategy? The answer is obviously not. **The sole advice it provides is to create and maintain friction through locking-in customers by creating switching costs. Porter's notion on mobility / entrance barriers needs to be enhanced by**

---

[335] Furthermore product and pricing indications become evident. The discussion in 3.3.4 will continue these investigations in a manner customized for the Internet environment.

the sources of how a firm can create these switching costs / barriers. This is obviously an area, which can be answered by **looking inside the firm.** Microeconomists traditionally only do this in a limited way. In the microeconomist's understanding, a firm's individual perform-ance is dependent on certain factor inputs and the underlying "technology", which determines the efficiency of the production. In this mindset two factors put into the production function are fully substitutional along the defined isoquants. Information is rational – at least "in the long run". Technology defines how much output a firm can produce in respect to certain fac-tor combinations. In this respect

> "Technology is society's [and a firm's, C. G.] pool of knowledge regarding the in-
> dustrial (...) arts. (...) The important thing about technology is that it sets the limits on
> the amount and types of goods that can be derived from a given amount of resources."
> (Mansfield 1991:8)

Differentiating aspects of a firm's internal structures are hidden in the term "technology" of the production function – an unsatisfying guideline from a standpoint of business strategy. Factor ratios and "technology" alone are saliently poor parameters to generate and orchestrate a strategy. Incomplete factor mobility and differentiated "production technologies" can main-tain asymmetrical allocation of resources over time. Dimensions like origin, endurance, non-substitutability, and non-limitability of resources are not sufficiently considered.[336] A firm's resources are a driver for successful strategy in the Internet and hence need to be integrated into business strategy considerations.[337] Hayek's notion of the distribution and use of knowl-edge resources points in this direction. For these purposes the following discusses insights from the resource-based view of business strategy. This inside-out approach will reveal how players can generate competitive advantage, differentiate themselves, and lock-in customers with products and services, by having unique capabilities which separate them from the pact.

3.2.2. Resource-Based View

The resource-based view follows an inside-out approach of business strategy focusing on the resources inside the firm. The term resources is more narrowly defined than in the neoclassi-cal framework. Only tangible and intangible resource which have a firm specific component, are defined as resources.[338] The original understanding of resources goes back to Penrose (1959) who points out that the uniqueness of a firm is caused by the heterogeneity of re-sources:

> "A firm is basically a collection of resources" (Penrose 1959:77)

A firm generates a superior margin because of two reasons. First, it is the availability of a unique set of resources and second is the efficient allocation of these resources. The approach was further developed by Teece, Wernerfelt, Rumelt and Barney. It ultimately became influ-

---

[336] See Hunt / Morgan (1995), p. 7, Osterloh / Grant (1994), p. 277-279. Although Rasche (1993), p. 425, is pointing out that also Porter was considering the role of specific firm resources in creating mobility barriers.

[337] See Dührkoop (1999).

[338] See Rasche (1994), p. 38.

ential in business practice through the article "The Core Competence of the Corporation" of Prahalad / Hamel (1990).[339]

As yet the resource-based view **does not exists as a conceptually closed school with a consistent terminology.**[340] In fact, the approach represents a host of quite heterogeneous studies. **Their smallest common denominator is the emphasis of the resource base of the firm.** Prahalad / Hamel primarily analyze larger industrial players and focus on technological aspects.[341] In order to give a wider base for the resource-based view Figure 3-5 gives an overview of authors and a description of their understanding of resources as a source to generate competitive advantage for a firm.

AUTHOR & DEFINITION	PARAMETERS OF DEFINED RESOURCES / CAPABILITIES / COMPETENCIES
Amit / Schoemaker Strategic Assets	• Strategic assets (resources and capabilities) are a set of scarce, dedicated, and specialized **resources and capabilities**, whereas the capabilities always refer to certain resources. • Strategic assets are hard to trade and imitate • Characteristics of strategic assets: specificity to the firm, enduring, scarcity of the resources • Enable firms to earn economic rents
Barney Firm Resources	• Resources are not or only hard to imitate due to historical matters, causal ambiguity and social complexity • Characteristics: scarcity, finite substitutional and value adding • Physical capital, organizational capital and human capital resources
Grant Capabilities	• **Resources** (financial, physical, technological, organizational, reputation) are the input into the production processes and the source of specific firm capabilities. • **Capability** (organizational routines) is the capacity of resource bundles to conduct certain **tasks** in order to achieve competitive advantage. • Resources and capabilities are characterized how enduring, transparent, transferable and easy to imitate they are.
Wernerfelt Resources	• Resources are all what can be considered as a strength or weakness of a firm • The term comprehends tangible and intangible assets
Pümpin Strategische Erfolgspositionen	• Firms have internal and external utility potentials • SEP's are **capabilities inside a firm which relate utility potentials to crucial factors of the market** and the firm environment • SEP's are not or only hard to imitate • SEP's fuel the long-term success
Prahalad / Hamel Core Competencies	• Potential access to a wide variety of markets • Significant contribution to the perceived customer benefits • Core competencies are difficult to imitate
Von Krogh / Roos Competence Configuration	• **Competencies** are the synthesis of **firm specific tasks and knowledge systems** • The **competence configuration** determines the potential of a firm

Figure 3-5: Authors and Definition of the Strategic Role of Resources[342]

---

[339] "I believe these authors were single handedly responsible for the diffusion of the resource-based view into practice." (Wernerfelt 1995:171).

[340] See Peteraf (1993), p. 180.

[341] See Tampoe (1994), p. 67.

[342] Amit / Schoemaker (1993), pp. 36- 40, Barney (1991), Grant (1991), Wernerfelt (1984), p. 172, Pümpin (1992), p. 34, Prahalad / Hamel (1990), p. 83-84, Krogh / Roos (1992), pp. 424-425.

The authors discuss how resources can be leveraged into competitive advantage. Imperfect factor markets result in constraint possibilities for the exchange and transaction of resources and capabilities. The asymmetrical allocation of resources between firms is the source for competitive advantages. One can trace this concept of competencies or capabilities driving the market development back to Hayek's idea of the – asymmetrically distributed – factor information being the fundamental driver of market development processes. Hence this approach implicitly uses his insights as they were introduced in 3.2.1. **Therefore the author recommends to mentally align the terms capabilities, competencies or resources with the concept of knowledge** while reading the discussion of the resource-based view. **It evidently reveals the subtle - but massive - power of Hayek's ideas.** Additionally it also reveals the difficulty of this approach: Knowledge is "software", hard to measure, difficult to manage often available only as tactic knowledge as Krogh / Venzin point out.[343]

One can think of this environment as an "ecology of ideas" (Kirsch 1997), which represents the available knowledge where some is carried by actors / firms in the industry system (endogenous variables of the competitive system), and some by actors / stakeholders in the in the social or political system (exogenous parameters of the competitive system). Finally, all information is carried by individual actors, who exchange information through various kinds of observations (ibid.). In the case of firms being the actor, they acquire, carry, utilize and protect information within the firms' boundaries. Informational advantages of firms can be described with the neo-classical term "imperfect information" or the strategic management term "competitive advantages". Montgomery (1995) points out that the management needs to ensure a **co-evolution of the resource base of the firm with the external environment**, in order to maintain a **competitive competence configuration** (Krogh / Roos 1992). Ultimately it represents the evolutionary spirit of Hayek's notion of asymmetrical distribution and the use of knowledge, which creates dynamics in economic and social systems, applied on firms in competitive market systems. Along these lines Prahalad / Hamel (1994) point out four success factors of resource-based management in respect to firms specific competencies:

- **Identification**: Potential analysis of the strategic value of the own competencies
- **Exploitation**: Focus on core competencies in existing markets and development of new markets
- **Maintenance**: Defense and protection of the portfolio of existing competencies
- **Development**: Expansion of the base of competencies by development of existing and gain of new competencies

Rasche points out that utilization does not exhaust core competencies but moreover their growing use increases their power.[344] If one applies the understanding of resources aligned to knowledge one can simply call this **learning**.[345] Of course the resource-based view defines

---

[343] See Krogh / Venzin (1995), p. 421.

[344] See Rasche (1994), p. 143. Kollmann (1998) is arguing along the same lines for the Internet framework, stating that informational advantages are creating competitive advantages through effective information acquisition (analysis of markets, customers, competitors), efficient internal information processing and effective use of information. Ultimately "Competitive advantage in the markets of the future is shifting from product edges (...) to informational advantages." (ibid.:49).

[345] For an overview about organizational learning in the context of business strategy in changing environments see Tischler (1999), pp. 74-84.

knowledge more specifically as resources, capabilities, or competencies as outlined in Figure 3-5. It uses this insight to explain why some firms are better off than other firms and are able to maintain this position over the time. But in its very core the focus on knowledge seems to be the essential aspect. **It shows how the asymmetrical distribution of knowledge and the capability to utilize this knowledge creates structures and dynamics in the competitive positioning of actors in markets. This is particularly valid in the information economy of the Internet.**

This is an important insight as most firms in the Internet framework build their business in an **information economy, with mostly very few fixed assets, based on ideas, intellectual property rights and exclusive knowledge** – hence on "software". If one compares the early position in the browser market in 1994 Netscape was a very small player without an existing customer base, in addition to few developers and a low cash flow. On the other hand Compu-Serve was – back then – a giant player with massive business and market access. In 1994 / 1995 an analysis based on pure economics would potentially support the thesis that Compu-Serve would beat Netscape after it had just acquired the first commercial browser player Spry. But looking at the data reveals that it happened very differently. Obviously it was the competencies of a "Silicon Valley Dream Team", Andreessen as technology visionary, Clark as experienced entrepreneur and executive, and Barksdale as the top executive to be a winner in this competition – at least for a few years. Competencies rooted in the particular knowledge of the executives – top executive personalities and competencies Midwest based CompuServe certainly did not call its own – evidently made a difference here. This would support an application of the resource-based view, because the different performance of these two players was certainly routed in a different inside-out conception of both firms. Nevertheless, the subsequent history shows how the better economics of scale and scope of Microsoft –a player with evenly great internal knowledge and capabilities - turned a new player into the winner. Evidently both views can contribute insights (see also Case Study 3-1 and Case Study 2-6).

This example also points to the widely agreed fact that in the Internet framework the crucial knowledge resource is by enlarge represented by the work force as a firms "human capital" resource (see also 2.1.4). Analyst Mary Meeker discusses the importance to master this "**human resource**" and the use of the "embedded knowledge" in the socially constructed context (Badarocco 1991) of Internet firms:

> "A recent study from Cornell University appears to indicate that employee-friendly companies tend to do better in the long run. (...)
>
> Over the years, we have watched companies start and flourish and then disintegrate. The clearest indicator of success seems to be a strong company culture. Strong management (...) *creates* the strong strategy. Overall, the most important thing a board can do is bring in good management and guide it.
>
> What is the most desirable corporate culture? Again, we see Silicon Valley leading the way. It's a culture where employees are valued and listened to, where they are encouraged to apply their intelligence.
>
> Most of the companies starting now have very little in the way of fixed assets; they're hoping to build up a customer list, a workforce, a set of strategic alliances. In some

cases, they may have contractual relationships with some of the individuals involved, but most of these assets depend only on people -- and their happiness, loyalty, enthusiasm and other intangibles that can't easily be bought.

It's easy to raise a billion dollars; it's much harder to build a billion-dollar company. (...) More than ever, people are something to invest in. As the overall quality of the workforce becomes poorer (and competition for trained, educated people becomes fiercer), companies will have to start investing more in training their own -- a contradiction perhaps in Silicon Valley culture where people move around easily." (Meeker 1996)

Meeker is empirically observing for the Internet exactly what Penrose was emphasizing in the context of to the resource-based view. She pointed out the **crucial role of the executive management**, as only the management resource is constraining the growth in the long run.[346]

"In Penrose's theory management is both the accelerator and the brake for the growth process." (Mahoney / Pandian 1992:366)

Meeker specifically points out that the ability to acquire and cultivate human resource and the according know-how applies much more as a resource constraint in the Internet economy than capital restrictions. [347] The ability to utilize this knowledge requires a corporate culture where the information can be acquired, shared, developed, protected, and ultimately utilized to generate competitive advantages. Again, an Internet specific insight which is not all that new is shown in the following Hayek citation:

"In ordinary language we describe (...) the complex of interrelated decisions about the **allocation of our available resources**. All economic activity is in this sense planning; and in any society in which many people collaborate, this planning, whoever does it, will in some measure have to be **based on knowledge** (...). The various ways in which the knowledge on which people base their plans is **communicated** to them is the crucial problem for any theory explaining the economic process, and the problem of what is the best way of **utilizing knowledge** initially dispersed among all the people is at least one of the main problems of economic policy- or of designing an efficient economic system (, firm, or business strategy, C. G.)." (Hayek 1945:520, emphasizes C. G.).

---

[346] See Penrose (1959), p. 5.

[347] One of the most recent, almost bizarre, examples is the start-up recruiting strategy of Goggle (www.google.com), one of the Silicon Valley hyped companies of 1999. After being "undercover" for more than a year, their first recruiting targeted seasoned top executives, a handful of professional experts and for job offerings number eight and nine: a chef (for "the happy, hungry Googlers", "the only cook with pre-IPO stock options") and a masseuse ("for our relaxed hard-working Googlers"). All job offers include notions on the cool cuisine, free massages and of course the "very cool" Palo Alto address and Stanford atmosphere, but also hardworking/professional jobs. This case is evidently a good example of where a start-up player understood the role of their personnel and start-up culture. Finally, it should be noted that first Netscape and then later Yahoo! were considered to be the "coolest" companies around. This is due to a significant recruiting incentive for the highest potential employees in Silicon Valley which they could afford to bring in by paying lower salaries – hence, these firms are able to recruit the best people of the market even when paying lower salaries just by selling their name as a "hot brand" leveraging that their company name on a resume becomes an asset in a person's future career.

This ultimately puts the people working in a firm in the foreground. They are the "containers" of knowledge and ultimately in charge of utilizing it appropriately. Given this knowledge-aligned resource, understanding it consequently, has to be concluded that **in the Internet the human resource available makes the difference if firms are successful or not.** Empirical and analytical observations discussed in this section strongly support this thesis.

Moreover Krogh / Roos (1992) point out the importance of generating "know-how" which is required for the "tasks" (ibid.:424) of the according market activities. This describes the firm's competence configuration as a relative term. Markets as well as the firm are dynamic systems and the fit of **the competence configuration describes the ability to survive on a competitive position** in a market. In the same context Prahalad / Hamel describe competencies as being the source of "competitive fitness". In this way the resource-based view implicitly catches up with Hayek's understanding of the evolutionary character of markets.[348] It basically means that at a given point firms have to be equipped with the capabilities to be more competitive relative to a certain environmental situation.

In respect to the development of the competitive Internet framework Booz Allen Hamilton emphasize the **proactive role of competencies in the evolution of markets**:

> "There is wide-ranging agreement that tomorrow's telecommunications [and other convergence, C. G.] industry will be far more competitive. One possible approach to this future environment is to examine core competencies and understand their role in the creation of markets" (Booz Allen Hamilton 1998)

This focus on knowledge as fundamental parameter, which is underlying resources, seems to be a wise focus **considering the uncertainty of the environment**, which was identified as another strategy challenge of the field (3.1.1), because

> "In an economy where uncertainty is the only certainty, the source of lasting competitive advantage is knowledge." (Nonaka 1991:96)

Or in other words: In rapidly changing environments firms more than ever need to know what they want, what is required to get there, and need to be able to conduct it, as the following notion of Hayek expresses:

> "If we can agree that the economic problem (...) is mainly one of **rapid adaptation to changes** in the particular circumstances of time and place, it would seem to follow that the ultimate decisions must be left to the **people** who are familiar with these circumstances, **who know directly of the relevant changes and of the resources immediately available** to meet them." (Hayek 1945:524) (emphasis, C. G.)

Barney (1991) and Grant (1991) define general requirements towards resources, which have to be fulfilled, in order to generate and protect competitive advantages over time:

---

[348] See Montgomery (1995, eds.). Salient in this context also Porter's (1991) notion on the relative strength of a resource, largely determined in its value by external forces, which underpins Krogh's relative definition of competencies as configuration according to tasks determined by external requirements.

- **Resources need to add value,**
- **Be scarce, and**
- **Constraint in respect to other players being able to imitate or substitute them and**
- **they have to exhibit limited mobility**

Firms only gain a long-term competitive advantage if resources exhibit these factors in a cumulative way.

The most problematic aspect in practical application is the **difficulty to identify relevant firm resources** and core competencies. Prahalad / Hamel define core competencies in the context of a tree of four levels. Competencies are leading to a set of core products. These core products result in a portfolio of business units which generate a host of end products.[349] In order to identify core competencies Prahalad / Hamel distinguish three general factors:

> First, a core competence provides potential access to a wide variety of markets (...)
>
> Second, a core competence should make a significant contribution to the perceived customer benefits of the end-product (...)
>
> Finally, a core competence should be difficult for competitors to imitate" (Prahalad / Hamel 1990:83-84)

Besides this general definition the core question for applied work is:

> "What does it mean in practice?" (Javidan 1998:60)

In regard to the Internet, Booz Allen & Hamilton has applied the competence concept for the new media area, and

> "(...) has identified eight core competencies: building a brand, segmentation, pricing, customer care, product development, distribution, technology, and strategic alliances. To set themselves apart, successful players must manage these core competencies better than their competitors in terms of time, cost, and value added for the client." (Booz Allen Hamilton 1998)

Based on practical expertise the author concurs with the suggested capabilities of Booz Allen Hamilton. But considering the analysis above the functional capability human resource to recruit, develop and retain personnel should be added. These factors consistently follow a functional categorization. One can basically attribute them to typical functional disciplines of an organization. Although it has to be stated that they do not consistently follow the requirements for core competencies as defined by Prahalad / Hamel (see citation above). They should be rather called **capabilities** as Javidan suggest:

> "The distinguishing feature of capabilities is that they are functionally based." (Javidan 1998:62)

---

[349] Prahalad / Hamel (1990), pp. 81-82. Rumelt (1994) points out that this structure of the core competence approach adds dynamic aspects to the pure mind set of resource portfolios.

The author argued with Hayek's points in an analytical way that knowledge should be considered as the fundamental **resource**. Furthermore, the author argues that in an industry with very limited fixed assets the human resource can be considered as the container for it. The acquisition, processing, utilization and protection of knowledge enables firms to generate the foundation for competitive advantage. Meeker's citation above furthermore confirms this from an empirical view for the Internet environment. She emphasized the factors of culture and management to leverage the knowledge, which is consistent with Penrose' initial statements.[350]

In respect to Krogh / Roos' definition of **tasks** they were identified for each layer of the online industry in part II (see Figure 2-27).

Players then need to be able to leverage their resources via their functional capabilities into competitive advantage about the according tasks of the layers. Javidan (ibid.) points this out and states that firms often fail in this respect.

> "Each corporation has a bundle of resources, but not every firm can put its resources
> into best use (to succeed in the particular tasks, C. G.). Companies vary how they can
> leverage their resources. Capabilities refer to a corporation's ability to exploit its re-
> sources" (ibid.)

Figure 3-6 summarizes these factors and illustrates this leverage of resources via functional capabilities into the tasks determined by the competitive market:

---

[350] The definition of these resources follows the requirements stated above (see Barney 1991 and Grant 1991):
Knowledge applied this way adds value. It is scarce if a firm acquires and protects the relevant knowledge.
Processing and developing it in a specific way makes it hard for other players to imitate it (in respect to the
required tasks of the particular layer, and if the resource is protected it exhibits also limited mobility).

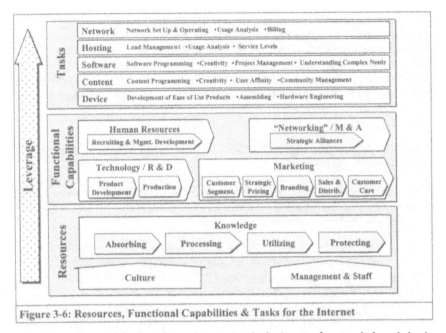

Figure 3-6: Resources, Functional Capabilities & Tasks for the Internet

Given the challenge of floating planning parameters in the Internet framework, knowledge is a factor which is (a) rather constant and (b) under the control of the firm. Along these lines Prahalad / Hamel (1994)[351] argue against artificial constraints created by existing industry definitions and market segmentations. They suggest focusing rather on the core competencies and derive a business strategy from this source. This solves the problem of blurring boundaries, which cannot be solved from a market-based view.

Knowledge resources enable firms to shift the focus from the rapidly moving product market competition to the rather stable resources of the firm. Therefore the author argues that next to customers needs and basic economic principles, the competencies of a firm are the third fixed factor for a business strategy planning framework.

Considering the forces of convergence the respective industrial sectors move together and extend the resource requirements. Furthermore the multi-layered constitution of the on-line industry requires a spread of activities and tasks in interconnected but distinct areas. As a result specific capabilities frequently need to be leveraged into new environments with different requirements. The resource-based view is critical in respect to expansion into diverse areas. Diversification into a variety of areas is only advised if players are able to leverage synergies.[352] The resource-based view assumes that in most cases **players will not be able to leverage their competencies into distinct markets successfully, if they cannot keep their**

---

[351] See Prahalad / Hamel (1994), p. 1 and furthermore Binder / Kantowsky (1996), p. 39.

[352] See Peteraf (1993), p. 188.

business focus.[353] **Cross-over strategies in the convergence area seem to be critical from that standpoint.** Although Colombo / Garrone / Seri describe that players from the convergence industries are able to partially leverage existing competencies they point out that players have to generate new capabilities for the Internet environment,[354] because

> "(...), interactive multimedia services do represent a change of paradigm (...) the strategic behavior of firms and the modes for organising economic activity will differ (...)" (Colombo / Nguyen / Perrucci 1997:209)

The required **capabilities have to be gained in the authentic environment.** This evidently underpins the necessity to hold the original perspective underlying this thesis (see 1.1.2) and not to fall into the trap of just looking to the Internet environment from a horizontal perspective trying to incrementally expand their competencies. This is a typical mistake being made by players from the convergence industries. In order to ensure their competitiveness they need to generate new competencies and a genuine market perspective:

> "(...) incremental adjustments in firms' core competencies, which have been developed cumulatively in their traditional business, be it telecommunication, media, electronic appliances, or whatever, do not allow them to capture the opportunities provided by the contextual (and intertwined) emergence of new needs and new technologies. A radical change in search patterns and market behavior will be required" (Colombo / Dang Nguyen / Perrucci 1997:222)

Part II shows that each of the horizontal market layers exhibits independent tasks and functional requirements (see Figure 2-27). This can be traced back to the resource level, where the functional capabilities and knowledge resources differ accordingly. The different requirements of each layer in return result in different strategic patterns according to capabilities and resources of the players positioned in the respective layer. But

> "Since excellence in all core competencies (capabilities, C. G.) is not achievable, a balance must be struck, with excellence sought only in those competencies (capabilities, C. G.) that are key to the company's future markets." (Booz Allen Hamilton 1998)[355]

This citation states the necessity to understand which resources a firm has to focus on, while developing all internally would result in an overspread. The author argues in respect to Krogh's notion of the fit of the competence configuration that firms need to match their existing resources with the requirements given by the market side. The analysis in 3.2.1 and 2.5 made a strong point in highlighting the needs and required tasks in this respect..

---

[353] See Mahoney / Pandian (1992), p. 368 and Nayyar (1992), pp. 229-230.

[354] Colombo / Garrone / Seri (1998), p.4. Colombo / Nguyen / Perrucci (1997), p. 226 point out that players from formerly deregulated, highly-competitive industries have smaller difficulties in expanding their competencies into the competitive Internet framework.

[355] Along these lines Colombo / Nguyen / Perrucci (1997), p. 222 point out that players from the convergence industries have difficulties in building a complete set of competencies covering all layers of the industry.

The analysis above outlined significant heterogeneity of the distinct layers of the on-line industry as a business environment. Leveraging the capabilities into these areas seems to be very difficult. The failure cases of classical telecommunications (e.g. AT&T Worldnet), media players (e.g. Time Warner's Pathfinder), hardware (e.g. Alcatel Screenphone, see Case Study 1-1) or software players (e.g. Microsoft Interactive Media Group) exhibit this difficulty very prominently. Mass market on-line packages are obviously extremely difficult to imitate as it requires a portfolio of very diverse tasks, capabilities and know-how resources. Therefore, **attempts for vertical integration aimed to achieve vertical network effects, become extremely difficult.** Managing the largest narrow band dial-up network of the world, the largest data center, the largest community, a full suite of content programming and the according software components require competencies from very different areas. No other player next to AOL was able to imitate or replicate these competencies. Nor has any other player from the highly determined convergence industries has been able to imitate this complex package.[356] The lesson from the resource-based view seems to prove itself in the case of the on-line industry. A cross over to the different layers seems to be an over-challenging spread of competencies. In addition, the underlying economics support large players which makes a market entry particularly difficult.

Therefore the combination of knowledge and capabilities in respect to the required tasks of the distinct market layers in firm network constellations needs to be seen as a key parameter.

> "Because no firm has a dominant position or first-mover advantage in these businesses, nor all the capabilities needed for success, firms jockey for advantage by forming partnerships." (Gomes-Casseres / Leonard-Barton 1996:364)

In other words **to utilize a complete set of competencies the players have to partner with one another.** This results in potential competitive advantages for all networked players. In this context Badarocco points out that complementarity of resources and firm specific know-how are a main motive for cooperation.[357] Prahalad / Hamel (1991) suggest to **cooperate with best practice players in order to expand and leverage the know-how of a firm.**[358] Colombo / Garrone / Seri observed this trend with players of the convergence industries in the Internet framework.[359] This refers to the capability to build strategic alliances mentioned above. Zerdick points out the change in perspective in this constellation. Players have to focus on their own competencies while they have to understand how to **combine a portfolio of complementary competencies in a value network** with such complementary players.

> "Die Wettbewerbsstrategie der Business Webs fordert einen strategischen Perspektivenwechsel für Medien- und Kommunikationsunternehmen. Der strategische Focus wird zugleich enger und breiter als bisher: Enger, da man sich im Wettbewerb auf

---

[356] Failure cases such as Microsoft, AT&T, Newscorp, Time Warner, Apple and so forth are prominently underpinning this argument. The success of French Minitel and German T-Online are strong examples for a noncompetitive approach to on-line services and multimedia, which was created in the exogenous environment (respective top down public planning) and not by competence and market forces as AOL.

[357] See Badarocco (1991), p. 25.

[358] See furthermore Rasche (1993), p. 424, Inkpen / Grossan (1995), p. 614.

[359] See Colombo / Garrone / Seri (1998), pp. 5-6.

seine Kernkompetenzen beschränkt, und breiter, da man die Bildung von Allianzen als strategsiches Element begreift" (Zerdick 1999, eds.:16)

This in return enables each player of the different layers of the network to leverage a superior resource portfolio. In the presence of vertical network externalities obviously a very crucial capability as players do not only combine their resources in a synergetic way but they also generate superior (network) economics.

Yet in addition to this cooperation with purely complementary partners Doz / Hamel (1998) generally point out to consider co-opetitive partnerships with potential competitors as well, if they can be temporarily seen in the role of a "complementor" (Brandenburger / Nalebuff 1997). They state this particularly in early stages of technology, hence it is highly relevant for the Internet framework. These kind of alliances can fuel the break even to critical mass of technologies and according networks. This was empirically observed by Mahrdt (1998) for the Internet environment. According to him new market structures particularly emerge in Co-opetiton networks (3.3.6). A temporary consortium to define a standard, which provides interoperability between the networks of several competitors is an example. In late 1999, a prominent case is the debate in regards to a technological standard for the buddy list and in-stant messaging applications at the Internet Engineering Task Force (IETF). Powerful players in the industry agreed to this mutual proceeding after several brutal force attacks of Micro-soft's "Messenger" against the AOL "Instant Messenger".[360]

The findings from the resource-based view are summarized as follows:

Competence is guiding firms in rapidly changing competitive markets: To the cus-tomer, against competitors and in the conduct with complementors. Firms shall focus their conduct on what they can do best and not on what they want to do best. Instead they should consider doing these things with the best player in this segment and partner with them. Cultivation, utilization, and protection of underlying knowledge resources and a fo-cus on the according customer needs are a crucial process.

Overall, it has to be stated that the resource-based view can provide at least a fixed parameter in the turbulent Internet environment. Although it also has to be noted that the resource-based view does not offer analytical instruments to identify core competencies and fails to provide a practical framework to derive a business strategy.[361]

Overall the following implications for the on-line industry can be summarized from the re-source-based view:

- **Resources can be traced back to the concept of knowledge.** Diffusion of innovative knowledge explains the connection to market dynamics and shows the individual handle for firms to generate frictions.

---

[360] See Houston (1999) and furthermore 0.

[361] See Campbell / Goold / Alexander (1995), pp. 120-121, and Rasche (1993), p. 424.

- A **knowledge-oriented resource approach requires a culture where people can acquire, process, utilize and protect information within the firm's boundaries.** Firms playing in the information economy frequently generate their competitive advantage not from fixed assets as in the industrial economy but on strategic knowledge which is kept inside the firm.

- **Firms need to identify, exploit, maintain, and develop knowledge resources, functional capabilities in respect to the required tasks of their market layer.** Competencies of a firm are relative factors, which are dynamically defined by the evolving requirements of the competition.

- **Competencies are guiding a firm.** A strategy focus on their knowledge resources puts firms into a position to handle the problem of rapid change of market structures, and uncertainty. The market evolution requires continuos learning.

- **Knowledge resources need to be leveraged via functional capabilities in the respective areas into competitive advantages in the tasks of the according market layer.** Knowledge alone is an abstract factor. It requires to be put into perspective with organizational functions and the respective tasks in the competitive market.

- **Players usually need to establish cooperative value networks with the best practice players to establish competitive vertical networks,** because the paradigmatic shift between the distinct market layers of the on-line industry requires different tasks which normally cannot be served with the same set of underlying resources.

The findings of these two mainstream approaches of business strategy will be summarized in 3.2.3 and put into perspective with the challenges for business strategy as analyzed above.

3.2.3. Lessons for Competition in the On-Line Industry

The **particular challenges** that business strategy is facing in the on-line industry environment are developed in 3.1 and at **first seemed to be quite novel and unique.** However, the discussion of mainstream business strategy revealed a host of insights and implications for business strategy corresponding to these challenges. **Many of the unique and innovative aspects are evidently not as novel as they appear from a first look. From a higher level of abstraction, many issues exhibit the same general characteristics as any other industry.** Nevertheless, due to the rapid change and the complexity involved, the surface frequently seems to show new phenomena. In an environment where clarity of a standpoint gets lost easily it appears wise to step back and look at the rather known, manageable, and certain aspects. The traditional concepts were not generally proven wrong so far and if applicable for the on-line industry, as discussed above, one should apply them. The practical as well as the theoretical discussion based on known concepts using widely shared terminology improves the understanding of the findings. Therefore an application of these theories itself enjoys network externalities, an in turn better economics of information / knowledge. In contrast to this, the seemingly new concepts are more a hypothesis rather than a seasoned strategy framework. Therefore, one focuses on relatively abstract, frequently old, insights of strategy theory, remaining on a high-level perspective, trying to avoid blurring it with a too detailed view.

If one considers the infant state of the industry it appears sensible to work with rather fundamental models and not sophisticated tools, which assume structures not yet exhibited in the industry. Moreover to focus on empirically analyzing microstructures of the competition seems not to be wise as structures on a very precise level of granularity usually adjust in very short timeframes. This would make empirical and descriptive work on this level obsolete in a short time, proven wrong by the rapidly moving business practice. Structures, which can be used for the more sophisticated instruments, will evolve over time with the maturing of the industry. But in any way even in a short-term perspective this work argues that at this point in time they would potentially not focus on the aspects which are crucial to be competitive at this stage of the industry. In this new field specific issues of business practice emerge in a very heterogeneous – and so far not foreseeable way. Thus, general guidelines promise higher added value as detailed analysis of specific practices. Creative and innovative entrepreneurs will solve issues occurring from a very detailed microperspective in various ways. This particularly holds true in concrete business situations, as the business practice seems to be more creative, experienced, and professionally advanced than the academic sector in this field at this point in time. These patterns will stabilize over time and future research will analyze it. Considering the fundamental indicators of the maturity processes, one can assume a rather long timeframe for this development. Adoption rates covering almost every potential customer will take several years. Usage patterns of the customers will adapt rather in decades. Technological innovation will not reach maturity in the fundamental technological systems characteristics in several years (see 2.1.). Therefore, rapid change and patterns of immaturity will remain for a very significant timeframe until consolidation will increase.

Overall, Hayek's notion of the role of knowledge was evidently a central concept. Integrated as underlying assumption the distribution and use of knowledge builds a bridge between the market-based view and the resource-based view. It comprehends opportunities and threats, given in the market environment, strength and weaknesses inside a firm, and their interconnection (see the SWOT aspect in 3.2). An application from both views puts firms in the position to use and generate the frictions, which are necessary to earn sustainable profits. A comparison of the challenges (3.1.4) and findings of 3.2.1 and 3.2.2 reveals that the majority of issues can be solved with these insights from the mainstream in strategy theory.

Nevertheless the analysis of strategy theory also shows some gaps and weaknesses of the academic mainstream in the areas of products and technology management and issues to comprehend the horizontal network effects in each market layer. Besides some advice from the resource-based view there is a knowledge gap how to strategically conduct in a constellation of vertically connected layers with various interdependencies. Hence particularly the network specific aspects are not covered by mainstream theory. Figure 3-7 puts this into perspective.

Challenges	Market-Based View	Resource-Based View
Premature Exogenous Parameters • Policy • Technology • Society • Industry	**Dynamic SCP – Paradigm** • Models the complex interplay and mechanisms between the factors in a market constellation • Seamless integration with network economics **Internalization of exogenous parameters** • Opens space for business strategy • Provides additional strategic variables • Effects on business model need to be analyzed	
Field Parameters • Growth • Change • Uncertainty • Complexity	**NEEDS as fixed parameter** • Can be used as anchor guiding business strategy **Competitive advantages for first movers** • Definition of rules • Creation of facts for other actors	**RESOURCES as fixed parameter** • Competencies are guiding a firm • Focus on internal knowledge resources, provides a stable factor for business strategy • The market evolution requires continuos learning
Product Market Area • Market Immaturity • Premature Business Models • Blurring Boundaries • Immature Products + Tec. • Horizontal Externalities	**ECONOMICS & theory of markets** • Predicts prospective profits of business models • Offers favorable options for a strategic positioning • Explains the economics & logic of the business **Creation of friction in a market** • Creates the potentials to earn profits. **Distribution and use of knowledge** • Key driver for market dynamics	**Resource Management** • Firms need to identify exploit, maintain and develop their resources **Leverage into the competition** • Knowledge resources need to be leveraged via • Functional capabilities into competitive advantages in the • Required tasks of the respective market layer
Vertical Externalities		**Vertical value networks with best practice players** • Each layer requires different capabilities • Individual firms cannot maintain a corresponding wide array of resources • Firms need to share complementary resources
Complementors & Co-opetition		
Dynamics of Interdependencies		
Overall insight for the dynamics of competitive market	**Distribution and use of knowledge** Firms need to generate, utilize and protect knowledge to define, create and maintain market structures which provides the possibility to generate sustainable profit	**Distribution and use of knowledge** A knowledge-oriented resource approach requires a culture where people can → absorb - process - utilize - protect information within the firm's boundaries
	➢ Resources can be traced back to the concept of knowledge. ➢ This connects the resource-based view to market dynamics. ➢ It shows firms how to generate frictions to gain profits.	

Figure 3-7: Internet Challenges for Business Strategy - Mainstream Insights & Gaps

Given this situation, one can assemble a general tool set which provides a cohesion for the singular tools necessary to work out a business strategy with the industry model.

3.2.4. Tool Set

The central issue form a planning standpoint is the identification of **fixed factors**, which can be used as a starting point to derive a strategy (see 3.1.4). Three parameters are suggested, which exhibit stable and foreseeable patterns and hence can be applied as fixed parameters for a business strategy planning process.

First, on the market side one can consider **needs** as a fixed point as they were analyzed in 2.3.2 (see Figure 2-23). This is a very strong aspect considering the economic effects discussed in section 2.2. A finding in the context of network economics was the role of complementary needs bundles as key reason for complementary composite goods. This factor being fixed then puts firms in the position to orchestrate their product – market strategy in a way that network externalities automatically occur – if well conducted.

Second, on the firm side, the firm's **resources** (knowledge, capabilities, abilities to perform tasks) are a factor which is rather fixed and particularly under the control of a firm. Hence an analysis of this factor and the comparison of the requirements of the field – in particular with the customer needs - reveals the competence configuration of a firm. Favorable strategic direction will become obvious in this way.

Third, the underlying forces and principles of **economics** are a stable factor. The analysis showed that these fundamental principles did not change. Furthermore all components in the strategic cohesion exhibit underlying economics: The firms, their chosen production "technology", the network / product technology, and last but not least the user. Moreover, if one considers the role of knowledge with the dynamics of the economic structure, it will become obvious. Finally, the specific economics of networks were analyzed in 2.2.1, which could evidently be outlined in a SCP-Paradigm. Given this structure they are easily translatable into the components of the tool set as the strategic cohesion can be modeled in a SCP – Paradigm as discussed in 3.2.1.

Ultimately these factors represent the market side, the resource-based (firm) side and the ubiquitously underlying aspect of the economics. Thus this approach has an inside-out and an out-side in view which comprehensively covers the field. **The key message is that firms need to observe themselves in respect to their capabilities, know about the customer needs and well understand the economics of all relevant players and components involved.** A business model should be built on these fixed points rather on some floating variables. They consider the utility functions of the customers, the underlying "technologies" of the production function and the economics of the firm under competitive aspects. Given these insights Figure 3-8 models a tool set 1 for this cohesion, which highlights the three fixed factors in capital letters.

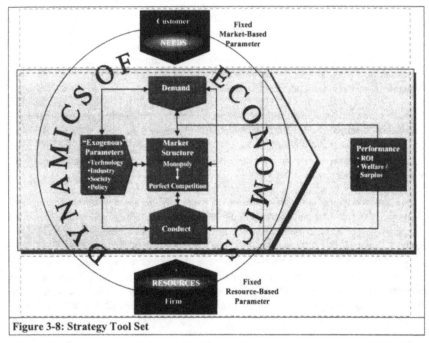

Figure 3-8: Strategy Tool Set

The strategy tool set shown in Figure 3-8 has to be seen under the following logic:

The strategic framework is determined by the tool set

- The tool set **models the components in a customized dynamic SCP – Paradigm.**

- It considers the **fixed parameters** and the adjustments in respect to dynamics and internalization of the "exogenous" parameters as discussed in 3.2.1.

- It is **aimed to maximize the performance** of the system as the target measure. From a firm standpoint this describes the returns, from an economic standpoint the overall welfare and surplus. Therefore, the tool set can not only be applied by firms, but also by the government and non-profit sector.

- **The endogenous factors** of the system need to be influenced by the strategic conduct of firms (see 3.3 for the according tools)

- **All components are** interconnected and **interdependent**

The conduct is based on the resources of the firms (see Figure 3-6) and opportunities in the market need to be analyzed in the light of the industry specifics. As criticized above, mainstream business strategy left open several of the required aspects for this component. Particular product and technology related issues, as well as the horizontal and vertical network effects could not be explained. For these reasons the following is discussing more novel and specialized strategy theories which are closely related to the Internet. The resulting insights will provide the individual tools for firms to conduct a strategy which can be derived from the fixed factors with this tool set.

3.3. Tools for Net-Centric Business Strategy

In recent times, there have been some very net-centric strategy approaches emerging, namely theories that take the Internet as the central research object. Some of the new ideas are hyped and fashionable arguments as criticized in 3.1.4, and some of them are stuck too focused on traditional and inflexible approaches as described as the horizontal perspective. But on the other hand, there are some concepts, which intelligently **apply and extend existing ideas of strategy to generate insights for the Internet framework**, as Varian / Shapiro point out:

"Old Ideas, New Applications" (Varian / Shapiro 1998b:114)

This has already been seen under the light of the parallels this work draws between **neoclassical economics, Industrial Economics**, and last but not least the ideas of Hayek. Aspects of **game theory**, which are discussed below, have always been part of strategy making, in economics as well as in other constellations. The most recent product and pricing strategies discussed under the key word "versioning" are ultimately also an industry specific application of existing economic methods. This, on the one hand, proves the underlying theories, but more importantly discloses the Internet and on-line industry as yet another industry, and not the threshold to a new economics. Nevertheless, in practice, many of the traditional concepts need to be re-interpreted and applied in a novel way to make sense.

Considering the **challenges to business strategy, which remained uncovered by the mainstream** market-based and the resource-based view as discussed above, the following debate will introduce net-centric concepts covering the gaps left open according to Figure 3-7. The unsolved issues in particular are:

- **Immature products**
- **Immature technologies**
- **Immature business models** – especially product and pricing issues
- **Horizontal network externalities**
- **Vertical network externalities**
- **Multiple interdependencies**

These aspects need to be solved for the particular situation of the Internet. For these purposes, the author has identified two conceptual approaches, which embrace the specifics of the Internet environment.

At first these issues imply the challenge to break down these field parameters into detailed issues of a **product – market – strategy**. Questions arise about **the proactive creation and leverage of network effects, product and pricing strategy, issues of adoption in an infant, but rapidly growing market**. The research in the context of network economics – in particular the work by Varian, Shapiro and Economides – provides corresponding insights with strategic implications **considering the economic and technological prerequisites** of the on-line business.

The second issue is how to react to the chaotic, unclear situation of an industry which is characterized by a host of players in several layers, where the **roles of friend or foe are unclear,** yet constantly adjusting. For these purposes Brandenburger / Nalebuff (1997) lay out a new mind set of business strategy, which is particularly relevant for immature and growing markets. **They understand strategy first as the cooperative aspect of creating a pie, and then the competitive aspect of dividing that pie into pieces.** This shortly describes **the mindset of co-opetition.** Their hybrid concept of business strategy particularly elaborates **on the role of "complementors",** which are an additional role to the typical roles of competitors, customers, and suppliers **who help creating that pie. This evidently provides a conceptual framework for a competitive strategy in value networks with complementary players.**

The following will introduce these two theories whereas business strategy derived from the microeconomic theory of network economics provides detailed insights how to enable a strategy based on network externalities (3.3.1). Furthermore, it will discuss how the strategic conduct of firms in respect to their product strategy (3.3.2), networking strategy (3.3.3), pricing strategy in respect to business models (3.3.4) and adoption strategies in growing areas (3.3.5), which can generate a big pie with the best network economics possible. Along these lines, the co-opetition approach provides an idea how players strategically position themselves the best in the process of creating and dividing this pie (3.3.6). [362] This will ultimately enable firms to play a virtuous game of business strategy in value networks in the Internet. 3.4

3.3.1. Enabling Externalities for a Network Strategy

This section will analyze the underlying causes and enablers for the creation of network externalities. **In extension to the findings from network economics of part II,** which observed the general, economic perspective and modeled a structure, mechanisms, and laws of the industry, **the following will analyze how these factors can be put into a relevant perspective from a firm's point of view.** The theory is particularly well suited, because it strategically analyses factors, which capture the specific economic aspects of technology, industry structure and content and communications products of the on-line industry. **The way these**

---

[362] The combination of these two theories is not uncommon in the research related to the Internet. See for example the Stanford Computer Industry Project, which analyzes the Internet framework primarily from a standpoint of hardware and software manufacturers. In this context the following description of business strategy challenges applies: "The team's projects have been focused on the following themes: - Competitive and collaborative strategies, - Understanding fundamental core capabilities, - New forms of corporate organization (...) The newest research theme involves the examination of competitive and collaborative strategies within the mega-computing industry. In particular, we have conceptualized the industry as a series of colliding oligopolies and examined how firms effectively compete in such settings. Our goal is to build on our understanding of industry evolution and firm competencies that we developed in our studies of product innovation, supply chain logistics, and new organizational forms, and to extend that work to include strategies." (http://www.stanford.edu/group/scip/strategy.html). This thesis is looking at the same object from a different perspective. Their findings suggest to see the Internet framework as a multi-layered environment which vertically connects players on distinct market layers with strong network externalities exhibited in all directions. Players need to find the strongest complementors to build up a value net. This research has, independently from this research project, developed a corresponding framework to model the industry using the same theoretical backgrounds (according to additional interviews with Francois Bar, Stanford University, 26th of April 1999, Stanford, and John Richardson, Stanford University, 6th of May 1999, Los Angeles). The European research cooperations conducted in this Ph.D. project revealed that studies in Switzerland (St. Gallen) and in Germany (Regensburg) apply ideas of network economics and co-opetition in their work accordingly.

factors are worked out can be seen in the wider context of the market-based business strategy, as network economics can be considered within this tradition. Therefore this section serves as a logical enhancement to 3.2.1. It will "translate" the network economic key terms, will lay out market structures in a way which reveals the causes and the role of network externalities and the implications for business strategy.

The author showed in 2.2.1 that the structure of the theory can be summarized in an SCP – Paradigm. Although the theory of network economics is usually not presented in this structure, it is possible to "reassemble" the theory in this traditional microeconomic business strategy pattern. This shows first the consistency of the approaches. But secondly, and more importantly, it allows to use the applied findings which were worked out in the discussion of the market-based view and concluded in a tool set following the adapted pattern of a dynamic SCP – Paradigm (see Figure 3-8).

Recalling the basic conclusion of network economics, one can understand the mechanisms in the following way: The key parameters are put in the center of a SCP – Paradigm while they follow a causal logic. Network externalities are the key factor in the market structure. Players who are able to leverage these externalities in their conduct need to aim the level of critical mass and will finally perform as a dominant player. Putting this into perspective with the findings from the market-based view, this constellation can be reassembled in a dynamic cohesion where firms can redefine this constellation in a way, that a firm's strategic conduct aims to create and leverage externalities proactively. Hence the "conduct" factors lock-in / switching costs, adoption rates, bottlenecks and compatibility become the moderating variables which need to be configured around the "market-structure" factors complementarity, demand and supply side scale and scope effects, horizontal (intra-layer) and vertical (inter-layer) network structures under the presence of imperfect information and coordination failures. These factors need to be managed by the firm's conduct based on their resources in a way that it reaches critical mass.

Furthermore the author suggested above to treat the "exogenous" parameters as "variables of the system as well, as long as they exhibit a rather fluid state. It then seems sensible for companies to carefully observe and influence the development process of the external environment, given possibilities provided by the particular resource situation of the firm.

Under this conditions the **causal logic can be formulated as follows:**

Firms need to create and utilize goods with network externalities and push them to fast adoption in order to reach critical mass. Once this level is achieved positive feedback will support this player to accomplish a dominant position with increasing returns. Path dependency will support this comfortable position, but instability of this market equilibrium requires according conduct to avoid the market to "tip" to a new dominant network.

Figure 3-9 illustrates this cohesion:

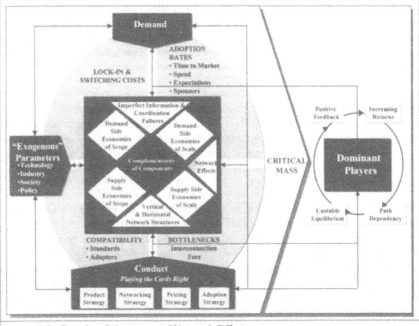

Figure 3-9: Creation & Leverage of Network Effects

Given this nature of the industry the following is aimed to further break down these factors to levels that are more concrete. It will discuss specific product, networking, pricing and market adoption implications for firms strategy. This will explain how firms can create and protect such a position.

Firms aimed to perform as a dominant player in the on-line industry need to master the economic laws leveraging the potential of network externalities and the underlying Industrial Economics. Figure 3-9 highlights network externalities as the factor which determines, if a player can achieve critical mass or not. Complementarity is set in the center as the crucial factor providing network externalities. In this sense Varian points out the **salient feature of the economics of network goods for business strategy**, as they are involved in the provision of on-line services:

> "What's quite striking for (...) goods with these kinds of network externalities we typically have both
>
> - supply-side Economies of scale so that the more you produce, the cheaper your unit costs of production and
> - demand side Economies of scale so that the more you sell, the more valuable the good is to the consumers
>
> If you look on the interaction of this demand-side Economies of scale with the supply side economies of scale, you can get an extreme form of positive feedback which has very interesting implications for business strategy" (Varian 1999b:27)

Therefore, the following **debate focuses on the way, how a firm can proactively create and enable these externalities**. This will put it into a position where it can achieve a dominant position, capturing monopoly rents. Bill Gates emphasized the power of the underlying forces back in 1994, when he explained Microsoft's dominance strategy:

> "We look for opportunities with network externalities – where there are advantages to the vast majority of consumers to share a common standard. We look for businesses where we can garner large market share, not just 30% to 35%" (Kwak 1998:5)

Gates highlights the two critical factors in the causal chain to become a dominant player. They are understanding how externalities are caused and secondly focusing on technology to enable them. The following will first analyze the factor **complementarity, which is the cause for network externalities** and then the factor **compatibility, which is the eventual enabler** for them.

> "The key reason for the appearance of network externalities is the complementarity between the components of a network." (Economides 1996:681)

Although there is vast amount of literature existing about network externalities, the **complementarity as underlying cause is rather poorly analyzed**. The majority of the literature looks at given constellations such as PC operating systems or telephone networks, where complementarity is already predefined, and discusses only the factor compatibility, frequently as a regulatory issue. Unfortunately, this discussion oversees the underlying conceptual cause, which is required for a proactive networking strategy for firms. The logic of a particular situation of components - whereas a "component" in general can be widely defined as a product part, a product, a product bundling, a firm, and even a complete competition – reveals the details of complementarity in a relation. Depending on how a situation is set up, according externalities will result. In this respect the author laid out an analysis of complementarity in 2.2.3. This discussion distinguished two main types of complementarity:

- **One-way complementarity**

- **Two-way complementarity**
  - **Asymmetrical**
  - **Symmetrical**

One-way complementarity results in a one-way network constellation and thus weak indirect network effects. **Two-way complementarity** results in a two-way network, which provides for stronger direct network effects. If one end perceives the complementarity stronger than the other end, one should call this asymmetrical complementarity. If the relation is perceived evenly from both ends one should call it symmetrical. The direction and power of the resulting network effects are following the symmetries accordingly. This has implications for the strategic constellation.

But if one considers the complementarity between components – given the wide definition of components – it results in tremendous leverage for network strategy. If players are able to create – or just even "see" – complementary relations to other players, either horizontally within the same layer of the industry, or vertically into other layers of the industry, firms can virtually generate network externalities. For example if one component, e. g. a firm, has large scale and is very complementary to other components, this component has a powerful bottleneck position. If the interconnections are defined compatible this component can charge for interconnecting. This short example shows the strategic influence of complementarity in networks. They will be further discussed under an economic perspective in 3.3.3 and from a game strategic perspective in 3.3.6.

The crucial aspect is to see a complementary relationship between components, that somehow can be networked. This can then be applied for products, bundled (composite) products, firms, and even industries, particularly in the Internet area as Economides points out:

> "Most products may be thought of as complex systems, or **networks**, composed of subsystems and components. This is especially true for many information technology products. Networks may be physical, as in the case of the (...) Internet communications network; or they may be logical as in the case of the different software modules / layers which must interact to support an application [or content, C. G.] such as (...) electronic mail or customer billing. " (Economides / Lehr 1994:1)

This is a crucial insight, because it builds the conceptual bridge to the idea of complementors, which Brandenburger / Nalebuff (1997) discuss as the **crucial role of complementors in a co-opetition mindset** (see 3.3.6). In this understanding, industries, firms or their products can be seen as complementors.

As mentioned in 2.2.1, such a network can be real or virtual. An example are the subscribed user of a buddy lists, a real – though intangible - two-way complimentary network, whereas the data traffic generated by the horizontal network of AOL subscribers exhibits a two-way complementary, virtual network with the vertically related data network of MCI Worldcom (see Case Study 2-5). The strategic aspect beyond the creation of network effects is shown in the position of the two ends in the latter relation. In a game scenario, one player will perceive the relation with a higher complementarity. Thus, he will gain the larger network effect. If the other player knows about this he can use this position by charging a virtual interconnection fee as remuneration for the provided externality. Microsoft has been mastering this for years in its co-marketing agreements. The ownership of the PC desktop can provide massive vertical externalities for any bundled component. Windows benefits usually only marginally. But in return, Microsoft usually charges exclusive use of another Microsoft product of another layer and co-marketing in the marketing activities of the partner. This strategic pattern was for example conducted in the bundling with content for the Microsoft Active Desktop Push Channels. The bundled providers gained a prominent position on each PC desktop and in return needed to exclusively deliver content for MS (and not Netscape's Netcaster Channels), distribute exclusively Internet Explorer and promote Microsoft as a partner in their Marketing. This strategy of leveraging market dominance into vertically related layers led to the large anti trust trial of the US DOJ against Microsoft. Nevertheless, Microsoft exhibits the same strategic patterns with the new Windows media player, although this example is so far widely overseen. 3.3.6 will introduce this mindset to show the strong leverage of these strategic networking effects.

Business strategy has to identify, create, and leverage these complementarities to generate situations, which exhibit network externalities. The question is how this can be done proactively in a high technology environment. Firm strategy has to develop a networking strategy, which connects complementary components. But

> "(...) Clearly, *compatibility makes complementarity feasible*" (Economides / White 1994b:6).

In this respect, **compatibility is the enabler** to put complementary components into a network constellation. **There are the two basic strategic options** how to conduct in respect to network effects:

▪ **Closed and vertically integrated,** where

> "(...), benefits of complementarity may be realized through vertical integration – one firm does all, as in the old (...) [CompuServe or AOL, C. G.] structure, where all the (...) components were made by the same company." (Economides 1998:3)

▪ **Open and virtually integrated,** where

> "Benefits of complementarity can be realized through **standardization** and **interoperability** among components. Such a structure is called an "open systems architecture." (Economides 1998:2) [emphasis, C. G.]

The open standard system architecture standardization of on-line applications and network technology in the Internet is a perfect example. Network protocols, host computer, content, client software, user hardware conform to the same set of technical standards and can share a mutual system architecture. Once a component is set up, it is functional with an enormous variety of compatible components, thereby reaping the benefits of complementarity. This can refer to level of integration or virtualization of the product as well as well as the firm aspect. In this mindset it does not matter if one analyzes the network effect in a product system, firm or even industry system. One can think of an vertically and horizontally integrated, proprietary standards based, on-line service such as Minitel in 1990 as opposed to an open standard, virtually networked Gateway 2000, Netscape, Yahoo!, MCI type of service. The future business practice exhibits players conducting strategies with various combinations of compatibility and virtuality in their conduct. Hence it needs to be further analyzed which approach is appropriate in which situation.

Reasons for horizontally and vertically integrated systems

▪ Network reasons
- Internalization of network externalities keeps positive feedback inside the firm
- Particularly attractive over level of critical mass
▪ Product and organizational reasons (non-network reasons) [363]
- Better coordination among components
- Quality benefits of joint use of integrated product

---

[363] See Economides 1998e, p. 4.

- Cost savings in joint production
- Better quality of integrated design
- Quicker information flow in a vertically integrated company
- Assurance of markets for components
- Easier vertical expansion to new components

The example of Windows showed the use of horizontal and vertical externalities. Windows gets positive feedback within the operating system market which is a horizontal externality, while Microsoft leverages this asset into other layers, such as browser, multimedia player, or email software. Due to critical mass Microsoft chooses to vertically integrate large portions of components. It chooses virtual structures only in cases where it has an "underdog" position, such as in the instant messenger market. There it makes sense for Microsoft to support open standards in this horizontal layer in order to utilize the network effects with the installed base of open standard components.

Reasons for virtually networked systems

- Network reasons
  - Participation of network effects with installed base of open system components
  - Small players can work around critical mass issues
- Product and organizational reasons (non-network reasons) [364]
  - Better access to resources and capabilities
  - Increased flexibility
  - Increased variety of products
  - Possibly higher demand for products
  - Lower capital requirements
  - Assurance of supply in case of very high demand

Consider every website fueled by vertically created network externalities. They are generated by large players, such as AOL, German Telekom, AT&T, Dell or Microsoft which are massively marketing Internet access. The more users that go on-line, the better for the reach of every website. Bundling deals of portal sites such as Yahoo! or Lycos with ISP's, follow this externality and try to leverage it by tying together two-way complementary layers in a virtual network: Portal sites need people going on-line and access provider need portal sites guiding the user. On the other hand AOL already has critical mass on both layers, and thus prefers to tie the layers together to keep the network externalities internally.

In respect to on-line services in the Internet framework the initial predominant paradigm was based on an open system. Whereas past proprietary on-line services had predominantly closed systems, Internet standards like tcp/ip, html, packet switching can be identified as sustainable standard technology trends. As a result, individual players can define closed and proprietary components of their technology which they combine with open standard components. The definition of technology at the interfaces of technological systems defines the degree of

---

[364] See Economides 1998e, p. 4.

interoperability with other systems. To give an example, one can think of an on-line service which uses open technology, e.g. Java, within a part of a community chat system in a way that user which are not customers can interact in a chat with customers of the on-line service with their standard browser. This creates mutual benefits for customers, non-customers and the on-line service. In order to create competitive advantage through technology the on-line service can define some value added components which are solely for customers, which are created in proprietary technology. This short example might illustrate the effects on interoperability of a network through use of open standard technology, while proprietary components maintain competitive advantages for the firm.

Overall this discussion shows that network externalities are certainly not a factor, which is given exogenous but that players can create and leverage them in their favor. Therefore, the following will work out the factors a firm has to master in its strategic conduct in order to be ahead of the wave to break through critical mass first. The goal is the creation and leverage of network effects. The following outlines the relevant factors to show how firm conduct can create, leverage, and protect network externalities:

▨ **Product** strategy addressing network effects

▨ **Firms** conducting a **horizontal and vertical networking strategy** strategically interconnecting with other players

▨ **Pricing strategies** and **business models** for a network economy

▨ **Adoption issues** with critical mass and tippyness

Firms intelligently orchestrating these factors will be able to create and leverage the network effects. Hence, the following analyzes how firms can conduct in a way to realize and leverage network externalities in their strategy starting with implications for product design.

3.3.2. Product Strategy

The product strategy predefines the possibilities of working with the concept of network effects or not. The discussion on network economics reveals that needs are a fundamental source of complementarity. Furthermore the analysis of the field came to the conclusion that needs are one of the few fixed elements in the floating framework of the Internet. Finally the analysis about pricing strategies below will reveal that incremental pricing should be set up according to the perceived customer benefit and corresponding needs rather than to costs. Therefore, the first general consequence is to **develop network goods according to the fundamental needs** communication, information, community and commerce, connecting users conveniently to according services (see Figure 2-23). This can be the provision an email service or more derived the provision of connectivity software, e. g. a dialer for communication. For information one can think of a news site or the underlying content management system. For community one can think of an instant messaging software or a subscriber management system which is handling the rights of community members.

In order to exhibit network economics the core features of the product need to entail two-way complementarities, hence they need to establish an interactive **two-way network relation**.

The market-based view and the specific economics recommended to **address large markets**, as this leverages the **returns to scale on the production side**, but due to the low cost **personalization** products should be personalized to virtually create bilateral monopolies. The following will brake down these issues into factors firms have in designing products.

■ First of all the technological structure allows to **offer several versions of virtually the same product**, which is basically the concept of low cost product differentiation, which in practice

> "(...) goes under a lot of names. It is sometimes called 'one-to-one marketing'. Sometimes it is called 'personalization'. We have the term versioning." (Varian 1999b:26)

This indicates the need to create a line of products at low variable cost, as for example

> "Windows NT Workstation 4.0 sells for about $260. It can be configured as a Web server, but only accepts 10 simultaneous connections. Windows NT Workstation Server can accept hundreds of simultaneous connections, and sells for $730–$1080, depending on configuration. According to an analysis by O'Reilly Software the two operating systems are essentially the same." (Varian 1997:7)

Another example is stock quotes, which sell for $50 in a real time version and are available for free with 20 minutes delay. Firms can differentiate their product in versions along the dimensions time (e.g. delay of stock quotes or "full version" of a software), quality (e.g. "webmaster" vs. "home" version), quantity (e.g. homepage including 20MB and 50MB server space). The additional costs for another version are zero or almost zero and the variety in quality allows for **differential pricing** (see below) which can capture a larger part of the rent in a market. Furthermore, this will result in a customer self-selection, as customers will pick the version, which matches their needs and price elasticity in the optimal way. As a consequence, firms can address an increased market scope at the same costs. Hence,

> "(...) make sure that you design the product so that it can be versioned. That is, the product should be designed in a way that it is easy to reduce its quality in order to sell to a particular market segment" (Varian 1997:12)

The high fixed costs and extremely low variable costs make this strategy extremely profitable as it allows the firm to sell additional units at a very high contribution. As a result, a firm can reach additional customer segments with a product under extremely attractive economics.[365] This approach describes the logic of a strategy of economies of scope with singular products, which exhibit massive economies of scale. The economics of a firm using this strategy will exhibit positive feedback effects. For an example positioned in the content layer see Case Study 3-5.

■ **Bundling with other components interconnecting complementary components form other layers or sublayers** adds to this internal scope effects. **Firms shall consider gen-**

---

[365] See Varian (1997) and Varian / Shapiro (1998a, 1998b).

erating scope effects in a virtual network as well. The components of each layer exhibit complementary relations from a customer perspective.[366]

> Bundling, that is the sale of two or more goods in combination as a package, is a common business strategy." (Economides 1993:3)

Bundlings offer a very large variety of strategic options to add value to the customer, enhance market access and improve the supply-side economics. One can assume that product bundlings assemble a product of components, which have a complementary relationship, often across firms' boundaries. Otherwise bundling would have no value adding effect and is useless. One can distinguish pure and **mixed bundling**, where **pure bundling** is a product combination, which is solely sold bundled whereas mixed bundling is selling goods, which are also sold separately.[367] Pure bundling then describes an integrated structure and mixed bundling a virtual structure. One can think of AOL which provides access, content, email and homepages as a pure / integrated bundling as opposed to an ISP with a co-marketing bundle of free Tripod homepages and a co-branded Lycos portal site as a mixed / virtual bundling.

Networking scenarios can be developed between the network, hosting, software and device layers of the on-line industry. Each of these main layers can be bundled together to generate network effects. For example, customers who by modems or PC's are happy to find free trials of on-line service providers, Internet software for content and email and so forth bundled with the modem or PC. The hardware experiences an added value as does the software and the access providers on the supply side. The firms network their marketing resources and can provide a more competitive pricing. Hence, the combination has demand side and supply side economies of scale and scope. Together they bundle a package across firms which completes a valuable product for a customer who wants to get online. This evidently describes a two-way complementarity between each component.[368] The users experience economies of scope by the bundling of complementary components from distinct layers and economies of scale if these networks attract many users.

Networking scenarios can also be developed within each layer bundling components or the sublayers. **Figure 3-10** shows a **scenario for the content layer** and compares the two-way, or in media term "interactive", content with a traditional media approach. Where traditional content addresses mass markets in a one-way relationship, new interactive media address mass markets in a two-way relationship with a host of interactive services which in fact focus on individual customers. It reflects the market situation of the end of the 1990s, where typical relationships between content components are characterized by the following networking and bundling patterns. Dominant horizontal portal sites (such as AOL.com or Yahoo!) bundle the interactive killer applications: search (e. g. Inktomi), chat (e.g. Yahoo! Pager or AOL Instant Messenger), a mailbox, and topical news (usually by standard providers as AP or Reuters). This "basic package" for the mass market is connected to more specialized vertical portal sites (e.g. financial portals

---

[366] See Bakos / Brynjolfsson (1996, 1997).

[367] See Adams / Yellen (1976).

[368] See Economides (1993), pp. 10-14.

such Yahoo! Finance or SportsLine USA), communities with message boards, and homepages (such as Geocities or The Well) and transaction commerce driven sites (such as eBay or Yahoo! Auction).

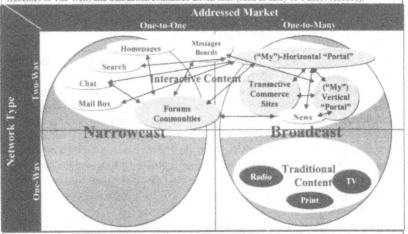

Figure 3-10: Virtual and Integrated Bundlings in the Content Layers

This scenario shows that at this point in time the portal sites play the role of the aggregator, networking the demanded components for the user. People receive their information, can meet their friends for a chat, use a mailbox, stay informed about their special interest topic, and are able to shop for their needs. The example also shows that some of these components are vertically integrated. Yahoo! has only recently been running auctions, acquired Geocities, and deployed its own messenger software. It also runs a few vertical portals such as Yahoo! Finance. In the past Yahoo! had just a general directory and licensed search technology (such as currently Inktomi) and over the years it has emerged into a company that vertically integrates all major layers of the content and interactive services area. The network effects of the complementary networked components have been internalized since then. Yahoo! has developed very limited connections to the vertically related hardware, software, hosting, and network layers.

In another example, CBS' executive, Michael Levy, describes a complementary network relationhip focusing on the marketing effects of a network. It connects AOL, which provides the on-line service platform, horizontal portal and "eyeballs", SportsLine, which provides the leading vertical portal site for sports, and CBS which provides a massive off-line medium connecting the virtual world and the real world. Each entity shifts users in a complementary way to the other entity: "SportsLine's America Online relationship actually encompasses a three-way deal with CBS. When CBS promotes our site on a sports event, it will say 'CBS SportsLine on AOL,' which not only promotes AOL, but also reminds the sports fans that are AOL users that they can easily get SportsLine through AOL. Long term, we believe that every sports fan in America is going to know about CBS SportsLine and how to get there. They are going to depend upon SportsLine's fantasy leagues, full line of sports merchandise, and exclusive real-time odds from the sports books in Las Vegas from its Vegas Insider site. We believe that no one will need a search engine of any type to find us or know about us, because we intend to be the best out there. Moreover, because of its changing nature, we believe that sports will be the biggest content category on the internet." (Goldman Sachs 1999:84)

Case Study 3-2: Bundling Strategies in the Content Layer

The reason why this "networking" is possible is the presence of standards. Even the most complementary components cannot capture a network externality, if they are not compatible.

A crucial step in product design is the **decision relating to open or closed technology and application of compatible standards, which exhibits a trade-off:**

> "From the point of view of the firm, compatibility and standardization are desirable since a firm can benefit from the externality of the total sales of all compatible firms." (Economides 1998:3)

> „[But, C. G.] Firms that compete in markets where network externalities are present face unique tradeoffs regarding the choice of a technical standard." (Economides / Flyer 1997:29

> "[Because, C. G.] On the other hand, compatibility implies more similar products, and therefore more intense competition among the firms that produce compatible products. To avoid the more intense competition, a firm may want to be incompatible with others. In deciding if its products will be compatible with those of others, each firm needs to balance these two opposite strategic incentives." (Economides 1998:3)

In this sense, adhering to an **open standard** puts a firm / product in the position to **capture the externality of the value added by a large network**. However, by doing so the firm loses direct control over the product development and faces more intra-platform competition. Alternatively, adhering to a **proprietary closed standard** allows the firm to face less or **no intra-platform competition**, but it sacrifices the added value associated with a large network.[369]

Recalling the fundamentals of the market theory the optimal position is to own a dominant position, which indicates to **own a de facto standard**. In other words, **a proprietary strategy generates potential profits. While** on the other hand, **critical mass issues require a dominant position.**

For these reasons, the next step in developing a product strategy is the **strategic decision about interface design.** Product design, therefore, needs to consider two-way flow functionality in its interface design, as potential network effects otherwise cannot be captured. The conclusion is that open interfaces to widely adopted standards denotes leverage particularly for smaller start-up players, while exclusive ownership of technology increase attraction with growing dominance in the market. But one should consider carefully at which point it is sensible to close technology as the rapidly growing environment then requires competition of innovation of the owned technology against the growth and innovative forces of the combined forces of all other players. The case of Microsoft's Windows versus Apple tells a great deal about the advantage of being the owner of a proprietary dominant system, but the serious threat by the open Linux technology, with its innovation fueled by a global community of developers, also shows the downside. **A common strategy is the development of adapters and converters** in order to work around the trade-off generated by the open versus closed technology decision. A firm can close the interfaces

---

[369] See Economides / Flyer 1997, p. 27 and furthermore Farrell / Saloner (1985) for an extensive analysis of technical standards and their effects on compatibility and the particular outcome for innovation.

to its network but can develop adapters to interfaces of related components. The design of these adapters can control compatibility. This is particularly crucial for asymmetrical compatibility as a virtuous lever in competitive strategy. An example might be the large player design adapters which connect users of small networks to its products only in a one-way relationship, but does not interconnect the users of the dominant network to the small network. The logical conclusion is that users of the small network travel into the large network, which in return keeps its own users inside. By doing so, the large player can benefit from the activities of small players and will incrementally "inhale" its base.[370] Depending on the strategic directive, asymmetrical compatibility can support or oppress the growth of certain networks. One must think of the manner in which Microsoft designed Office 97 in such a way so that those new files could not be used with old software. The design decision against making the file format not downwardly compatible should pull users to the new structure. As this left customers unsatisfied, Microsoft developed converters to use new files with the old software. However, in order to maintain the force to upgrade, the quality of the converted files remains inferior.

▪ The final point, which needs to be considered, is the aspect of **friction**. Market-based strategy theory teaches that this is the cause of profits. Furthermore, network economics revealed that networks do not exhibit a stable equilibrium and can tip over into a new dominant network structure. Customers typically experience lock-in effects into a certain network because leaving this network entails switching costs. Hence, players **lock-in the installed base by generating switching costs for switching away from the network**.[371] In fact, product design has a significant influence on this factor.[372]

The product design can fundamentally influence these switching costs by:

▪ Offering **converters** for existing assets generated in other networks, such as an email folder converter from Eudora Mail to Microsoft Outlook

▪ Offering **complementary product components** which are only compatible with the own product system and would be lost if users would switch, such as a personal web based "to do list" on the personalized version MSN

▪ Implementing features where **users need to get used to the product**, such as a particular user interface, such as the auction interface of eBay

▪ Implementing functionalities where **users generate their own value**, such as generating a web based folder with emails and contacts and calendar functions such Yahoo! Mail and Yahoo! Calendar and Contacts.

In the current Internet terminology, the later features are usually called "sticky applications" which stick the users to the product web of a certain vendor and then they use the

---

[370] See Farrell / Saloner (1992) and Economides / Woroch (1992), Economides / Lehr (1994). For a discussion of the bottleneck function of standards see Katz / Shapiro (1985), pp. 436-437 and Economides (1996), p. 29 who analyze the strategic influence of adapters to realize compatibility in non-standard networks.

[371] See 2.2.1 for a definition and explanation of the terms switching costs and lock-in as well as an illustration of the according effects.

[372] See Varian / Shapiro (1998a), pp. 135-171. Varian / Shapiro (1998b) and Farrell / Shapiro (1988, 1989).

services more often. Finally, increasing the installed base of a product generates switching costs caused by demand side externalities:

> An increased **installed base** makes switching unattractive, as for example, when a user looses the possibilities of connecting to AOL users if he switches to Microsoft's messaging software.

As this discussion from a product perspective implicitly assumes competitive forces only in a one-dimensional way the following will put this in a perspective with the multi-layered architecture of on-line services in the Internet.

3.3.3. Networking Strategy

Considering the multi-layered nature of the industry the next step is to distinguish the positioning of the product component in a wider system structure as shown in Figure 2-34. This positioning reveals the potential components in horizontal and vertical dimension, which exhibit a natural interface. This interface carries a potential network effect but also a potential substitution relationship. The design decision about compatibility enables these effects. The content example above (see **Figure 3-10**) illustrated this for the currently most important components of the content layer. But as the scope of the on-line industry also covers the other layers, additional network effects apply, where the vertical dimension plays a crucial strategic role.

After the proprietary on-line service bundled all components into one closed technology platform, the World Wide Web initially exhibited open system bundlings, with a mixed bundling approach in the mid 1990s.[373] At this stage of start-up, almost every player networked with any other player. Later, with increasing competition, the players shifted their strategy to more "exclusive" pure bundling approaches. This established the first vertically integrated network structures, although they remained by-and-large in virtual structures. In the late 1990s the strategies are increasingly shifting away from virtual vertical structures to more integrated networks. The growing merger and acquisition activities in the Internet arena indicate that after a start-up period of virtual networks, concentration following an intense merger period become increasingly common.

The different strategic implications cause one to analyze the **horizontal and vertical dimensions** in separate ways. The following will lay out the **parameters** a firm should consider in such a networking strategy. This discussion will reveal that the most likely outcome caused by the economic mechanisms of the industry leads to **scenarios of horizontally and vertically concentrated structures**, which can happen in a virtual or integrated way. For these purposes, the **competitive levers for firms to conduct** in such a constellation have to be laid out as well.

Horizontal network perspectives

Horizontally located components seem at first to be natural substitutes.

> In general there will be a number of elementary goods of each type. Elementary goods of the same type are obviously substitutes. (Economides 1991:3)

---

[373] See Varian / Shapiro (1998a), p. 187.

But as each **horizontal layer** itself faces **critical mass issues** and an interconnection of these components will help to expand the network effect of compatible components within this layer. One can, for example, think of GSM cellular telephone technology or instant messaging software. Interconnection of competing players on one horizontal layer can interconnect competing components to increase the overall network size. This describes the complementary aspect in their relationship. But the players will compete within the layer to be the dominant player to gain stronger positive feedback than the competitors, which describes the competitive relationship. This is the situation of co-opetition (see 3.3.6). The decision about the application of open or closed standards enables these effects. Again critical mass and growth issues of a closed network have to be seen in the trade-off to open systems and competition.

Network economics provides three recommendations for this situation. In the presence of a critical mass problem, a **monopolist can invite new players to enter the competition** and to develop the network with combined resources. However, in this constellation it is crucial that the increased competition is based on the technological control of the incumbent player.[374] The second option is to interconnect horizontally competing networks both of which exhibit critical mass issues. This practice of **combining substitutable networks to shared networks** leverages network effects. The third option is to **interconnect existing incompatible networks**, which exhibit a substitution relationship. In order to achieve compatibility an adapter has to be developed. The interconnection of the networks increases demand-side externalities as users benefit from a larger network. The crucial aspect is to control the technology for the adapters and capture the larger portion of the interconnection rate.

- **Invite new players and sell licenses of proprietary technology**

A player, such as a provider of a new network technology, can invite other players to enter the intra-network competition. Economides (1995b) points out that additional players will expand the network externalities as more users will be on the network which will in turn increase the overall value of the network.

> "Entry of competitors reduces prices and profits ceteris paribus. But the addition of their production to the size of the network increases the demand functions (willingness to pay) facing all network members, including the innovator (former monopolist). This allows the innovator to sell higher quantities and charge a higher price. Thus, if the externality is strong, the network effect overshadows the standard competitive effect of entry. As a result, the innovator is better off as one of a oligopolistic firms rather than as a monopolist." (Economides 1995b:2-3).

In addition, Varian (1994) argues that players entering the competition will also result in costs reduction for all involved players. While volumes will increase at decreasing costs, the down side of such a move is the increased competition, which will drive down prices, as considered by Economides (ibid.). Furthermore, Rumer argues in this respect that li-

---

[374] See Economides / Himmelberg (1994), and Economides (1992, 1995b) for an extensive argumentation why the large monopolists have incentives to invite small competitors with licensed technology to expand the network effects to a broader basis while creating competition.

censees might turn into competitors or provider of substitutes after the licensing period.[375] In anyway it is **crucial to maintain the control over standards and licenses through contractual relationships.**[376]

▨ **Create shared networks**

In the presence of several horizontally located, competing component networks, it can be beneficial to connect these networks to generate network externalities.

> "Many networks start of as self-contained (proprietary) networks. It is often the case that over time networks link up to form shared networks." (Economides 1991a:1)

Although this **creates intra-platform competition** the **creation of network externalities** can have greater positive effects with an additional **costs reduction** due to scale effects.[377] Economides points out

> "(...) that when the demand for transactions across private networks is as large as the demand for transactions within the private networks, each private network has an incentive to establish compatibility with other private networks and facilitate hybrid (across networks) transactions. (...) When the demand for transactions within only one of the two private networks is high, this network chooses to maximize incompatibilities, while the other private network desires compatibility. The result is partial incompatibility of the two private networks." (Economides 1991a:25)[378]

Hence, the following conditions define the rules of scenarios with shared networks, which will be illustrated with the standards fight between AOL, which owns a closed technology serving 80 million customers with 750 million messages a day, competing against Instant Messaging networks such as Microsoft Messenger with 1 million users:[379]

▪ An assumption that demand for inter-network traffic is large, such as the demand of ICQ users to connect with Yahoo! Pager, Microsoft Messenger and AOL Instant Messenger and vice versa.

▪ Strong incentives for smaller networks, such as Microsoft's relatively small Messenger network benefits a large amount from sharing the customer base with the giant

---

[375] See Rumer (1994), pp. 24-27.

[376] Another example of how the entrance of additional players can help to push a network market to critical mass, is the following statement of Tim Jackson, founder of QXL, commenting on eBay's and Yahoo!'s move into the European on-line auction business creating positive effects for on-line auctions as a whole: "The market is growing so fast so having strong players with good marketing skills will have a positive effect on the number of people using online auction sites. Of course we're hoping that once they've tried other services people will go with us because of our stronger proposition." (n a. 1999a:10).

[377] See Varian (1994).

[378] Without explicitly using the tern "asymmetrical" Economides refers to the aspects of asymmetrical complementarity and its strategic implications as analyzed above.

[379] See Economides for an analytical microeconomic approach and from an empirical perspective Squire, Sanders, Dempsey (1998b), pp. 180-182 and 240-250 analyzing the European multimedia sector. See Vonder Haar (1999) for the data about instant messaging network illustrating the different interest in the particular case of the Messenger competition.

AOL buddy list. This incentive drove Microsoft and Yahoo! to "hack" the AOL network to interconnect their smaller user base with the huge AOL community.

- Weaker incentives for larger networks, which is exhibited by AOL's struggle to keep Microsoft and Yahoo! customers outside the AOL Messenger network.

- Stronger incentives for the network with predominantly ingoing traffic, such as Yahoo! and Microsoft to increase their processed messages by a much larger factor as AOL.

- Weaker incentives for the network with predominantly outgoing traffic, such as AOL, which already handles 500 million messages a day and hence would increase its volumes relatively less.

> "These results show the significance of the relative scale of the demand for transactions within and across private networks for the decision of compatibility and for the emergence of shared network. The best scenario for the emergence of a shared network is one of equal demands for all four types of transactions, within each private network and across them. The worst scenario for the emergence of a shared network is when the demand for transactions across the private networks is small." (Economides 1991a:25)

Case Study 3-3 outlines one example of how a licensing strategy and interconnection agreements to establish shared network structures using adapters support the growth to critical mass in an internationalization strategy.

CompuServe was set up as a closed network based proprietary technology. Given this, each business partner and customer had to agree to the service terms which obliged the third party to use the technology components delivered by CompuServe, which were protected by copyrights.

The advantage of CompuServe was the exclusive capability to provide an integrated on-line service package. As competing on-line services, such as AOL emerged CompuServe strove to remain the leader in a business / professional / technical market segment, and to develop an international growth strategy, while AOL aimed to capture more the entertainment oriented consumers in the US.

Both AOL and CompuServe had the luxury of no competition due to closed proprietary network technology as discussed above. The disadvantage was the constraint of internal resources to growth rates at 10-20%, around 1994 and 1995 even with growth opportunities of almost 100% per annum.

The decision of CompuServe to remain a closed proprietary platform with global market definition faced the following challenges:

- Distribution of proprietary user software
- Programming in proprietary technology
- Programming of international content and localized software
- Building up operations in foreign markets
- International access network roll-out

For the first two issues CompuServe, just as AOL, developed the following strategy, typical for proprietary players:

Distributing software under the bandwidth limitations of the early 1990s, usually required classical offline marketing such as direct mailing or magazine cover inserts of diskettes. However, there were natural allies: computer, software and modem companies. All of them had existing marketing activities and were happy to add an on-line service to their product bundling. PC manufacturer such as Compaq could enable their computers with interactive services, Microsoft could claim Windows came with on-line services, and modem companies like US Robotics needed a connectivity provider in any case. Hence, each player who wanted to enhance its product with the addition of an on-line service bundle and thus was open to marketing the CompuServe or AOL network technology. In the absence of many alternatives to CompuServe or AOL, marketing alliances could be set up easily. In order to allow distribution partners to copy the version they had to sign a license agreement for the client software package. Driving this policy online services were virtually integrating the missing components into a completely vertically integrated system. The combined players could deliver to the customers a complete package for using interactive services based on a proprietary technology.

The programming of content was organized in such a way that CompuServe offered a portfolio of business models (see Figure 2-22) serving different type of content providers. Each content provider had to sign a licensing agreement as well as ensue the provision of content in the proprietary formats, programmed with proprietary content programming tools.

Ultimately the user had to agree to the software license as well.

In this way, the component network of hardware, software, content, data network, and users was set up. The challenge for this proprietary strategy was that it remained a resource consuming plan. All efforts to distribute the technological platform were driven by internal resources. In the case of the client software the two-step approach with channel marketing partners (complementors) leveraged their distribution power. CompuServe had to convince partners from all areas to agree to the technology.

Coming on the heels of the decision to launch an ambitious internationalization strategy, the primary challenge was to prioritize and allocate resources depending on the potential of the respective international markets. Decisions needed to be made if the roll out was driven by internal organizations, with large partners or small partners, which depended on market prioritization. Corresponding programs needed to be developed. These internal or shared resources needed to develop a network of business partners providing content, access network, and distribution channels. Finally, the localization issues needed to be address as a pure US service offering was not sufficient for larger customer groups. CompuServe decided to invest its own resources into the development of the European market, which was considered the central area for growth of interactive services outside the US. However, other markets partners needed to be located and the development corresponding programs was required. In addition, CompuServe tried to find a large partner for the Japanese market, and small partners for the smaller regional markets in Asia, Latin America, and Eastern Europe.

A duel-track licensing program was pursued. The track for the smaller markets such as Hong Kong or Singapore was called an "affiliate program", where complementary affiliates (complementors) established small CompuServe business units within their business. For the Hong Kong market, Motorola was the chosen as partner, while Fujitsu became the partner for Singapore and Australia. Sega developed the Brazilian market and a private entrepreneur developed Mexico. These companies developed regional content, network agreements with local vendors, and conducted marketing with their resources. Pricing decisions were under local control and the local partner pursued differential pricing policies. Due to the higher incremental costs, these prices were significantly higher. The affiliates were completely tied into

CompuServe's technology and at the same time, expanded the global reach of the content and network presence for the global player, CompuServe. Overall, these markets could acquire only 10-20,000 customers each. [380]

The other track was pursued in the Japanese market, where NiftyServe, now part of Japanese NTT, was chosen as a partner. CompuServe signed a deal to license the entire technological platform as outlined in Figure 2-24. NiftyServe, hence, did not need to develop its own technology to provide a complete on-line service offering. On the other hand, NiftyServe became locked into CompuServe as their technology vendor. The Japanese business operation was completely under the control of NiftyServe and the licensing fee was negligible.

Theoretically, there should have been a network effect from the increased use of platform. In fact, this occurred with an increased number of network POP's (point of presence) and the generation of increased traffic. This lowered the costs for the network infrastructure and had demand side scope effects for the travelling part of the CompuServe community members. Unfortunately, the content-side of the network effects was not employed, neither service connected its content to the other, which makes sense if one considers the limited number of users who could use both Japanese and Latin symbols. A rare exception was the presence of Spanish language content from Mexico, which was supporting the European division in developing the Spanish subscriber base. Considering the technology oriented CompuServe community, a lot of the American computing content was used in the European markets, especially the UK. Overall, these demand-side network effects were weak. The reason was the mistake to increase scale and scope into new areas, which did not have a very high propensity to interconnect with the existing network components. In other words, only a few customers traveled and requested a bigger scope of the network. Moreover, only few international communities crossed the national boundaries and interconnected with others. The increased installed base of client software was an improvement for this network technology, but it did not reach critical mass, if compared with the dimensions common internet client technologies scale up to in the late 1990s. Taking the standpoint of the US core market, the expansion had some compelling successes. However, this only refers to the aspect of internationalization, which in fact was impressive in the cases of UK, Germany, France, Mexico, and Japan. But the aspect of strategic management focusing network effects through interconnecting to shared networks and licensing technology has to be assessed as a failure. Network effects were not generated over a level of critical mass. The reason for this failure was that management drove a traditional internationalization strategy without acknowledging possible network effects. The focus was set on standard parameters of industrial economics putting the firm in the center. The mistake was to overlook the aspects of the economics of communities (network externalities) (see Case Study 2-2) aligned with the corresponding production externalities of the underlying production functions (see Case Study 2-4, Case Study 2-5, Case Study 2-6, Case Study 3-5). There is a critical mass issue with a new community in New Zealand and there is also a break even issue with the costs for the network provision in New Zealand. If one compares this with the parallel development of AOL in the US one can see that they fueled their growth via the NYSE and grew reached the level of critical mass. Their growing community was providing positive feedback from the market side and at the same time improved the economics of the underlying production function.

Nevertheless, the NiftyServe case is a good example of monopolist inviting competitors by licensing a proprietary technology. For an economic discussion of this network constellation see Economides (1992,

---

[380] Stemming from determination and entrepreneurial spirit, the same constellation resulted in successful penetration of the Mexican market, where the local affiliate grew to almost 100,000 members in 1997 – the leading branded ISP of Mexico.

1995b). The problem for CompuServe was that NiftyServe, although developing a subscriber base of more than 2 million users, never created positive feedback in the home market. Japan was completely disconnected from the US market. Moreover, CompuServe did not dare to capitalize on the bottleneck position of the technology it owned and basically gave the technology to NiftyServe for free. Hence, it did not leverage the technology via licensing into positive feedback on the home market nor the bottleneck position into an interconnection fee for the technology license.

Case Study 3-3: Licensing Strategy, Interconnection & Network Effects[381]

Vertical network perspective

At this point, the perspective of the analysis shifts to the vertical dimension of network structures, which will be put into perspective with the competition in each horizontal layer. This step is the pivotal one in a competitive networking strategy for a multi-layered industry. At a first glance, component networks, which are vertically aligned, appear as natural complements. This is also true for a non-network industry. Car manufacturers need the tire companies and the distribution networks and so on. However, as discussed in 2.2.1 these value chains follow the rules of one-way networks with indirect network effects. The reason is that there is a one-way flow. Nobody would buy tires or car seats with the absence of cars. These value chains have a clear one-way flow of logic. This is different in the on-line industry. Computers are sold also with the absence of the Internet, and so are most software components, content, and communications networks. But the unique complementary bundling of components form the perspective of an on-line services adds a different perspective. Devices need content, content needs software, and the host network needs traffic and vice versa. This establishes a two-way complimentary relationship, in a complex value-web with strong two-way network effects. If firms are able to connect the vertical layers in the correct way, they can generate positive feedback between the distinct layers. Of course, to be able to do so and see the leverage, firms have to look at the situation from the perspective of an on-line player and not like a telecom player or media company.

Four perspectives need to be considered to fully develop networking forces for a firm. The first two can be derived along the lines of Figure 3-9. It highlights the complimentary relationship, as the fundamental source of network externalities. The externalities extend to the demand-side of the user and to the supply side of the firm.

Economies of scale and scope on the demand side

The argument for economies of scale on the demand side from a vertical perspective follows the lines of the discussion regarding product bundling discussed in 3.3.2. Customers generate a network effect when there is a large number of people using email. They also benefit from a greater network effect, when the network of users is connected to the biggest network of email software. This refers to email devices (today mostly PC's, while in the future it will be all the enabled telephones, personal assistants and so forth) spread over the entire access network including, a buddy list connecting all these people to the devices, software, hardware and network layers. In other words, one must strive to pro-

---

Background information by the interview with Bill Truesdale, VP International CompuServe, 25th of March 1997, Columbus.

vide a one-stop shop of dominant network components for customers. This networking on the marketing side enables firms to provide the best products in one bundle, which leverages the externalities of each horizontal layer in a vertical scope. Each player enjoys a complementary marketing effort. The purchase of the PC has the world's largest on-line service community "back-packed", and the on-line service direct mailing comes with the most popular messenger and email software and connects to the largest ISP network. This generates additional competitive advantage for each bundled player at no incremental costs.

Hence from the demand side perspective, a company has to scale-up in each particular horizontal layer, and network these layers along a scope vertically related to the components. These components play a dominant role in their respective layer. The perceived added value from the customer's perspective defines the dimensions of the scope of such a network.

▣ **Economies of scale and scope on the supply side**

On the supply side firms need to utilize their interconnected "production chain" (Borrus / Zysman 1997). This can occur in a closed integrated system, such as attempted in the late 1990s by AT&T with TCI, and Excite@Home, or in a more virtual way, as occurred with the AOL bundling with Gateway 2000 hardware, Netscape and SUN software, plus the MCI Worldcom Network. Gateway sells the hardware and places people in front of the PC screen; AOL is the "on-line brand" configuring all the components (such as the dialer, browser, and mail client), which provide the "on-line experience" with content (horizontal and vertical portal sites, communities, instant messaging etc.). For strategic purposes, AOL also hosts the data. The components run on Netscape's front-end and SUN's back-end software over the network of MCI Worldcom. Due to the network, each layer provides scale in the particular layer and scope to the virtually integrated "production chain". As each of the layers provides positive externalities for the other layers, the right combination of components in such a vertical network provides the self-dynamic of positive feedback. This results in an enhanced competitive position for the players and the networked constellation, as a whole, will become the dominant paradigm for the industry.[382]

In addition to this leverage stemming from improved economics, the third perspective is grounded in the resources of the firm and hence relates to the discussion regarding the resource-based view, found in 3.2.2.

▣ **Complementary network of firm resources and capabilities according to tasks in horizontal layers**

The resource-based discussion shows that a portfolio of resources and complementary capabilities for a diverse set of tasks can be developed in and delivered through a network of firms. Furthermore, the analysis of the capabilities in the different horizontal layers of the on-line industry shows that players can not develop the complete scope of required capabilities. The missing competencies require an internalization through networking

---

[382] See Borrus / Zysman (1997).

with other firms.[383] Therefore, the third perspective is to consider the resources and capabilities of network Therefore, the third perspective considers the resources and capabilities of network partners required for the tasks of vertically-related but distinct horizontal layers. The discussion will not further emphasize the mainstream business strategy sufficiently covered when it was summarized the on-line industry in Figure 3-6.[384] In the real-world case of the AOL-Netscape-SUN cooperation, Goldman Sachs correctly identifies the combined complementary skills of the three players as the fundamental strength, which will enable it to succeed. Each one is positioned in a separate horizontal layer, which is virtually interconnected in the vertical dimension. Finally, Goldman Sachs points out how this virtual alliance is poised to attack typical vertically related giants such as IBM and Microsoft, and then writes:

> "AOL-SUN-NETSCAPE ALLIANCE BRINGS COMPLEMENATRY SKILLS TOGETHER. The alliance brings together the unique strength of the three different companies, all focused on the Internet as a key part of the new economy – SUN's relationships with ISP's and hardware strength, AOL's audience accumulation ability and Netscape's Internet backend software. By bringing together key skillsets and technology into a focused effort, the alliance should be very competitive in going after formidable companies such as IBM and Microsoft, both which are providing a full suite of software and services to build the new Internet commerce infrastructure." (Goldman Sachs 1999c:49)

Finally, the last rationale for vertical interconnections in the on-line industry is the aspect of strategic relevance.

▨ **Ownership of or access to strategically relevant components as an internal resource**

In addition to establishing a network with the best economics of scale and scope on the demand and supply-side with players combining the most competitive skills, it is a crucial factor to have control over strategically relevant components. These components should be internalized, or at least access to these resources should exist. The discussion in new institutional economics has widely discussed this topic.[385] Scholars from the academic as well as the business sector clearly identify the factor **customer relationship** as the crucial factor.[386] These can be seen from the **quantitative aspect** as Barry Schuler, president of AOL's on-line service, points out, for its on-line service approximately 20 million customer relationships exist with an approximately 80 million relationships when all properties are considered. He says:

---

[383] See Colombo / Nguyen / Perrucci (1997).

[384] See Prahalad / Hamel (1991) to find an elaboration of the argument on building "best practice" networks, that leverage network competencies. Then combine this with the argument of Krogh / Roos (1992) to put this into perspective with the tasks required by the competition. See Badarocco for a discussion on complementary resources from the standpoint of strategic alliances. See Colombo / Garrone / Seri (1998) for the corresponding empirical observations of the Internet framework. See Wüthrich et. al (1997) for aspects of the virtual nature of a network of firms.

[385] See Williamson (1975, 1986, 1999, eds.).

[386] For a discussion in the academia see Hagel / Lansing (1994), Hagel / Sacconaghi (1996), Sacconaghi / Abela (1997), Hagel / Rayport (1997a, 1997b) and Hagel / Singer (1999).

"In the next chapter of the computing industry - where consumers increasingly will tap into applications via online networks - AOL is betting that its growing set of customer relationships will be more central to building market share than owning the keys to standardized software such as the Windows operating system. (...)

The reason Microsoft has failed in the online services business and hasn't been able to get it going," said Barry Schuler, president of AOL's interactive services unit, 'is that they don't have that relationship with the customer.' " (Vonder Haar 1999)

The second factor is the **qualitative aspect** about customer relations such as the ability to (a) know what the customers do and want, which predominantly controlled in the content or hosting layer and (b) to own instruments to commercialize this relation such billing systems & collection processes via credit card or direct debit. Telecom provider or Internet service provider can leverage this capability particularly strong as they have a solid billing relation with the customers, which can be translated from the on-line service or telephone bill into e-commerce billing options.[387]

Considering the economic and strategic forces, one has to analyze which industry structure will most likely result and what the competitive conduct of players will likely be.

Considerations of the most likely industry structure

A look at the above discussion indicates **a trend towards concentration in the horizontal and vertical dimensions.** Each horizontal layer follows a trend towards concentration or a networking of components, which results in a larger scale. The vertical dimension is similar, as it supports integration among of the complete scope of the layers.[388]

"As explained in our economic analysis, convergence will create an incentive to vertical integration, (...) as a result of which firms will be able to gain access to higher margin areas in the developing value chain. This may result in economies of scale and scope for the vertically integrated firm, and may also produce consumer benefits.."
Squire, Sanders, Dempsey (1998b), p. 144

When writing about the vertical and horizontal dimension, Bakos / Brynjolfsson refer to the concentration effects as bundling and describe the effects on industry structure in the following manner:

---

[387] See Colombo / Garrone (1998), pp. 24-25. A widely overseen aspect is that these billing tools are somehow proprietary. Opposed to this banks in fact control the only widely adopted standards for billing which are credit cards. According to Henry Liechtenstein, VP of Citicorp, banks and the credit cards they issue will dominate electronic commerce for the foreseeable future. "'Transactions in the virtual world will be cleared and settled by the same institutions already doing the clearing and settling in the in-person world, using the same techniques.' Banks have a monopoly over narrowly defined payments systems and markets (i.e., checks and credit cards). The growth of electronic commerce, however, inserts virtual mediation between purchase transactions and the machinery of settling and clearance of payments. These innovations will drive incremental change in existing payments systems, rather than overturning and eliminating them. Although these changes may be (eventually) far-reaching, banks will maintain their preeminent position in the payments system for the foreseeable future." (Cioffi 1999a:15-16).

[388] See Economides (1993, 1994, 1995c) Farrell/ Munroe/ Saloner (1994) and Bakos/ Brynjolfsson (1996, 1997).

"Our analysis shows that a multiproduct monopolist of information goods can often achieve higher profits and greater efficiency by using a bundling strategy than by selling the goods separately. If it would be difficult (or illegal) for a collection of single-good monopolists to coordinate on a unified bundling strategy and price, our analysis suggests that they may benefit from merging or from selling their information goods to a single firm. Thus, bundling creates non-technological economies of scope; for instance, an information good that is unprofitable (...) if sold separately could become profitable when sold as part of a larger bundle. These effects of bundling have implications for (...) [the, C. G.] market structures." (Bakos / Brynjolfsson 1996)

This analysis reveals the forces of concentration, although Bakos / Brynjolfsson give a higher priority to monopolization and, thus an integrated, structure. In a collaborative manner, the same effects can be generated by a virtually integrated monopoly although the authors refer to a collusion agreement between firms may be illegal. Nevertheless, both cases do emerge in practice. The implications for the industry structure and the competitive conduct of firms in this structure remains the open question.

"First, the dynamics of bundling could create a winner-take-all market. Multiproduct firms that successfully sell a suite of information goods may find it more profitable to introduce new information goods than will single-product firms. (...) Bundling may therefore enable a multiproduct firm to charge lower prices while remaining profitable. Furthermore, a single-product firm may find it profitable to sell all rights to its product to the multiproduct firm to reap a share of the benefits from bundling. This suggests that an equilibrium with a single multiproduct monopolist will be stable in the face of the introduction of new information goods or even small bundles of new information goods. This winner-take-all effect from bundling is distinct from technological economies of scope or scale or learning (...), network externalities (e.g. Farrell and Saloner, 1985), or financial market imperfections." (Bakos / Brynjolfsson 1996)

The initial state of the Internet-based on-line business was predominantly a virtual structure, as is shown in 2.5. The main cause was the presence of open standard components and systems. Many small start-up players created new components of the network and dominated this sub-layer, such as the ICQ network. In the beginning, they competed with each other and because of network externalities, one player began to dominate the competing substitutes. The early phase of the browser market and Netscape's road to temporary dominance is an excellent example (see Case Study 2-6). The competing players in these horizontal layers are usually connecting via an integrator in a vertically layer in order to enhance the value of their product with the customer. Generally it bundles together marketing resources and internalizes the vertical network effects on the production side as well. These

"Network services are created by packaging separate components in combinations demanded by users. Typically, production of individual components exhibit strong scale economies, and so their supply tends to be monopolized. Consequently, unless a single firm provides all components, disjoint networks must interconnect to ensure users a full array of services." (Economides / Woroch 1992:1)[389]

This was exactly the case in the on-line industry in the open standards world of the Internet in the mid to late 1990s. Case Study 2-5 and Case Study 2-6 demonstrate how these forces unbundled the formerly integrated proprietary on-line services, when AOL used a Microsoft browser and the Worldcom network was bundled under the AOL brand. This in return established **virtual networks, which exhibit vertical integration**, as stated by Noam:

> "Some companies are likely to follow a systems integration approach, in which they (...) select optimal elements in terms of price and performance, package them together, manage the bundles and offer it to the customers on a one stop basis" (Noam 1996:22)

Generally, one can state that

> "(...) there will be a number of elementary goods of each type. Elementary goods of the same type are obviously substitutes. The different combinations of elementary goods create systems that are also seen by the consumers as substitutes." (Economides 1991:3)

The later part of Economides' citation refers to **vertical systems, which creates networks of complementors**. The crucial point is that this is in the plural, because it is to be stressed that the **competitive forces result in several networks in the vertical dimension,** which in return exhibit competitive relation along the vertical dimension.

> „Production and distribution networks often are composed of both competing and complementary brands of components. The complementary components then can be combined to produce composite products or systems, which are substitutes for one another." (Economides / Salop 1992:2)

The result is formerly complementary components exhibit competitive relationships when they belong to different coalition structures. This occurred in the on-line industry as described below.

The economics and vertical forces described above, including the **concentration and consolidation processes** are observable over the time. Players started to consolidate their networks driven by the economic forces. **The initial virtual structures are increasingly replaced by integrated structures in the late 1990s,** as measured by intense merger and acquisition activities. This leads to two strategic options:

> "- One is the strategy to make [virtual, C. G.] alliances – trying to create group of firms that adhere to a common standard and all the stresses and strains that come along with the process of making those alliances.

---

[389] See Economides / Woroch (1992) or Economides / Woroch / Lopomo (1997) and focusing on the Internet data network, hardware, service and content conditions Srinagesh (1995) and Varian / MacKie-Mason (1992).

- On the other side there are standards wars. Because large [vertically integrated, C. G.] network contains a lot of value, dominating such a network can be a very attractive price, leading to winner-take-all a battles for standards." (Varian 1999b:27) [390]

Therefore, **the two fundamental structural options for business strategy are:**

▓ **Virtual vertical structures** or

▓ **Integrated vertical structures**

While the former structure will depend on an **open standard system,** the later will tend to close its system structure with **proprietary standards** (although theoretically it can work with open standards the goal is to reduce competition, which supports proprietary structures). Depending on requirements and the corresponding option, each constellation exhibits advantages and disadvantages. Nevertheless, it is doubtful that a complete vertical integration in one firm is feasible considering the heterogeneity of the character of the resources in the distinct layers (see 2.5.1), which results in an enormous stretch of the resources of a vertically integrated firm. In other words: cultures and competencies vary too much to integrate the complete vertical scope in one structure. Each vertical structure will exhibit certain virtual types of integration at the boundaries. As discussed in 3.3.2, there is a trade-off between the possibilities of an open, virtually integrated system, which can leverage the externalities created by the size of the industry as a whole, versus the advantage of the reduced competition and internalized externalities in closed, integrated structures, which sacrifices the added value associated with a large network.

> "The tension between these economic forces shapes the coalition formation equilibrium in these markets." (Economides / Flyer 1997:29)

In return, this creates three outcomes:[391]

▓ **The concentration in the industry as a whole increases** through vertical integration, (regardless if it is virtual or not).

▓ **Only a few players on each horizontal layer and a few vertical networks** will remain. They will be more or less virtually integrated, which is caused by the economics and market requirements as discussed above.

▓ **The coalition structures reduce the strategic options,** because formerly complementary components on vertically related layers belong to different coalition structures.

  ▪ This reduces the potential complementors and

  ▪ increases additional indirect competitors in the vertical layers

Figure 3-11 illustrates such a concentrated structure with the case of two vertical network structures. In this duopoly one is established virtually and the other one is set up in an inte-

---

[390] See furthermore Arthur (1994), David (1986), Varian / Shapiro (1998a) and Kenney / Curry (1999).

[391] See Economides (1991a, 1991b, 1994, 1995, 1998e), Economides / Flyer (1997), Economides / White (1994a, 1994b) and Economides / Wildman (1995).

grated closed network.[392] Although this concentration into two coalition structures decreases the competition, it introduces additional competition between vertically related components of distinct vertical coalition structures.

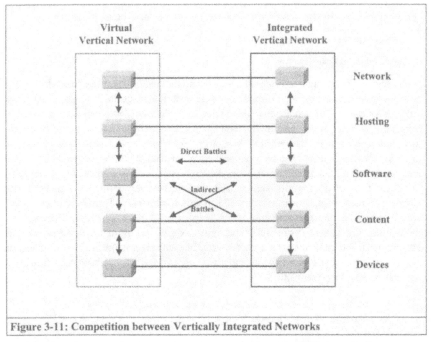

Figure 3-11: Competition between Vertically Integrated Networks

In such a constellation, the individual components (firms) in coalition structures have several ways to leverage the vertical network effects in a competitive strategy.[393]

When considering the horizontal layer, the rational move is to become the dominant player as described above. The goal is to be the first player with critical mass. If this is not possible with one's own resources and the resources of the coalition structure, then firms need to consider tendering invitations to enter the shared network (see above).

When considering the vertical layer, individual firms are suddenly confronted with new competitors. Vertically related firms of competing vertical coalition structures exhibit the competitive patterns leveraging their strategic network goals through their product design (see 3.3.2) as described in Figure 3-12:

---

[392] See Economides (1994). See KPMG (1996a), p. 106-109 for an overview of vertical and horizontal coalition structures in the European convergence and multimedia area.

[393] See Economides / Salop (1992). Economides (1993) points out that a mixed bundling approach, or in other words, a virtual integration in an open system structures is the more viable structure if complementarity is higher, but with an increase in the competitiveness of the relation an integrated closed system, or pure bundling in his terminology.

STRATEGIC GOALS	INSTRUMENTS
• **Raising rivals costs**: a component from one layer can supply a component for the rival's system. Hence, the upstream position and control over the interconnection of this will put one coalition in the position of influencing the rival's costs. One can think of a data network provided to the community of the rival, i.e. in the debate regarding higher telecommunications rates for German AOL users compared to Deutsche Telecom's T-Online users, as both groups use the Deutsche Telecom's local loop. [394]	**SYSTEM COMPATIBILITY**
• **Cutting rival of the market**: if one component of the coalition is able to provide market access for a vertically related component of the competing network this can be used as a bottleneck to strangle the rival. The Window's desktop is just such an example of a bottleneck. [395]	**ADAPTERS**
• **Reducing a rival's quality**: The quality of a competing component can be influenced in connection with a system. For example, does the Microsoft Hotmail experience a decrease in functionality and quality if used with something other than the latest Microsoft Outlook version. [396]	**INTERCONNECTION RATES**
• **Raising rival's prices**: Ownership of a downstream component, which is necessary to complete the rival's system, establishes a bottleneck, which can be used to increase the prices for the compatible component of the network in such a way as to drive up prices for the competitor, and decrease his volume and his economies of scale. [397]	

Figure 3-12: Cross-Layer Goals and Instruments in Vertical Coalition Structures

The design of **system compatibility, control over interconnection rates** and **strategic use of adapters** are the instruments, which can be used to reach these strategic goals. The ideas found in 3.3.2 regarding product strategy show the strategic relevance of product design in these markets, because this ultimately puts a firm in the position to play these strategic games.

Therefore, incompatibility with the interconnecting vertical layer results in a potentially fatal problem: "The component is useless for on-line services." A computer without browser software can not use the content of the web. A website programmed with the latest technology is not compatible downward to older browsers, and so forth. Therefore, **vertical networking is conditional**. The issue is to **develop compatible interconnections in a manner, which provides the strategic alternatives to control the interface in order to become the gatekeeper of a bottleneck**. Considering the discussion about vertical interdependencies, it is a strategic advantage to **control the interfaces, which allows one to play strategic games**, with respect to complementary components of a vertical layer belonging to a hostile vertical network.

Firms, then, need to leverage these factors to their favor and to the favor of their coalition structure. The virtuous use of these vertical levers in one layer can be used to control several layers, or as Borrus / Zysman note, even to **control the entire industry**:

---

[394] See Economides / Wildman (1995) and Economides (1998d) for the Microsoft strategy with the Windows operating system bundled with the Internet Explorer browser and local telecommunication providers entering into the long distance market.

[395] See Economides (1998e).

[396] See Economides (1997, 1998c) and Economides / Lehr (1994).

[397] See Economides (1998a) and Economides / Wildman (1995).

> Those constituent system elements – from components and subsystems (...) – become
> separate and critical competitive markets with the potential to control competition in
> the industry as a whole" (Borrus / Zysman 1997:1)

This can result in divergent interests, if one considers a small content player of a the virtual network offered a position in the bundle of the dominant software layer by a player of the competing coalition structure. If the current coalition structure does not provide such a powerful component, the decision not to leave the initial coalition and to fail to partner with the competitor is painful. In the long run, such weaknesses in a coalition structure of an individual component will threaten the stability and power of the network. Hence, the network partners should be as complementary and as dominant as possible in their layer. As a result **each vertical coalition has to leverage its most dominant component in the structure as the central piece and bundle the other components revolving around this central dominant component**, such as in the case of Microsoft's PC operating system and Office Suite, in order to expand its network.

> "The other opportunity it [Microsoft, C. G.] has is to go out and buy little companies
> that wouldn't normally be successful, bundle them into their Windows or Office hair-
> ball and use their lock-in and monopoly leverage to make them successful and drive
> everyone else out of business," (Gonsalves 1999)

As a reaction from the competing vertical coalition structure based around AOL-Netscape-SUN, SUN's Scott McNealy describes the gravity of the dominant and integrated Wintel structure in the following manner:

> "That makes everybody want to sell their company for a price lower than they want
> to, because if you're not the one bought, you're done." (ibid.)

McNealy's reaction shows how he perceives the threat of loosing his smaller network partners. They are bundled around his SUN empire, which establishes the large alliance with AOL/Netscape and a host of small players in a virtual structure under the Java headline. Microsoft's closed and integrated approach keeps its interfaces ("API's") controlled and by leveraging its scale, it is able to break up parts of AOL/SUN's open vertical structure.

Considering this discussion and relating it to the discussion on the interplay with the political sector, the argument of considering regulators as a strategic player gains in credibility, because this discussion indicates that **successful strategies in this environment are susceptible to anti-trust and anti-competitive charges**. Therefore, a strategy always needs to consider how far the forces of the network can reach without getting in trouble with public policy and local authorities.[398]

> "Because of the effects of lock-in, network externalities, and returns to scale there is a
> tendency to have a winner take it all structures in these markets. Therefore you have

---

[398] See Varian / Shapiro (1998a), pp. 297–325. This is the argument Varian (1999b), p 28, which leads to why Varian / Shapiro (1998a) were basically forced to discuss policy issues in a book about business strategy. The simple point is, if a firms is able to master the economic principles it will end up in such a dominant position in the long-run that it will be confronted with anti trust issues.

to think very carefully about issues of anti trust (...) and the proper rules for competition (...) (Varian 1999b:28).

Overall the conclusion is that – due to significant sunk costs – there will be very few players on each horizontal layer and also very few vertical networks. These coalition structures cover the complete scope of the on-line industry with the underlying economies of scale. Furthermore, it is expected that speed of change of markets and technology and the diversity of required competencies and cultures will drive a significant portion of these vertical coalition structures to remain as virtual structures rather than integrated in a single firm.

This does not sound all that new but clearly indicates that a rather "macro" approach such as Industrial Economics is well suited for the requirements of the infant on-line industry as opposed to rather the rather "micro" views of business administration as it is mired in too many details. **From a standpoint of Industrial Economics, the novel aspect is the economics of bundling components into networks.** The authors in the context of network economics accurately work out **the network aspect, which enables players to use the compatibility of complementary components to generate scale and scope effects in a virtual constellation,** which is a specific characteristic of networks. In this arena, a player focuses on one component, reaches critical mass to dominate that market layer, and bundles with other dominant components to expand the scale effects in an even wider scope. This well-structured business strategy framework is applicable to firms in each layer regardless of their size. Players, who are able to drive a business strategy embedding them in a dominant vertical network will leverage network effects into their horizontal layer, which is ultimately contingent for "their" competition.

The advice from mainstream business strategy should be recalled at this point: firms should not focus on temporary market structures but rather on the underlying customer needs and drive to figure out which added value they can add based on their resource situation. They should **consider not only complementary economics, but also complementary competencies in their virtual networks, designing them in a way that the firm focuses on its core competencies.** This composite system of competencies should focus on the complementary bundle of customer needs. Each partner serves a portion of a need. The result is a superior composite product delivered in a value network. At the same time, the organization of value creation will occur in a flexible manner.[399]

In order to enhance this economic consideration of a networking strategy and the product strategies discussed above, the following sub-section will discuss corresponding pricing strategies and the remaining issues of business models in the on-line industry.

3.3.4. Pricing Strategies & Business Models

Of all the aspects discussed within this work, the **issue of business models and pricing are the most difficult.** This is stems from the facts introduced in part II, where the point was ar-

---

[399] See Friedrich / Hinterhuber (1995), p. 41.

gued of the **sheer absence of stable and sufficient business models in the Internet framework**. For these reasons, analysis of past on-line services provided an overview regarding business models, which worked for on-line services in the past.

Five years after the emergence of the web it seems to be a valuable exercise to analyze what happened with respect to business models since that time, as illustrated in Case Study 3-4:

"At a deeper level, the great debate between partisans of the Internet and champions of proprietary on-line services is really about business models. There is a far more important question than which technology will win, namely: which of the competing business models represented by these networks will prove most successful at creating economic value for participants?" (Hagel / Bergsma / Dheer 1996:57-58). A few years after this citation it is possible to compare the front runners for both type of players. On the side of closed proprietary on-line service, by-and-large, only AOL remains significant. On the side of the new interactive media models which emerged with the world wide web, the old number one is still the dominant player: Yahoo! A surface glance already reveals that the situation regarding pricing and business models is highly problematic.

The dominant business model, and certainly the one providing the most substantial revenue streams, is AOL's, where Goldman Sachs identifies "STRONG FUNDAMENTALS: We remain positive about AOL given the economics of scale from its subscriber, traffic and network infrastructure. AOL continues to enjoy strong market share versus its competitors, with over 55% of the Internet/Online service market. Financially, AOL has the opportunity to execute and add several high-margin revenue streams from subscriptions, advertising, direct marketing, transactions, and daytime business services" (Goldman Sachs 1999c:48)

Goldman Sachs refers to the slowly emerging business models providing new revenue streams. In fact, in the end of the 1990s one sees the first business models based on advertising and e-commerce – particularly the auction model.[400] which seems well-suited to interactive on-line services – developing some stability and sustainability. Along these lines, Goldman Sachs emphasizes the sustainable development of the advertising model with respect to the market leader Yahoo! and refers to its "MATURING NEW MEDIA MODEL. Yahoo!'s business is just beginning to mature from a page view/CPM driven model, and it is flourishing into a diverse multiple revenue stream story with large growth opportunities on all fronts. These opportunities include direct marketing, sponsorship, promotions, hosting, placement/distribution, merchandising, member acquisition, transactions and advertising. We expect Yahoo! to layer in these additional revenue streams both organically and through new acquisitions." (Goldman Sachs 1999c:114)

It seems that regardless of actual revenue the assessment of the category leaders is very positive, which in It seems that regardless of actual revenues, the assessment of the category leaders is positive, which in return supports the notion of dominant players and increasing returns. But significant is the idea of acquisitions, which are needed to create the abilities to generate new revenue streams over different layers of the interactive content business for a horizontally positioned player like Yahoo!. This runs along the lines of the network strategy considerations above. Although it has to be stated that the positive assessment of

---

[400] See Klein (1997) for an analysis of the auction model, which seems to be a very sustainable and appropriate model for the Internet. Additional information from the interviews with eBay executives Brian Sweetie (Exec. Vice President Marketing), Scott Barnum (Vice President International) and Reed Malzman (Business Development Director), 12th of May 1999, San Jose.

Yahoo! as the biggest Internet brand needs to be enhanced with the idea of the great future challenges which face this player, as illustrated by the following statement from a Yahoo! strategic planning executive: "Our biggest question is how we can translate over 200 million page views a day or over 50% of the Internet community into a business model. (...) Our goal is to be the biggest toll keeper of the world. The question is how." [401] In other words Yahoo! achieved leadership in an attractive market segment but does not know how to capitalize on this position. Identifying the same problem Linda Lawrence, Vice President International Netcenter at Netscape, stated in the interview with reference to Yahoo!: "What is their business model? When will they have one?"

If one examines this situation it appears that having no sustainable business model is still acceptable in the Internet and that AOL is running a sustainable business model. But, is this a sustainable prediction for the future?

In respect to the "FREE" model, Bill Gates' remark on the still very low adoption rates compared to traditional media appears very sensible: "You have to see a lot more growth (of the Internet) before the advertising model becomes profitable" (Zenith 1999). Along the same lines are his statements on the evolution of business models: "The long-run business model in this industry is unclear." (Yoffie et. al. 1996:1)

With respect to the multiple revenue stream model of AOL, which is based on a two-part tariff, (see below) focusing on the connectivity side of the business, one can be skeptical as well. These concerns with models based on connectivity arise because of the erosion of these revenue streams in the growing presence of "FREE" connectivity providers. Considering that the advent of broadband will cause a disruption of this model, the near future risk becomes evident. [402]

Finally, one can expect to have a completely new setting in the first years of the next century, when people will access a large variety of differentiated on-line services with a host of devices on a broadband infrastructure. Therefore, it has to be concluded that no sufficient answer to the business model and pricing issue can be derived from current conduct of the industry.

Case Study 3-4: AOL On-line Service Powerhouse vs. Yahoo! Internet Giant – Business Models revised

With respect to this unsatisfying situation, this work provides an overview of the current research on this topic and places it in a perspective with the comments regarding product, networking and adoption strategies.

In a recent attempt, Dührkoop (1999) analyzed the future potential business models of the Internet, concluding that there is no "dominant design" yet. Bailey (1998) had similar findings. In other words, there are no stable business models. This supports the thesis of this work: market share is the strategic goal and revenue generating business models remain in the background. In such a situation it is important to consider the lessons of the market theory as discussed in 3.2.1.

---

[401] Interview with Matt Rightmire, Director Strategic Planning at Yahoo!, 28th of April 1999, Santa Clara.

[402] Additional information from the interview with Chris Hill, Executive Vice President Corporate Development AOL Europe, 23rd of June 1999, London.

Another recent approach in the European area was conducted by Zerdick (1998, eds.)[403] who states that, although highly relevant, there is no overview of business models exist in the media area which firms can apply in their strategic planning process today. He identifies the lack of necessity as the reason for this. He goes on to state that there has always been a given set of generally accepted business models. Thus, he derives a possible portfolio of business models by approaching the issue via two paths. First is the **general pricing decision** regarding a **costs or needs-based** pricing. Based upon this decision, he refers to pricing strategies based on regional, temporal or segmentation aspects. Basic insights regarding pricing strategy are derived from standard marketing management.[404] The other path outlines **industry specific models**: subscriptions, kiosk transactions, advertising and other, business models, which have traditionally dominated the media industry.

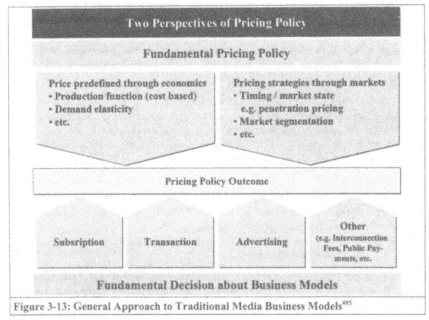

Figure 3-13: General Approach to Traditional Media Business Models[405]

Because of differences given in the Internet environment, this set of experiences provides room for enhancement with additional models. Thus, he concludes that the **emerging options**

---

[403] See Zerdick (1998, eds.), pp. 24-28. Direct citation in German: "Trotz des hohen Relevanzgrades ist bislang keine Strukturierung der Erlöstypen für den Medien- und Kommunikationssektor erfolgt, die Unternehmen bei der strategischen Planung Ihrer Geschäfte nutzen können. Dies ist allerdings leicht zu erklären: Es bestand kein Bedarf für eine solche Strukurierungsleistung, da der Markt für jedes Medienangebot ein bestimmtes „Korsett" an Erlösformen vorgab. Ein Spielraum für diesbezügliche Entscheidungen war kaum vorhanden und damit auch kein Bedarf. Durch das Internet verändert sich dieser Entscheidungsraum in hohem Maße, da nicht nur eine weitere Verwertungsstufe der Inhalte, sondern auch weitere Erlösmodelle hinzutreten, die bei einem Produzenten von Inhalten zur Anwendung kommen können. Aus der Konstante der Festlegung von Erlösformen für Medienangebote wird eine Variable, deren Einsatz Unternehmen unabhängig von der bisherigen Konstellation planen können." (ibid.:24-25).

[404] See Kotler / Armstrong (1998).

[405] Zerdick (1998, eds.), p. 25.

for new business models in the Internet open possibilities to play this strategic card and to include this **new parameter in business strategy.**[406] Therefore, he outlines the following fundamental distinctions for potential models, which he expects to occur in the course of the Internet:[407]

DIRECT			INDIRECT	
Usage Based			**Via Enterprise**	**Via Government**
Transactions ■ Quantity based ■ Time based	One Time ■ Connection fee ■ Licensees ■ Usage device (e.g. set top box)	Regularly ■ Subscription ■ Broadcasting fees ■ Other	■ Advertising ■ Data mining ■ Commissions ■ Other	■ Subsidies

Figure 3-14: Clusters of Business Models in the Internet[408]

His analytical approach does not consider past on-line business experience and reflects the range of future options incompletely. The analysis "got stuck in the experience gap" described in Figure 2-21. Although Zerdick refers to some business models from the telecommunications and information technology sectors[409], he is not able to give a comprehensive overview of future business models. He refers rather generally to the need to incorporate network effects with positive feedback into business models[410] but it seems sensible that he discusses the aspects of data-mining and co-marketing[411] to generate the community driven business models for the new infomediaries, which he omits.

In order to present a more complete answer to the issues of pricing and business models this work refers to the empirical findings of past on-line services (see Figure 2-22) and advises players to gather data from the past to inform new business ventures. This can tell a great deal about strength and weaknesses of certain models. Not a very fashionable argument but for those who follow its logic, it will pay back.

In addition to this empirical, piecemeal approach, it is worthwhile considering an **analytical approach based on economics**. It was predominantly Varian/Shapiro[412], who analyzed the pricing specifics of communications, information products, and technologies in network markets. They deliver an analytical approach consistent with the theoretical framework above. It can be seen through the lens of the microeconomic discussion in 3.2.1. Their pricing considerations accompany their discussion of product **versioning** as discussed in 3.3.2.

Their findings highlight two aspects. First, as opposed to non-network markets, the efficient pricing strategy differs in the marginal willingness to pay, and not the marginal costs determined by the production function.

---

[406] Ibid.

[407] Ibid., p. 25.

[408] Zerdick (1999, eds.), p. 25.

[409] Ibid., pp. 92-94 and 124-125.

[410] Ibid., pp. 165-166.

[411] Ibid., pp. 165-170.

[412] See Varian / Shapiro (1998a, 1998b) and Varian (1999a, 1998a, 1998c, 1997, 1996, 1995, 1993, 1978) and Varian / MacKie-Mason (1994a, 1994b, 1994c).

"One prominent feature of information goods is that they have large fixed costs of production, and small variable costs of reproduction." (Varian 1997:1)[413]

"The classic prescription for economically efficient pricing---set price at marginal cost---is not relevant for technologies that exhibit the kinds of increasing returns to scale, large fixed costs, or economies of scope found in the telecommunications and information industries." (Varian 1998a)

Therefore, **pricing should be needs-based,** because cost-based pricing does not lead to reasonable results.[414] In the words of Varian:

"Cost-based pricing makes little sense in this context; value-based pricing is much more appropriate." (Varian 1997:1)

"The appropriate guiding principle in these contexts should be that the marginal willingness to pay should be equal to marginal cost. This condition for efficiency can be approximated using differential pricing, and will in fact, be a natural outcome of profit-seeking behavior." (Varian 1998a)

Secondly, Varian points out that since uniform pricing at marginal cost is not efficient in this industry, suppliers must devise other pricing strategies. He advises that one such strategy is to **employ differential pricing schemes** for different consumer groups, when offering the corresponding product versions. Different consumers of a certain product place a different value on that product and, therefore, the willingness to pay for the product varies across the consumer population.

"Different consumers may have radically different values for a particular information good, so techniques for differential pricing become very important." (Varian 1997:1)

Offering several versions of almost the same product at different prices **leads to a self-selection of customers,** depending on their individual willingness to pay.[415]

"(...) the producer provides different qualities/versions of a good which sell at different prices. (...) the point of versioning is to get the consumers to sort themselves into different groups according to their willingness to pay. Consumers with high willingness to pay choose one version, while consumers with lower willingnesses to pay

---

[413] This shows the major difference to "normal" industries as assumed in neoclassical economics where goods are traded under perfect competition and neoclassical economic theory determines that firms will end up pricing at marginal costs. In a perfectly competitive market structure, there are a large number of suppliers, none of which is large relative to the overall market and the output of these suppliers are homogeneous and there are no barriers to entry (see Katz / Rosen 1991). It is assumed that the industry exhibits diminishing returns to scale and that the fixed costs are relatively small. However, this is different in the telecommunications and information services industries, which require huge fixed costs in the deployment of their required infrastructure and low variable costs and thus exhibit increasing returns to scale. Therefore, it is not efficient for them to apply the classic economic practice of pricing at marginal cost, which is close to zero.

[414] See also Monroe (1994).

[415] See Economides / Lehr (1994) for an analytical modeling of alternating consumer willingness to pay depending on levels of product quality.

choose a different version. The producer chooses the versions so as to induce the consumers to "self select" into appropriate categories. (Varian 1997:1)

This practice of product versioning with differential pricing schemes puts firms in the position of **extracting as much of this value from the consumers as possible**. The amount extracted is limited by the consumers' willingness to pay for the product. For these reasons

> „Network participants should devote their effort to selecting the **business model** that best meets the **needs** of network users" (Hagel / Bergsma / Dheer 1996:67) [emphasis, C. G.]

Considering these aspects one can formulate the thesis: that as an input factor, the long term commercial success of firms in the Internet framework is not driven by technology or market dominance alone, but:

Business models make the difference.

According to the above considerations, differential pricing schemes leveraging a line of product versions seem to be key to the design of successful business models. They can be divided into two-part tariff schemes, price discrimination schemes, and bundling schemes.

■ In a **two-part tariff scheme**, users are charged a flat fee to connect to the network, and a usage fee for their incremental use of the network. This can refer to the connectivity services, such as ISP's, or also content services, such as subscription and pay per view models. **Two-part tariffs can be applied to align a needs-based pricing scheme to the costs structures**. The flat-fee should be set to cover the fixed costs of the network infrastructure or content provision; in addition to any consumer surplus derived from the attachment. The usage fee may be metered by time, packets, bandwidth used etc., and should also include the marginal consumer surplus derived from that usage.[416]

■ In a **price discrimination scheme**, consumers are divided into segments and are charged according to the segment to which they belong.[417] In terms of microeconomics, this is basically the idea of **product differentiation** combined with the idea **discriminatory pricing**, where the rent is captured by the producer. This not a new idea, but "versioning" is more than just a technological and web-centric term.[418] In the Internet business, this fore-

---

[416] See Varian (1999a, 1998c 1997, 1996) and Economides / Wildman (1995).

[417] There are three types of price discrimination schemes: **first-degree price discrimination.** Each consumer is charged for his individual willingness to pay. This scheme extracts the maximum consumer surplus from each individual consumer. However, this scheme is usually difficult or impossible to implement, and sometimes its implementation may be illegal. **Second-degree price discrimination is where** consumers are divided into segments based on some attribute that the consumers are induced to reveal. For example, airline fare restrictions are devised in such a way that consumers reveal their willingness to pay for airplane tickets. Another example of second-degree price discrimination in a network context would be the versioning of a network service. For example, regular e-mail may be free, but with no delivery time guarantees, while urgent e-mail may have an attached fee, with certain delivery guarantees attached. **Third-degree price discrimination is where** consumers are divided into segments based on some verifiable attribute, such as students or senior citizens. See Varian (1998a).

[418] See Varian (1997) and Varian / Shapiro (1998b).

going would be called mass customization and personalization as Case Study 3-5 illustrates with the example of a website:

One can think of a financial web service. The basic version offers just news and stock quotes. The service is free and advertising is the business model for this version. Mass-market consumers select this offering.

A personalized version offers customized stock quotes and news according to the selected stocks. This version is also free for the customer but the advertising is sold at higher rates. The advertiser pays for the added value as users selecting this version disclose themselves as customers with higher affinity for the advertiser's products.

A third version offers real time quotes and a personal stock trading account offered at a monthly subscription. Here the customer pays for the added value of the package and the monthly fee covers the fixed costs for customer management and the non-delayed stock quotes.

In another premium version, customers can purchase stocks and other financial products, which is a fourth, transaction-based, version, where the customer is charged a margin for the transactions to cover the variable costs for the transaction.

A final offering is an on-line access service with a branding of the site, which bundles all components together and uses the technology platform of an on-line service. The site acquires customers for the on-line service provider and appears as the one stop shop for his vertical market segment.

In each case, the firm charges a premium to capture the customer surplus.

The overall suite of versions is based on one technological platform, composed of one product based on the most complex version. The offering including access is considered a cross-selling business, which derives additional revenue. The other versions are just slimmed down version of it. Customers of the first version just use components of the fourth version, but are not able to see the rest. Given this combination and the provision of certain financial products, and exclusive content offerings, the example assumes a unique product combination, which no other competitor is able to offer. It is a monopoly of a line of products, which offers an endless number of personalized version of one product. Customers choose one version according to their needs and willingness to pay and hence self-select the appropriate version.

Case Study 3-5: Personalization, Mass Customization and Pricing[419]

Although addressing mass markets this strategy of differential pricing and versioning of products is a hybrid strategy, which questions the concept of cost leadership and mass market strategies for the information goods and services.

> "I have my doubts about this strategy. I think that the "mass market" is going to be
> less significant in the future than it has in the past." (Varian 1998c:17)

These terms need to be interpreted in a more open way as for typical industrial good as it is described here and in 3.3.2.

---

[419] If one translates this example into microeconomics it leads back to discriminatory pricing and product differentiation. Each personalized product serves one customer. The market type for each combination would be a monopson (see 3.2.1). But as each of the product version creates no incremental costs it follows the same production function. One can treat it as one product serving many customers. Therefore, it is as a monopoly with discriminatory pricing. The technological possibilities of the Internet provide options to implement this model with highly efficient economics.

In a **bundling scheme,** users are charged for the bundling of complementary goods.[420]
Consumers may exhibit a willingness to pay for individual components, which does not
concur with the their cost structures. **The bundling can cross-subsidize the cost structures of several components of a integrated (monopoly) bundle.**

> "Even if an information good introduced by as part of a bundle by the multiproduct
> firm is intrinsically less valuable to consumers than a similar product that might be
> sold by single-product firms, our analysis shows that the multiproduct firm may, in
> equilibrium, achieve a higher market share and earn higher profits from that good."
> (Bakos / Brynjolfsson 1996)

This describes the typical leverage of vertical networking of components as described in
3.3.3. Contingent for such a constellation is the complementarity of needs, which underlie
the combined components. For example, on-line service customers pay a monthly fee by-
and-large for the connectivity and support the content bundled in this offering. Both
components combined differentiated traditional on-line service providers from ISP's. The
on-line service providers cover their additional content costs by the increased willingness
to pay for access.[421]

> "However, if a consumer's type is correlated [which describes complementarity of
> needs, C. G.] with an observable behavior, such as time spent on-line or willingness
> to wait for "stale" information, then this behavior can be used to segment the market.
> This enables a form of second-degree price discrimination (Varian, 1996b), in which
> consumers self-select by purchasing different versions of the bundle. (...) [A firm, C.
> G.] can pursue a mixed bundling strategy of offering several bundles, each including
> a subset of the available information goods; this menu of bundles will screen consum-
> ers by type." (Bakos / Brynjolfsson 1996)

In conclusion, **bundlings,** such as the AOL on-line service, **assume a certain set of
needs** which demand for bundled products and **mixed bundlings offer the consumers
the potential to self-select,** as for example described in Case Study 3-5.

With price discrimination schemes, firms can maximize their profits from several segments,
because each segment is charged an optimal price based on the segments willingness to pay.
For example, stockbrokers, who rely on stock information services, are willing to pay, and are
charged higher rates than private individuals investing in stocks. Furthermore, a two-part tariff can align needs-based pricing closer to the costs structures and reduce the commercial risk.
A good example is the monthly subscription for on-line services like AOL, which covers a
large amount of the fixed costs.

Four types of charges should be considered with respect to pricing networks, and which can
be applied to the pricing schemes described above:

---

[420] See Bakos / Brynjolfsson (1996).

[421] See Varian (1995) and Varian / MacKie-Mason / Shenker (1996).

- **Fixed or access charge.** This charge is independent of the user's use of the network, and should ideally cover the network's fixed cost plus the customer's surplus. Note that this is very similar to the flat fee under a two-part tariff scheme. This access charge is very similar to the monthly fee charged by on-line services, where the user pays this fee regardless of the monthly usage. It provides a very stable and predictable revenue stream in the case of Internet and on-line service providers.[422]

- **Usage charge.** This charge is a function of the amount of use. Internet access providers have usage charges that depend on the duration of connection. Other ways to measure this charge can be the amount of data transmitted over the connection. This charge should ideally be the marginal consumer surplus plus the marginal cost of the usage, i.e. the cost of the network resources (routers, switches, maintenance) incurred by the connection.[423]

- **Congestion charge.** This charge depends on the load in the network at the time or the customer's network connection. These charges become higher as the network becomes more congested, and drop to zero when the network is not congested. The purpose of congestion charges is to prevent quality degradation. In the current narrowband world of on-line services these charges are not common. In the past, these charges were connected to modem technology (see Figure 2-22). This kind of charge may return particularly in the course of the deployment of broadband services. Ideally this charge would be equal to the value that the customer places on each individual connection or service (e.g. a piece of electronic mail), although the implementation issues are not trivial.[424]

- **Service quality charge.** This charge reflects the differences in resource utilization for different types of services. For example, real-time video requires more resources than real-time audio, which requires more resources than electronic mail. These kinds of charges reflect the perceived customer value, such as a high value of sports results in a certain timeframe or with a delay. These charges are currently uncommon in the telephone and data networks, but common in the content industry, which provides content in different formats and time delays. For example, a best selling book is later released as a paperback or the chain: movie theaters, video purchase and video rental, pay TV, free TV, TV rebroadcast).[425]

Overall, the conclusions on pricing strategies and business models are limited to the advice to study comparable past experiences and to focus on needs-based pricing with a differentiated product versioning and pricing strategy, where customers can position themselves in a self-selection process. At the end of the day, insights, which appear more as common sense than scientific arguments, might be the best guideline. Along these lines it has always been good advice position oneself as the sole supplier of a good, which is perceived as a scare resource by a host of customers on the demand side. Profitable business models easily evolve out of such a situation.

---

[422] See Varian (1999).

[423] See Varian / MacKie-Mason (1994a, 1994c) and Varian (1996).

[424] See Varian / MacKie-Mason (1994b).

[425] See Varian (1999).

The following Case Study 3-6 extends these concerns regarding business models. It outlines a hypothetical situation based upon current business issues and highlights some billing and pricing issues, which will occur in the course of broadband deployment. The core issue, which will become evident, is that the broadband world will be accompanied by some usage patters, which have divergent implications on revenue and costs with respect to the different standpoints of media, telecommunications, and electronic commerce players.

The main thesis of this hypothetical case is that telecommunications carriers as well as media players should worry about pricing schemes in a high bandwidth world. The reason is that the underlying economics of their respective business models exhibit conflicting directions for this future market.

The result will be a battle for value between these industries.[426] This case will illustrate the implications of distinct usage types, which will occur in the future and will prove this thesis.

The assumed pricing scheme in the first step is the unbundled model of the narrowband world of on-line services in the Internet. Each component is charged separately. A monthly flat rate for access, no charge for the majority of the content, some subscriptions for content and a few service charges per download of contents. E-commerce transactions are handled via a credit card or a direct debit. This describes a scenario of a distributed system in the absence of a unifying billing and pricing technology as it was present in the old on-line service world.[427]

The following will lay out four usage types. This scenario will reveal the conflicting positions of network service providers, content providers, ecommerce vendors in respect to the four usage types.

First one can assume users which predominantly use the web for browsing and multimedia entertainment. Users will go to multimedia fashion shows of Macy's and preferably downloading massive advertising clips. Hence, no revenue generated for content while the backbone and access network was massively congested. The ecommerce player distributed its advertising messages. The question is who should be paying? The costs are obviously mainly on the end of the network provider.

Secondly, others might favor to read text dominated in depth stock analysis for investment purposes. With a substantial payment for the content and almost no use of network capacity for the simple text file.

The third type of user might use value added on-line based services as banking. The bank would be happy to reduced the process costs by "going direct" with its service substituting the costly efforts in the branches. The customer would enjoy increased availability of the banking services.

The fourth user type wants to conduct purchases on-line. The user is browsing the video library of an on-line video store and is downloading massive video clip samples. Finally a video is purchased for a bargain price via credit card. The network provider is facing substantial costs for the data transport, the "etailer" is conducting his business model and a bank is processing the transaction with a small margin.

The connectivity costs as well as content costs for these usage patterns will differ drastically. At the same time the described revenue streams, which resemble the pricing schemes of the current narrowband Internet, do not allocate the costs and revenues in a fair way. While the viewer of an advertising spot will cause high network costs and no content costs the investment analyst will cause marginal connectivity costs but uses highly valuable content. The analysis of the non-concurring business logic of bandwidth as

---

[426] See Middelhoff (1998).

[427] See Figure 2-22 and Hagel / Bergsma / Dheer (1996), p. 64.

a limiting factor in the telecommunications perspective and content as a limiting factor in the media industry, and customers relation in electronic business processes needs to be brought in sync as soon as the broadband world enables massive throughput and provision of massive multimedia content. Upon a cost based pricing approach it is an open issue how business models should reflect these different cost as neither a telecommunication nor a content dominated approach would be sufficient. Hence a combination is required. As telecommunication as well as content provider are potentially not the same player a third party must be involved. This party could be a pricing mechanism which would be the broker of the scare resources bandwidth, quality content, customer relationship. This would require a market and the according technology. First the markets with different channel steps do not exist from a standpoint of industrial structure. Second the according technology is not available. Therefore, there is currently a gap which leaves the question of conducting the broadband business models an unsolved issue. This gap could be filled by a player who is specializing on these complex constellations with a corresponding billing and customer management technology. This third party, let's call him "service provider" would focus on customers and could come to different conclusions based upon a needs based pricing. Powerful billing & collection systems, subscriber management systems of such a service provider would justify the existence and the particular problem of the business model illustrated above could be solved. This gap is unfilled yet and the only sector which hosts players with corresponding resources is the telecommunications industry. Telco provider own and operate complex billing and customer management systems in a large scale. This asset can be leverage into the broadband Internet space. In fact AT&T as one of the dominant players supports this hypothesis by developing the @Home network as potential future broadband on-line service. [428] In this case @Home is positioned right at the bottleneck of the value creation between media and telecom players. As ownership of @Home is on the telecom side media players have to worry. In fact Time Warner is running Road Runner as a competing player. The leader of the low bandwidth world is obviously AOL. Hence AOL tries to retain his position by accessing the broadband space. First partnerships with RBOC's using their DSL technology are in place. AT&T and TCI do not give access to their cable infrastructure and keep @Home as the sole player. Time Warner with its cable business and the Road Runner service would be a third option to enter the broadband arena for AOL. As the US regulation is reluctant to increase competition in this infant area – which is a superb example for the influence of the exogenous parameters of the industry model - @Home can leverage its early mover position. Depending on the behavior of the players the outcome may vary. Cooperation between AOL and Time Warner would combine Warner cable business and AOL interactive services and billing capabilities with combined customer relationships. This constellation would threaten the @Home position.[429]

Which business models would work for this somewhat problematic complex needs in such a scenario where e.g. @Home is the broadband on-line service provider for millions of consumers? These are all issues that have to be resolved from the scratch in the Internet framework. Past experience could tell stories about a world were valuable content was distributed over a network where bandwidth of the local loop was a precious bottleneck (see model 13 of Figure 2-22). The main difference is that in the past numbers leveled on 2.4 Kbit and to 9.6 Kbit according to old analog modem technology. In the future the issue will be discussed on levels of 56Kbit modem or 128Kbit ISDN versus 300Kbit to several Mbit DSL technol-

---

[428] "@Home is the leading provider of high speed Internet services to consumers over the cable television infrastructure. (...) With over 460.000 subscribers and its proposed merger with Excite, @Home is striving to become the network of the next century" (Goldman Sachs 1999c:51).

[429] See interviews with Peter Cowhey, professor at UC San Diego and former Chief Negotiator for the FCC at the WTO telecom negotiations, 20th of April 1999, Berkeley and Francois Bar, professor at Stanford University and academic advisor to Pacific Bell in the DSL role out project, 26th of April 1999, Stanford.

ogy. If players consider past examples they will find proof of concept for some models. Significant experience will indicate directions. The past would indicate that large customer bases were manageable over a host of business models. The requirement would be a third party service provider between users, content and telecommunication part of the business. The crucial aspect would be the aggregation of customers and a bundling of services under powerful commercial infrastructure.

A player, conducting a "clearing function", could bundle a host of services with a huge variety of underlying business models. E. g. Business model 11-13 of Figure 2-22 would consider premium fees for faster connections (e.g. DSL) and business model 10 would consider the costs for telecommunication based on throughput. For a given base fee the whole package could be purchased based on a monthly subscription which would consider average usage patterns (model 14). For certain high value components, such as company analysis or large data transport, individual particularities could be charged on top (model 4). Obviously this is just a scenario but it shows that a wise approach to design future business models will take into consideration past models with comparable constellations.[430]

Case Study 3-6: Billing & Pricing Issues in Broadband On-line Provision

Besides these rather critical considerations about pricing strategies in the Internet the last component of the Net-centric strategy discusses the particular adoption patterns in network markets, which needs to consider critical mass issues to become a dominant player and the threat of this dominant position being an unstable equilibrium.

3.3.5. Adoption Strategy

Adoption patterns in network markets differ from non-network markets. These differences have mission critical implications for business strategy. Moreover, markets in the frame of the Internet can be entirely seen as **"start-up markets"** in a sense that their adoption rates are moving towards the **early majority** (USA, Scandinavia), **early adopters** (Europe, some Asian markets) or are still within the innovators (rest of the world).[431] Therefore, the adoption aspect is highly relevant. For these two reasons it is a fundamental aspect to analyze the way network technologies experience different adoption (Katz / Shapiro 1986a, Moore 1995, Albers / Peters 1995) than business strategy would presume this for non-network markets (Rogers 1995).

The following **assumptions** need to be fulfilled to create a situation as described below.

▪ **The good exhibits network externalities** (demand side economies of scale and scope)

▪ **The technology exhibits high initial and fixed costs which are sunk, while incremental costs are low (supply side economies of scale)**

▪ **Expectations about the future adoption influence today's adoption**

▪ **Information and coordination is imperfect**

▪ **Adoption and usage creates switching costs and lock-in into the network**

---

[430] „Transactions and payment technologies. Content vendors and aggregators usually prefer to get paid for their offerings, and network users like to feel that their payments are secure. Payment technologies will need to be able to handle both large and small (less than $10) payments." (Hagel / Bergsma / Dheer 1996:63). This citation underpins the need for a secure institution clearing the markets of different pricing schemes.

[431] See Cioffi (1999b).

In this sense Kenny / Curry point out that the **rules for competitiveness in such a situation are underlying a path dependent development, increasing returns for a dominant player which captures a dominant position in his segment**.

> "Competitiveness in Internet commerce appears at this time to have many of the characteristics described (...) of being path dependent, increasing returns, and evolutionary. One outcome of these characteristics is that first-mover advantages are enormous and the occupation of a niche is critical. Conversely, the capture of "mindshare" provides a powerful advantage and it is difficult to dislodge an entrenched competitor using the same business model." (Kenny / Curry 1999:32)

However, they also point out that technological shifts result in evolutionary processes in which the dominant equilibrium position of players erodes due to a new environment. External changes support the development of a new – substitutional – network. In the technology environment it is usually the fitness of a dominant design is predominantly shaping a certain period.[432]

The following will lay out **four different stages in the adoption of network technologies** and will put this into perspective with discussion on product, pricing and networking conduct described above. Due to the five assumptions above each of these stages has different requirement to the strategic conduct of firms:

- **Start-up phase**
- **Point of critical mass**
- **Gaining the dominant position**
- **Retaining the dominant position**

Each of these steps is contingent. The goal is to survive the start-up period and to reach the level of critical mast as the first player. The positive feedback will reward the player which reaches this stage at first. At this breaking point, demand-side will make marketing increasingly easier and the production externalities will fuel the economics of the business. The goal changes from mutual growth more towards building a dominant position and capitalizing on this position. But, as the technological environment is threatening the design of this network with invention of superior technology the system has to create start-up problems for new entrants. Moreover, it needs to be able to co-evolve with the overall technological innovation of vertically related components to make sure not to drop out of vertically related structures due to incompatibility. In this process there is a lot of movement and speed involved.

Players will have it easier if they have a head start against other players. Therefore, **moving early** is important, being late is punished by the market. For example, CompuServe could well leverage its early internationalization strategy which resulted in dominant market position in Europe in the mid 1990s (see Case Study 3-3) as it was in an excellent position at the start of the Internet age, which occurred around this time.

---

[432] See Utterback (1994).

But in addition players need to stay at high-speed to maintain the distance over the competition. Therefore, **moving fast** and not being surpassed by faster competitors is crucial in the growth process. In the case of CompuServe the misunderstanding of the marketing requirements of a growth market opened the door to the late-comer AOL, who understood the marketing challenges. In an alliance the on-line marketing champion Bertelsmann, AOL moved rapidly in the European on-line consumer space taking over CompuServe.

Finally gaining market dominance in a start-up industry is not a consolidated position. Owning 80% of a market, which has only reached 15% of a population, requires a firm to **keep moving**. On these grounds, one can postulate the following thesis:

> Be first – Be fast – And keep growing faster than the market.

If firms neglect this, a constellation will work around the dominant player. It will target precisely the remaining 85% with another system, which suits the needs of the new customers better. This will cause a disruption in the development path with the network shifting to a substitute system design.[433] Considering the immature product and technology of on-line services in the late 1990s this "make it easy for the masses" strategy is well positioned to reach the rest of the population with a product that offers services while technology is increasingly kept invisible in the background. In addition to these product issues, the marketing issue is to provide the resources needed to develop these markets. The examples of Freesurf in the UK or Yahoo! in Europe show that a virtual bundle with massive telecom, retail and hardware players designed for end consumers constitutes a massive threat to AOL. Easy to use, slimmed down products accompanied by massive marketing cooperation develop the momentum needed to keep growing. For example Yahoo! in Germany works with the largest retailers in mass market industries, such as C & A, Internet by call ISP's, such as Talknet, and print media publishers, and wireless players such as Mannesmann, D2 privat, and Nokia to work around AOL, or in the case of Germany T-Online dominance. In reaction, the dominant players have to regain speed and develop activities to react to the new designs of on-line service bundlings.[434] From their standpoint, first mover advantages and learning curves have to be extended to move into new segments of customers.[435]

How can this be done in practice? In the presence of such particularities business strategy has to react differently, and differently over time in order to **build and sustain a solid business development path**. Figure 3-15 shows the four stages and demonstrates that firms have to move early and fast and need to keep growing with the market growth. The following paragraphs work out a set of strategic factors and put them into perspective over time, as adoption changes the rules in network markets. The factors being analyzed are expectations of market

---

[433] See Christensen (1997) and Christensen / Bower (1995).

[434] According to interviews with Chris Hill, Executive Vice President Corporate Development AOL Europe, 23rd of June 1999, London, Fabiola Aredondo, Vice President Yahoo! Europe, 4th of June 1999, London, and Peter Würtenberger, Managing Director Yahoo! Germany, 2nd of June 1999, Munich. See Yoffie / Cusumano (1999), pp. 71-76 for the role of speed and the leverage of the positions as a small start-up player and a dominant player.

[435] See also Mueller (1997).

participants, the creation and leverage of network effects, pricing strategies, and product management over time. The smallest common denominator of these factors is that **strategic intentions need to shift at the breaking point of critical mass**. The collaborative aspect shifts more to competitive mindset, which describes the co-opetition mindset (Brandenburger / Nalebuff 1996), which build successful players in this industry:

"Business is cooperation when it comes to creating the pie and competition when it comes to dividing it up." (ibid:4)

Figure 3-15: Strategic Conduct in Different Adoption Stages & Braking Point of Critical Mass

Work with expectations

The theory of network economics and the analysis of business practice in the Internet explains how players at first need to fight against the start-up forces, rather than competitors. Many of these mechanisms are controlled by expectations of all market participants and coordination failures are also based on their expectations. Therefore, players need to **signal to all market participants** that they are willing to create and sustain a network market on a certain technology.

As a start-up phenomenon, a player has to convince the market participants that the network will make it. Besides verbal commitments, the crucial aspect is **sponsoring** of a new network. The pricing strategy (see below) reflects this pattern. Katz / Shapiro find that in the absence of players sponsoring the start-up costs of a network, a technology which is superior today will dominate the market tomorrow. If two rival technologies are competing, the sponsored one will have the advantage, even if it is inferior. Finally, if competing technologies are sponsored, the one which will be superior tomorrow will have the strategic advantage.[436] The sponsoring of on-line services via wireless applications by players like Nokia, Yahoo!, and service providers is a typical example, which will take place in the first years of the new decade.

As a dominant player, **pre-announcements, intended to shape the expectations** in the market, can create barriers for start-up players, which tend to offer a new – substitution – network technology.[437] If customers, for example, believe the incumbent will upgrade to new technology, there is no longer a need to switch to a small start up network.

"The aura of inevitability is a powerful weapon when demand-side economies of scale are strong." (Varian / Shapiro 1998: 181)

Create & leverage network effects

This factor is in fact identical with the considerations about networking strategy discussed in 3.3.3. But again, firms need to handle this factor differently according to the stage of the market

* A start-up is interested in **sharing a network** collaborating with other start-up network or **give licenses** to others, in order to fuel growth with additional external resources.

* A dominant player rather closes its network and **charges for interconnection**. This can be a monetary charge or marketing values in order to translate this position into future growth. In addition, because it is dominant in the horizontal layer, its **attention shifts to vertical layers to acquire smaller player**. This can be for protective reasons – in order to destroy potential virtual structures which work around the own network, or to expand its own network into additional vertical layers. Furthermore, other **large players on vertical layers have to be identified as friend or foe,** whereas a small player considers any large vertical player as an attractive partner.

Needs-based penetration pricing[438]

* In a start-up period, players sponsor their products at no or low fees in order to increase demand. Potential lock-in effects, which decrease demand, can be overcome by offering free services. This basically describes a strategy where a player is **buying market share** in order to skim that profit later and rather **invest in an installed base.**[439]

---

[436] See Katz / Shapiro (1986a).
[437] See Farrell / Saloner (1986).
[438] See Economides (1996), p. 29 and Varian (1997), p.1.
[439] See Economides 1998b.

Alternatively, a **large player will segment the market** and will **charge the existing locked-in customer** a premium depending on their switching costs. In order to grow with the adoption of the overall market, a **trading down** strategy will offer downgraded version for new customers in order to **extend the installed base into late adopting customers segments.**

> "(...) design for the high end of the market first, and then downgrade the product to
> get the versions for the other segments of the market." (Varian 1997:12)

■ **Open standard products versus vertically compatible proprietary products[440]**

* Corresponding with the networking strategy small start-ups need to drive open standard product development to be able to interconnect with other horizontally and vertically system components in order to generate network effects.

* Once becoming the dominant player, it will change its standards focus by driving a control standards strategy where it tries to establish a de facto standard on their layer driving small players out of business. In order to co-evolve with the technological and market development, successful players have to be able to maintain compatibility of interfaces to the vertical layers in a way that ensures that they can close these links to cut of competitors or open to interconnect with complementors.

Given this shift in the strategic mind set of a firm in the business development path and the complex coalition and competitive structures disclosed in 3.3.3 the following presents a hybrid mind set for business strategy, which applies the corresponding game theory for such situations.

3.3.6. Co-opetition Games with Your Complementors

This section introduces the concept of co-opetition (Brandenburger / Nalebuff 1997) as a **new mindset for business strategy** and will combine it with the findings of network economics. It conceptually applies game theory, emphasizing the cooperative and competitive aspects of business and how players can play their cards in the best way in such constellations.

> **"Business is cooperation when it comes to creating a pie and competition when it
> comes to dividing it up.** (...) It is simultaneously war and peace. (...) You have to
> compete and cooperate at the same time. The combination makes a more dynamic re-
> lationship (...). This is why we've adopted Noordas's word co-opetition (...)." (Bran-
> denburger / Nalebuff 1997:5, emphasis C. G.)[441]

The authors explicitly discuss the role of complementors as a key role in business strategy, which extends the complementary aspect of network economics into business strategy.

---

[440] See Bar / Borrus / Steinberg (1995) and Katz / Shapiro (1985), pp. 435-436 for further discussion on the consequences of the adoption of standards.

[441] Brandenburger / Nalebuff (ibid.) disclose that they picked up the word "co-opetition" from Ray Noorda, founder of Novell, who initially coined the term.

While 3.3.3 outlined the economic rationale for a networking strategy, it employed a **multi-layered vertical duopoly coalition structure**. These considerations imply game structures between the different parties. This seems not only a sensible move in the empirical light of the industry, but also takes into consideration the methods of the underlying Industrial Economics. The predominant approach to business strategy in the microeconomic tradition has traditionally been game theory driven. Sutton points out that traditional game theoretical models in economics usually formulate a "Bertrand" or "Cournot" condition or a "joint-profit-maximization" as the starting point to games.[442] Factors in the market structure are usually analyzed as implications for conduct and performance as Schmalensee points out.

> "The game-theoretic revolution in industrial economics has taught us that unobservable details of market structure may have large effects on conduct and performance" (Schmalensee 1992:133)

This is exactly what was shown in part II, which analyzes and conceptually models the networked structure of the on-line industry and part III, which discusses implications for firm strategy.

Traditional microeconomists model a situation by focusing on one aspect (e.g. pricing, quality, market access, and so on), while holding the other factors fixed. Then they incrementally play with all the factors. The reason for this *ceteris paribus* approach is rooted in their methodology, which has always been based on mathematical equations, and is thus an **analytical approach**. If they were to make all factors dynamic, it would produce too many variables and the system of equations would not be solvable. As a result, the output of the system would be ambiguous.

> "Game theory sounds tailor-made for the analysis of business strategy. But historically, there's been an obstacle preventing the world of business from embracing game theory. The problem is that academics and business people speak two different languages: equations versus experience." (Brandenburger / Nalebuff 1997:40-41)

Different to this **Brandenburger / Nalebuff present a conceptual approach that renders all factors dynamic**. By doing so, they do not generate or model equations, but they can work around the *ceteris paribus* constraint. This improves the likelihood that they are modeling something closer to the practical world. Furthermore, this thesis, although employing insights from Industrial Economics and generating Network Economics as its offspring, works around the analytical methods and to present a conceptual model, which delivers the analytical insights of network economists. The approach of Brandenburger / Nalebuff is a purely conceptual approach, which **focuses on growing environments and assumes change and dynamics in complex situations**. Moreover, it **focuses on the role of complementors**. Therefore, it is a consistent explanation of how firms can strategize in the omnipresent friend – foe – complementor situations of the Internet. The following will introduce relevant game structures for the on-line industry and applies their approach.

---

[442] See Sutton (1995), pp. 35.

In order to connect the general ideas of Brandenburger / Nalebuff Figure 3-16 charts a matrix of the most common constellations firms will face in the on-line industry. It presents the menu of choices outlining potential co-opetitive alliances, which is a crucial factor in network industries as Varian / Shapiro point out:

> "To compete effectively in network markets you need allies. Choosing and attracting allies is a critical aspect of strategy in the network economy." (Varian / Shapiro 1998a:258)

Considering the nature of the industry, it will be populated with the following predominant types of players:

Small start ups: trying to find a favorable position, innovating with technologies and business models, creating new markets and aiming to become the dominant player in that area by virtuously playing games with the right complementors.

Large giants: who have achieved critical mass, became dominant players and trying to retain this position by growing with large complementors and protecting boundaries against (frequently by acquiring) small complementors.

The horizontal and vertical network structure, as laid out in Figure 3-16, tends toward large, vertically integrated structures. Therefore, the following analyzes the most common situations for small players (usually start-ups) and large players and how their relationship can be characterized from both the horizontal and vertical perspective. The following two matrixes show the alternating settings:

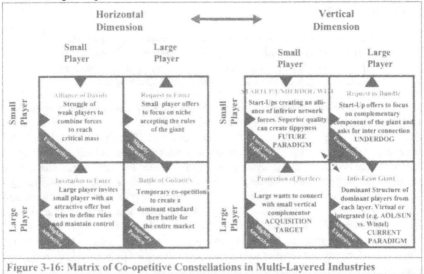

Figure 3-16: Matrix of Co-opetitive Constellations in Multi-Layered Industries

This matrix defines eight generic, co-opetitive relationships, which occur in a multi-layered industry. It has distinct implications for both the horizontal and vertical perspective. The arrows indicate the order and direction of actions, for example, large player invites small player as opposed to small player requests the large player's entrance. This distinction exhibits the asymmetrical relationship of the players, and depends on who has the larger / earlier interest.[443]

Horizontal Dimension[444]

* **Co-opetition between small player and small player.** This is the **"alliance of Davids"**. Two small start-ups find themselves in the same competition and face the mutual critical mass issues, hence the need to form a coalition to generate network effects. This is an **unattractive** team of weak players struggling to reach critical mass. One can for example think of two smaller stock trading communities lacking the required marketing resources.

* **Co-opetition request from small player to large player.** The small player realizes the need to leverage network externalities. It approaches the large player with a **"requests to enter"** promising to extend its network, focusing on a niche, and accepting his rules for interconnection or licensing. This can be **slightly attractive** for both players if they are basing their game on complementarity rules, otherwise the small player ekes out a marginal existence, such as many of the CompuServe affiliates who requested licenses for smaller markets such as Australia or New Zealand, where CompuServe did not provide the support required from a large player.

* **Co-opetition request from large player to small player.** The large player realizes it has limited resources and sees the need to generate network effects. It starts a licensing program similar to the one described in Case Study 3-3, where CompuServe licensed its technology in the Asia / Pacific region in the context of its internationalization strategy. The large player gives the small player an **"invitation to enter"** based on the large player's terms and conditions. This can be **slightly attractive** for both players if they base their game on complementarity.

* **Co-opetition between large players.** Two large players realize they have limited resources to reach critical mass independently. Therefore, it is **temporary attractive** to create a shared network and a dominant standard. Shortly after critical mass of the shared network is reached, a **"battle of Goliath's"** erupts for the entire market – most likely in price wars. The battles for wireless telephony standards are a good example for this case.

---

[443] Empirical back-up information by interviews with Tony Philipp, Christoph Mohn, Karsten Weide, Ned Taylor, Reed Maltzman, Dave Bezair and Bill Truesdale (see Appendix).

[444] See European Commission (1997), p. 8 outing the following main rational in the convergence area for horizontal cooperations: Reach of critical mass and increase of market dominance, sharing of entry costs of new technologies, risk sharing in case of unclear demand for new products or services, internationalization and taking advantages of deregulation.

Vertical Dimension[445]

- **Co-opetition between small player and small player.** A small, vertically located, player tap into the power of complementarity by building a virtual network. In the start-up stage they establish an **"underdog web,"** which can turn out to be the **future paradigm,** if their resources, configuration, and product bundling meets future demand better than the existing paradigm. One can think for example a virtual bundling of ISP's with free webmail boxes and a Yahoo! portal site as opposed to the integrated on-line services bundling in 1995-1997.

- **Co-opetition request from small player to large player.** A small player wants to generate network effects and **"requests to bundle"** the small complementary component with the large player. One can think for example of Lycos approaching the AOL and CompuServe on-line services in 1996-1998 offering Internet search functionality in an AOL or CompuServe design and a small "Lycos powered" co-branding to gain access to the large communities behind the on-line services. Due to the underdog position of the small player the relationship is **unattractive to the large player.**

- **Co-opetition request from large player to small player.** A large player needs to react to changes in the environment and vertical extensions to the product bundling are necessary. Compatibility on the vertical interfaces assumes that the large player bundles a small player's offering for **"protection of the vertical borders".** The small players is a **natural acquisition target.** This would be when a small software firm offers specialized applications to AOL like the buddy list and is later acquired and integrated within the large player's organizational and product structures.

- **Co-opetition between large players.** Two vertically located large players interconnect their structures. These **"Info-Econ Giants"** define the **current predominant industry paradigm** and control the market. Here one has AOL/Netscape bundling with SUN and Worldcom to become the largest on-line user community management, content and hosting player, largest client software player, largest back end software player, and largest network player.

If one considers the **instability of the market equilibria** as outlined in the discussion on network economics (2.2.1) **the reason why dominant networks tip is based in the vertical relationship of the future paradigm** (a virtual bundle of vertically related small start ups) **and the current paradigm** (vertically integrated info-econ giants). This is represented by the arrow between the two corresponding quadrants of the vertical matrix. Small players crave this tippyness as they can serve new customer needs better, faster and more flexibly with the

---

[445] See European Commission (1997), p. 8 outing the following main rational in the convergence area for vertical cooperation: risk sharing in the case of unclear demand for new products or services, market positioning, access to know-how, control of customer access, attempts to increase higher levels of value added, and protection against competition of firms positioned in substitution markets. Gomes-Casseres / Leonard-Barton (1996:364) emphasize the salient role of alliances in the on-line industry and point out a two-stage action – reaction effect, which is the result of insufficient competencies of singular players to grasp the complete vertical industrial scope: "As a result [of incomplete resources, C. G.], when one firm forms an alliance, others often follow. The bandwagon effect then gathers its own momentum as firms begin competing over partnerships, hedging against the uncertain future with portfolios of alliances and forming preemptive alliances."

most recent technology and virtually create scope. Large players can leverage scale and scope but have to continuously reinvent themselves, all the while retaining evolutionary fitness by co-evolving with the requirements of the market and underlying technological innovations.

Considering both dimensions in the light of the market dynamics and network adoption (3.3.5) one can consider it to be a **two step game.**

- **In the first step, focus lies on wining dominance in the horizontal dimension.** After reaching critical mass and reaping the rewards of dominance, **grown up players will change their conduct after the breaking point of critical mass** (see Figure 3-15).

- **In the second step the focus shifts to the vertical perspective.** Large players need to find ways of **growing faster than the market.** The have to keep pace with the adoption rates of the overall industry in order to retain their dominant position.

In both cases the role of complementors is key and players need to know how to play the game right. As a successful player you will need to know how "To find your natural allies (...)" (Varian / Shapiro 1998a:258), which requires understanding the complementarities hidden in the market structure. **This is exactly where the power of co-opetition comes in play.**

Brandenburger and Nalebuff's central thesis is that in **deciding how to conduct a business in an increasingly complex world, it seems an oversimplification to limit one's analysis to the competitive environment.** Furthermore, the reliance on competitive analyses implies the existence of purely adversarial relationships between the players in a given industry. In reality, there may be cooperative relationships within a competitive industry that has not resorted to unfair or non-competitive monopolistic practices. In fact, cooperation and competition often exist concurrently between the same two players.[446] For example, Microsoft and AOL are able find ways to cooperate in client software and distribution by bundling Internet Explorer with AOL and AOL with Windows, while their respective portal sites (MSN.com, AOL.com) and on-line services (AOL and MSN) clearly exhibit a competitive relationship. Cooperative strategies can be used to create a new market (or expand an existing market), and once it is created, competitive strategies can be used to divide it up amongst the players. Industry-wide standards negotiations, where all participants try to launch a new technology, reveal a great deal about this complementary relationship. This is based on the premise that **business is not necessarily a zero sum game,** where each situation is solely win-lose.[447] Or as Mike Homer, Executive Vice President and General Manager of Netcenter[448], puts it:

> "One of the "tricky" things to remember about the internet is that a lot of these opportunities are not "zero-sum" games. For example, if SportsLine can aggressively grow its membership services and secure the credit card information that enables additional purchases, then its revenues will grow. Instead of thinking this will take busi-

---

[446] See Brandenburger / Nalebuff (1997), pp. 12-16.

[447] See (ibid.), p. 59.

[448] Netcenter is the end user business of Netscape. It includes the Netscape portal business www.netcenter.com, the international entities, as well as the Netscape client software products like the communicator browser (interview with Linda Lawrence, Vice President International Netcenter, 25th of March 1999, Mountainview).

ness from the vertical portals, I think that there are going to be "multiple hands on the wheel."" (Goldman Sachs 1999:83-84)

There are scenarios in which **win-win is achieved by cooperation** and others in which **lose-lose occurs without it.** Players arrive at a win-win situation by jointly increasing the size of the pie (=increase of market volume) rather than a win-lose situation (=increase in market share at no growth). In the early market stage of network industries, creating value is more important than capturing value since having a large market share is useless if the market is not a pie but only crumbs. However, once a technology has reached critical mass, capturing market share is crucial in order to survive the battle zone (Figure 2-12). Without cooperation, a lose-lose-lose situation exists, not only because the competitors end up losing a potential market, but in typical critical mass situation, the market gets under-served as consumers lose a potentially useful product or service. In industries with strong network effects, such as the information technology industry, cooperation and competition, or co-opetition, may be the only way to conduct business. Because of strong network effects it is often difficult in the information technology industry to launch new products and break through to critical mass. In addition, the market demands increasing interoperability and this requires technical standards. However, the establishment of technical standards by competitive market forces in and of themselves is usually a challenging aim. Frequently, it leads many start-up companies to bankruptcy and established companies to product abandonment before their products reach the stage of positive feedback. Many years competition in which no clear winner emerges slows down development of the overall industry, in terms of company profitability and in terms of interoperability. It also requires high customer investments which become obsolete once a clear winner does emerge. Strategies are needed to avoid this undesirable situation for all participants. Co-opetition, which has its theoretical foundations in game theory, does just that. [449]

The classical formulation of game theory was presented in 1944 by John von Neumann and Oskar Morgenstern in 1944.[450] This theory studies the "game of strategies" in a social exchange economy including complexity and dynamics of interaction in a multi-factor scenario. In a social exchange economy, a participant tries to reach an optimal result. But in order to achieve this, participants must enter into relationship of exchange with others. If two or more persons exchange goods with each other, then the result for each one will depend not merely upon his own action but on those of the others as well. Thus each participant attempts to maximize a function of which he does not control all variables. This is certainly no maximization problem, but a peculiar and disconcerting mixture of several conflicting maximization problems. Every participant is guided by differing principles and no one determines all the variables which affect his interest.[451] This perfectly describes the complex co-opetitive situation in the Internet as analyzed in part II.

This characterization leads to the primary insight of game theory for business strategies:

---

[449] See Brandenburger / Nalebuff (1997), pp. 4-5.

[450] See v. Neumann / Morgenstern (1964).

[451] See Brandenburger / Nalebuff 1997), pp. 5-8.

> "The underlying principle is (...): you have to put yourself in the other players' shoes. You have to be allocentric. This doesn't mean you can ignore your own position. The skill lies in putting the two vantage points together: in understanding both the egocentric and the allocentric position." (Brandenburger / Nalebuff 1997:61)

This emphasizes the **importance of focusing on others and trying to play through all the reactions to their actions as far ahead as possible**. The authors suggest looking at a situation from both perspectives to see the added values, rules of the game, and perceptions of the situation from both sides:

> "Put yourself in the shoes of the other players to assess how valuable you are to them (...) to anticipate the reactions (...) to understand how they see the game." (Brandenburger / Nalebuff 1997:62)

By adopting this perspective, a player can, for example, discover that its chances for success are greater if it **creates a win-win, rather than a win-lose, situation** with other players. In other words, **firms should consider both cooperative and competitive ways** to change the game. **Looking at situations from both perspectives reveals the complementarities to generate and leverage network effects.**

In this sense co-opetition comes down to communication and ways to negotiate win-win scenarios. When examining at which stage of the game a business is and deciding how to conduct the game, players should evaluate the existence of potential win-win situations. If a firm is negotiating from a position of weakness, then it may be in its interest to cooperate. If a firm is negotiating from a position of great strength, then it may be its best interest to compete all-out. However, this strategy should not be pursued without properly addressing the possibility of a win-win scenario. With respect to the on-line industry Figure 3-16 outlines the potential situations for co-opetition. When evaluating the stages outlined above, players need to consider in which stage of the game they would put themselves and how the co-opetitor would see this.

According to game theory as Brandenburger / Nalebuff lay it out, the game has five components: players, added values, rules, tactics, and scope, and "PARTS"[452] as they call it. **Each of these components is dynamic.**

Players are customers, suppliers, substitutes (competitors), and complementors. It is important to realize that **none of the players are fixed, including the company itself**. An effective business strategy may entail bringing in new players or pushing out existing ones. For example, if a firm only has one supplier, it may want to pay for other suppliers to enter the game in order to make the raw material market for its business more competitive, or even to turn its supplier's products into commodities. On the other hand, if a firm is considering becoming a new player as a supplier to big companies, it should try to get compensated by the future customer for the competition you create. Within the players' element, **the concept of the Value Net expresses the relationship amongst the**

---

[452] PARTS is the acronym for the five game components players, added values, rules, tactics and scope.

players.[453] In this sense, the Value Net is a sub-component of PARTS, which explains who the game's players are.

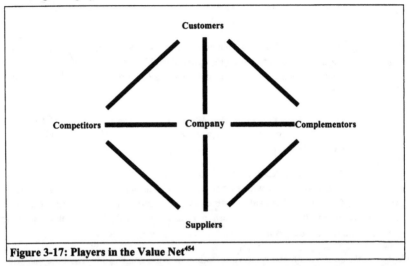

Figure 3-17: Players in the Value Net[454]

Brandenburger and Nalebuff also **use the Value Net to explain the interdependencies amongst the players**. They argue that there are both vertical and horizontal symmetries in the Value Net. Vertically, it demonstrates that customers and suppliers are both equal partners in creating value. Firms need to listen to the needs and wants of both sides. They cannot follow the convention of always placing the customer first. They must also nurture supplier relationships, a strategy which, at present, is not always the norm. Listening to suppliers allows firms to create partnerships and possibilities for improving the supply process. In this sense in the vertical dimension "Customers and suppliers play symmetric roles." (Brandenburger / Nalebuff 1997:22). While on the horizontal dimension "Competitors and complementors play mirror-image roles" (ibid.).

> **"A player is your complementor if customers value your product more when they have the other player's product than when they have your product alone."**
> (Brandenburger / Nalebuff 1997:18)

whereas

> **"A player is your competitor if customers value your product less when they have the other player's product than they have your product alone."** (ibid.)

Understanding this relationship highlights a deficiency in current competitive practices – focusing only on how to eliminate one's competitors. Firms should also attempt to develop complementors, which in the long-term increases a firm's overall value to a customer. **A single player can be in multiple roles at the same time, with all roles interdependent.**

---

[453] Brandenburger / Nalebuff (1997), pp. 16-39 and 71-109.

[454] Brandenburger / Nalebuff (1997:17).

By understanding these two symmetries, the Value Net carries potential for greater successful application. Instead of focusing on only the conventional players like customers and competitors, the Value Net shows that firms really have four positions to choose from when developing business strategies. The Value Net gives a company a competitive advantage over other players playing the game, particularly by widening the scope of defining competitors:

> "The traditional approach defined competitors as the other companies in your industry-those that make product similar to yours (...). As people think more in terms of solving their customers' problems, the industry perspective is becoming increasingly irrelevant. Customers care about the end result, not about whether the company that gives them what they want belongs to one industry or another. The right way to identify your competitors is, again, to put yourself in the customers' shoes." (ibid.:18-19)

In this sense the Value Net describes competitors in a way which is not defined by the positioning in one industry, in the terminology of this work – within one horizontal market layer, but by the level of complementarity or substitution level. By doing so, players from separate competitions, such as other vertical layers, become relevant in formulating a strategy. The level of complementarity therein defines the immediate strategic relationships. Crucial in this respect is the customer perspective. This understanding is perfectly concurrent with the structure of the on-line industry as described above. Players in the same market layer can be a complementary player in a vertical layer at one moment, and then can turn into competitors during another stage of the game, e.g. when they belong to a different vertical coalition structure.

Added values are what each player brings to the game. It is

> "The size of the pie when you are in the game minus the size of the pie when you are out of the game" (ibid.:45)

Trying to raise a player's added value or lower the added values of other players can make a player more valuable. Some ways to raise the added value are tailoring products to customer needs, building a brand, or using resources more efficiently. One the other hand, creating competition among suppliers, controlling production to generate a shortage of products, using commodity parts in one's products, etc, are some possible ways of lowering the values of others.[455] For example Windows as well as the AOL on-line service have enormous added value of bringing a product in front of the customers eyeballs and hence are a complementor in many on-line services. Their direct relationship is competitive. **A particular effect in network industries is that scale always results in potential value added as it entails network externalities.**

Rules are just as mutable as are the players and added values of the game. In business, most of the rules people play by are well-established laws and customs. This is different **in the on-line industry where rules are often waiting to be written.** But in general, the rules that exist, can be changed or negotiated with other players, such as contracts. Players

---

[455] See (ibid.), pp. 45-49 and 111-158.

may want to revise the rules to their advantage. For example, a meet-the competition (MCC) clause in many contracts gives the incumbent seller the right to make the last bid, which allows the producer to sustain a higher price and reduces the chance of a price war. This in turn also helps give the challenger some room to raise prices to its own customers. And for the customers, their producers are more willing to invest in serving them since MCC guarantee producers a long-term relationship if they so choose. In addition, the imitation of MCC allows the producers to push the prices up further, so they have even more to lose from starting a price war. This is a typical case in which co-opetition creates a win-win situation. From game theory point of view, the function of rules is to limit the possible reactions to any one action. **To analyze the effect of a rule, a player must look forward and reason backward.** Given the effects a player can then start changing the rules in its favor.[456]

■ **Tactics** are the fourth component in a game. Business is a complicated game, riddled by uncertainty. Tactics are used to influence the way other players perceive the uncertainty and thus influence their behavior. Some tactics work by reducing misconceptions, other work by creating or maintaining uncertainty. For example, if Netscape decided not to compete directly with Microsoft in the browser business, and just go after a niche market, it would have been able to avoid the price war on browsers. To do this, it would have had to make it clear to Microsoft that it was not going after the whole market. Hence; both companies could have co-existed and divided the market. If Microsoft had been convinced, it would not have reduced the price of Internet Explorer to nothing and tried to drive Netscape out of business.[457]

■ **Scope** describes the boundaries of the game. Games are not static, they evolve over time and are linked across space. Managers should constantly evaluate the possibility of expanding or shrinking those boundaries.[458] For the Netscape example discussed above, when Netscape lost market share to Microsoft on the browser market, it extended the scope by developing the Netscape homepage "Netcenter" as independent business which was interconnected with the browser client software.[459]

The Value Net and PARTS are important frameworks for locating co-opetition opportunities. The standard framework for the most common situations in the on-line industry was laid out in Figure 3-16. However, there are many potential traps that must be avoided. First, players must realize that they do not have to accept the game in which they find themselves. The bottom line is that players can change the game to their advantage and **it is far more rewarding to be a game maker than a game taker.** Secondly, it is important to note that **changing the game does not have to come at the expense of others.** This mind-set is critical for finding the win-win strategy. The third trap is to only focus on part of the game. **If players fail to see the whole game, they cannot change the part they do not see.** Lastly,

---

[456] See (ibid.), pp. 49-52 and 159-197.

[457] See (ibid.), pp. 198-233. Furthermore Yoffie / Cusumano (1999) on tactics in the case of a small player and a large player illustrating with the case of Netscape vs. Microsoft.

[458] See (ibid.), pp. 45-49 and 234-260.

[459] According to interview with Linda Lawrence, Vice President International Netcenter, 25th of March 1999, Mountainview.

players should always keep in mind that business is a dynamic process. Other player are also trying to change the game. Their changes could result in positive effects or not. Players often need to change the game again in order to maintain a game maker position. This is a continuum as **there is no end of the game.**

Overall it can be summarized that co-opetition provides significant advantages in a network industry where complementors play a salient role. It provides firms with a portfolio of potential **advantages** if used properly.

▪ **Co-opetition leverages network externalities.** By explicitly focusing on complementors co-opetition is the strategic complement to the economic rational of network externalities as it was laid out in this thesis. In this sense **co-opetition is a necessary pre-condition to grasping the vertical scope of the on-line industry.** Co-opetition across the vertical dimension results in pooling of resources and players can bundle their products into a composite system of higher perceived value and improved economics. Moreover **co-opetition is contingent in the horizontal layers reaching critical mass issues in early market stages.**

▪ **Co-opetition describes the strategic shift during adoption stages.** Particularly before reaching the point of critical mass and receiving positive feedback is where co-opetition has its greatest value, e. g. creating a market as a start-up. Up until then partnering has the best leverage, and after that the strategic intentions start shifting (see Figure 3-15). Since each of the segments of the technology adoption life cycle (Moore 1995) has a different response to a new technology, and industry structures vary over adoption cycles, a company must steadily change its business strategies and tactics in order to deal with the alternating behavior of the different segments and different horizontal and vertical competitive settings.

▪ **It provides firms with a new model which formulates strategies that incorporate both competitive and cooperative tactics.** Traditional firms, which rely exclusively on competitive models, will be at a disadvantage to their, peers who are willing to consider a new model revealing new and perhaps even better strategies. These strategies could even lead to win-win situations where all competitors receive some benefit from their participation in the industry.

▪ **It provides firms with a systematic approach to manipulate their business environment.** It thus can be seen as an extension to the dynamic SCP – Paradigm (Figure 3-9). This new conceptual framework consists of the Value Net and PARTS. Both aspects of the framework apply game theory principles to business situations and provide ways to change the game, if it is more beneficial to a firm and if others allow it.

▪ **Co-opetition could result in greater profits.** If co-opetition increases the total market, then firms can compete for market share of a "bigger pie". In cases with network externalities, this can turn out to be more profitable than having a larger market share of a smaller pie. Without considering co-opetition, a firm could have settled for lower profits, without realizing it had the capacity to earn even more money.

■ **Co-opetition is particularly relevant in growing markets,** such as the on-line industry, where adoption rates are in an early stage and mutual growth creates win-win situations as opposed to competing for a static pie.

But co-opetition also incorporates some **disadvantages** as it can turn out to be a double-edged sword. In some instances, it can give firms a larger market share and even a larger market. In other cases, it can lead to legal disputes or it can create stronger competitors who seize market share. Therefore, great care should be taken in selecting when and how to use co-opetition to a players advantage.

■ **Potential for legal disputes:** Along the same lines as argued by Varian / Shapiro (1998a) and Varian (1999b) networking, particularly under the presence of complementarities / network, externalities carry the potential for **anti trust issues.** Firms engaging in co-opetition run the risk of employing anti-competitive tactics such as controlling prices, discriminator pricing, driving out their competition, or developing a monopoly. The unfortunate aspect of co-opetition is that it could be perceived as **tacit collusion.**[460]

■ **Strengthening competitors at your expense:** In the process of co-opeting, a player may find themselves in a worse position than when they started. They may actually discover that co-opetition has led to stronger competitors or new entrants into the market. Inviting players to compete automatically results in increased competition, which carries the risk of generating a powerful new competitor. This is especially true if the complementors have strong competitive and innovative culture, which can turn transferred know-how back against the originating firm.[461] Ultimately **in a rapidly changing environment, as the Internet is today, allies can be tomorrow competitors.** While Microsoft chose AOL as a complementor to integrate interactive services in the operating system and distribute the Internet Explorer browser in the mid 1990s, it now faces future competition in the mass market with AOL having acquired Netscape and collaborating with SUN directly against Microsoft.

■ **Igniting additional dynamics:** The advice that games do not stand still induces players to continuously change the rules in a proactive way. If a larger number of players follows this strategy it can in fact lead to increased market dynamics and erosion of stabilized laws of the market place.

---

[460] Brandenburger and Nalebuff (1995) describe for example how the New York Post was able to get the New York Daily News to raise its price ten cents above the original price at which both competitors had been selling newspapers. Rather than explicitly agree to a price hike, the Post used an ingenious method to tacitly get the Daily News to agree to a price hike. As Brandenburger and Nalebuff explain it, the two newspapers were not colluding to raise prices so much as avoiding a price war. But the same scenario could be seen from a collusionary perspective. Nalebuff and Brandenburger (1997), pp. 192-195 address this issue in the discussion of the game component "rules" of their PARTS model. They argue that players engaging in co-opetition should consider the legal and regulatory environment in which they operate, which considers this threat to co-opetitive strategies. But in reality crossing the legal boundaries may be a very sensitive issue. The case of the German digital pay TV plans of Bertelsmann and Kirch Gruppe colliding with the European regulators are a recent example.

[461] See Rumer (1994), pp. 24-25 and the corresponding discussion about cooperations in the context of the resource-based view (3.2.2).

270

After this final tool for net-centric strategic conduct, the above summarizes the instruments which were worked out in the course of this thesis.

3.4. Summary of Tools, Tool Set and Industry Model

This section summarizes the developed instruments and puts the model, the tool set and the individual tools into perspective. The instruments are constructed in the following way: The **industry model** (see Figure 2-38) outlines the **industrial structure** in a way which presents the data of the field in a clear outline. The **framework of the tool set** (see Figure 3-8) is used for processing of this data. The fixed factors (symbolized by) of the framework are used to guide the strategy formulation process derive and formulate a strategy which refers to the components of the model. In order to **conduct** this strategy the **set of individual tools** (symbolized by ✖) for a product, networking, pricing, adoption, policy, and complementor strategy work on the specific factors of the **layers of the industry structure**.

The tool set laid out the setting of the fixed factors by putting it into perspective with the endogenous variables. In this sense the endogenous variables need to be **moderated by the strategic conduct** of firms, whereas creation and leverage of horizontal and vertical network externalities is central to the strategy. Network economics explain the **creation and leverage of horizontal and vertical network externalities as endogenous variables of the system** in the sense of the tool set (see Figure 3-9). Along these line the following summarizes the forgoing of formulating and conducting a business strategy in the on-line industry.

The industry model delivers structured data input. The strategy tool set puts these factors into a strategic perspective. Whereas a strategy formulation can be anchored by an analysis of the fixed factors:

Resources

Needs

Network Economic Principles

Horizontal and vertical network effects are a central anchor in the strategy. In order to conduct the formulated strategy, firms need to apply tools in respect to

✖ Product Strategy

✖ Networking Strategy

✖ Pricing Strategy

✖ Adoption Strategy

✖ Policy Strategy (The "Exogenous" Parameters)

✖ Complementor Strategy

These tools are orchestrated by applying the multi-layered industry model.

Figure 3-18 visualizes this dynamic interplay of industry structure and firm strategy:

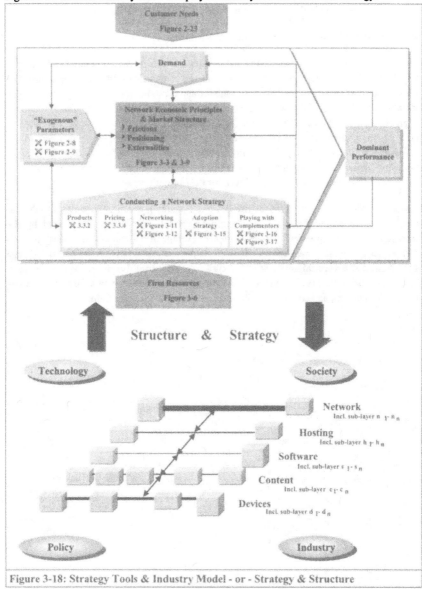

Figure 3-18: Strategy Tools & Industry Model - or - Strategy & Structure

Being equipped with business strategy insights from the market-based view, the resource-based view and the net-centric strategy tools a comprehensive tool set can be applied in practical situations. The model of the industry which was worked out in part II can be applied to model specific situations. A strategy planning process then needs to consider the individual data of the field in order to bring the model alive. Deriving a strategy then needs to apply the strategic framework of the tool set. In return strategy which is already formulated can be tested upon its plausibility of the underlying thesis and can be conducted in the field. In an example this will be conducted with a brief case which plays through the situation of AOL in Europe.

The following case study will cross-check the prospects of the strategy of AOL in Europe for 1999/2000 and will apply the relevant factors of the instruments worked out in this thesis. AOL Europe has formulated its strategy for entering the "**third phase of Internet evolution**" (Bar / Cohen / Cowhey / DeLong / Kleeman / Zysman 1999:10, emphasis, C. G.) of on-line services in the Internet framework. This stage will be dominated by three main aspects:[462]

- Advent of broadband
- Evolution into a mass market
- Large variety of on-line services via multiple devices

This entails enormous opportunities and threats. AOL aims to be the dominant paradigm in this next evolutionary stage of on-line services.

The case illustrates the current industrial situation, applies the significant factors of the theoretical framework of this thesis and involves the relevant strategic factors of the industry such as adoption rates, industry maturity processes, technological innovations of software, hardware and network platform and the evolution of new services. Applying this case includes the perspectives of hardware, content, hardware, software, hosting, and network players.

AOL entered the European market as a late comer in early 1995 in a joint venture with Bertelsmann (initially also a 10% minority stake of Axel Springer Verlag). AOL is the on-line player with the highest level of vertical integration. It provides a relatively complete package of services under one bill. Until 1998 it could reach 1 million subscribers in Europe and after the acquisition of CompuServe the combined customer base went over 2 million subscribers. In 1999 a new strategy was formulated after a change in the executive team of the firm.

Strategy Thesis: "**We can repeat what AOL did in the US from 1995 until 1998 and grow faster than the market and gain market dominance in 1999-2001.**"

Underlying Assumption: Europe will face the same adoption patters in the 1999-2001 as the US in 1996-1998. AOL in the US took the opportunity to capture the major share of new users reaching a dominant position of almost 20 million subscribers in 1999. Extensive marketing expenditures in branding and distribution were key to reach this goal.

Strategy Goal: Capture the majority of new adopters and be the dominant player.

Strategy Plan: Investing massive resources in marketing and organization and develop the market with a "Multi-Brand-Strategy" with the integrated AOL bundling for the mass market, CompuServe for the sophisticated and semi-professional users, Netscape as Internet access service and portal site, the branded killer application Instant Messenger, and an attempt to develop a portfolio of portal sites under the respective brands.

---

[462] See Bar / Cohen / Cowhey / DeLong / Kleeman / Zysman (1999), p.6.

Strategy Issue: Are the underlying assumptions of this strategy correct and is it possible to translate the historical scenario from the advanced US market in the lagging European market? Where are the mission critical factors in this strategy?

The author will compare the strategic factors being part of the framework of the strategy tool set in order to **analyze the plausibility of the European strategy and to disclose strengths and weaknesses**. Each factor will be rated in order to show the strategy fit with the market structures and organizational structures.

Overall Situation - Analysis of the Wider Industrial Structure

* **Industrial framework.** The US market was mainly dominated by the convergence processes described in 2.4 and a **similar situation** is exhibited in the European market. (+)
* **Technology framework** in the US was a relatively stable framework of Computer based (predominantly windows PC's and app. 10% Macintosh), narrow-band dial-in structure for proprietary services and standard html on-line services. Fundamentally different is the situation AOL Europe is facing in 1999: The technology platform will shift to multi-device, multi-access network and multi-standards (html, XML, Java, WAP etc.) while still using partially old proprietary technology components. This is a **massive technology challenge**. (- -)
* **Policy framework** in the US was characterized by a predominately unregulated Internet (content and software) market and a very stable telecom market regulated by the FCC with the predominant revenue stream for the Internet access resulting in very solid and stable economics. This is a large difference in Europe: Privacy and tax regulation demands for certain standards and the telecom regulation resulted in eroding access driven revenue streams (see Case Study 2-1) with AOL rolling out a free Netscape branded ISP offering. Therefore the **economics are completely different** in the European scenario compared to the US case. (- -)
* **Socio-economic framework:** The US market was characterized by massive demand, availability of capital over the stock market (AOL was offered not at the NASDAQ but at the NYSE and was the first Internet stock in the indices) and issues to build up a skilled work force in AOL's headquarter in Virginia. The **European market exhibits indeed a similar development** in each factor. Furthermore AOL in Europe received massive corporate funding (app. $500 Mio.) and plans to go public in a second stage to fuel the required conduct of the strategy formulation. Overall these factors rather support the European plans. (++)

As an intermediate result one can state that an analysis of the wider industrial structure already shows **significant differences to the underlying assumptions**. Nevertheless the **core aspect on adoption patterns is correct**. But the **political and technological framework exhibit major industrial forces which work against AOL's European** strategy whereas the US strategy had these forces supporting them. **Consequently the strategy incorporates high risk to fail as the underlying assumptions are partially incorrect**.

The following is considering the empirical **fixed points in the strategic framework of the tool set** in order to analyze if the fixed factors in fact support the fundamental grounds of the strategy thesis. The first fixed point is the analysis of the chosen strategy under the light of the (network) economic principles:

Industrial Structure / (Network) Economies

* **Market Type:** AOL in the US was the leader in a **narrow oligopoly** (four player) but increasingly confronted with a **growing number of specialized competitors**, particularly in distinct value layers.

Netscape and Microsoft for Software, players like Yahoo! or Geocities for content and community, UUNet for hosting and networks and so forth. As a reaction the software was first integrated then acquired, the network was unbundled. A similar situation is valid for Europe. But there is a large difference: **AOL in the US was the by far largest player** and could leverage its dominance. **AOL Europe is in best case the number two in each regional market usually with a large distance to the market leader in this country**. Although AOL claims to be the largest pan-European service it has to be stated that this market definition is absolutely irrelevant for most business relations. It is rather a public relations hook to claim at least this leadership position. In fact there are only very few supply relations in the network layer were European scope can be leveraged. Therefore AOL in the US had **massive positive feedback** effects and **AOL in Europe is usually in the downtrend of the network market share battle zone** fighting against the stronger positive feedback of a larger player (see Figure 2-12). This is valid for the overall bundling in the case where there are competitors with the same bundling approach, but this is also valid for each individual layer in respect to content, software, hosting and networks, while devices are not integrated into the bundle yet. (- -)

- **Market Position** (Bargaining Position): Due to its dominance AOL in the US had a strong bargain position against suppliers in all layers and due to its large community also to the customers. As a result AOL had the lowest inbound costs for network, (hosting was done in internal operations), software, content and to device players (PC and modem) and the highest prices to the customer (prices for AOL were $25 dollar which is $5-10 higher than the market average). Different in Europe: The bargaining position of the customer is weak with prices going down (for example, the free offering in UK or the $6 base rate in Germany). Furthermore the prices for network are higher than the costs of the competitors. (- -)

- **Supply Side Economies of Scale**: AOL in the US is the largest player on each layer: Largest dial-up network traffic (rented at MCI/Worldcom / Case Study 2-5), largest data hosting center (internal hosting for scale reasons and strategic customer information reasons), largest client software player (Netscape, integrated AOL-Internet Explorer Instant Messenger, ICQ, back-end alliance with SUN), largest content player (AOL proprietary content, AOL.com, Digital Cities), attempts to integrate devices. Therefore it can realize the components of all layers at the lowest costs. This situation is very different for AOL in Europe, where particularly the network costs are always higher as the market leader. Because in each market the telecommunications players can offer better consumer ISP rates due to scale and scope effects. As a result of the scope effects with AOL in the US (the proprietary) hosting is realized at very low costs although the local Internet content hosting is realized on low scale which exhibits inferior economics compared to larger local competitors which can bundle larger traffic on their hosts. The software layers exhibits very positive economics due to the scope effects with the US. The content layer can leverage scope effects with other Bertelsmann interactive units and is frequently realized at low or no costs, although this is a common position among the larger aggregators such as Yahoo!. Overall the **European scale effects are much weaker than in the US**. (--)

- **Supply Side Economies of Scope**: No other player is able to bundle interactive services components in a scope such as AOL. Microsoft has similar opportunities with Windows, MSN, MSN.com and Explorer but overall plays on a smaller scale in each component. This is true for AOL in Europe, as well, as there is virtually no competitor delivering equivalent scope. In addition the European unit can benefit from additional scope effects by interconnecting with other Bertelsmann units. Therefore **AOL Europe benefits from strong economies of scope**. (+)

- **Demand Side Economies of Scale**: These effects are by enlarge determined by the size of the community of users on the on-line service. Due to the enormous subscriber base the US service can generate a much better externalities in this respect. Hence wherever US components are relevant from a user side the European unit can utilize the US scale, but in most cases the US components are not relevant for the users (language and cultural barriers to software, content (and hence also hosting), community and regional barriers to the network). **Europe has weaker positive feedback from the demand side**. (- -)
- **Demand Side Economies of Scope**: This aspect is determined by the complementarity of underlying needs for the scope of components. See the discussion of needs below.

Given these facts there is a **massive difference in the economics between the past US position and the current European position.** The US unit could leverage network externalities as a whole and actually reach a dominant position and therefore **AOL enjoys enormous positive feedback in the US**. The European entity is far from reaching critical mass to get the equivalent positive feedback. In fact in some respect the **European entity receives negative feedback** as it has to compete against larger players. Particular if one considers the real market definitions the position of a European player is relatively irrelevant as each market has a distinct and independent competition. Therefore the scale and scope effects have to be measured by enlarge in terms of regional markets where AOL usually has a position of a first line underdog as opposed to AOL in the US which has always been the dominant giant. The European unit exhibits smaller scale than comparable players in each layer but can use the advantage of supply with several US components (namely hosting of proprietary content, software development, international content) at low rates and can leverage some scale in Pan-European network deals. Particularly the weaker position to the customer results in weaker network effects on the demand side and in a painful price cut. Overall the **economics and network economics of AOL in Europe are significantly worse as in comparison to the US. Therefore the only way to perform accordingly is to grow even stronger than the US service as the income side is less efficient. But in any case to realize this growth will be tougher as positive feedback is weaker. For these reasons the EUROPEAN MARKET WILL BE SIGNIFICANTLY LESS EFFICIENT. Furthermore the aimed position under the given strategy carries the risk of developing a DEFICIT BUSINESS in a large scale given the aimed LARGE VOLUME of the business.**

The second fixed factor are the firms resources which have to be seen under the light of requirements of the field:

Resources
- **Resources:** AOL in the US has been the player with by far the largest experience curve in the US market. The same can be stated for AOL in Europe. Their accumulated know-how in all market layers puts them in a very strong position. Furthermore AOL Europe could recruit an excellent work force with the support of the shareholder Bertelsmann. Although a significant number of senior executives left the company after the reformulation of the strategy as it is analyzed this case. But overall the know-how and personnel situation is **excellent, particularly in comparison to the resource situation of competitors.** (+ +)
- **Capabilities:** AOL in the US has enormous capabilities in marketing, technology and R & D, as they have recruited and developed an enormous human resource of 12,000 people and went through a series of successful acquisitions. The European unit has strong capabilities **Marketing, M & A, human resource** management and **general management**, particularly through the **influence of**

Bertelsmann which is a best practice player in these functional areas. The large downside is that **AOL in Europe does not own significant technology and R & D capabilities** as these components are based in the US unit. This dependence is a significant weakness in a competition which will be dominated by several disruptive technology shifts. Given the functional strength of the player required, **technological weakness will be a crucial factor in a period which will be characterized by technology shifts in each major product components** (multiple devices, multiple operating system, increased flexibility of client software, new content technologies for multiple devices and multiple access networks, broadband and wireless access network technologies) **(-)**

- **Tasks:** AOL in the US is able to master all the tasks which are required in all layers, while starting to generate practices in devices. AOL in Europe has mainly focused tasks in the content layer and just localization of the other layers. The network was mainly outsourced. Assumed AOL in the US is delivering the components as in the past this is not a weakness, although the European management is required to continuously assign resources or their developments in the US. **(+)**

As a consequence the **internal resource situation of AOL in Europe is good.** Nevertheless it is a high risk aspect that the **missing technological capabilities can turn out to be a contingent factor** for the success of the strategy. In this case **AOL is equipped with all resources for a market success but does not have a dynamic and flexible competitive product.**

The third fixed factor are the needs which define if the product bundle is actually able to establish a market and secondly if the bundling is relevant.

Needs

- **"Connected to communication, information, community, commerce in a convenient way"** is in fact the bundle AOL serves. In order to get on-line a product such as the **AOL on-line service is demanded by users.** The **configuration of the bundling is relevant.** The question is, if it has to be in an integrated way and other players can provide the same **bundling in a virtual way** on new technologies in a better way. The **demand side scope effects are certainly an advantage of AOL** in Europe as in the US. **Dependent on the quality level** (technology restrictions of proprietary AOL technology for example with operating system compatibility, email functionality, access technology support) **determines if these demand side scope effects can be leverage over time.** But the needs are obviously there and accumulate to an overwhelming demand as it is the underlying thesis of the strategy formulation. **(+)**

One can state that the demand side and underlying needs actually support the strategy of AOL in Europe. Their multiple brand strategy will enable it to segment the market in a sophisticated way by offering bundles (AOL, CompuServe), unbundled access (Netscape on-line), content only (AOL, CompuServe, Netcenter portal sites) and unbundled communities (Instant Messenger, ICQ). Nevertheless the flagship business are the two on-line services which are based on **technology which will not match the future quality demands.** In this sense AOL Europe is **dependent on the delivery of better products by AOL in the US,** which is dependent on their overall resource situation.

The analysis of the fixed factors of the on-line industry in respect to the chosen strategy of AOL in Europe can be summarized in the following conclusion. The strategy is based on a correct basic assumption in respect to the demand side but fails to consider the different economic situation. The strategy has a high incorporated risk but due to the assigned resources it is **highly likely that AOL Europe will grow significantly.** Although the product and technology weaknesses carry a large potential risk. Nevertheless, in the presence of supply side and demand side market forces which work against AOL this growth direction will be a thorny path resulting in an **INEFFICIENT AND POTENTIALLY NOT SUSTAINABLE BUSINESS.**

At this point the author notes that the model of the industry supported part of the thesis of the strategy but declined several salient assumptions of this plan. The detailed analysis in application of the framework of the strategy tool set came to the conclusion that the strategy has a high risks to fail and in case of success may result in a rather unattractive business. Furthermore the consecutive analysis of the potential conduct according to this strategy shows that it by - and - large constrains the creation and leverage of network effects. Given this analytical result **the author would recommend not to conduct this strategy and to develop an alternative strategic scenario.** Such a scenario would need to consider the enormous resources of the firm, the overwhelming demand for interactive services. But given the technological weaknesses of the product as well as the resource situation **another product - market position would be more favorable.** Such a scenario should furthermore consider the marketing muscle, the portfolio of brand and state of the art **open technology** which is available on the market. In this sense AOL would be able to **become the new dominant paradigm** and to **drop the current dominant players** in each market. This would be a forward looking strategy with larger future potentials. In fact such a strategy of virtually bundling the best product components, realizing the best economics and network economics and bundling this package with a strong brand under the right market position cab be seen with Yahoo! in Europe. If Yahoo! is able to find the key to the new dominant design of business models in the next stage of the Internet it will be able to become the dominant player in the new paradigm of on-line services. Nevertheless Yahoo! would need to develop further resources to accomplish this goal. But as both firms are aligned to the development of the US market the European development is not independent.

Considering this critical position towards the **structural prerequisites** in respect to the strategy formulation of AOL in Europe, the following will lay out the consequences for the **strategic conduct** in the areas of product, pricing / business model, networking, adoption and co-opetition strategy **tools** in order **to influence on the market structure and improve the position** and **enable and leverage network effects** as much as possible.

✖ Product Strategy

In fact the product bundling as well as the singular product components of AOL are network goods with the corresponding supply side economics and particularly the demand side **network externalities.** Users of AOL have significant switching costs if changing the network as they would also loose their email addresses, address books, email folders, bookmarks and so forth. In order to provide **a set of versions** AOL can use its multiple brand / product strategy where customers can self-select. The major issue is the decision about open and closed technology, whereas their technologies for the on-line service bundling and the messenger products are proprietary. **The issue is to be potentially able to interconnect to third party components on horizontal and vertical layers.** This is possible via the example with the messenger where the considerate decision of the AOL management today in 1999 is to keep the gates closed. But the option to open is there. The current technology of the on-line services has one-way open interfaces to Internet content but not to open email technology and a host of new operating systems and production standards such as WAP or XML. **Overall the flexibility to interconnect with other components is limited for the flagship on-line services. The portal sites, browser software and messenger software do exhibit better interoperability.**

(+) in respect to the most recent products and

(-) for the flagship on-line services

✖ Pricing Strategy & Business Models

The **pricing strategies are in fact the most critical issues** as in the past all components were offered in a bundle and the users at first (in the absence of the Internet) mentally aligned the charges for the content usage. Later in the presence of free Internet content the charges were perceived for the access. In the late 1990ies the charges for access are dropping, while the content, hosting and software components are considered to "be there", because the market rule is "free". This issue plays in fact against every player but **AOL can play from a position of a large paying customer base. Furthermore it owns a portfolio of products and sub-products which can be offered in several versions and pricing schemes.** Customers can self select what they want. Overall this is a critical issue for AOL, just as it is for many other players but **AOL can leverage multiple brands, products, and pricing schemes on the base of a substantial (but eroding) revenue stream. New revenue streams** (namely advertising, ecommerce and value added services) need to be developed. AOL is driving this path in a very determined way.

(+)

✖ Adoption Strategy

The bundle "on-line service" is established but in an uncomfortable "distant follower" position AOL has long past a start-up phase and is in the stage of **regaining a dominant position** after it has lost it already. One can describe this revamp position similar to start up position, while the service needs to be redefined and reinvented in order to be re-launched under a new paradigm gaining market dominance in a new constellation. In other words AOL has to play with two faces. In order to play with the expectations of the market participants it has to argue like a dominant player using predatory pre-announcements but at the same time sponsoring the revamp strategy. It has to control the growth by charging interconnection where possible and acquiring start-up complementors and bundling it to the system. But it has to also find complementors which can help AOL transfer into a new paradigm where it has to share resources and interconnect. Introductory pricing with low / no charges is used to attract new adopters. Finally it has to find ways to role out open products which can be interconnected to complementors of the revamp strategy. In fact AOL is conducting these tactics whereas the technological development will determine the success.

(+)

✖ Networking Strategy

AOL's networking strategy is stuck in the middle! – in the middle between the need to interconnect with other large players on other layers to grow with the market, or in best case faster, and the decision to be vertically integrated. **The reason is that the vertical integration establishes a closed vertical structure which is creating a host of additional indirect competitors.** In other words: Vertical integration is powerful if you are the dominant leader in all layers and deadly if you are a distant follower. For example would an ISP be happy to get a good portal site for his offering, such as Lycos or Yahoo! with some co-branding for both players. Theoretically AOL could offer a family of portal sites with different excellent brands. The problem is that AOL stays in a direct competition with the ISP in his core business of consumer access. Hence the network will not happen. The same happens if AOL talks to a content provider playing the role of the connectivity provider of choice. The content player will perceive the competition by the portal sites. This is again the problem of indirect competition. It will work to the advantage of plain ISP, such as a telco. The same applies in the case of software companies which offer email clients, browser and messenger software. **Therefore AOL is not able to generate network effects in virtual horizontal and vertical coalition structures on the content, software, hosting and (consumer) net-**

work layer. As a result it is damned to generate these effects mainly independently which is determined by the number of AOL subscribers.

A choice could be the creation of a shared network in a horizontal way, for example by developing AOL bundlings with rebranding for some large vendors (private labels). Another way would be to cross sell community access and charge interconnection. For example the instant messenger network could be opened for third parties but they would need to distribute AOL on-line services in a certain amount.

In a vertical perspective AOL can hardly network with other players due to its own high vertical integration. The only ways which are left open are to connect to a wholesale data network, the device area or some non-substitutional software players (such as games or office productivity software). In fact the network is already established with a wholesale ISP (UUNet and Mediaways) and the device layer offers a wide choice of computer, modem, PDA, cellular phone and game console players. In order to drive this strategy technological compatibility is a prerequisite. In respect to the software layers the games market is complementary to the AOL brand while the productivity software market is dominated by Microsoft which is a competing vertical coalition structure. Future plans with open SUN architecture could work for AOL here.

Furthermore AOL has to clearly define the competitors and raise their costs, reduce their quality, raise their prices and cut them off the market access in **indirect battles over vertical relations.** This can be done only in a limited way as the Internet community would react very sensitive to these practices by a large player. But the subtle ways of "not linking to competitors", slowing down connections, being partially incompatible to competitors value added features and so forth are tactics which should be considered.

(-) in respect to the most recent products due to the indirect battles

(--) for the flagship on-line services

✖ Co-opetition Strategy

AOL has a somewhat **awkward position by being on the verge to be the past paradigm.** The underlying technology is from the past, the product and business concept is from the past and the business is loosing relative market share. In this position AOL is no longer large enough to be playing the role of a real dominant player, but it is too large to play the role of the junior partner with many other players. As a consequence it can easily find very small players which want to interconnect vertically or horizontally but they would actually prefer to work with the larger player. As the networking analysis showed above most of the potential network complementors can not be seen in this role as the vertical integration creates indirect competitions and furthermore in cases where players want to interconnect closed technology does not enable this. For this reason the **networking and complementor strategies have to be redefined** at the same time when the **technology / product concept needs to be designed for the new technological situation of the "broadband mass market".** This can be done by **looking for complementors in a wider industrial spectrum. Hardware** players were mentioned above and **broadband** players can be seen as a logical complement in the field of the future where rules are not yet defined. Furthermore the mass market development requires to consider partners from **lateral industries** as well, particularly as partners have to become larger to **pool large resources for the according large mass markets.** One can think of retail chains, banks, automobile manufacturers or any player who needs an interactive medium to enhance customer relationships to its customer base. In order to realize this it is required to **reinvent the product concept and to redesign the technology. AOL may consider to play two roles. In the old narrowband business it has to close the markets and play the tough game of a large player. In the new world it has to behave cooperative like a start up utilizing the focus and knowledge advantages against rather unskilled players from lateral industries.** The "AOL anywhere" strategy of AOL in the

US is aiming this way. The issue for AOL in Europe is to make sure that the European components will be available in time. Only this ensures that AOL can take the future opportunities in order to **reinvent the old paradigm to be the new paradigm.**

(-) Massive problems will occur in the course of conducting the chosen strategy

(+) An alternative strategy might have a better potential to be translated in the third phase of the Internet

It can be concluded that AOL needs to reinvent itself and translate itself into the new broadband, multiple devices, multiple services and the "brand" world. Although it has to be stated that the economics do not support the current AOL / CompuServe on-line service offerings under the flagship brand. This is exactly where the company puts the majority of the resources. Driving the narrow-band proprietary on-line services with all the resources seems to be contradictory in the verge to the third evolutionary stage of the Internet. In this sense it might be of value to reconsider the strategic thesis and consider fall back strategies. They could be based on more individual unbundled components and AOL could "virtually" bundle them giving the users the choice of self selection and shift the resources to such a strategy.

Case Study 3-7: Analysis of the European AOL Strategy

Part IV: Summary & Outlook

4. Summary & Outlook

4.1. Summary – Dynamic Structure & Strategy

The predominant goal of this thesis is to analyze the industrial structure and business strategy of the on-line industry in the dynamic Internet environment.

The author describes the **multi-layered structure of the industry** and **its virtual construction by the convergence industries.** Due to the multiple horizontal and **vertical network effects** and its particular industrial economics, business in the industry performs in different patterns than in non-network industries. The author lays out its particular layering and the role of the exogenous parameters and the competing firms in the industry with respect to their impact on the developmental trajectory of this future growth area. References to the industrial past indicate many future potential patterns when the rate of change in the industry will slow down and consolidation processes will take place. In application of empirical and theoretical findings the **crucial industrial mechanisms, namely network externalities, critical mass issues and (unstable) dominant players** are laid out under consideration of a set of **impacting parameters** on a layered structure.

The particular challenges for business strategy leads to a discussion of mainstream business strategy theories and the introduction of some more recent concepts. The interesting finding is the **comprehensiveness of the most issues by the mainstream theories,** although the object is frequently perceived as a "new economic paradigm". Obviously, it is not that different. The author presents a **framework for business strategy, which enables firms to derive a strategy** by focusing on the **fixed factors of the rapidly changing industry.** In this sense, the role of underlying **(network) economic principles, the fundamental structure of needs and the resources and competencies of a firm are set up as a triangle of starting points for business strategy.** In an analysis of the most recent business strategy concepts, which are developed around the Internet, the author presents a **set of tools to conduct a strategy** within this strategy framework. These tools consider **product, pricing, networking, adoption and co-opetition to impact the industry structure** as it is modeled in the first part of this dissertation, **leveraging the structural mechanism.** In this sense, the classical interplay between structure and strategy is developed for the on-line industry.

The combination of these two components delivers the instruments required to solve the defined research problem.

Aside from these applied results, the author **translates the analytical framework of network economics into a conceptual framework** with strong empirical foundations. Furthermore, the **combination with the game theory idea of co-opetition and the role of complementors** adds significant value when compared to both approaches in isolation. Moreover, the **author reveals the majority of network economic concepts to be purely adapted industrial economics, which can be reduced to the new finding of demand side economies of scale.** Nevertheless, this extends this fundamental microeconomic concept from the analysis of the production function of the firm to the **economics of the utility function of the household.** If a market exhibits on both sides these returns to scale it performs in very particular patterns.

This is particularly relevant for many future industries. However, the current research has widely overseen the **demand side economies of scope**, which is rooted in structures of correlated needs and has to be addressed with bundling strategies in order to leverage these effects. The author enhances the network economic framework with this factor. Furthermore, **conclusions about patterns of the development of the industry structure and according game theoretic implications** about start-ups and large established players in horizontally and vertically related competitions are derived. The conduct of all involved players in this framework of structure and strategy will determine the future development of the industry.

However, it has to be pointed out that several issues can be addressed in further research.

4.2. Outlook – Further Research Issues

With respect to the research aim of delivering an applied framework, it has to be stated that pricing and **development of business models,** as one of the crucial issues, was solved only in a purely analytical way and explicit answers were left open. Current business practice does not show consistent patterns in this respect while it is an, if not the, most prominent unsolved issue. It is probably a question of time, which is dependent on the competitive behavior of all market participants until certain dominant models will be stabilized. Ultimately these models will determine the answer to a second unsolved issue: **Which sector of the convergence industries will capture the value.** At this point in time, particularly on the verge of the mass market broadband world, the cards have yet to be played. Intelligent conduct and positioning will determine a large portion of the future state of these large industrial sectors.

Moreover, the presented multi-layered model was initially created by **unbundling processes,** which were caused by technological innovation and a shift in industrial sectors. Caused by the two-way complementarities, a massive dynamic of vertical network effects between horizontal layers has dominated this industry since then. If one were to consider comparable unbundling processes in other industries, which end up in a multi-layered constellation with two-way complementarities, then it should be possible to **generalize this framework.**

Finally, the **discussions on industry structure and organizational structure** support the **thesis of scale and scope as a dominant structure**. In other words, large aggregates of horizontally and vertically integrated firms exhibit the best economics, with the economics of information as the predominant cause. This is – at least in the long-run – a different finding as in **the virtualization debate on decreased transaction costs in ICT environments, which recommends focusing on core competence and tends to support small flexible units.** There might be in fact a tension of converging and diverging forces of economic aggregates, which might indicate inconsistencies in the theoretical framework. In fact, if business processes are becoming unbundled, then they automatically have to be bundled with another process. If these unbundling and deconstruction processes follow the economics of the information value chain, it should be considered that many physical value chains will be assembled around information value chains, which itself follows economics of scale. If this thesis is valid the complete virtualization debate is in fact a large industrial "reconstruction" debate, which will end up in an equilibrium state of large industrial aggregates based on the economics of information – in other words this would determine the **transition from industrial economics to information economics.**

Glossary / References

Glossary

The knowledge of readers of this work regarding the extensive, complex and rapidly changing technical terminology is presumably heterogeneous. The following listing provides several websites, which define technical terms on an ongoing basis.

- PC Webomedia. An online encyclopedia and search engine dedicated to computer technology. http://www.pcwebopaedia.com
- ILC Glossary of Internet Terms
  http://www.matisse.net/files/glossary.htm
- McGraw-Hill The McGraw-Hill Internet Training Manual
  http://www.marketing-coach.com/mh-guide/glossary.htm
- Netdictionary - Alphabetical Reference Guide to Internet Terms
- http://www.netdictionary.com/html/index.html
- Yahoo! Collection of links to On-line Glossaries
  http://www.yahoo.com/Computers_and_Internet/Internet/Information_and_Documentation/Internet_Glossaries/

Sources of reference - telecommunication terms:

1. John Graham, revised and updated by Sue J. Lowe (1991). Dictionary of Telecommunications. Penguin.
2. Jim Chalmers (1995). Pocket Telecommunications. The Economist Books.
3. E.A. Edis & J.E. Varral (1992). Telecommunications Pocket Book. NEWNES.
4. Fred Halsall (1995). Data Communications, Computer Networks and Open System. Addison-Wesley.

References

Abbate, J. (1994), From ARPANET to Internet: A History of ARPA-sponsored Computer Networks, 1966-1988, dissertation, University of Pennsylvania

Abernathy, W. / Clark, K. (1985), Innovation: Mapping the Winds of Creative Destruction, in: Research Policy, Vol. 14, Feb. 1985, pp. 3-22

Abernathy, W. / Utterback, J. (1978), Patterns in Innovation in Technology, in: Technology Review, Vol. 80, No. 7, 1978, pp. 40-47

Adams, W. / Yellen, J. (1976), Commodity Bundling and the Burden of Monopoly, in: Quarterly Journal of Economics, Vol. 90, pp. 475-598

Agor, W. H. (1986), The Logic Of Intuition: How Top Executives Make Important Decisions, in: Organizational Dynamics, Winter 1986, pp. 5-18

Albers, S. / Peters, K. (1995), Schätzung von Diffusionsmodellen für den Dienst Btx/Datex-J, in: Stoetzer, M.-W./Mahler, A. (1995, eds.), pp. 167-194.

Allensbach (1997), ACTA – Allensbacher Computer und Telekommunikationsstudie 1997

Allensbach (1998), ACTA – Allensbacher Computer und Telekommunikationsstudie 1998

America Online (1996), AOL Demographics & Research, Internal Study

Amit, R. / Schoemaker, P. J. H. (1993), Strategic Assets and Organizational Rent, in: Strategic Management Journal, Vol. 14, S. 33-46

Andrews, E. L. (1998), France Telecom plans update for Minitel – IBM to develop Network for a new On-Line Information Service, in: New York Times, Oct. 7th 1998, C2

Ansoff, H. I. (1965), Corporate Strategy, New York, Prentice Hall

Antonelli, C. (1997), The Economics of Path-Dependence in Industrial Organization, in: International Journal of Industrial Organization, Vol. 15, No. 6, pp.643-661

Antonelli, C. (1992), The Economic Theory of Information Networks, in: Antonelli (1992, eds.), pp. 5-28

Antonelli, C. (1992, eds.), The Economics of Information Networks, Amsterdam

Applegate, L. M. (1997), Network Computing - The Third Era of Information Technology. Harvard Business School, September 24, 1997, on-line at: http://www.hbs.edu/-applegate/090997/nc/index.html

Andersen (1998a), Your Choice – How eCommerce Could Impact Europe's Future, Chicago

Andersen (1998b), Ecommerce - Why Now!, on-line at: http://www.ac.com/showcase/ecommerce/ecom_whynow.html

Andersen (1998d), Screen All Calls, in: Outlook Online Magazine, 06/98, on-line at: http://www.ac.com/overview/Outlook/6.98/over_currents4.html

Andersen, (1996), Electronic Publishing - Strategic Developments for the European Publishing Industry towards the Year 2000 (Study for the European Commission)

Arthur, B. W. (1996) Increasing returns and the new world of business, in: Harvard Business Review, Vol. 74, No. 4, July - August 1996, pp. 100-109

Arthur, B. W. (1994), Increasing Returns and Path Dependency in the Economy, University of Michigan Press, Ann Arbor 1994

Arthur, B. W. (1990), Positive Feedbacks in the Economy, in: Scientific American, Vol. 80, pp. 92 - 99

Arthur, B. W. (1989), Competing Technologies, Increasing Returns, and Lock-In by Historical Events, in: Economic Journal, Vol. 99, pp. 116-131

Arthur, B. W. (1988), Self-Reinforcing Mechanisms in Economics, in: Anderson / Arrow / Pines (198, eds.)

AT Kearney (1998a), Digital Pioneers – A White Paper on the Practical Applications of Electronic Commerce: Separating Hype from Reality, Chicago

AT Kearney (1998b), Converging Technologies and Value Creation – A Look At the Internet and the Opportunities it Offers, Chicago

Baack, C. (1999), Anmerkungen zum Internet von Morgen, in: Baack / Eberspächer (1999, eds), pp. 1-14

Baack, C. / Eberspächer, J. (1999, eds.) Das Internet von Morgen – Neue Technologien für neue Anwendungen, conference documentation of the according conference held in Munich on the 19th and 20th of November, Hüthig, Heidelberg

Badarocco, J. L. (1991), Strategische Allianzen - Wie Unternehmen durch Know How Austausch Wettbewerbsvorteile erzielen, Wien, Überreuter

Bailey, J. P: (1998), Intermediation and Electronic Markets – Aggregation and Pricing in Internet Commerce, dissertation, MIT

Bain, J (1956), Barriers to New Competition, Cambridge, Harvard University Press

Baker, S. A. (1999), Security and the Infrastructure for Electronic Commerce, manuscript in BCLT (1999)

Bakos, Y, / Brynjolfsson, E. (1997), Aggregation and Disaggregation of Information Goods: Implications for Bundling, Site Licensing and Micropayment Systems, Sloan MIT working paper, on-line at; http://www.gsm.uci.edu/~bakos

Bakos, Y, / Brynjolfsson, E. (1996), Bundling Information Goods: Pricing, Profits and Efficiency, Sloan MIT working paper, on-line at; http://www.gsm.uci.edu/~bakos/-big/big.html

Bane, P.W. / Bradley, S.P. / Collis, D.J. (1997), Winners and Losers – Industry Structure in the Converging World of Telecommunications, Computing and Entertainment, in: Yoffie (1997, eds.), pp. 159-200

Bar, F. / Borrus, M. (1997), Why Competition is Necessary in Telecommunications and How to Achieve it – The Experience of Advanced Economies, BRIE working paper 102, UC Berkeley

Bar, F. / Borrus, M. (1995), The Future of Networking, BRIE research paper, UC Berkeley

Bar, F. / Borrus, M. / Coriat, B. (1989), Information Networks and Competitive Advantage – Issues for Government Policy and Corporate Strategy Development, BRIE/OECD Report, Paris, Brussels

Bar, F. / Borrus, M. / Steinberg, R. (1995), Islands in the Bit-Stream, Charting the NII Interoperability Debate, BRIE working paper 79, UC Berkeley

Bar, F. / Cohen, S. / Cowhey, P. / DeLong, B. / Kleeman, M / Zysman, J. (1999), Defending the Internet Revolution in the Broadband Era: Why Open Policy Has Been Essential – Why Reversing That Policy Will be Risky, BRIE / E-conomy working paper 12, on-line at: http://e-conomy.berkeley.edu/pubs/wp/ewp12.html

Bar, F. / Reed, R. R. / Hart. J. A. (1992), The Building of the Internet – Implications for the Future of Broadband Networks, BRIE working paper 60, UC Berkeley

Barney, J. (1991), Firm Resources and Sustained Competitive Advantage, in: Journal of Management, Vol. 17, No. 1, pp. 99-120

Bartlett, C. A. / Ghoshal, S. (1992), Transnational Management – Text, Cases, and Readings in Cross-Border Management, New York, Irwin McGraw-Hill

Barlow, J. P. (1994), The Economy of Ideas, in: Wired, March 1994, on-line at: http://www.hotwired.com/wired/2.03/features/economy.ideas.html

Bamford, R. S. (1997), Netscape Communications Corporation in 1997, Case Study, Graduate School of Business, Stanford University

BCG (1999), E-Commerce in Deutschland: Vom Goldrausch zur Goldgewinnung, Munich

BCG (1998), The State of Online Retailing, BCG study

BCG (1995a), The Information Superhighway and Retail Banking, Vol. I,   Chicago

BCG (1995b), Project California – Backup Material – A Detailed Industry Analysis of Telco/Cable, Wireless, OLSs/Internet, LAN/WAN, November 1995, San Francisco

BCLT (1999), The Legal and Policy Framework for Global Electronic Commerce, Conference Syllabus, UC Berkeley, 5th – 6th March 1999

Beardsley, S. C. (1998), Full Telecom Competition in Europe is Years Away, in: McKinsey Quarterly No. 2, 1998, pp. 32-37

Beardsley, S. C. / Evans, A. L. (1998), Who will connect you?, in: McKinsey Quarterly, No. 4, 1998, pp. 18-31

Benson, G. S. / Farrell, J. (1994), Choosing How to Compete: Strategies and Tactics in Standardization, in: Journal of Economic Perspectives, Vol. 8, Spring 1994, pp. 117-310

Bernstein, P. L. (1998), Are Networks Driving the New Economy, in: Harvard Business Review, Vol. 76, No. 6, November – December 1998, pp. 110-115

Bertelsmann (1997), Die Medienmärkte der Zukunft, in: Meyn, H., Massenmedien in der Bundesrepublik   Deutschland,   on-line   at: http://www.bertelsmann.de/deutsch/news/reden/text/medien.html

Binder, A. B. / Kantowsky, J. (1996), Technologiepotentiale – Neuausrichtung der Gestaltungsfelder des Strategischen Technologiemanagements, Deutscher Universitätsverlag, Wiesbaden

BMWi (1996a), Wirkungsanalyse der Förderung von kleinen und mittleren Unternehmen der informationstechnischen Industrie in den neuen Bundesländern auch im Hinblick auf die Entwicklung der globalen Informations-Infrastruktur, Berlin 1996

BMWi (1996b), Elektronischer Geschäftsverkehr - Initiative der Bundesregierung, Bonn 1996

BMWi (1996c), Info 2000 – Deutschlands Weg in die Informationsgesellschaft. Fortschrittsbericht der Bundesregierung, Bonn 1996

BMWi (1997a), Stellungnahme der Bundesrepublik Deutschland zum Grünbuch der EU-Kommission „Konvergenz der Branchen Telekommunikation, Medien und Informationstechnologie und ihre ordnungspolitischen Auswirkungen", Berlin 1997

BMWi (1998), Anhörungen von Wirtschaft und Verbänden, online at: http://www.bmwi.de/-infogesellschaft.html#bench

Booz Allen & Hamilton (1995), Zukunft Multimedia - Grundlagen, Märkte und Perspektiven in Deutschland, Frankfurt/M.

Booz Allen & Hamilton (1995a), Insights - The Promise of New Media, 1, 4, September 1995

Booz Allen & Hamilton (1997), Telekommunikation in der Welt von morgen - Marktstrategien, Konzepte und Kompetenzen für das 21. Jahrhundert, Frankfurt/M.

Booz Allen & Hamilton (1998a), Insights - The Promise of New Media: Core Competencies, on-line at: http://www.bah.com/viewpoints/insights_old/cmt_core_comp.html

Booz Allen & Hamilton (1998b), Product Offering to Internet Service Providers, Munich July 1998, proprietary of Booz Allen Hamilton, CompuServe internal data

Booz Allen & Hamilton (1998c), Strategies for Cyberspace - The iWorld Future: Strategy for a New Telecom Environment, on-line at: http://www.bah.com/viewpoints/-insights/cmt_cyberspace.html

Bork, R. H. (1999), The Case against Microsoft, on-line at: http://www.procompetition.org/-research/bork.html

Borrus, M. / Zysman, Z. (1997), Globalization with Borders: The Rise of Wintelism as the Future of Industrial Competition, BRIE working paper 96B, UC Berkeley

Borrus, M. / Zysman, Z. (1994), From Failure to Fortune – European Electronics in a Changing World Economy, BRIE working paper 62, UC Berkeley

Bowers, T. / Singer, M. (1996), Who will Capture Value in On-Line Services ?, in: McKinsey Quarterly, No. 2, 1996, pp. 78-83

Brandenburger, A. M. / Nalebuff, B. J. (1995), The Right Game: Use Game Theory to Shape Strategy, in: Harvard Business Review, Vol. 73, No. 4, July- August 1995, pp. 57-71

Brandenburger A. M. / Nalebuff, B. (1997), Co-opetition, New York, Doubleday

Bruck, P.A. / Selhofer, H. (1997), The Ignored User - Critical Factors Determining User Demand for New Information Services, in: IDATE: Communications & Strategies 26, 1997, pp. 277-303.

Burda (1997), Typologie der Wünsche 1997/98, Munich

Burda (1998), Typologie der Wünsche 1998/99, Munich

Burg, U. v. (1998), Plumbers of the Internet: The Creation of the Local Area Networking Industry, dissertation, University of St. Gallen, St. Gallen, Switzerland.

Burkert, H. (1994), Legal Uncertainty and Electronic Markets, in: Electronic Markets Journal, Vol. 4, No. 11, pp. 1-3

Campbell, A. / Goold, M. / Alexander, M. (1995), Corporate Strategy: The Quest for Parenting Advantage, in: Harvard Business Review, Vol. 73, No. 2, March-April 1995, pp. 120-132

Case, S. (1998), Vom Marktpionier zum Marktführer: Die Erfahrungen von America Online, summary of a speech at the mcm forum St. Gallen 1998, 23-24 June 1998, on-line at: http://www.mediamanagement.org/netacademy/publications.nsf/all_pk/969

Castells, M. / Aoyama, Y (1993), Paths Towards The Informational Society – A Comparative Analysis of the Transformation of Employment Structures of the G7 Countries 1920-2005, BRIE working paper 61, UC Berkeley

Caves, R. E. / Porter, M. E. (1977), From Entry Barriers to Mobility Barriers – Conjectural Decisions and Contrived Deterrence to New Competition, in: Quarterly Journal of Economics, Vol. 91, pp. 241-61

Chalmers, J. (1995), Pocket Telecommunications, London, The Economist Books

Christensen, J. (1997), The Innovator's Dilemma: When New Technologies Cause Great Firms to Fail, Boston, Harvard Business School Press

Christensen, C. / Bower, J. L. (1995), Disruptive Technologies: Catching the Wave, in: Harvard Business Review, Vol. 73, No. 1, January - February 1995, pp. 47-59

Church, J. / Gandal, N. (1993), Complementary Network Externalities and Technological Adoption, in: International Journal of Industrial Organization, Vol. 11, No. 2, pp. 239-260

Church, J. / Gandal, N. (1992a), Network Effects, Software Provision and Standardization, in: Journal of Industrial Economics, Vol. 40, No. 1, pp. 85-104

Church, J. / Gandal, N. (1992b), Integration, Complementary Products, and Variety, in: Journal of Economics & Management Strategy, Vol. 1, No. 4, pp. 653-675

Church, J. / Gandal, N. (1996), Strategic Entry Deterrence: Complementary Products as Installed Base, in: European Journal of Political Economy, Vol. 12, pp. 331-354

Cioffi, J. (1999a), The Legal and Policy Framework for Global Electronic Commerce, Conference Report and Summary, BRIE, UC Berkeley

Cioffi, J. (1999b), The Digital Economy in International Perspective, Common Construction or Regional Rivalry, Analytical Summary and Report, BRIE / E-conomy working paper 1, UC Berkeley, on-line at: http://e-conomy.berkeley.edu/events/deip/-summary.html

Cioffi, J. / Berg, C. (1999), Conference on Issues in Global Electronic Commerce, Conference Summary of the E-Conomy Conference held at the University of Southern California, Los Angeles, May 6. / 7. 1999

Clark, J. (1995), The Herring Interview with Jim Clark, The Red Herring, November 1995

Coase, R. H. (1937), The Nature of the Firm, in: Economica, 4 (13-16), November 1937, pp. 386-405

Coffman, K. / Odlyzko, A. (1998), The Size and the Growth Rate of the Internet, AT&T Research Labs Paper, also in: First Monday, on-line at: http://www.firstmonday.dk/-issues/issue3_10/coffman/index.html

CompuServe (1995), CompuServe Annual Financial Report, Columbus, Ohio

CompuServe (1996), Customer Satisfaction Analysis

CompuServe (1997), Kündigerbefragung

CompuServe (1998), Kundenanalyse

CompuServe / Gartner Group (1997), Lost Customer Analysis

CompuServe / Gartner Group (1998), Lost Customer Analysis - Business Accounts

CompuServe / GfK (1998a), Marketing Collateral Audit

CompuServe / GfK (1998b), CompuServe User Profiles- Gfk Online Monitor

CompuServe / Teleperformance (1997), Subscription Cancellation Survey for France

CompuServe / W3B (1996), CompuServe Demoskopie

Cohen, S. S. / Fields, G. (1998), Social Capital and Capital Gains, or Virtual Bowling in Silicon Valley, BRIE working paper, UC Berkeley

Cohen, S. S. / Fields, G. (1999), Social Capital and Capital Gains in Silicon Valley, in: California Management Review, Vol. 41, No. 2, Winter 1999, pp. 108-130

Colombo, M. G. / Dang Nguyen, G. / Perrucci, A. (1997), Multimedia, Paradigmatic Shift and Distinctive Competencies of Firms: an Empirical Analysis, in: IDATE: Communications & Strategies 26, 1997, pp. 207-254

Colombo, M.G. / Garrone, P. (1998), Common Carriers' Entry into Multimedia Services, forthcoming in: Information Economics and Policy, 1998

Colombo, M. G. / Garrone, P. / Seri, R.G. (1998): Firms' Heterogeneity and Dynamics of Entry in a New Sector: Analysis of the Multimedia Service Provision Sector, Paper presented at the ITS'98 Conference, Stockholm, June 21st – 24th 1998

Communic (1997a), 5. Forum Telekommunikation – Strategien neuer Anbieter im deutschen und internationalen Markt, 18th and 19th of February 1997, conference documentation, Königswinter

Communic (1997b), Interactive Services '97, 25th and 26th of February 1997, conference documentation, Hamburg

Datamonitor (1998), Corporate Internet Services in Europe: Value Added Service Strategies for Survival, London

D'Aveni, R. (1995), Hypercompetitive Rivalries: Competing in Highly Dynamic Environments, New York, Free Press

David, Paul A., (1989), A Paradigm for Historical Economics: Path-Dependence and Predictability in Dynamic Systems with Local Network Externalities, in: Proceedings of the Second International Cliometrics Society Meetings.

David, P. (1986), Understanding the Economics of QWERTY: The Necessity of History, in: Parker (1986, eds.), Economic History and the Modern Economist, New York, Basil Blackwell

David, Paul, A., (1985), "Clio and the Economics of QWERTY," American Economic Review, Papers and Proceedings, Vol. 75, pp. 332 - 337

Davidow, W.H. / Malone, M.S. (1992), The Virtual Corporation, New York: Harper Collins, 1992

Deloitte (1998), Global CIO Survey, Deloitte Consulting, on-line at: http://www.dc.com/research/announcements/rlscopy.html

Dempsey, J. et. al (1998), The last mile to the Internet, in: McKinsey Quarterly, No. 4, 1998, pp. 6-17

Derian, J. D. (1999), Technologies Enabling E commerce: a French Perspective, paper presented at the conference on issues on global electronic commerce, University of Southern California, May 6-7 1999

Dery, M (1996), Escape Velocity: Cyberculture at the End of the Century, New York, Grove Press

DIW (1994), Gesamtwirtschaftliche Position der Medien in Deutschland 1982-1992, in: Beiträge zur Strukturforschung, Heft 153

DIW (1996), Künftige Entwicklung des Medien- und Kommunikationssektors in Deutschland, in: Beiträge zur Strukturforschung, Heft 162

Dixit, A. K. / Nalebuff, B. J. (1991), Thinking Strategically: The Competitive Edge in Business, Politics, and Everyday Life, New York, Doubleday

DOJ (1999), United States vs. Microsoft, on-line at: http://www.usdoj.gov/atr/cases/-ms_index.htm

Donahue, D. J. (1997), The NII in the Home, in: NRC (1997), pp. 165-167

Dowling, M. / Lechner, C. / Thielmann, B. (1998a), Industry Structure in Converging Markets – An Analysis of the European TV and On-line Services Industries, Paper presented at the Consortium for Research on Telecommunications Policy and Strategy (CRTPS) – 4th annual Conference "Promoting Investment in the Digital Telecommunications Infrastructure", June 5 and 6, 1998, University of Michigan Business School, Ann Arbor, Michigan

Dowling, M. / Lechner, C. / Thielmann, B. (1998b), Convergence – Innovation and Change of Market Structures between Television and Online Services, in: International Journal of Electronic Markets, Vol. 8, No. 4, 1998, pp. 31-35

Doz, Y.L. / Hamel, G. (1998), Alliance Advantage - The Art of Creating Value through Partnering, Boston, Harvard Business School Press

Drucker, P. F. (1985), The Discipline of Innovation, in: Harvard Business Review, Vol. 63, No. 3, 1985, pp. 76-72

Dührkoop, T. (1999, forthcoming), Die Entstehung und die Durchsetzung des Internet – Medienwandel aus Betriebswirtschaftlicher Sicht, dissertation, St. Gallen

Dyson, E. et. al. (1998), Protecting Yourself Online : The Definitive Resource on Safety, Freedom, and Privacy in Cyberspace, New York, Harper Collins

Dyson, E. (1999), without title, on-line at: http://www.edventure.com/pcforum/pcforum.html

Dyson, E. (1998), Privacy Protection: Time to Think and Act Locally and Globally, in: Release 1.0 April 1998

Dyson, E. (1997), Release 2.0: A design for living in the digital age, New York, Broadway Books

Dyson, E. (1996), Intellectual Property on the Net – Release 2.0, in: Release 1.0 Jan. 1996

Dyson, E. (1994), Intellectual Property on the Net, in: Release 1.0 Dec. 1994

Eberspächer (1999), Wege zum Breitband-Internet, script of a panel discussion, in Baack / Eberspächer (1999, eds), pp. 183-227

Economides, N., (1998e), Competition and Vertical Integration in the Computing Industry, in: Competition, Innovation, and the Role of Antitrust in the Digital Marketplace,. Eisenach, J. A. and. Lenard, T. M. (eds.), Kluwer Academic Publishers 1998, on-line at: http://raven.stern.nyu.edu/networks/papaers.html

Economides, N. (1998d), Raising Rivals Costs in Complementary Goods Markets - LECs Entering into Long Distance and Microsoft Bundling Internet Explorer, on-line at: http://raven.stern.nyu.edu/networks/papaers.html

Economides, N. (1998c), Quality Choice and Vertical Integration, in: International Journal of Industrial Organization, on-line at: http://raven.stern.nyu.edu/networks/papaers.html

Economides, N. (1998b), Letter to the Wall Street Journal on Path Dependency, on-line at: http://www.stern.nyu.edu/networks/wsj.html

Economides, N. (1998a), Competition and Vertical Integration in the Computing Industry, in: Eisenach / Lenard (forthcoming, eds.)

Economides, N. (1997), Quality Choice and Vertical Integration, research paper NYU, September 1997, on-line at: http://raven.stern.nyu.edu/networks/papaers.html

Economides, N. (1996), The Economics of Networks, in: International Journal of Industrial Organization, Vol. 14, No. 2, pp. 675-699

Economides, N. (1995a), Principles of Interconnection – A Response to "Regulation of Access to Vertically-Integrated Natural Monopolies", research paper NYU, on-line at: http://raven.stern.nyu.edu/networks/papaers.html

Economides, N. (1995b), Network Externalities, Complementarities, and Invitations to Enter, in: special issue on The Economics of Standardization of The European Journal of Political Economy, Vol. 12, 1996, pp. 211-232

Economides, N. (1995c), The Incentive of a Multi-Product Monopolist to Provide All Gods, research paper NYU, on-line at: http://raven.stern.nyu.edu/networks/papaers.html

Economides, N. (1994), The Incentive for Vertical Integration, discussion paper NYU, on-line at: http://raven.stern.nyu.edu/networks/papaers.html

Economides, N. (1993), Mixed bundling in duopoly, discussion paper NYU, on-line at: http://raven.stern.nyu.edu/networks/papaers.html

Economides, N. (1992), A Monopolists Incentive to Invite Competitors to Enter in Telecommunications Services, research paper NYU, on-line at: http://raven.stern.nyu.edu/networks/papaers.html

Economides, N. (1991a), Compatibility and the Creation of Shared Networks, chapter 3 in: Wildman et. al. (1991, eds.)

Economides, N. (1991b), Compatibility and Market Structure, Discussion Paper, NYU, on-line at: http://raven.stern.nyu.edu/networks/papaers.html

Economides, N (1989), Desirability of Compatibility in the Absence of Network Externalities", in: American Economic Review, Vol. 79, No. 5, pp. 1165-1181

Economides, N. / Flyer, F. (1997), Compatibility and Market Structures for Network Goods, discussion paper, NYU, on-line at: http://raven.stern.nyu.edu/networks/papaers.html

Economides, N. / Himmelberg, C. (1995), Critical Mass and Network Size with application to the US Fax market, research paper NYU, on-line at: http://raven.stern.nyu.edu/networks/papaers.html

Economides, N. / Himmelberg, C. (1994), Critical Mass and Network Evolution in Telecommunications, research paper NYU, on-line at: http://raven.stern.nyu.edu/networks/papaers.html

Economides, N. / Lehr, W. (1994), The Quality of Complex Systems and Industry Structure, research paper NYU, on-line at: http://raven.stern.nyu.edu/networks/papaers.html

Economides, N. / Salop, S, C. (1992), Competition and Integration among Complements, and Network Market Structure, in: Journal of Industrial Economics, Vol. 40, No. 1, pp. 105-123

Economides, N. / White, L. J. (1994a), Networks and compatibility: Implications for Antitrust, in: European Economic Review, Vol. 38, 1994, pp. 651-662

Economides, N. / White, L. J. (1994b), One-Way Networks, Two-Way Networks, Compatibility, and Public Policy, research paper NYU, on-line at: http://raven.stern.nyu.edu/networks/papaers.html

Economides, N. / Wildman, S. S. (1995), Monopolistic Competition with Two-Part Tariffs, research paper NYU, on-line at: http://raven.stern.nyu.edu/networks/papaers.html

Economides, N. / Woroch, G. (1992), Benefits and Pitfalls of Network Interconnection, Discussion Paper NYU, on-line at: http://raven.stern.nyu.edu/networks/papaers.html

Economides, N. / Woroch, G. / Lopomo, G. (1997), Strategic Commitments and the Principle of Reciprocity in Interconnection Pricing, Discussion Paper, NYU, UC Berkeley, on-line at: http://raven.stern.nyu.edu/networks/papaers.html

Edis, E.A./ Varral, J.E. (1992), Telecommunications Pocket Book. NEWNES

Egan, E. A (1996), The Era of Microsoft? – Technological Innovation, Network Externalities, and the Seattle Factor in the US Software Industry, BRIE working paper 87, UC Berkeley

Eisenach, J. A. / Lenard, T. M. (forthcoming, eds.), Competition, Innovation, and the Role of Antitrust in the Digital Marketplace, Kluwer Academic Publishers 1998

Eisenhardt, K. (1989), Building Theories form Case Study Research, in: Academy of Management Review, Vol. 14, No. 4, 1989, pp. 532-550

EITO (1995), The European Information Infrastructure and the Convergence of Information Technology, Telecommunications and Media, a study of the European Information Technology Observatory, Frankfurt

Ecker, H. A. / Mobley, J. G. (1997), The Evolution of the Analog Set-Top Terminal to a Digital Interactive Home Communications Terminal, NRC (1997), pp. 168-177

Elixmann, D. / Kürble, P. (1997, eds.): Multimedia - Potentials and Challenges from an Economic Perspective, Proceedings des Wissenschaftlichen Instituts für Kommunikationsdienste (WIK), Bad Honnef 1997

Esser, W. / Ringlstetter, M. (1991), Die Rolle der Wertschöpfungskette in der strategischen Planung, in: Kirsch (1991, eds.), pp. 511-537

Eugster, C. C. et. al. (1998), Builders for a new Age, in: McKinsey Quarterly 1998, No. 3, pp. 92-105

Europe (1997), Presseerklärung zur Europäischen Ministerkonferenz "Globale Informationsnetze: Die Chance nutzen, Bundespresseamt Juli 1997

European Commission (1997a), Grünbuch zur Konvergenz der Branchen Telekommunikation, Medien und Informationstechnologie und ihre ordnungspolitischen Auswirkungen, Brussels 1997

European Commission (1998d), Inventory of Dispute Resolution Mechanisms – What are the Choices for the Telecommunications Sector?, Brussels

European Commission (1998c), Study on Technical and Regulatory Requirements for Open Access to Broadband Telecommunications Networks and Services for Customers, Service Providers and Content Providers, Brussels

European Commission (1998a), Provisional list of comments on the Green Paper, submitted in response to the public consultation and accessible through the World-Wide Web

Evans, A. L. et. al. (1998), The Future of Satellite Communications, in: McKinsey Quarterly 1998, No. 2, pp. 6-17

Evans, P. B. / Wurster T. S. (1997), Strategy and the New Economics of Information, in: Harvard Business Review, Vol. 75, No. 5 September/October 1997, pp. 70 - 85

Farrell, J. / Saloner, G. (1992), Converters, Compatibility, and the Control of Interfaces, in: Journal of Industrial Economics, Vol. 40, No. 1, pp. 9-36.

Farrell, J. / Saloner, G. (1986), Installed Base and Compatibility: Innovation, Product Preannouncement, and Predation, in: American Economic Review, Vol. 76, pp. 940-955

Farrell, J. / Saloner, G. (1985), Standardization, Compatibility and Innovation, in: Rand Journal of Economics, Vol. 16, pp. 70-83

Farrell, J. / Shapiro, C. (1988), Dynamic Competition with Switching Costs, in: Rand Journal of Economics, Vol. 19, pp. 123-137.

Farrell, J. / Shapiro, C. (1989), Optimal Contracts with Lock-In, in: American Economic Review, Vol. 79, pp. 51-68.

Farrell, J./ Munroe H. K. / Saloner, G. (1994), Systems Competition versus Component Competition: Order Statistics, Interface Standards, and Open Systems, Stanford University working paper, July 199

Feldman, S. I. (1999), Keynote: Electronic Commerce – Technology Directions, Research Opportunities, Policy Concerns, in: BCLT (1999)

Fisher, R. / Ury, W. / Patton, B. (1991), Getting to Yes, Negotiating Agreement Without Giving, in: The Harvard Negotiation Project, New York, Penguin Books

Forrester (1996), Online Unravels – Vol. II, No. 9, London

Forrester (1997a), The Limits of Convergence, in: The Forrester Report http://www.forrester.com/excerpts/pt9709.htm)

Forrester (1997b), Web TV and Beyond, in: The Forrester Report http://www.forrester.com/excerpts/pt9714.htm

Fortune (1996), The End of TV as We Know It, (12/23/96), pp. 58-68

Fost, D. (1999), Web's Threat Prompts Newspapers to Put Up Money-Losing Sites, in: San Francisco Chronicle, April 15, 1999, B1, B4

Freese, E. (1995), Profit Center und Verrechnungspreis, in: ZfbF Vol. 47, 1995, pp. 943-954

Freese, E. (1995a), Profit Center - Motivation durch internen Marktdruck, in: Reichwald / Wildemann (1995, eds.), pp. 77-94

Friedrich, S. A. / Hinterhuber, H. H. (1995), Führung mit Kernkompetenzen - Gewinnen im Wettbewerb der Zukunft in: Gablers Magazin, No. 3 1995, pp. 37-41

Frost, D. L. (1999), Old and New Issues in the Taxation of Electronic Commerce, in: BCLT (1999)

Gartner Group (1997a), Internet Security

Gartner Group (1997b), The Internet Infiltrates the Home: A Study of Wired U.S. Households

Gartner Group (1997c), Getting out of the Box: Future Internet Access Trends

Gartner Group (1997d), The Race of Content Supremacy: Fighting for Local Hearts and Minds (and Wallets)

Gartner Group (1997f), Internet and Online Strategies Market Share Guide and Definitions

Gartner Group (1997g), North American Internet and Enterprise Strategies Market Share

Gartner Group (1997h), 1997 Internet and Enterprise Strategies Market Forecast

Gartner Group (1997i), Worldwide Internet and Enterprise Strategies Market Share

Gartner Group (1997j), Internet Development in Eastern and Central Europe

Gartner Group (1997k), Internet and Enterprise Strategies and Digital Commerce Market Share Guide

Gartner Group (1997l), The Browser War: Third Quarter 1997

Gartner Group (1997m), Internet and Intranet Plans in European Organizations

Gartner Group (1997n), Will Internet Profiling Standards Open End Users' Kimonos?

Gartner Group (1997o), The joys (and perils) of Freemail

Gates, W., et. al. (1996), The Road Ahead, New York, Penguin

Gauthronet, S. / Nathan, F. (1998), On-Line Services and Data Protection and the Protection of Privacy, Study for the European Commission

Gerpott, T.J. (1996), Multimedia - Geschäftssegmente und betriebswirtschaftliche Implikationen, in: WiSt Nr. 1, 1996, pp. 15-20

Gerpott, T.J. / Heil, B. (1998), Wettbewerbssituationsanalyse von Online-Diensteanbietern, in: Schmalenbachs Zeitschrift für betriebswirtschaftliche Forschung (zfbf) 50, Nr.7/8, 1998, pp. 725-746.

Gerpott, T.J./Hermann, H. (1997): Supplier Groups and Strategies in Emerging Multimedia Market Segments, in: Elixmann, D. / Kürble, P. (1997, eds.): Multimedia - Potentials and Challenges from an Economic Perspective, Proceedings des Wissenschaftlichen Instituts für Kommunikationsdienste (WIK), Bad Honnef, pp. 233-255

GfK (1998), GfK – Online Monitor, Nürnberg

Glatzer, R. (1997), The Internet – A Model: Thoughts for a Five - Year Outlook, in: NRC (1997), pp. 237-240

Goldman Sachs (1999), Internet Portals in Europe, London, Goldman Sachs Investment Research

Goldman Sachs (1999b), GS Net Metrics, New York, Goldman Sachs Investment Research

Goldman Sachs (1999c), Internet Quarterly – The Force is still with the Net, May 1999, New York, Goldman Sachs Investment Research

Goldman Sachs (1999d), Internet Retailing, New York, Goldman Sachs Investment Research

Gomez, P. et. al. (1999), Neue Organisationsformen in den konvergierenden Medien-, Tele-kommunikations-, und IT-Branchen, presentation at the association of professors of business administration, commission for organization, workshop in Zurich 26th and 27th of February 1999.

Gomes-Casseres, B. / Leonard-Barton, D. (1997): Alliance Clusters in Multimedia - Safety Net or Entanglement?, in: Yoffie (1997, eds), pp. 325-369.

Gong, J. / Srinagesh, P. (1995), The Economics of Layered Networks, paper presented at MIT workshop on Internet economics, March 1995, online at: http://www.press.-umich.edu/jep/works/GongEconLa.html, also in: NRC (1997), pp. 74-79

Ghoshal, S, / Bartlett, C. A. (1990), The Multinational Corporation as an Interorganizational Network, in: Academy of Management Review, Vol. 15, No. 4, 1990, pp. 603-625

Ghoshal, S. / Westney, D. E. (1993, eds.), Organization Theory and the Multinational Corpo-ration, New York

Gräf, L. (1997), Locker verknüpft im Cyberspace – einige Thesen zur Änderung sozialer Netzwerke durch die Nutzung des Internet, in: Gräf / Krajewski (1997, eds.), pp. 99-124

Gräf, L. / Krajewski, M. (1997, eds.), Soziologie des Internet: Handeln im Elektronischen Web-Werk, Campus, Frankfurt, New York

Graham, J. (1991). Dictionary of Telecommunications, revised and updated by Sue J. Lowe, New York, Penguin

Grant, A.E. / Shamp, S.A. (1997), Will TVs and PCs Converge? - Point and Counterpoint. New Telecom Quarterly, No. 2, 1997, pp. 31-37

Grant, R. M. (1991), The Resource-Based Theory of Competitive Advantage - Implications for Strategy Formulation, in: California Management Review, Vol. 33, No. 1, Spring 1991, pp. 114-135

Grant, R. M. (1992), Contemporary Strategy Analysis - Concepts, Techniques, Applications, Blackwell, Oxford

Graumann, C. F. (1956), Social Perception. Die Motivation der Wahrnehmung in neueren amerikanischen Untersuchungen, in: Zeitschrift für experimentelle und ange-wandte Psychologie 3, 1956, pp. 605-661

Greenstein, S. / Khanna, T. (1997), What does industry convergence mean?, in: Yoffie (1997, eds.), pp. 201-224

Gruner & Jahr (1998), MarkenProfile7 - Telekommunikation / Computer Online

Hagel, J. (1996), Spider vs. Spider, in: McKinsey Quarterly No. 1, 1996, pp. 4-19

Hagel, J. / Armstrong, A. G. (1995), Real Profits from Virtual Communities, in: McKinsey Quarterly, No. 3, 1995, pp. 126-141

Hagel, J. / Armstrong, A. G. (1996), The Real Value of On-line Communities, in: Harvard Business Review, Vol. 74, No. 3, May/June 1996, pp. 134 - 141

Hagel, J. / Armstrong, A. G., (1997a), Net Gain - Expanding Markets Through Virtual Com-munities, in: McKinsey Quarterly No. 1, 1997, pp. 140-153

Hagel, J. / Armstrong, A. G., (1997b), Net Gain - Expanding Markets Through Virtual Com-munities, Boston, Harvard Business School Press

Hagel, J. / Bergsma, E. E. / Dheer, S. (1996), Placing your bets on electronic networks, in: McKinsey Quarterly No. 2, 1996, pp. 56-67

Hagel, J. / Eisenmann, T. R. (1994) Navigating the Multimedia Landscape, in: McKinsey Quarterly, No. 3, 1994, pp. 78-91

Hagel, J. / Hewlin, T. / Hutchings, T. (1997), Retail Banking: Caught in a Web, in: McKinsey Quarterly No. 2, 1997, pp. 42-55

Hagel, J. / Lansing, W. J. (1994), Who Owns the Customer?, in: McKinsey Quarterly No. 1994, pp. 63-68

Hagel, J., / Rayport, J. F. (1997a), The Coming Battle for Customer Information, McKinsey Quarterly, No. 3, 1997, pp. 64-76

Hagel, J., / Rayport, J. F. (1997b), The New Infomediaries, in: McKinsey Quarterly, No. 4, 1997, pp. 54-70

Hagel, J. / Sacconaghi, A. M.(1996), Who will Benefit From Virtual Information?, in: McKinsey Quarterly, No. 3, 1996, pp. 22- 55

Hagel, J. / Singer, M. (1999), Private Lives, in: McKinsey Quarterly, No. 1, 1999, pp. 6-15

Halsall, F. (1995), Data Communications, Computer Networks and Open System. Addison-Wesley, New York

Hamel, G. (1991), Competition for Competence and International Learning within International Strategic Alliances, in: Strategic Management Journal, Vol. 12, pp. 83-103

Hamel, G. / Doz, Y. L. / Prahalad, C. K. (1989), Mit Marktrivalen zusammenarbeiten - und dabei gewinnen, in: Harvard Manager, No. 3, 1989, pp. 87-94

Hamel, G. / Heene, A. (1994, eds.), Competence Based Competition, Chichester et. al., John Wiley & Son

Hansch, S. (1998), Amazon Ponders Effects of Rivals Planned Mergers – On-Line Retailers tight for Market Share, in: The New York Times, Oct. 7th 1998, C2

Harrington, L. / Reed, G. (1996), Electronic Commerce (Finally) Come of Age, in: McKinsey Quarterly No. 2, 1996, pp. 68-77

Harrington, L. et. al. (1998), Electronic Commerce: Three Emerging Strategies, in: McKinsey Quarterly, No. 1, 1998, pp. 152-159

Hayek, F. A. (1945), The Use of Knowledge in Society, in: American Economic Review, Vol. 4, 1945, pp. 519-530

Hayek, F. A. (1937), Economics and Knowledge - Presidential address delivered before the London Economic Club; November 10 1936, Economica IV, 1937, pp. 33-54

Haynes, M. a. (1999), Black Wholes of Innovation in the Software Arts, in: BCLT (1999)

Higgins, P. (1998), The Web Lifestyle, Session 8, in: Microsoft (1998)

Hinterhuber, H. A./ Levin, B. M. (1994), Strategic Networks - The Organization of the Future, in: Long Range Planning, Vol. 27, No. 3, pp. 42-63

Houston, P. (1999), Peacemakers take on MS-AOL, on-line at: http://www.zdnet.com/zdnn/-stories/news/0,4586,2307997,00.html

Hunt, S. D. / Morgan, R. M. (1995), The comparative advantage theory of competition, in: Journal of Marketing, No. 59, p. 1-15

ICANN (1999), About ICANN, on-line at: http://www.icann.org/abouticann.html

IDATE (1997), Communications & Strategies 26, Idate, Paris

IDATE (1999a), The Wold Atlas of the Internet, Idate, Paris

IDC (1997a), Internet Commerce in Europe

Inkpen A. C. / Grossan, M. M. (1995), Believing is Seeing: Joint Ventures and Organizational Learning, in: Journal of Management Studies, Vol. 32, No. 5, Sept. 1995, pp. 595-618

Inktomi (1997), Inktomi Corporation White Paper, on-line at: http://www.inktomi.com/Tech/-EconOfLargeScaleCache.html

IUKDG (1997), Federal Act Establishing the General Conditions for Information and Communication Services - Information and Communication Services Act - (Informations- und Kommunikationsdienste-Gesetz - IUKDG), on-line (in English) at: http://www.iid.de/rahmen/iukdgebt.html

Jarillio, J. C. (1988), On Strategic Networks, in: Strategic Management Journal, Vol. 9, 1988, pp. 31-41

Jarillio, J. C. (1990), Comments on 'Transaction Costs and Networks, in: Strategic Management Journal, Vol. 11, 1990, pp. 497-499

Jarillio, J. C. (1993), Strategic Networks - Creating the Borderless Organization, Oxford et. al., Butterworth-Heinemann

Javidan, M. (1998), Core Competence: What Does it Mean in Practice?, in: Long Range Planning, Vol. 31, No.1, pp. 60 – 71

Johnson, B. A. et. al (1995), Banking on Multimedia, in: McKinsey Quarterly, No. 2, 1995, pp. 94-106

Jupiter Communications (1996), The 1996 Online Advertising Report, New York

Jupiter Communications (1998), Paid Content: Limited Revenue Opportunities for Mass-market Web Ventures, New York

Kahneman, D. / Slovic, P. / Tversky, A. (1982, eds.), Judgement under Uncertainty: Heuristics and Biases, Cambridge, Cambridge University Press

Kalakota, R. / Whinston, A. B. (1996): Frontiers of Electronic Commerce, New York, Addison-Wesley

Katz, M. L. / Shapiro, C. (1994), Systems Competition and Network Effects, in: Journal of Economic Perspectives, Vol. 8, No. 2, pp. 93-115

Katz, M. L. / Shapiro, C. (1992), Product Introduction with Network Externalities, Journal of Industrial Economics, Vol. 40, No. 1, pp. 55-84.

Katz, M. L. / Shapiro, C. (1985), Network Externalities, Competition and Compatibility, in: The American Economic Review, Vol. 75, No. 3, pp. 424-440

Katz, M. L. / Shapiro, C. (1986a), Technology Adoption in the Presence of Network Externalities, in: Journal of Political Economy, Vol. 94, pp. 822-841.

Katz, M. L. / Shapiro, C. (1986b), Product Compatibility Choice in a Market with Technological Progress, in: Oxford Economic Papers, Vol. 38, pp. 146-165.

Katz, M. L. / Rosen, H. (1991), Microeconomics, Boston, Irwin

Kavassalis, P. / Solomon, R. J. (1997), Mr. Schumpeter on the Telephone - Patterns of Technical Change in the Telecommunications Industry before and after the Internet, in: IDATE: Communications & Strategies 26, 1997, pp. 371-408.

Kelly, K. (1997), New Rules for the New Economy: Twelve dependable principles for thriving in a turbulent world. Wired, Issue 5.09, September 1997, 09/97, on-line at: http://www.wired.com/wired/archive/5.09/newrules.html

Kelly, K. (1998), New Rules for the New Economy - 10 Radical Strategies for a Connected World, New York, Viking Press

Kenney, M. / Curry, J. (1999), E-Commerce: Implications for Firm Strategy and Industry Configuration, BRIE / E-conomy working paper 2, on-line at: http://e-conomy.-berkeley.edu/pubs/wp/ewp2.html

Ketelhöhn, W.(1995), Take Time to think out Your Business Challenges, in: European Management Journal, Vol. 13, No. 4, pp. 443-451

Ketelhöhn, W.(1993), International Business Strategy, Oxford, Nichols Publishing Company

Kirsch, W. (1997), Wegweiser zur Konstruktion einer evolutionären Theorie der strategischen Führung, Munich, Verlag Barbara Kirsch

Kirsch, W. (1988), Betriebswirtschaftslehre – Eine Annäherung aus der Perspektive der Unternehmensführung, Munich, Verlag Barbara Kirsch

Kirsch, W. (1991, eds.), Beiträge zum Management strategischer Programme, Munich, Verlag Barbara Kirsch

Klein, S. (1997), Introduction to Electronic Auctions, in: International Journal of Electronic Markets, Vol. 7, No. 4, 1997, pp. 3-6

Kleinsteuber, H. J. / Rosenbach, M. (1997), Regulation in the USA – A lesson for Europe?, in: Zerdick (1997, eds.), pp. 229-236

Knyphausen, D. zu / Ringlstetter, M. (1991), Wettbewerbsumfeld, Hybride Strategien und Economies of Scope, in: Kirsch (1991, eds.), pp. 539-574

Knyphausen, D. zu (1993), "Why are Firms different" - Der "Ressourcenorientierte Ansatz" im Mittelpunkt einer aktuellen Kontroverse im strategischen Management, in: Die Betriebswirtschaft, Vol. 53, No. 6, pp. 771-792

Koll, T. (1999), The Evolution of the Internet, conference manuscript, in Baack / Eberspächer (1999, eds.), pp. 39-54

Kollmann, T. (1998), The Information Triple Jump as the Measure of Success in Electronic Commerce, in: International Journal of Electronic Markets, Vol. 8, No. 4, 1998 pp.44-49

Kotler, P. / Armstrong, G. (1998), Principles of Marketing, 8th ed., New York, Prentice Hall

Köster, P. H. (1983), Ökonomen verändern die Welt, Hamburg, Gruner & Jahr

KPMG (1996a), Public Policy Issues Arising from Telecommunications and Audiovisual Convergence – Report for the European Commission, 1996

KPMG (1996b), Appendix 4 – Country Reports, in: KPMG (1996a)

KPMG (1996c), Appendix 5 – Structure of the IT and Telecommunications Sectors, in: KPMG (1996a)

KPMG (1996d), Appendix 7 – Revenue Model, in: KPMG (1996a)

KPMG (1998a), Electronic Commerce – Research Report, London 1998

KPMG / Yahoo! (1998), Europe Gets Wired, London 1998

Krogh, G. v. / Roos, J. / Aadne, J. H. (1996), Representationism - the Traditional Approach to Cooperative Strategies, in: Krogh / Roos 1996 (1996, eds.), pp. 9-31

Krogh, G. v. / Roos, J. (1996a), Managing Strategy Processes in Emerging Industries – The Case of Media Firms, MacMillan Publications, London

Krogh, G. v. / Roos, J. (1996, eds.), Managing Knowledge: Perspectives on Cooperation and Competition, London, Sage

Krogh, G. v. / Sinatra, A. / Singh, H. (1994, eds.), The Management of Corporate Acquisitions, Ipswitch

Krogh, G. v. / Venzin, M. (1995), Anhaltende Wettbewerbsvorteile durch Wissensmanagement, in: Die Unternehmung, No. 6, 1995, pp. 417-436

Krogh, G. v. / Roos, J., (1992), Figuring out Your Competence Configuration, in: European Management Journal, Vol. 10, No. 4, pp. 422-427

Krogh, G. / Roos J. (1996b), The Epistemological Challenge: Managing Knowledge and Intellectual Capital, in: Special Issue, European Management Journal, Vol. 14, 1996, pp. 333-337

Krogh, G. / Roos, J. / Aadne, J. H. / Schweinsberg, M. (1996), The Berlingske Group: Looking at the future of electronic media. IMD Case GM656

Krogh, G. / Aadne, J. H. (1996), In Search of Successful Strategies in the Emerging Media Industry, in: Junior consult - Wirtschaftsmagazin ESPRIT St. Gallen, Vol. 1, No. 1, 1996, pp. 11-13

Kwak, M. (1998), The Browser Wars, 1994 – 1998, Case Study, Harvard Business School

Lado, A. A. / Boyd, N. G. / Wright, P., (1992), A Competency-Based Model of Sustainable Advantage - Toward a Conceptual Integration, in: Journal of Management, Vol. 18, No. 1, pp. 77-91

Lappin, T. (1996), FedEx is piloting the next phase, in: Wired, no. 4, December 1996, p. 236-290, on-line at: http://www.wired.com/4.12/fedex/

Leibenstein, H. (1950), Bandwagon, Snob and Veblen Effects in the Theory of Consumer's Demand, in: Quarterly Journal of Economics, Vol. 64, 1950, pp. 183-207

Leitherer, E. (1985), Betriebliche Marktlehre, Schäfer-Pöschel, Stuttgart

Leonard-Barton, D. (1992), Core Capabilities and Core Rigidities, A Paradox in Managing New Product Development, in: Strategic Management Journal, Vol. 13, Summer Special Issue, 1992, pp. 111-125

Lessig, L. (1999), Code, and Other Laws of Cyberspace, Basic Books

Lessig, L. (1998a), The Architecture of Privacy, Essay, Harvard Law School

Lessig, L. (1998b), The Laws of Cyberspace, Essay, Harvard Law School

Lessig, L. (1997a), Intellectual Property and Code, in: 11 St. Johns Journal of Legal Commentary 635

Lessig, L. (1997b), The Constitution of Code: Limitations on Choice-based Critiques of Cyberspace Regulation, in: 5 CommLaw Conspectus 181

Lessig, L. (1995), The Path of Cyberlaw, in: 104 Yale Law Journal 1734

Liebowitz, S. / Margolis, S. (1995), Path Dependence, Lock-In and History, in: Journal of Law, Economics and Organization, April, 1995, on-line at: http://wwwpub.utdallas.edu/~liebowit/paths.html

Lorange, P. / Roos, J. (1993), Strategic Alliances - Formation, Implementation and Evolution, Cambridge, Blackwell

Lynch, R. P. (1989), The Practical Guide to Joint Ventures & Corporate Alliances, New York, John Wiley & Sons

MacKie-Mason, J. K. / Varian, H. (1997), Economic FAQs about the Internet, in: McKnight / Bailey (1997, Eds.), Internet economics. Cambridge, MIT Press, pp. 27-62. also: in: Journal of Electronic Publishing, May 1995, Vol. 2, Issue 1, online at: http://www.press.umich.edu/jep/works/FAQs.html

Mahrdt, N. (1998), Strategische Allianzen bei digitalen Informations- und Kommunikationsdiensten - Eine wettbewerbspolitische Untersuchung, Baden-Baden,

Mahoney, J. T. / Pandian, J. R. (1992), The Resource-Based View within the Conversation of Strategic Management, in: Strategic Management Journal, Vol. 13, pp. 363-380

Mansfield, E. (1991), Microeconomics – Theory and Application, Norton, New York, London

March, J.G. / Simon, H.A. (1958), Organizations, New York et. al., Blackwell

Margherio, L. et. al. (1997), The Emerging Digital Economy, Washington 1997

McKenna, R. (1995), Real-Time Marketing, in: Harvard Business Review, Vol. 73, No 4, July – August 1995, pp. 87-95

McKnight, L. / Bailey, J. (1997, Eds.), Internet economics. Cambridge, MA: MIT Press

McKnight, L. / Bailey, J. (1995), An Introduction to Internet Economics, Presented at MIT Workshop on Internet Economics March 1995, on-line at: http://www.press.umich.edu/jep/works/McKniIntro.html

McWilliams, A. / Smart, D. L. (1993), Efficiency v. Structure-Conduct-Performance - Implications for Strategy Research and Practice, in: Journal of Management, Vol. 19, No. 1, pp. 63-78

Meeker, M. (1996), Hot Stocks – Some Assembly Required, on-line at: http://www.edventure.com/pcforum/96pcf/agenda/panel9.html#meeker

Merges, R. et. al. (1997), Intellectual Property in the New Technological Age, San Francisco, Panel Publishing

Merrill, C. R. (1999), Proof of WHO, WHAT and WHEN in Electronic Commerce – Under the Digital Signature Guideline, manuscript in: BCLT (1999)

Messerschmitt, D. G. (1996), The Convergence of Telecommunication and Computing – What are the Implications Today?, Paper for the IEEE, UC Berkeley, August 1996

Metcalf, R. (1993), Metcalf's Law and Legacy, in: Forbes ASAP, September 13, 1993

Microsoft (1999), Microsoft Legal Issues, on-line at: http://www.microsoft.com/presspass/doj/doj.htm

Microsoft (1998), Microsoft Global Internet Summit 1998, Seattle November 2nd – 3rd, conference documentation, on-line at: http://www.microsoftisn/events/nses (pw: NTUSER)

Middelhoff, T. (1998), Wer bestimmt die Multimedia-Wertschöpfungskette?, on-line: http://www.bertelsmann.de/bag/deutsch/news/reden/text/ witte.html

Miles, R. E. / Snow, C. C. / Coleman, H. J. (1992), Managing 21st Century Network Organizations, in: Organizational Dynamics Vol. 20, 1992, pp. 5-20

Miles, R. E. / Snow, C. C. (1993), Internal Markets and Network Organizations, in: Halal (1993, eds.), pp. 67-86

Monroe, K. B. (1994), The Pricing of On-line Services, in: Advances in Telecommunications Management, Vol. 4, pp. 165-176

Montgomery, C. A. (1995), Of Diamonds and Rust: A New Look At Resources, in: Montgomery (1995, eds.) pp. 251-268

Montgomery, C. A. (1995, eds), Resource-based and Evolutionary Theories of the Firm – Towards a Synthesis, Kluwer, Boston et. al.

Morgan Stanley (1995), The Internet Report - U.S. Investment Research, New York, December 1995

Morgan Stanley (1999), The European Internet Report, New York et. al., June 1999

Moore, G. A. (1995), Inside the Tornado, Harper Business, New York

Murphy, M. (1996), Note on the Consumer On-Line Services Industry in 1996, Case Study, Graduate School of Business, Stanford University

Mueller, D.C. (1997), First Mover Advantages and Path Dependency, in: Journal of Industrial Organization, Vol. 15, pp. 827-850

Nayyar, P. R. (1992), On the Measurement of Corporate Diversification Strategy – Evidence from large US Service Firms, in: Strategic Management Journal, Vol. 13, pp. 219-235

Neumann, J. v. / Morgenstern, O. (1964), Theory of Games and Economic Behavior, New York, Science Editions, John Wiley & Sons, Inc.,

Netaction (1997), Consumer Choice on Web Browsers, on-line at: http://www.netaction.org/-msoft/browsers.html

Netcraft (1999), Web Server Survey, on-line at: http://www.netcraft.com/Survey/

Network Wizards (1999), Internet Domain Name Survey, on-line at: http://www.nw.com

Nohria, N. / Eccles, R. G. (1992, eds.), Networks and Organizations - Structure, Form and Action, Boston, Harvard Business School Press

Noam, E. M. (1996): Media Concentration in the United States: Industry Trends and Regulatory Responses, in: IDATE: Communications & Strategies (1996), pp. 11-25

Noam, E. M. (1992), A Theory for the Instability of Public Telecommunications Systems, in: Antonelli (1992, eds.), pp. 107-127

Nolan, R. L. / Bradley, S. P. (1998), Sense and Respond – Capturing Value in the Network Era, Harvard Business School Press, Boston

Nortel (1998), Network Trends, presentation at the Microsoft 1998 Internet Network Summit, Seattle

Nonaka, I. (1991), The Knowledge-Creating Company, in: Harvard Business Review, Vol. 69, No. 6, November – December 1991, pp. 96-104

n. n. (1999a), Peer to peer auctions on Yahoo, in: New Media Investor No. 45, May 19 1999, p. 10

NRC (1998a), Internet Counts – Measuring the Impacts of the Internet, study be the national research council, National Academy Press, Washington

NRC (1998b), Fostering Research on the Economic and Social Impacts of Information Technology, National Academy Press, Washington

NRC (1997), The Unpredictable Certainty – Information Infrastructure through 2000, study be the national research council, National Academy Press, Washington

OECD (1999), Communications Outlook 1999, Paris

OECD (1998a), The Economic and Social Impacts of Electronic Commerce – Preliminary Findings and Research Agenda, Paris

OECD (1998b), Internet Infrastructure Indicators, Paris

OECD (1998c), France's Experience with the Minitel – Lessons for Electronic Commerce over the Internet, Paris

OECD (1998d), Content as a New Growth Industry, Paris

OECD (1996), Information Infrastructure Convergence and Pricing: The Internet, Paris

Oren, S. S. / Smith, S. A. (1981), Critical Mass and Tariff Structure in Electronic Communications Markets", in: Bell Journal of Economics, Vol. 12, Autumn 1981, pp. 467-87

Osterloh, M. / Grand, S. (1994), Modelling oder Mapping? – Von Rede- und Schweigeinstrumenten in der betriebswirtschaftlichen Theoriebildung, in: Die Unternehmung No. 4 1994, pp. 277-293

Paterson, R. (1997), Policy Implications of Economic and Cultural Value Chains, in: Zerdick (1997 eds.), pp. 169-186

Penrose, E. G. (1959), The Theory of the Growth of the Firm, New York, et. al., Wiley

Peteraf, M. A. (1993), The Cornerstones of Competitive Advantage - A Resource-Based View, in: Strategic Management Journal, Vol. 17, pp. 179-191

Perrine, T. (1997), Thoughts on Security on the NII, in: NRC (1997), pp. 416-421

Phlips, L. (1995, eds.), Applied Industrial Economics, Cambridge University Press, Cambridge

Picot, A. / Reichwald, R. (1994), Auflösung der Unternehmung - Vom Einfluß der IuK Technologien auf Organisationsstrukturen und Kooperationsformen, in: Zeitschrift für Betriebswirtschaft, No. 64, 1994, pp. 547-570

Picot, A. / Reichwald, R. / Wigand R. T. (1996), Die grenzenlose Unternehmung: Information, Organisation und Management, Wiesbaden, Gabler

Pine, J. (1993), Mass Customization, Boston, Harvard Business Press,

Porter, M. E. (1980), Competitive Strategy, New York: The Free Press

Porter, M. E. (1981), The contributions of industrial organization to strategic management, in: Academy of Management Review, Vol. 6, No. 4 1981, p. 606-620

Porter, M. E. (1985), Competitive Advantage, New York: The Free Press

Porter, M. E. (1987), Wettbewerbsstrategie – Methoden zur Analyse von Branchen und Konkurrenten, Campus, Frankfurt / M.

Porter, M. E. (1989), Wettbewerbsvorteile – Spitzenleistungen erreichen und behaupten, Campus, Frankfurt / M.

Porter, M. E. (1990), The Competitive Advantage of Nations, New York, The Free Press

Porter, M. E. (1991), Towards a Dynamic Theory of Strategy", in: Strategic Management Journal, Vol. 12, pp. 95-117

Poundstone, W. (1992), Prisoner's Dilemma, Doubleday, New York

Prahalad, C. K. / Hamel, G. (1989), Strategic Intend, in: Harvard Business Review, Vol. 67, No. 3, May-June, 1989, pp. 63-76

Prahalad, C. K. / Hamel, G. (1990), The Core Competence of the Corporation, in: Harvard Business Review, Vol. 68, No. 3, May-June 1990, pp. 79-91

Prahalad, C. K. / Hamel, G. (1991), Nur Kernkompetenzen sichern das Überleben, in: Harvard Manager, Vol. 13, Heft 2, 1991, pp. 66-78

Prahalad, C. K. / Hamel, G. (1994), Competing for the Future, Boston 1994

Pümpin, C. (1992), Strategische Erfolgspositionen - Methodik der dynamischen strategischen Unternehmensführung, Bern, Haupt

Rasche, C. (1993), Kernkompetenzen, in: Die Betriebswirtschaft, Vol. 53, No. 3, pp. 423-425

Raab, C. D. et. al. (1998), Final Report – Application of a Methodology Designed to Assess the Adequacy Level of Protection of Individuals with Regard to Processing Personal Data, Brussels

Rasche, C. (1994), Wettbewerbsvorteile durch Kernkompetenzen - Ein ressourcenorientierter Ansatz, Dissertation, Bayreuth, Wiesbaden

Rayport, J. F. / Sviokla, J.J (1994), Managing in the Marketspace, in: Harvard Business Review, Vol. 72, No. 6, November – December 1994

Rayport, J. F. / Sviokla, J. J. (1996), Exploiting the Virtual Value Chain, in: McKinsey Quarterly, No. 1, 1996, pp. 20-37

Rayport, J. F. / Sviokla, J. J. (1995), Exploiting the Virtual Value Chain, in: Harvard Business Review, Vol. 73, No. 6, November-December 1995, pp. 75-85.

Reidenberg, J. R. (1999), Restoring Americans' Privacy in Electronic Commerce, manuscript in: BCLT (1999)

Reidenberg, J. R. / Schwartz P. M. (1998), Dataprotection Law and On-Line Services: Regulatory Responses, A Study for the European Commission DG XV

Reichwald, R. / Wildemann, H. (1995, eds.), Kreative Unternehmungen - Spitzenleistungen durch Produkt- und Prozeßinnovation, Stuttgart, Poeschl

Richardson, J. (1999), Competition Policy, Structure and Conduct in the Internet Industry, Conference Contribution at the E-Conomy Conference on Global Electronic Commerce, in: Cioffi / Berg (1999)

Rogers, E. M. (1995), Diffusion of Innovations, New York, Free Press

Rohlfs, J. (1974), "A Theory of Interdependent Demand for a Communications Service", in: Bell Journal of Economics, Vol. 5, No. 1, Spring 1974, pp. 16-37

Rumelt, R. P. (1994), Foreword, in: Hamel / Heene (1994, eds.)

Rumer, K. (1994), Internationale Kooperationen und Joint Ventures, Wiesbaden, Expert

Sacconaghi, A. M. / Abela, A. V. (1997), Value Exchange: The Secret of Building Customer Relationships On Line, in: McKinsey Quarterly, No. 2, 1997, pp. 216-219

Samuelson, P. (1999), Intellectual Property and Contract Law for the Information Age, in: California Law Review, Vol. 87, No. 1, January 1999 1

Schoemaker, J. H. (1994), A Pyramid of Decision Approaches, in: California Management Review, Vol. 36, No. 2, 1994, pp. 9-32

Schmalensee, R. (1992), Game-Theoretic Models of Market Concentration – Sunk Costs and Market Structure, in: Journal of Industrial Economics, Vol. 40, June 1992, pp. 125-134

Schumpeter, J. (1964), Business Cycles, as abridged by Reindig Fels, New York, McGraw-Hill

Schumpeter, J. A. (1952), Theorie der wirtschaftlichen Entwicklung. 6th ed., Berlin

Schumpeter, J. (1943), Capitalism, Socialism, and Democracy, London, George Allen & Uwin

Schutzer, D. (1997), Electronic Commerce, in: NRC (1997), pp. 521-537

Seidman, O. (1997), The Browser War is over, in: Seidman's Online Insider, March 1997, online at: http://www.onlineinsider.com/html/archives/031697.txt

Seidman, O. (1999a), AOL: Don't be Sad 'Cos Two Out of Three Ain't Bad, in: Seidman's Online Insider, January 1999, online at: http://www.onlineinsider.com/html/-january_31__1999.html

Seidman, O. (1999b), Rekindling the Browser Wars, in: Seidman's Online Insider, April 1999, online at: http://www.onlineinsider.com/html/march_21__1999.html

Seidman, O. (1999c), AOL vs. FAT PIPES, in: Seidman's Online Insider, April 1999, online at: http://www.onlineinsider.com/html/april_18__1999.html

Selz D. / Klein S. (1997): Emerging Electronic Intermediaries - the Case of the Automotive Industry, in Proceedings of 10th Bled EC Conference, Bled, Slovenia, 1997, pp. 316-336.

Selz, D. / Klein S. (1998): The Changing Landscape of Auto Distribution, in: Proceedings of the 31st HICSS Conference, Hawaii, 1998

Selz, D. (2000), Value Webs, Ph.D. thesis, St Gallen, forthcoming

Simon, H. A. (1957), Models of Man, New York et. al. 1957

Slouka, M. (1995), War of the Worlds: Cyberspace and the High-Tech Assault on Reality New York, Basic Books

Smith, B. (1995), The Internet and the Online Services Segment - Content, Access and Equity Valuations, o.O.

SPA (1999), Competition in the Network Market: The Microsoft Challenge, Report by the Software Publishers Association, on-line at: http://www.procompetition.org/research/server/index.html

Spectrum (1996), Development of the Information Society – An International Analysis, an analysis for the UK Department of Trade and Industry, HMSO Publications Center

Spectrum (1997) Moving into the Information Society – An International Benchmark Study, an analysis for the UK Department of Trade and Industry, HMSO Publications Center

Spectrum (1998), Moving into the Information Age – An International Benchmark Study, an analysis for the UK Department of Trade and Industry, HMSO Publications Center

Stoetzer, M.-W. / Mahler, A. (1995, eds.), Die Diffusion von Innovationen in der Telekommunikation, Berlin et al.,

Squire, Sanders & Dempsey (1998a), Study on Adapting the EU Telecommunications Regulatory Framework to the Developing Multimedia Environment - A Study for the European Commission (Directorate-General XIII), ECSC - EC - EAEC, Brussels - Luxembourg

Squire, Sanders & Dempsey (1998b), Summary Report, in: Squire, Sanders & Dempsey (1998a)

Squire, Sanders & Dempsey (1998c), Comparative Overview of Current Regulatory Environment in Telecommunications and Broadcastings Sector - A Study for the European Commission (Directorate-General XIII), ECSC - EC - EAEC, Brussels – Luxembourg

Srinagesh, P. (1995) Internet Cost Structures and Interconnection Agreements, paper presented at MIT workshop on Internet economics, March 1995, online at: http://www.press.umich.edu/jep/

Styles, P., (1996), Media Business File, KPMG

Sutton, J. (1995), Game Theory and Industry Studies, in: Phlips (1995, eds.), pp. 33-51

Sutton, J. (1991), Sunk Costs and Market Structure: Price Competition, Advertising, and the Evolution of Concentration, Cambridge, MIT Press

Sydow, J (1992), Strategische Netzwerke - Evolution und Organisation, Wiesbaden, Gabler

Sydow, J. (1992a) Strategische Netzwerke und Transaktionskosten - Über die Grenzen einer transaktionskostentheoretischen Erklärung der Evolution strategischer Netzwerke, in: Stähle / Conrad (1992), pp. 239-311

Tampoe, M. (1994), Exploiting the Core Competencies of Your Organization, in: Long Range Planning, Vol. 27, No. 4, pp. 66-77

Tapscott, D. (1996), The Digital Economy - Promise and Peril in the Age of Networked Intelligence, New York, McGraw-Hill

Teletalk (1998a), Wir gehen unseren eigenen Weg, Interview with Klaus-Dieter Schäuerle (German Telecom Regulator), in: Teletalk, February 1998, pp. 8-11, on-line at: http://www.teletalk.de/archiv/9802/9802interview.html

Teletalk (1999a), Ganz normale Vorgänge, Interview with Gerd Tenzer (German Telecom), in: Teletalk, March 1999, pp. 8-11, on-line at: http://www.teletalk.de/archiv/-9903/html/interview.html

Teletalk (1999b), Marktkräfte brauchen Zeit, Interview with Klaus-Dieter Schäuerle (German Telecom Regulator), in: Teletalk, July 1999, pp. 8-11, on-line at: http://www.teletalk.de/archiv/9907/html/interview.html

Tischler, T. (1999), Strategie und Change – Ein Ansatz zur Strategiegenerierung im Unternehmen, Wiesbaden, Gabler

Turkle, S. (1997), Life on the Screen : Identity in the Age of the Internet, New York, Touchston

Tversky, A./ Kahneman, D. (1974), Judgement under Uncertainty: Heuristics and Biases, in: Kahneman et. al. (1982, eds.), pp. 3-20

USA (1998), U.S. Government Sites on Electronic Commerce Policy, on-line at: http://www.ecommerce.gov/Default.htm

USA (1997), A Framework for Global Electronic Commerce, The White House

Utterback, J. M. (1994), Mastering the Dynamics of Innovation - How Companies can Seize Opportunities in the Face of Technological Change, Boston, Harvard Business School Press,

Ury, W. (1993), Getting Past No: Negotiating Your Way from Confrontation to Cooperation, New York, Bantam Doubleday Dell

Verdin, P. / Williamson, P. (1994), Successful Strategy: Stargazing or Self-Examination, in: European Management Journal, Vol. 12, No. 1, pp. 10-19

Varian, H. R. (1999a), Buying, Sharing and Renting Information Goods, Working Paper, UC Berkeley, May 1999

Varian, H. R. (1999b), Internet Economics, in: Baack / Eberspächer (1999, eds.), pp. 25-38

Varian, H. R. (1998a), Differential Pricing and Efficiency, in: First Monday, on-line at: http://www.firstmonday.dk/issues/issue2/different/

Varian, H. R. (1998b), Information Policy, lecture charts from the class "Strategic Computing and Communications Technology, BA 296, Spring 1998, UC Berkeley, on-line at: http://www.sims.berkeley.edu/~hal/courses/eecsba1/sp98/policy.pdf

Varian, H. R. (1998c), Markets for Information Goods, Working Paper, UC Berkeley, October 1998

Varian, H. R. (1997), Versioning Information Goods, Working Paper, UC Berkeley, March 1997

Varian, H. R. (1996), The Information Economy - How much will two bits be worth in the digital marketplace?, in: Educom Review, No. 1, January – February 1996, pp. 44-46

Varian, H. R. (1995), Pricing Information Goods, Working Paper, University of Michigan, June 1995

Varian, H. R. (1994), Entry and Cost Reduction, Working Paper, University of Michigan, February 1994

Varian, H. R. (1993), Economic Incentives in Software Design, Working Paper, University of Michigan, June 1993

Varian, H. R. (1989), What Use is Economic Theory, Working Paper, UC Berkeley, August 1989

Varian, H. R. (1978), Microeconomic Analysis, Norton, New York

Varian, H. R. / Shapiro, C. (1998), Information Rules – A Strategic Guide to the Network Economy, Harvard Business School Press, Boston, MA

Varian, H. R. / Shapiro, C. (1998b), Versioning – The Smart Way to Sell Information, in: Harvard Business Review, Vol. 76, No. 6, 1998, pp. 106-114

Varian, H. R. / MacKie-Mason, J. K. / Shenker, S. (1996), Service Architecture and Content Provision – The Network Provider as Editor, Working Paper, University of Michigan, UC Berkeley, Xerox PARC, June 1996

Varian, H. R. / MacKie-Mason, J. K. (1994a), Some Economics of the Internet, Working Paper, University of Michigan, February 1994

Varian, H. R. / MacKie-Mason, J. K. (1994b), Pricing Congestible Network Resources, Working Paper, University of Michigan, November 1994

Varian, H. R. / MacKie-Mason, J. K. (1994c), Pricing the Internet, Working Paper, University of Michigan, February 1994

Vonder Haar, S. (1999), Case gets Microsoft's attention, on-line at: http://www.zdnet.com/-zdnn/stories/news/0,4586,2301807,00.html

W3B (1996), WWW Benutzeranalyse, Hamburg 1996

W3B (1997), WWW Benutzeranalyse, Hamburg 1997

W3B (1998), WWW Benutzeranalyse, Hamburg 1998

Wäsche, N. (1999), Die Chancen der Neuen – Das Internet und die Formierung eines neuen Dienstleistungssektors in Deutschland 1995 – 1998, Conference Paper for the Conference „Printmedien im Wettbewerb", Berlin, Oktober 23rd and 24th

Welsch, W. (1993), Ästhetisierungsprozesse. Phänomene, Unterscheidungen, Perspektiven, in: Deutsche Zeitschrift für Philosophie 41, 1993

Werbach, K, (1999), The Architecture of Internet 2.0, in: Release 1.0

Werbach, K. (1997), Digital Tornado: The Internet and Telecommunications Policy, OPP Working Paper at the FCC, on-line at: http://www.fcc.gov/Bureaus/OPP/-working_papers/oppwp29.pdf

Wernerfelt, B. (1984), The Resource-Based View of the Firm, in: Strategic Management Journal, Vol. 5, pp. 171-180

Wernerfelt, B. (1995), The Resource-Based View of the Firm - Ten Years After, in: Strategic Management Journal, Vol. 16, pp. 171-174

Wienandt, A. (1994), Die Entstehung, Entwicklung und Zerstörung von Märkten durch Innovation, Stuttgart, Poeschl

Wiesman, D. (1989), Management und Ästhetik, München, Verlag Barbara Kirsch

Wildman, S. S. et. al (1991, eds.), Electronic Services Networks, New York, Praeger

Williamson, O. E. (1975), Markets and Hierarchies – Analysis and Antitrust Implications, New York, Free Press

Williamson, O. E. (1986), Economic Organization – Firms, Markets, and Policy Control, New York, New York University Press

Williamson, O. E. (1990, eds.), Industrial Organization, New York, Free Press

Whitman, M. (1999), Ms. Billionaire: Interview with Ebay CEO Meg Whitman, in: upside, June 4 1999, on-line at: http://www.upside.com/texis/mvm/story?id=37541fc00

Wössner (1999a), Zukunftsperspektiven der Medienmärkte, class material, Hochschule St. Gallen / MCM

Wössner (1999b), Bertelsmann Multimedia, class material, Hochschule St. Gallen / MCM

Wössner (1999c), Medienwirtschaft in Europa, class material, Hochschule St. Gallen / MCM

Wüthrich, H. A. et. al. (1997), Vorsprung durch Virtualisierung, Wiesbaden, Gabler

Yankee Group (1997), The European Internet – Enter the Telco

Yoffie, D. B. (1997, eds.), Competing in the age of digital convergence, Boston, Harvard Business School Press

Yoffie, D.B. (1996), CHESS and competing in the age of digital convergence. California Management Review, Summer 1996, pp. 31-53, & In Yoffie (1996, eds.), pp. 159-200.

Yoffie, D. B., et. al. (1998), Microsoft Goes Online: MSN 1998, Harvard Business School Case Study, Boston, HBS Publishing

Yoffie, D. B., et. al. (1996), Microsoft Goes Online: MSN 1996, Harvard Business School Case Study, Boston, HBS Publishing

Yoffie, D. B. / Cusumano, M. A. (1999), Judo Strategy: The Competitive Dynamics of Internet Time, in: Harvard Business Review, No. 1, Jan – Feb 1999, pp. 71-81

Zakon, H. R. (1999), Hobbe's Internet timeline v.4.1, on-line at: http://info.isoc.org/guest/zakon/Internet/History/HIT.html

Zaret, E. / Meeks. B. N. (1999), AOL's epic aim: to slay Microsoft, on-line at: http://www.msnbc.com/news/280218.asp

Zenith (1999), Zenith Media's New Media Quotes Page, on-line at: http://www.zenithmedia.com/quotes.htm

Zerdick. A. (1997, eds.), Exploring the Limits, Berlin, Springer

Zerdick, A. et. al (1998, eds.), Die Internet Ökonomie, Berlin, Springer

Zerdick, A. et. al (1999, eds.), Funding the Future of Communications: Markets, Users, Economics, ECC Report 1998 (European Communication Council Report), Berlin, Springer

Zimmerman, A. B. (1998), The Evolution of the Internet, in: Coopers & Lybrand IT Magazine, Jan. 1998

Sources Consulted - Interview Partners

Academia / USA

<table>
<tr><td rowspan="8">University of California at Berkeley</td><td colspan="2">Prof. Michael Borrus</td><td>BRIE</td><td>Berkeley, CA</td><td>04/10/99</td><td>45 min.</td></tr>
<tr><td colspan="2"></td><td></td><td>San Francisco, CA</td><td>04/21/99</td><td>60 min.</td></tr>
<tr><td colspan="6">
• Evolving business models
• Stock market rationality / investor types for Internet stocks
• New business opportunities
• Start Up Funding
• Critical Internet core competencies
</td></tr>
<tr><td colspan="2">Prof. Hal Varian</td><td>Dean of SIMS
Haas School of Business</td><td>Berkeley, CA</td><td>03/05/99</td><td>15 min.</td></tr>
<tr><td colspan="6">
• Microeconomic focus of the theory of network economics
• Absence of resource based aspects into network economics due to microeconomic roots
• Insufficiency of network economics to provide comprehensiveness
</td></tr>
<tr><td colspan="2">Prof. John Zysman</td><td>BRIE</td><td>Berkeley, CA</td><td>02/18/99</td><td>45 min.</td></tr>
<tr><td colspan="2"></td><td></td><td></td><td>04/27/99</td><td>45 min.</td></tr>
<tr><td colspan="6">
• Discussion of the model of the industry (chapter 2)
• Discussion of the institutional & political framework (specifically regulatory environment)
• Development of industry size and structure and the influence of public policy
• Discussion of the strategy approach
• Discussion of the industrial development (vertical and horizontal monopolies)
(Plus many brief discussion at BRIE)
</td></tr>
<tr><td rowspan="4">Stanford University</td><td colspan="2">Prof. Francois Bar</td><td>Communications Department</td><td>Palo Alto, CA</td><td>04/26/99</td><td>120 min.</td></tr>
<tr><td colspan="6">
• Media business models in the Internet
• Deployment of DSL Technology (Prof. Bar was representing the Stanford Computer Industry Project in the advisory board of Pacific Bell, especially in respect to he economic modeling of the high bandwidth business with DSL technology)
• Cable deployment
• Discussion of the multi layered model presented within this thesis
</td></tr>
<tr><td colspan="2">John Richardson</td><td>Director International Computer Services Research</td><td>Los Angeles, CA</td><td>05/06/99</td><td>25 min.</td></tr>
<tr><td colspan="6">
• Multi-Layered constitution of the Internet industry
• Application of network economics in the Internet and on-line industry framework
• Application of the co-opetition approach in the Internet and on-line industry framework
• Current state of the scientific community of strategic management regarding the Internet
</td></tr>
<tr><td rowspan="2">University of California Davis</td><td colspan="2">Prof. Martin Kenney</td><td>BRIE</td><td>Berkeley, CA</td><td></td><td>120 min.</td></tr>
<tr><td colspan="6">
• E-conomy research agenda
• Market rules US vs. Europe
• "Geography" marketspaces
• DSL s. cable broadband
</td></tr>
<tr><td rowspan="2">University of California San Diego</td><td colspan="2">Prof. Peter Cowhey</td><td>Former chief advisor to the FCC and US negotiator at the WTO telecommunications talks 94-97</td><td>Berkeley, CA</td><td>04/20/99</td><td>45 min.</td></tr>
<tr><td colspan="6">
• Evolution of wireless technology standards
• Competition of alternative network technologies
• WTO telecom negotiation process
• International competition in telecommunication. Interconnection
• Current US Telecom Regulation in 1999 in respect to broadband network technology
</td></tr>
<tr><td rowspan="2">University of Southern California</td><td colspan="2">Prof. Jonathan Aronson</td><td>Dep. Of Int'l Relations</td><td>Bel Air, CA</td><td>05/07/99</td><td>30 min.</td></tr>
<tr><td colspan="6">
• Issues of public policy
• Velocity of adoption processes of the scientific community
</td></tr>
</table>

Academia / Europe

Freie Universität Berlin	Prof. Axel Zerdick	Communications & Economics, European Communications Council	Berkeley, CA	03/01/99	45 min.
	• State of the art of the European scientific community in respect to the new information economy • Comprehension of the theory of network economics in the German scientific community • Missing resource-based view in the Internet economics debate				

University of St. Gallen	Hans-Dieter Zimmer-mann	Research fellow, media com-munications management	St. Gallen	08/07/98 02/12/99	180 min
	• State of the scientific community in Europe • Network economics • Layered model (part II) of this thesis • Strategy approach (part III) of this thesis				

Consultants

Price Waterhouse Coopers	Stefano Bosisio	Senior Manager	Milan	06/09/99	90 min.
	• Leverage of wireless penetration into multimedia in the Italian case • Telecom entrance strategies • Role of multimedia in new telecom strategies • Required investments • Planning timeframes				

BCG	Mike Kleeman	Principal	San Francisco	05/10/99	15 min.
	• Experiences of top management consulting companies in the e-commerce and Internet area (telephone and email interview)				

Roland Berger	Christian Frank	Principal	Munich	07/23/99	90 min.
	• Multimedia expertise of European top management consultancies				

Analysts

	Josef Dietel	Senior Consultant / W3C	Hannover	03/17/98	30 min.
	• W3C standardization processes • Accomplishment of mutual buy-in • Other standardization institutions				
	Esther Dyson	Edventure Holding / Release 1.0 / ICANN	Munich	09/18/98	20 min.
	• Internet Economics • New business models • Buddy lists • Future of the online industry				
	Stuart Feldman	Director IBM advanced research labs	Berkeley	03/05/99	15 min.
	• Value of quantitative research data • Adoption drivers / enablers				
	Eliot Maxwell	Special advisor to the US admini-stration on the digital economy	Berkeley	03/04/99	45 min.
	• Regulatory policy in Europe and the US • Challenges for the regulatory environment of the on-line industry • Pros and cons of early regulation of infant industries				

Executives / USA

<table>
<tr><td rowspan="32" style="writing-mode:vertical-lr">CompuServe</td></tr>
</table>

Steve Litzow	**VP Channel Marketing**	**San Jose, CA**	**04/04/97**	**180 min.**
• Negotiations with RBOC's • Roll out expectations • CompuServe corporate culture • Internet locations (Silicon Valley, Seattle, Dulles, Columbus, Europe)				
Oscar Turner	**Director Strategic Planning**	**Columbus, OH**	**03/27/97**	**60 min.**
• Network economics • Business models • Convergence and competition				
Bill Truesdale	**VP International**	**Columbus, OH**	**03/25/97**	**45 min.**
• Internationalization strategy • Affiliate program • NiftyServe partnership • Global network interconnection agreements				
Bob Horton	**VP Technology**	**Columbus, OH**	**08/19/97**	**60 min.**
		London	**10/02/97**	**30 min.**
• CompuServe system architecture • Internet system architecture • Microsoft Internet technologies • Product development life cycles				
Bob Kington	**VP Content**	**Columbus OH**	**08/18/97**	**60 min**
• Content business models • Branded content (e.g. Pathfinder) • Communities, user generated content • Deal making with media companies				
Dave Bezair	**Director Product Mgmt.**	**Columbus, OH**	**03/26/97**	**60 min.**
			08/18/97	**60 min.**
• CompuServe online service system architecture • CompuServe network structures • Business models • Convergence and competition				
Carl Schafer-Junger	**Director Channel Mktg.**	**Santa Cruz, CA**	**04/04/97**	**120 min.**
• Negotiations with RBOC's • Market development • Role of momentum in markets and leverage				

Brian Sweete	**Exec. VP Marketing**	**San Jose, CA**	**05/12/99**	**45 min.**
• Growth Strategy • "Roadblocks" • Internationalization strategy • Acquisition strategy				
Scott Barnum	**VP International**	**San Jose, CA**	**05/12/99**	**45 min.**
• Growth Strategy • "Roadblocks" • Internationalization strategy • Acquisition strategy				
Reed Maltzman	**Director Strategic Planning**	**San Jose, CA**	**05/12/99**	**45 min.**
• Auction business models • Alternative revenue streams, such as selling market access (e.g. for shipping or escrow services) and using purchasing power • Market definition and market dominance				

eBay

	Linda Lawrence	VP Int'l Netcenter	Mountain View, CA	03/25/99	45 min.
Netscape	• Netscape / Netcenter International Strategy • Integration of Netcenter international group in AOL Europe • Business models • Competition with other portal sites • Competition with Microsoft Internet Explorer				
	Peter Harter	Global Public Policy Counsel	Berkeley, CA	03/05/99	30 min.
			Mountain View, CA	03/25/99	60 min.
	• AOL takeover • Relationships to regulators • Anti Trust policy				

	Ronah Edelin	VP International	Cupertino, CA	04/12/99	20 min.
PointCast	• Turnaround strategy of PointCast (telephone interview)				

	Patrick Bonaire	Business Development Manager	Palo Alto, CA	04/05/97	60 min.
Web TV	• Web TV adoption rates • Web TV success factors • Content business models • Access business models				

	Matt Rightmire	Director Strategic Planning	Santa Clara, CA	04/28/99	60 min.
Yahoo!	• New business models • M & A strategies • Stock market relations • International marketing coordination				
	Ned Taylor	Director Business Development	Santa Clara, CA	04/06/99	90 min.
	• New business models • M & A strategies • New marketing tools • Co-Marketing distribution deals • Strategic positioning • International marketing coordination				

Executives / Europe

AOL CompuServe Europe	**Chris Hill**	**Exec. VP Corporate Development**	London	06/23/99	60 min.
	• Broadband strategy • Alternative device strategy • "AOL everywhere" strategy • Strategic partnerships • Fuzziness in business strategy for the on-line environment • UK interconnection regulation and the "Freesurf" case				
	Konrad Hilbers	**CEO CompuServe Europe, COO AOL Europe**	Munich	02/09/99	60 min.
	• Take Over of CompuServe Europe by the Joint Venture AOL Europe (Bertelsmann AG, AOL Inc.) • Network negotiations with Worldcom • UK telecom interconnect regulation and the Freesurf phenomenon				
	Klaus Hommels	**Assistant Managing Director AOL Germany**	Hamburg	09/19/97	45 min.
	• Business strategy • Marketing rationale • Business economics • Bargaining power in content deals				

Alcatel Europe	**Benoit Raimbault**	**Marketing Manager Internet Screenphone**	Paris	07/24/98	60 min.
	• Business models • Partner bundling + subsidizing • Service bundling • Pricing • Time to market • Competition				

Apax Europe	**Klaus Hommels**	**Investment Manager Internet Ventures**	Munich	08/19/98	45 min.
	• Funding of European Internet ventures (via telephone)				

Compaq Europe	**Andrew Wyatt**	**Director Electronic Commerce**	Munich	06/21/99	60 min.
	• Integration of web site business into Compaq business processes • Integration of web site business into Compaq organization • "How to be the better Dell ?" • Integration of on-line service business to computer manufacturer value chains • "Free PC"-model • Partnering with Microsoft				
	Roar Stroem	**Director Strategic Bus. Dev. & Planning**	Munich	07/21/99	30 min.
	• Threat of new business models such as free PC's • Competencies in e-commerce and interactive services				

Grundig Europe	**Matthias Herfet**	**Project Manager Grundig Internet TV Set Top Box**	Munich	08/19/97	30 min.
	• Set Top Box Technology • TV Set Top Box Success Factors				

	Martin Stahel	Vorstand (EVP) Strategic Planning, Corp. Dev., Multimedia	Hamburg	06/10/99	90 min.
Gruner + Jahr	<ul><li>G & J multimedia strategy</li><li>Conversion strategy of a print publishing group</li><li>Strategic partnerships</li><li>M & A and New Business in the multimedia market</li><li>Competencies of media players</li></ul>				
	Tom Tischler	Director Corporate Development	San Francisco, CA	03/17/99	60 min.
	<ul><li>Shift of content distribution platforms and technologies according to content categories</li><li>Challenges for print media in the presence of the Internet</li></ul>				

	Christoph Mohn	CEO Lycos Europe	Munich	11/21/97	60 min.
Lycos Europe	<ul><li>European strategy of Lycos</li><li>Co-marketing distribution deals</li><li>Costs for content</li></ul>				
	Tony Philipp	COO Lycos Europe	Munich	01/15/97	60 min.
	<ul><li>Business models</li><li>Co-marketing distribution deals</li><li>Product features</li><li>Search engines vs. Catalogs</li></ul>				

	Rony Vogel	Marketing Manager Siemens Online Terminal	Munich	07/27/98	90 min.
Siemens Germany	<ul><li>Subsidizing business model</li><li>Product / Technology bundling</li><li>Market entrance, timing</li></ul>				

	Jan Traenkner	Managing Director Pro7 Digital Business TV	Munich	03/09/98	90 min.
Pro7	<ul><li>Integration of Internet technology and digital TV set top boxes (d-box)</li><li>Cooperative business models</li></ul>				

	Klaus Mantel	Business Development Manager Network Solutions Group	Munich	06/15/99	60 min.
	<ul><li>Windows OEM's</li><li>Streaming Media</li><li>Strategy against Real Networks</li><li>Content management systems</li><li>Cooperative partner marketing</li></ul>				
	Rainer Linder	Product Manager Windows & Internet Explorer	Munich	07/17/99	30 min.
Microsoft Germany	<ul><li>Consumer operating system strategy</li></ul>				
	Wolfgang Schneider	Business Development Manager Internet Customer Unit	Munich	06/16/98	120 min.
	<ul><li>WebTV usage</li><li>WebTV success factors</li><li>Browser strategy</li><li>Standardization efforts at the W3C (e.g. dynamic html, document object model, Jscript)</li><li>Strategy of software and content integration</li><li>MSN cross-platform content strategy</li><li>Streaming media</li></ul>				

	Fabiola Aredondo	Vice President Europe	London	06/04/99	20 min.
	• Organizational challenges • Growth strategy Yahoo! Europe • New business models				
	Steve Boom	Director Business Development Europe	London	06/04/99	60 min.
	• Marketing strategy Yahoo Europe • New business models • International marketing coordination				
Yahoo! Europe	Peter Würtenberger	Managing Director Germany	Munich	06/02/99	60 min.
	• Marketing cross-over strategy of Yahoo! • M & A strategy • Market structure • Market development				
	Karsten Weide	Sr. Producer Germany	Munich	06/23/99	90 min.
			San Francisco, CA	05/03/99	120 min.
	• Costs for content • Co-marketing distribution deals • Negotiation patterns with content providers • International coordination of Yahoo! • San Francisco start-up climate • Communities and the power of word-of-mouth for the growth of start ups				

GPSR Compliance
The European Union's (EU) General Product Safety Regulation (GPSR) is a set
of rules that requires consumer products to be safe and our obligations to
ensure this.

If you have any concerns about our products, you can contact us on

ProductSafety@springernature.com

In case Publisher is established outside the EU, the EU authorized
representative is:

Springer Nature Customer Service Center GmbH
Europaplatz 3
69115 Heidelberg, Germany